Table of Contents

JAN 1 1 2013

Cottage Country Ontario

Image © David Lee (Just Outside Algonquin Park)

Backroad Mapbooks

"One of the most comprehensive outdoor guidebooks on the market!"

~ **Federal Publications, Toronto**

"Discover so many places to go: trails to hike, campsites to visit and rivers and lakes to fish and paddle."

~ **Northern Life**

"They provide everything you need to know on camping, canoeing, fishing, hiking and biking"

~ **Toronto Sun**

www.backroadmapbooks.com

Ontario
Land Area...1 076 395 km²
Population...13 373 000
Capital...Toronto
Largest City...Toronto
Highest Point...Ishpatina Ridge
693 metres (2 274 feet)
Tourism info...1-800-ONTARIO
www.ontariotravel.net

 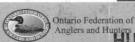
I

Acknowledgements

Published by:

Backroad Mapbooks

Mussio Ventures Ltd.
#106 - 1500 Hartley Ave,
Coquitlam, BC, V3K 7A1
Toll Free: 1-877-520-5670
E-mail: info@backroadmapbooks.com
www.backroadmapbooks.com

Backroad Mapbooks

DIRECTORS
Russell Mussio
Wesley Mussio
Penny Stainton-Mussio

ASSOCIATE DIRECTOR
Jason Marleau

VICE PRESIDENT
Chris Taylor

COVER DESIGN & LAYOUT
Farnaz Faghihi

COVER PHOTO
David Lee
(Just outside of Algonquin Park)

CREATIVE CONTENT
Russell Mussio
Wesley Mussio

PROJECT MANAGER
Andrew Allen

PRODUCTION
Sean Conway
Shaun Filipenko
Oliver Herz
Dale Tober

SALES / MARKETING
Joshua Desnoyers
Chris Taylor

WRITER
Russell Mussio

Library and Archives Canada Cataloguing in Publication

Mussio, Russell, 1969-
Backroad mapbook, cottage country Ontario [cartographic material] :
outdoor recreation guide / Russell Mussio. -- 4th ed.

Includes index.
Third ed. by: Trent Ernst.
ISBN 978-1-926806-37-2

1. Recreation areas--Ontario--Maps. 2. Outdoor recreation--Ontario--
Guidebooks. 3. Ontario--Maps. 4. Ontario--Guidebooks. 5. Algonquin
Provincial Park (Ont.)--Maps. 6. Algonquin Provincial Park (Ont.)-
-Guidebooks. I. Mussio Ventures Ltd II. ˚Ernst, Trent. Backroad
mapbook, cottage country Ontario. III. Title.

G1147.S61E63M88 2012   796.509713   C2012-904399-0

Acknowledgement

This book could not have been compiled without the help of a tremendous team of individuals working for Mussio Ventures Ltd. This is a big thank you to the growing team of researchers and writers that includes Sean Anderson, Johan Axen, Leslie Bryant-McLean, Robert Causley, Trent Ernst, Carmine Minutillo, Mike Manyk and Jason Marleau. When combined with the efforts of Andrew Allen, Sean Conway, Joshua Desnoyers, Farnaz Faghihi, Shaun Filipenko, Oliver Herz, Chris Taylor, and Dale Tober we were able to produce the most comprehensive guidebook available for Cottage Country Ontario.

We would also like to thank the following for making a significant contribution to the latest version of the project: Scott Weaire for his terrific Massassauga Provincial Park campsite updates, Ken Hoeverman at the Ontario Federation of Trail Riders, Maria Micallef at the County of Haliburton, Pavel Gmuzdek with Haliburton Forest & Wild Life Reserve, Ltd., Keith Mewett at Samuel de Champlain Park, Christine Bolton of the Ministry of Natural Resources in Peterborough and Jeff Ball Georeferencing Data Specialist for the Ministry of Natural Resources. These individuals stood out, but there were countless other clubs and organizations, government officials, tourism personnel and store owners or outfitters who we asked to send us information or who helped us find the right people to talk to. We do apologize if we forgot to mention you by name or did not write your name down.

As always, we could not have done this book without the help that was provided to us by various folks who live, work, and play in this area. A special thanks to Algonquin Bound Outfitters, the Friends of Algonquin Park, the Ontario Federation of Anglers & Hunters, the Ontario Trails Council and the many other outfitters in the area. Their time to send information to us has been a tremendous asset in compiling the bountiful number of outdoor opportunities in the region.

We would like to express our gratitude to Geobase, Statistics Canada and Ontario Ministry of Natural Resources for their help as data source providers. Our maps also contain public sector Datasets made available under the City of Toronto's Open Data Licence v2.0. When combined with the countless updates, GPS tracks and map links loyal customers sent us over the years, we were able to provide the most up to date information for virtually every corner of the province.

Finally, we would like to thank Allison, Devon, Jasper, Madison, Nancy and Penny Mussio for their continued support of the Backroad Mapbook Series. As our families grow, it is becoming more and more challenging to break away from it all to explore our beautiful country.

Sincerely,
Russell and Wesley Mussio

Distributed by
Gordon Soules Book Publishers Ltd.
1359 Ambleside Lane,
West Vancouver, BC, Canada V7T 2Y9
books@gordonsoules.com
604-922-6588 Fax: 604-922-6574

Disclaimer

Mussio Ventures Ltd. does not warrant that the backroads, paddling routes and trails indicated in this Mapbook are passable nor does it claim that the Mapbook is completely accurate. Therefore, please be careful when using this or any source to plan and carry out your outdoor recreation activity.

Please note that traveling on logging roads, river routes and trails is inherently dangerous, and without limiting the generality of the foregoing, you may encounter poor road conditions, unexpected traffic, poor visibility, and low or no road/trail maintenance. Please use extreme caution when traveling logging roads and trails.

Please refer to the Fishing and Hunting Regulations for closures and restrictions. It is your responsibility to know when and where closures and restrictions apply.

Help Us Help You

A comprehensive resource such as Backroad Mapbooks for Cottage Country Ontario could not be put together without a great deal of help and support. Despite our best efforts to ensure that everything is accurate, errors do occur. If you see any errors or omissions, please continue to let us know.

All updates will be posted on our web site: www.backroadmapbooks.com

Please contact us at:
Mussio Ventures Ltd.
#106 - 1500 Hartley Ave,
Coquitlam, BC, V3K 7A1

Email: updates@backroadmapbooks.com
P: 604-521-6277 F: 604-521-6260
Toll Free 1-877-520-5670
www.backroadmapbooks.com

Cottage Country Ontario

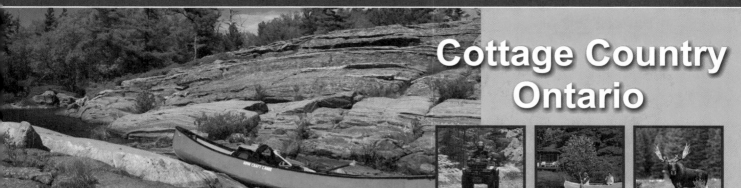

Image © David Lee

Welcome to the fourth edition of the Cottage Country Ontario Backroad Mapbook. Followers of the series will be happy to note the many new changes and updates. There are now separate sections for Hunting, ATV and Snowmobile Trails along with countless additions or tweaks in everything from Fishing, Parks and Wildlife Viewing. The maps have also been given a thorough review to add more Trails, fine tune the roads and add even more recreational activities.

Known as the heart of Ontario's outdoors, Cottage Country is home to thousands of scenic lakes and valleys making it one of the most popular outdoor destinations in North America. While the region is visited by thousands of travellers each year, with the Backroad Mapbook, it is easy to find a place to get away from it all.

With the inclusion of Algonquin Provincial Park, this book becomes even more indispensable to backroad travellers and outdoor adventurers. Algonquin is ground zero for adventure in Ontario, and every year, hundreds of thousands of hikers, mountain bikers, campers and canoeists come here to explore and experience the best of what Ontario has to offer. In fact, Algonquin is the world's most popular canoeing destination and people come from around the globe to experience this magical place.

But for all its glory, Algonquin is only one piece of this phenomenal area. Visitors can take an orienteering trip deep into the Massasauga Provincial Park or fish for the unique strain of Haliburton lake trout. And canoeists looking for places a little less crowded, can try places like the Gibson River Route and the Frost Centre Institute. There are all manner of trails that will keep hikers and bikers and skiers and ATVers occupied for days.

The main artery for travel through Cottage Country is Highway 400. This large highway stretches from the metro Toronto area north to Parry Sound with a branch (Highway 11) leading past Bracebridge and Huntsville. If you want to make good time in your travels it is best to include the large highway whenever possible. To the east and northeast, Highway 115/35 is the main artery that leads into the Kawarthas.

Branching from these larger highways are many scenic backroads and true bush roads. These roads skirt countless lakes as they wind through the rugged country that makes this region a favourite travel destination. The paved or hard packed gravel roads provide a more leisurely alternative to explore the area. For travellers that are not in a rush and simply want to enjoy the countryside, this is a real advantage. In the fall, the spectacular array of colours is a real motivator for visitors to get out and explore.

To many, our unique maps are the main reason for picking up the book. We emphasize the intricate backroad network, trail systems and recreation opportunities in Ontario. The emphasis on recreation activities allows for quick and easy referencing when researching a specific area.

However, not to be out done is the comprehensive listing of outdoor recreation activities. We include information on paddling routes, lake and stream fishing, camping (parks and conservation areas), multi-use trails (hiking/biking, and off road trails), wildlife viewing and winter recreation. Countless hours have been spent in researching this book, making it the most complete compilation you will find on the region anywhere. This information can be enjoyed by anyone who spends time in the great outdoors.

If you enjoy the outdoors, we are sure you will have as much fun using the Backroad Mapbook as we did in developing it!

History

The Backroad Mapbook idea came into existence when Wesley and Russell Mussio were out exploring. They had several books and a few maps to try to find their way through the maze of logging roads around southern BC. The brothers were getting very frustrated trying to find their way and eventually gave up. Not to be outdone, the two ambitious brothers started brainstorming. Eventually the Backroad Mapbook idea was born.

It was in BC that Jason Marleau eventually met Russell and Wesley from Backroad Mapbooks. This monumental meeting not only changed the career path of Jason but has also benefited many outdoor enthusiasts in Ontario and across the country. Jason has written and researched over a dozen Backroad Mapbooks and Fishing Mapbook titles. Not only has each of these titles gone on to become a national bestseller, they have also helped thousands of outdoor enthusiasts find that coveted fishing lake or hidden trail.

Jason Marleau with Russell & Wesley Mussio - Founders of Backroad Mapbooks

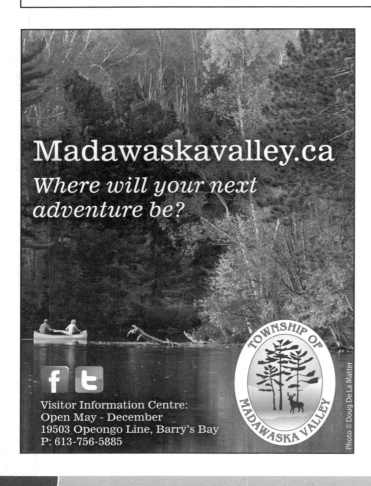
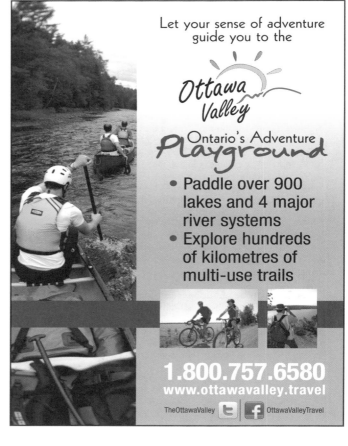

GET ANSWERS TO YOUR TRAVEL QUESTIONS!

- ❖ What to see
- ❖ What to do
- ❖ How to get there
- ❖ Transportation
- ❖ Accommodations
- ❖ Tours
- ❖ Attractions
- ❖ Special Events
- ❖ ...and more

Image © David Lee

Bancroft & District
CHAMBER OF COMMERCE TOURISM & INFO CENTRE

Ontario's Playground - For sport, for fun, for rejuvenation! White water challenges to calm serene lakes. Endless trails to cliffs of ice. Mineral collecting. Unique shopping. A rich heritage to experience, Abundant arts and the Rockhound Gemboree – Canada's largest Gem and Mineral Show. Yes...we DO have it all!

**Bancroft & District
Chamber of Commerce**

Bancroft, Ontario, K0L 1C0
613-332-1513 Phone
613-332-2119 Fax

www.BancroftDistrict.com

Visit Barrie and discover all the unique and exciting things that our vibrant city has to offer; quaint shops, award winning dining, live entertainment, attractions and excellent accommodations – all just a few steps away from beautiful beaches wrapped around Kempenfelt Bay, Lake Simcoe.

Tourism Barrie

205 Lakeshore Drive
Barrie, Ontario, L4N 7Y9

705-739-9444 Phone
1-800-668-9100 Toll Free

www.tourismbarrie.com

Just 90 minutes from Toronto with over 250 lakes and waterways to enjoy. Linked by the scenic Trent-Severn Waterway, with countless recreational choices for boaters, paddlers and anglers. Breathe the fresh air as you hike, cycle or ski over 600 km of trails through our fabulous rural landscape.

City of Kawartha Lakes

180 Kent Street West,
Lindsay, Ontario, K9V 2Y6

705-324-9411 Phone
1-866-397-6673 Toll Free

www.explorekawarthalakes.com

A wonderful year round destination with sparkling blue lakes and fascinating waterways. A charming heritage city, fascinating villages, exciting adventure and a world class Casino are all awaiting for you. This is the place to be, your vacation starts here!

Ontario's Lake Country
Orillia, Oro-Medonte, Rama, Ramara, Severn

705-325-9321 Phone
1-866-329-5959 Toll Free

www.OntariosLakeCountry.com

Come to Haliburton County and discover why the Highlands is your first choice for outdoor fun -- naturally! Your year round adventure destination featuring hundreds of kilometres of trails and hundreds of lakes for endless outdoor fun.

Haliburton Highlands Tourism Info Centre
12340 Hwy 35
Minden, Ontario, K0M 2K0

705-286-1777 Phone
1-800-461-7677 Toll Free

www.haliburtonholidays.com

Legend

C A N A D A

Scale Bar

Scale 1:150 000 1 Centimetre = 1.5 Kilometres

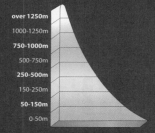

1.5km 0km 3km 7.5km

Map Information

Map Projection:
Universal Transverse Mercator Zone 17

Map Datum:
North American Datum 1983 (NAD 83)

Elevation Bar:

over 1250m
1000-1250m
750-1000m
500-750m
250-500m
150-250m
50-150m
0-50m

Area Indicators:

Provincial / National Park	City
Conservation / Natural Area	First Nations
Swamps	Crown Land
Water	Private / Restricted / Minning Areas

Contour Lines:

20m Intervals
100m Intervals
Contour Intervals approximately 20m

Line and Area Classifications:

═══	Freeways	▬◈▬	Trans Canada Trail
━━━	Highways	-------	Long Distance Trail
━━━	Secondary Highways	--------	ATV / Duo Sport Trails
━━━	Arterial Paved Roads	--------	Snowmobile Trails
───	Local Paved Roads	– – – –	Developed Trail
───	Forest Service / Main Industry Roads	· · · · ·	Routes (Undeveloped Trails)
───	Active Industry Roads (2wd)	– - – -	Ferry Routes - Trent Severn Waterway
───	Other Industry Roads (2wd / 4wd)	═══	Lake / River Paddling Routes
───	Unclassified / 4wd Roads	───	Portage Routes
-----	Deactivated Roads	–·–·–·	Powerlines
├─┼─┤	Railways	– – –	Pipelines
		▬▬▬	Wildlife Management Zones

Recreational Activities:

⚓ Anchorage   🚶 Hiking
🛥 Boat Launch   🐴 Horseback Riding
🌊 Beach   🏍 Motorbiking / ATV
⛺ Campsite / Limited Facilities   🚣 Paddling (canoe-kayak)
🚐 Campsite / Trailer Park   ⛱ Picnic Site
⛺ Campsite (back country / water access only)   Ⓟ Portage
🛶 Canoe Access Put-in / Take-out   Ⓡ Resort
⛷ Cross Country Skiing / Back Country Ski Touring   🧗 Rock Climbing
🚴 Cycling   🏂 Snowmobiling
🤿 Diving   ❄ Snowshoeing
🪂 Downhill Skiing   TH Trailhead
⛳ Golf Course   🔭 Wildlife Viewing
🪁 Hang-gliding   🏄 Windsurfing

Miscellaneous:

✈ Airport / Airstrip   ⊢ Dam / Lock
AP Algonquin Park Access   🚩 Long Distance Trail
↗ Arrow / Location Pointer   ⚘ Marsh
☼ Beacon   ⚓ Microwave Tower
🏠 Cabin / Hut   ☒ Mine Site (abandoned)
◎ City, Town, Village Indicator   Ⓟ Parking
🏞 Conservation Area   ✛ Pictograph
✂ Customs   ★ Point of Interest
⛴ Ferries   P50m Portage Distance
🛩 Float Plane Landing   🏛 Ranger Station
Ⓖ Gate   ▱▱▱▱ Snowmobile Route Trail Number
🛡 Highway: Trans Canada   🚆 Train Station
🛡 Highway: Primary   ⓘ Travel Information
▽ County Road   🚵 Viewpoint / Forestry Lookout (abandoned)
◇ Interchange   🏙 Waterfalls
🗼 Lighthouse   🦅 Wilderness Area / Wildlife Area / Wildlife Reserve
    🍇 Winery

Map Features

Recreational Features

You will find the maps mark points of interest, paddling routes, parks and conservation areas, trail systems and even wildlife viewing opportunities. **ATV, snowmobile trails** and **long distance trails** are highlighted with a background colour to aid users in tracking these systems. Hunters and anglers will also be happy to see that we have included the **Management Units** on the maps. The big green number notes the zones while the boundaries are marked with a faint green border. For a complete list of symbols and what they mean please refer to our Map Legend.

Road Features & Map Legend

By combining city and rural roads with current forestry and logging road maps our maps are designed for people wishing to get outdoors. However, they are very detailed and the myriad of current logging and industrial roads in addition to the various trail systems can be confusing. We provide a **map legend** at the start of each section of the maps to illustrate the region we cover as well as how to decipher the various grades of roads and symbols used on the maps.

Below are some more common features of our maps:

Roads & Trails

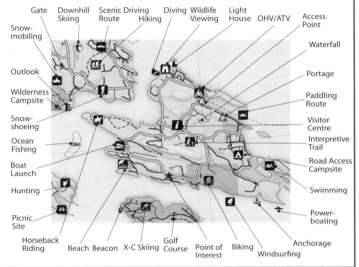

Recreational & Misc

UTM Grid & Longitude and Latitude

A useful navigational feature on our maps is the small numbers provided around our map borders. These blue numbers represent UTM Grids and the black numbers represent Longitude and Latitude reference points. Although most GPS units are set to longitude and latitude, switching the unit to UTM (NAD 83) is both easier and more accurate for land-based travel. Since our maps provide UTM grid lines that are 10,000 metres apart (both east & north), users can accurately pinpoint the location of features by dividing the grid into 10 equal parts (both east & north). Counting the number of tics from the nearest coordinate value and multiplying by 1,000 will give you the UTM coordinate. Do this for both the Easting (the numbers along the top and bottom of the map border) and the Northing (the numbers along the side) and you will have an accurate GPS waypoint.

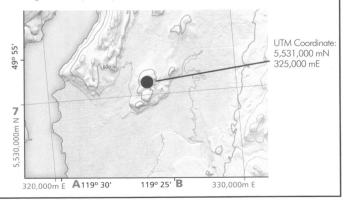

UTM Coordinate:
5,531,000 mN
325,000 mE

How to use the Scale Bar

To use the scale bar provided for each map, you can do one of the following things:

1) Use a piece of paper & mark the distance intervals from the scale bar. Then put that piece of paper on the map and measure the distance between two points. In example below the distance between "Adventure" & "Discovery" is 2 units or 3 kilometres.

2) Measure your distance with a piece of string, then place the string on the scale bar to find out the kilometres.

3) You can draw the approximate unit lines on the map itself (the green bars below) and then estimate the distance.

Note that all measurements are approximate.

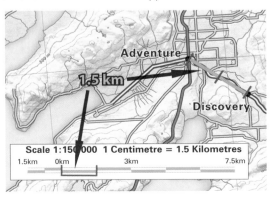

Inset Maps

Huntsville Map 34/C1

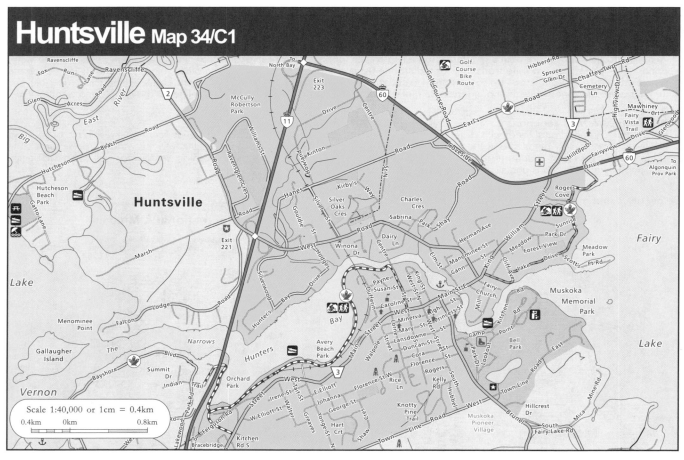

Scale 1:40,000 or 1cm = 0.4km
0.4km   0km   0.8km

North Bay Map 62/D2

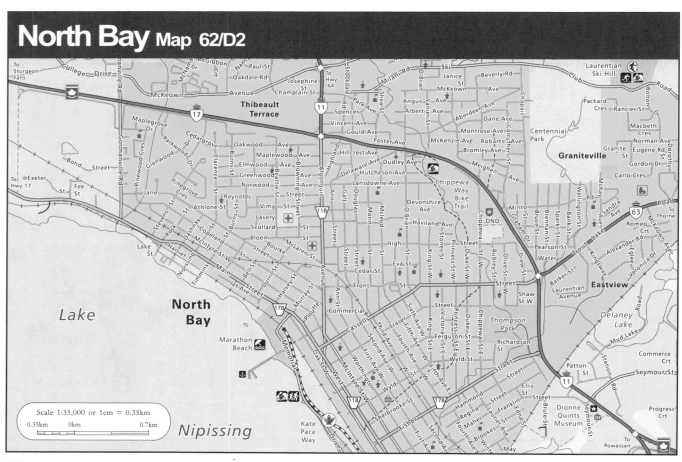

Scale 1:35,000 or 1cm = 0.35km
0.35km   0km   0.7km

Cottage Country Ontario

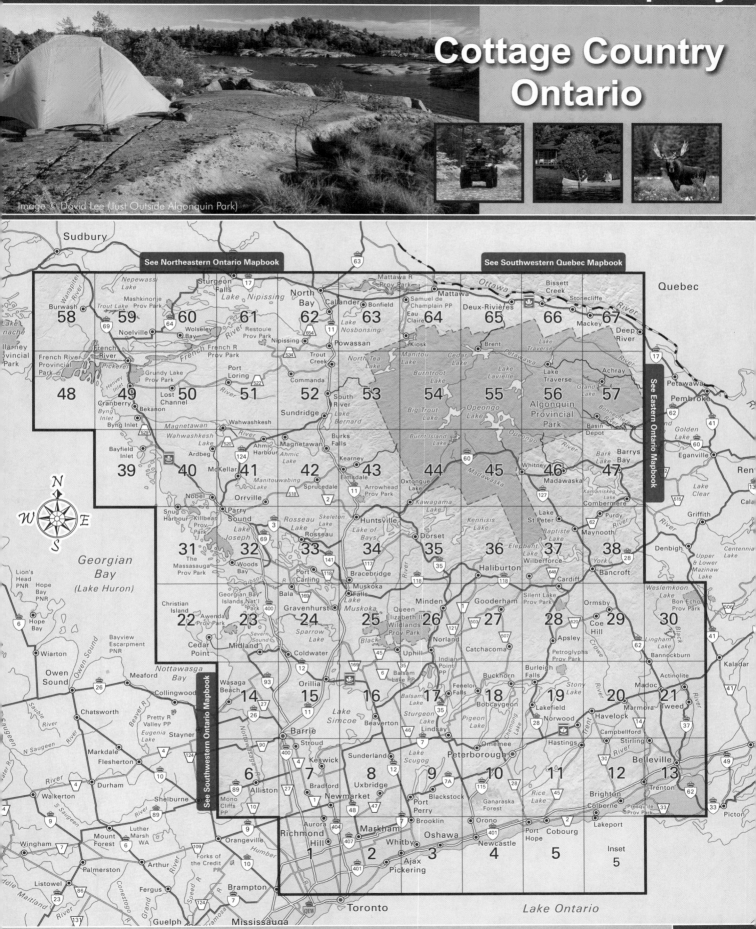

Image © David Lee (Just Outside Algonquin Park)

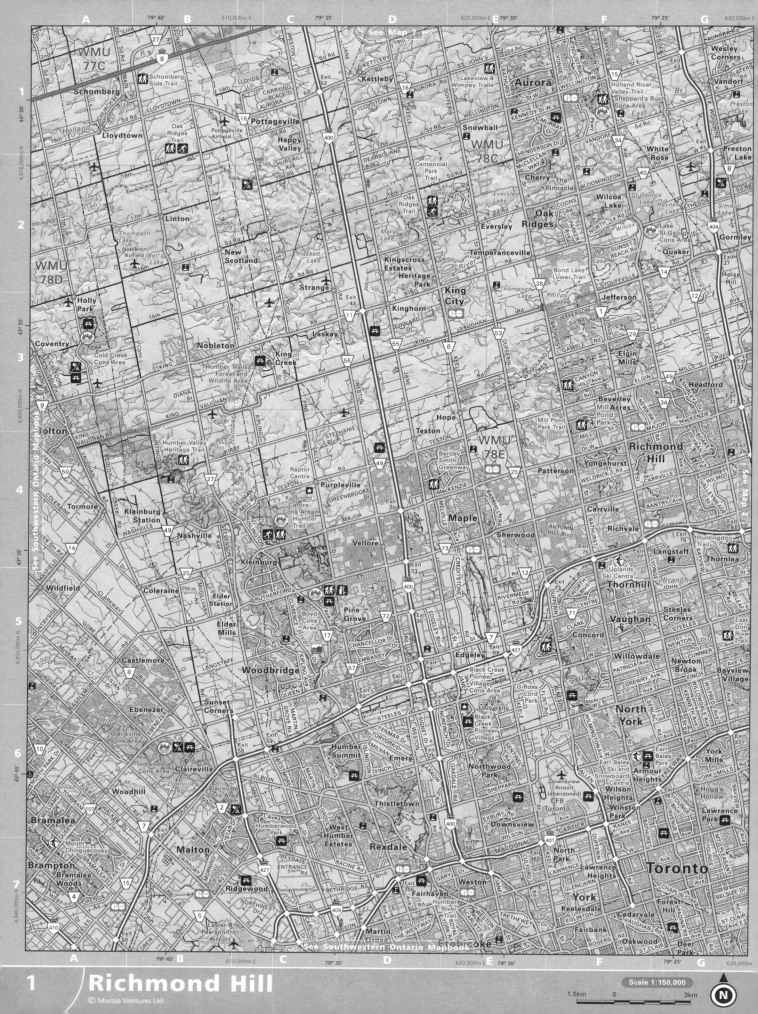

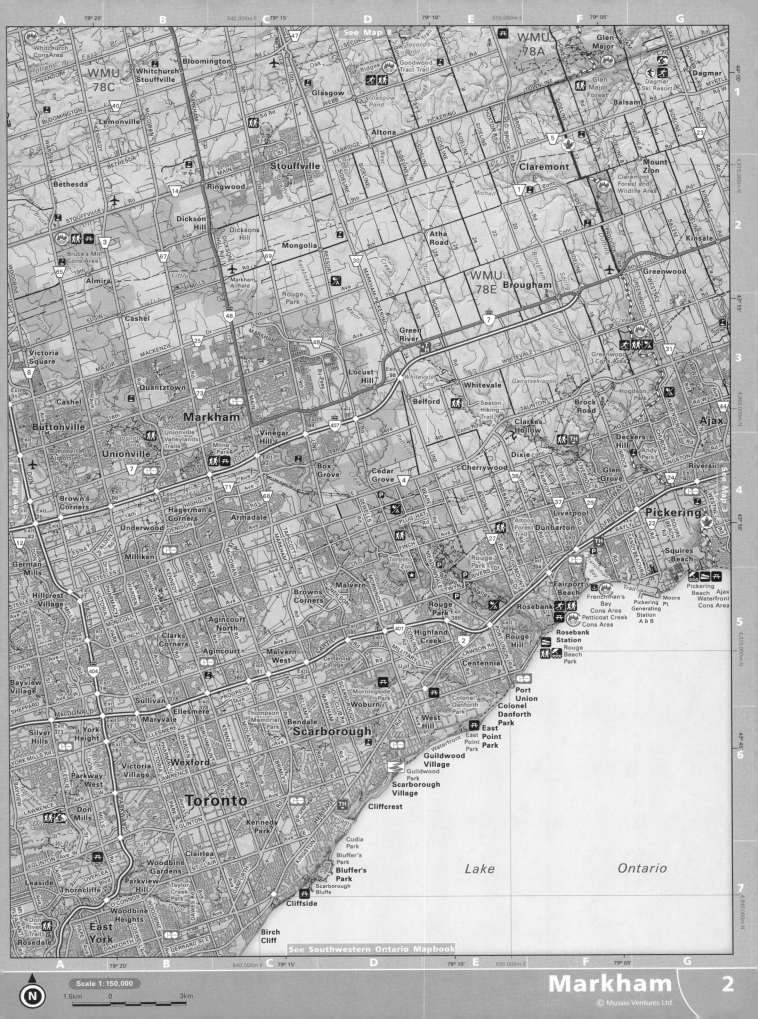

Scale 1:150,000

1.5km   0   3km

© Mussio Ventures Ltd.

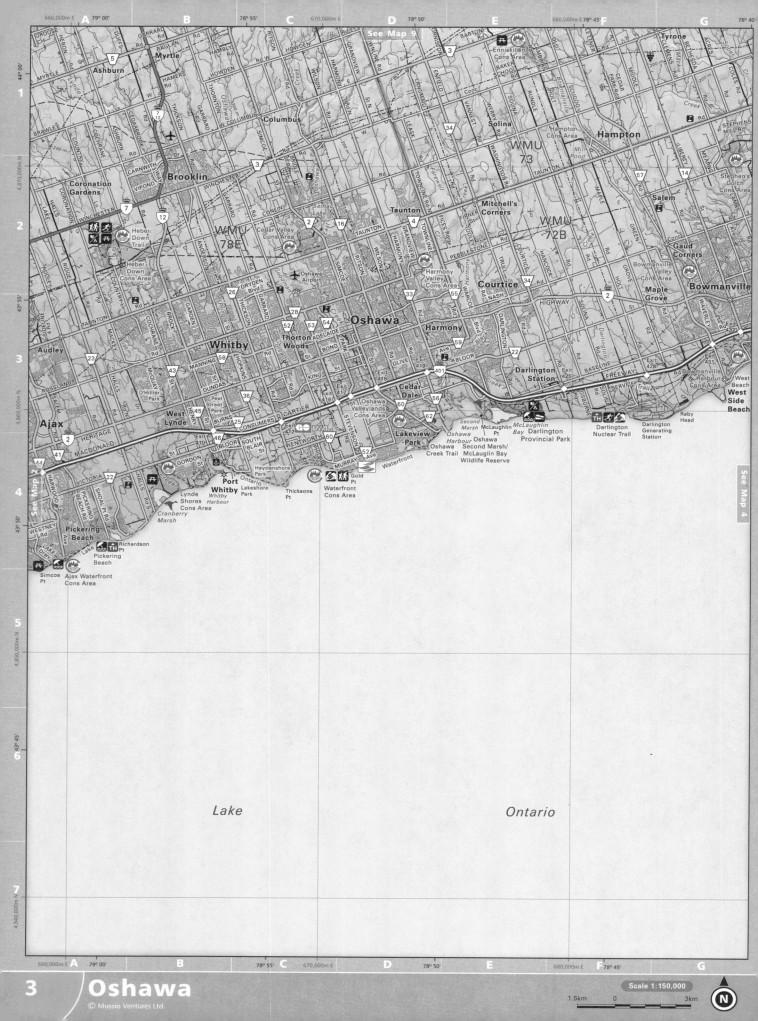

Oshawa

© Mussio Ventures Ltd.

Scale 1:150,000

1.5km 0 3km

N

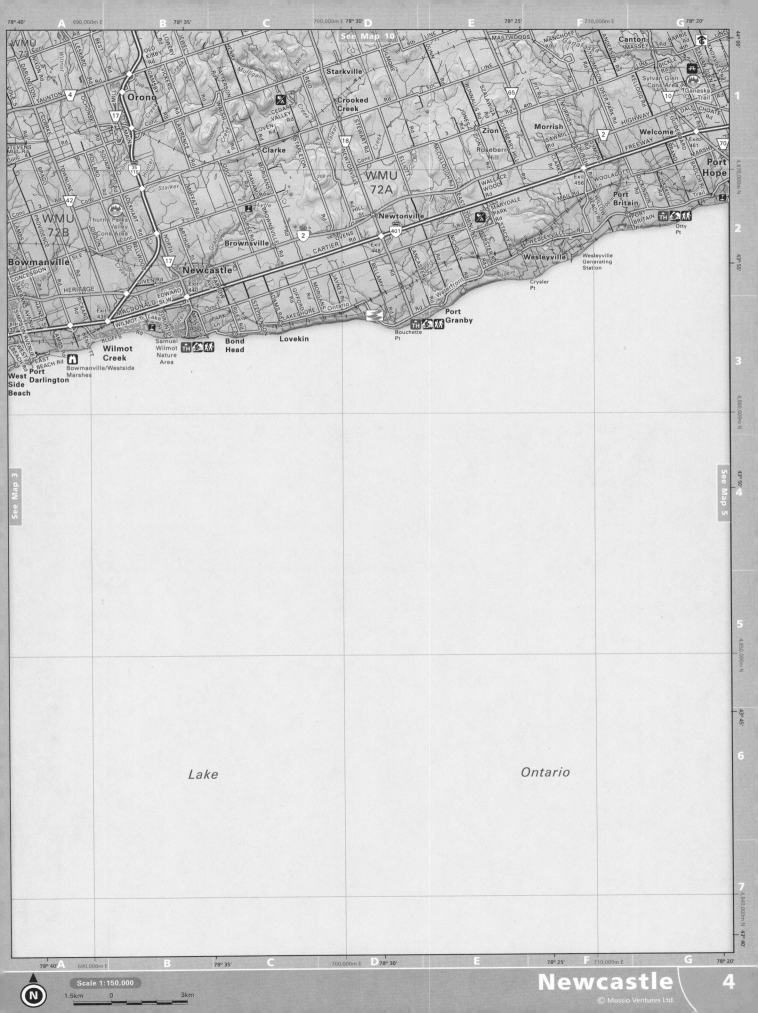

Scale 1:150,000

1.5km   0   3km

WMU
72A

Grafton

Haldimand
Cons Area
& Jubilee
Beach Park

Brookside

Coverdale

Spicer

Chub
Pt

Lucas
Point

Cobourg
Harbour

Cobourg

Carr's Marsh
Cons Area

Peter
Rock

**Port
Hope**

Dale

Ganaraska
Millenium
Trail

Ganaraska
Fishway

Lakeport

Victoria Beach
Loughbreeze

Sebastopol
Pt

Gull Island

Presqu'ile Provincial Park

Proctor
Pt

High Bluff
Island

The Bluff

Haldimand
Cons Area
& Jubilee
Beach Park

Wicklow
Beach
Boat Launch

McGlennon
Pt

Lake Ontario
Waterfront
Trail

Ogden
Pt

Lake

Ontario

Lake

Ontario

Scale 1:150,000

1.5km   0   3km

N

Alliston

6

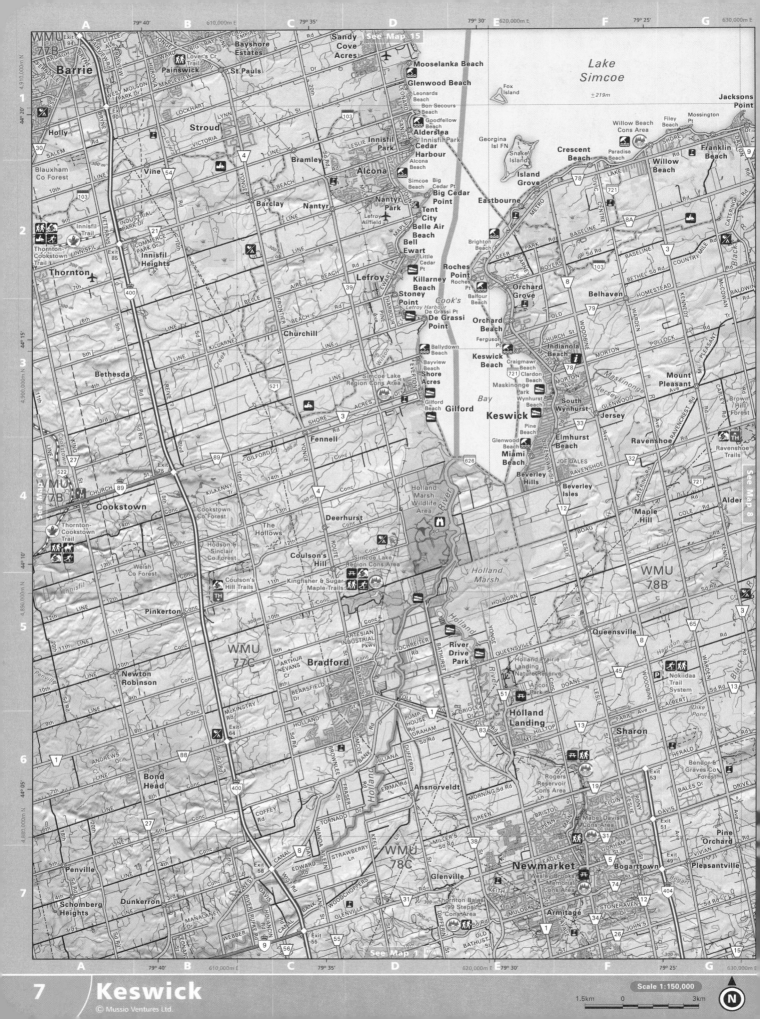

Scale 1:150,000

1.5km   0   3km

© Mussio Ventures Ltd.

Scale 1:150,000

1.5km 0 3km

N

Port Perry

© Mussio Ventures Ltd.

Scale 1:150,000

1.5km   0   3km

N

Peterborough

Scale 1:150,000

1.5km 0 3km

N

© Mussio Ventures Ltd.

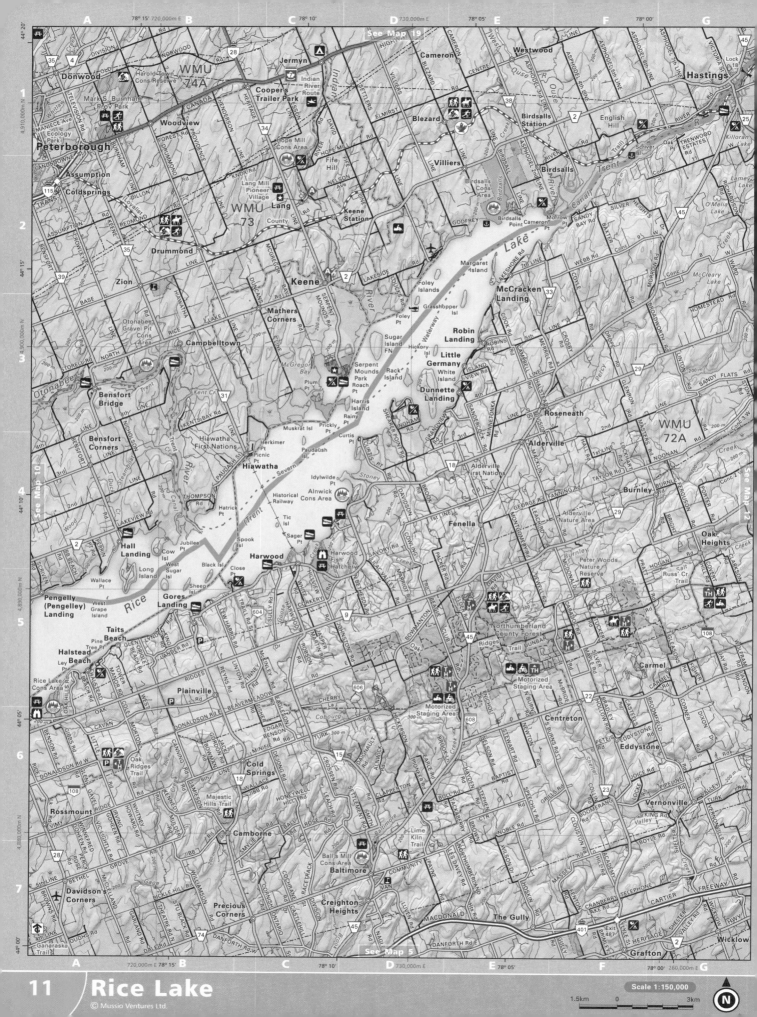

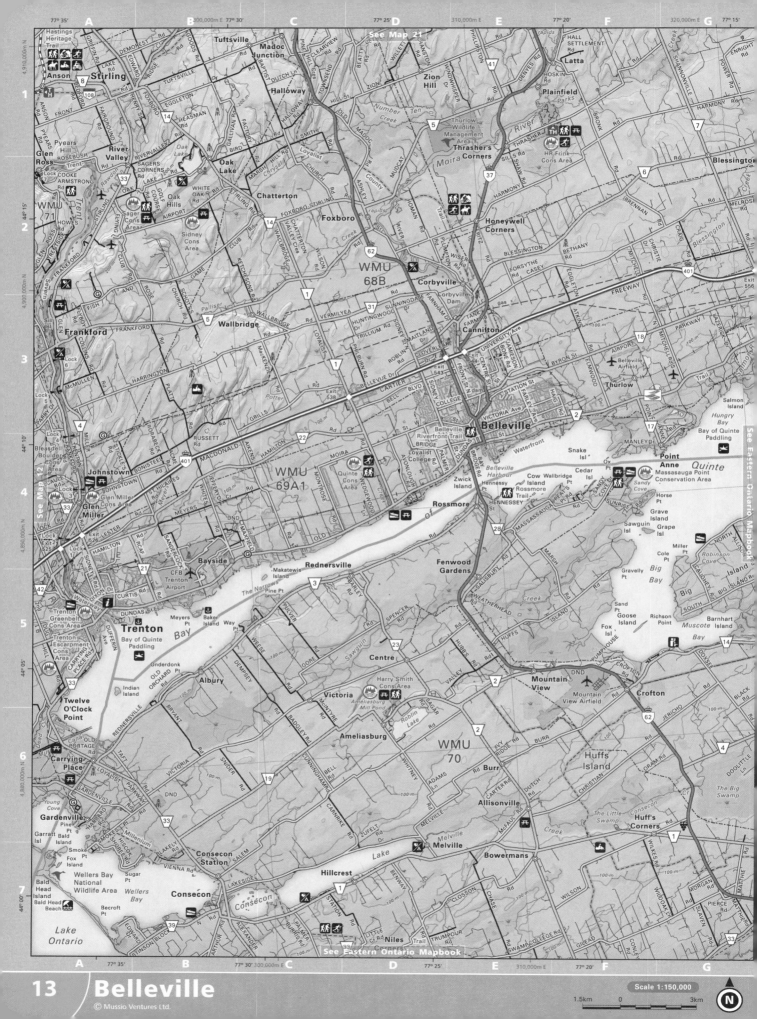

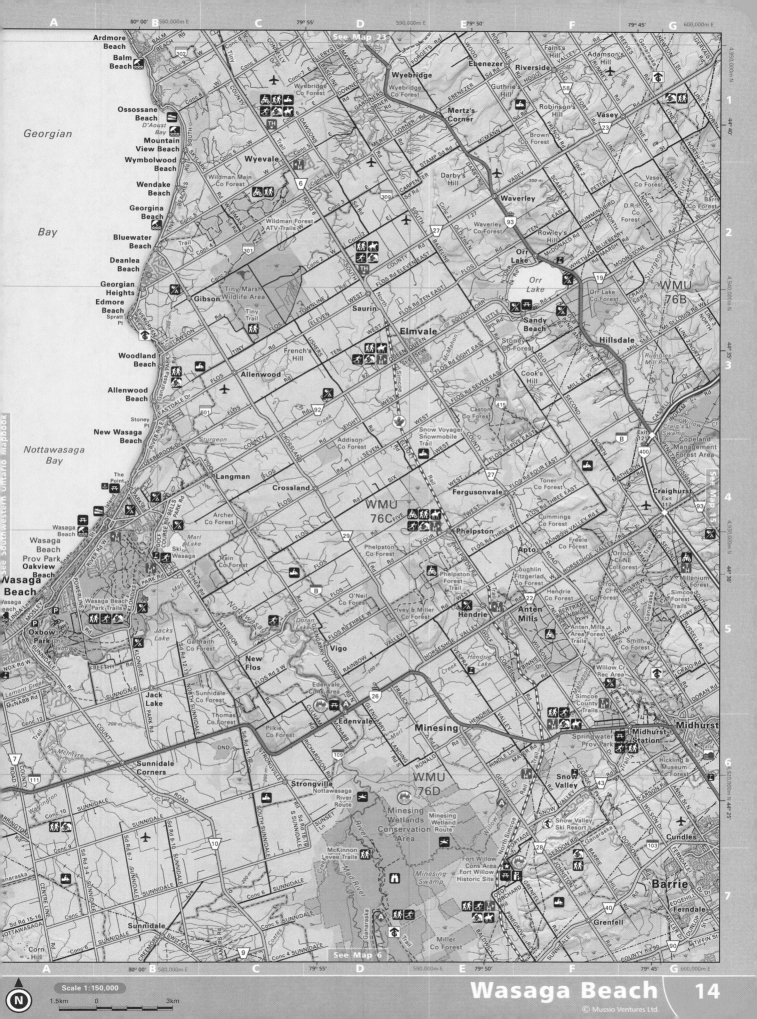

Scale 1:150,000

1.5km 0 3km

N

© Mussio Ventures Ltd.

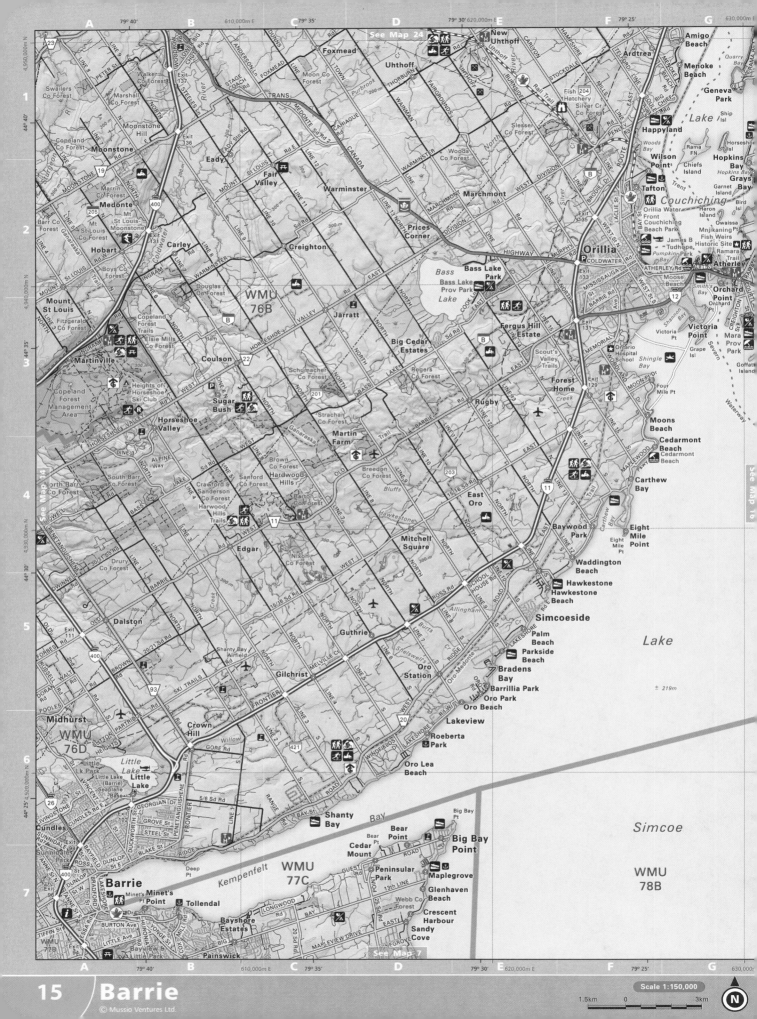

© Mussio Ventures Ltd.

Scale 1:150,000

1.5km   0   3km

N

Scale 1:150,000

1.5km   0   3km

© Mussio Ventures Ltd.

17 Lindsay

© Mussio Ventures Ltd.

Scale 1:150,000

Scale 1:150,000

1.5km 0 3km

© Mussio Ventures Ltd.

Scale 1:150,000

1.5km　0　3km

N

Havelock

20

Scale 1:150,000

1.5km   0   3km

N

© Mussio Ventures Ltd.

© Mussio Ventures Ltd.

Scale 1:150,000

1.5km 0 3km

N

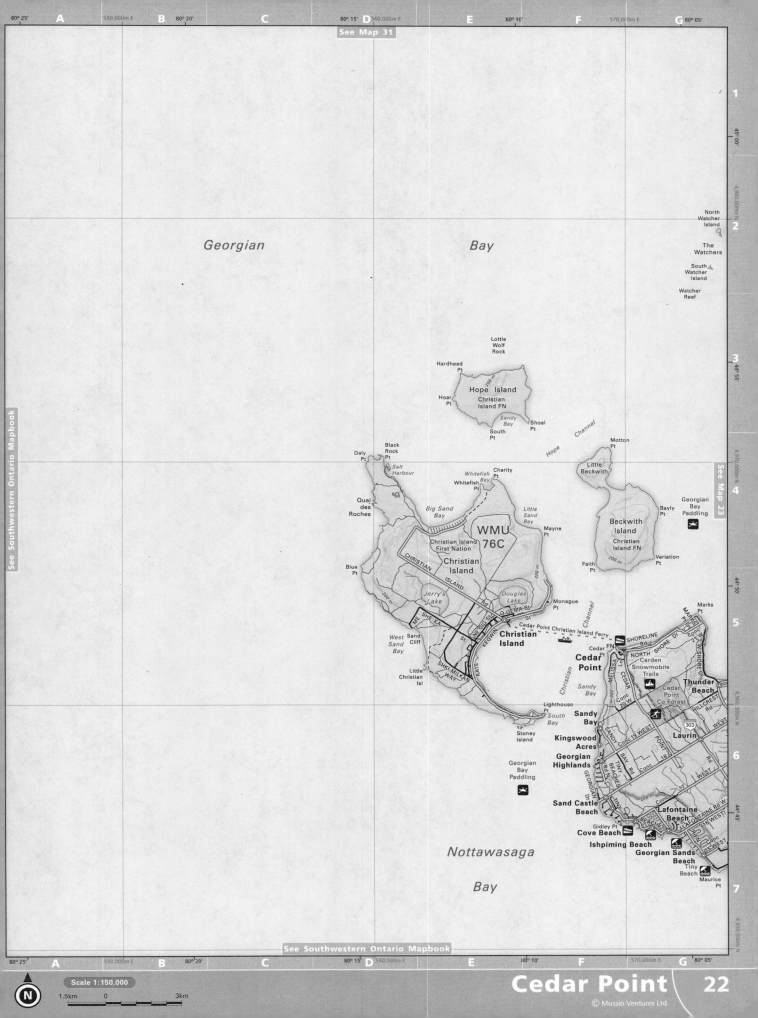

A · B · C · D · E · F · G

80° 25' 550,000m E 80° 20' 560,000m E 80° 15' 80° 10' 570,000m E 80° 05'

1

45° 00'

4,980,000m N

North
Watcher
Island

2

The Watchers

South
Watcher
Island

Georgian   *Bay*

Watcher
Reef

Lottie
Wolf
Rock

3   44° 55'

Hardhead
Pt

200 m

Hope Island

Hoar
Pt

Christian
Island FN

Hope Channel

Motton
Pt

Sandy
Bay

Shoal
Pt

Little
Beckwith

South
Pt

Daly
Pt

Black
Rock
Pt

Salt
Harbour

Whitefish
Bay

Charity
Pt

Bayly
Pt

Georgian
Bay
Paddling

4   4,970,000m N

Whitefish
Pt

Little
Sand
Bay

See Map 23

Quai
des
Roches

Big Sand
Bay

**WMU
76C**

Mayne
Pt

Beckwith
Island

Christian
Island FN

200 m

Christian Island
First Nation

Variation
Pt

Blue
Pt

CHRISTIAN ISLAND Rd

**Christian
Island**

Faith
Pt

200 m

200 m

Jerry's
Lake

Douglas
Lake

Monague
Pt

5   44° 50'

NE-SHE-KA St

O-GEMA St

KEGWIN

Cedar Point Christian Island Ferry

Marks
Pt

West
Sand
Bay

Sand
Cliff

St

**Christian
Island**

Christian

Channel

Cedar
FN

SHORELINE Rd

NORTH SHORE Dr

MARINA

SHORE DR

Conc 21 W

KATE

Little
Christian Isl

SHKI-MILKAN WAY

Cedar
Pt

**Cedar
Point**

NORTH
Carden
Snowmobile
Trails

Thunder
Beach

4,960,000m N

Sandy
Bay

Cedar
Point
Co Forest

HILLCREST Rd

Lighthouse
Pt

South
Bay

Sandy
Bay

**Sandy
Bay**

Conc 20 W

CEDAR

MELISSA

303

WEST

Laurin

Stoney
Island

**Kingswood
Acres**

Conc 19 WEST

SANDY BAY Rd

TINY BEACHES

POINT Rd

Conc 18

6

**Georgian
Highlands**

GEORGIAN DR

TINY

Georgian
Bay
Paddling

Conc 17

200 m

Conc 16

Nottawasaga

**Sand Castle
Beach**

BEACHES

**Lafontaine
Beach**

LAFONTAINE Rd W

44° 45'

Gidley Pt

Cove Beach

Conc (16) WEST

LAFONTAINE Rd W (16) WEST

Bay

Ishpiming Beach

**Georgian Sands
Beach**

Tiny
Beach

Conc 15 WEST

7

Maurice
Pt

4,950,000m N

A · B · C · D · E · F · G

80° 25' 550,000m E 80° 20' 560,000m E 80° 15' 80° 10' 570,000m E 80° 05'

N

Scale 1:150,000

1.5km   0   3km

Cedar Point   **22**

© Mussio Ventures Ltd.

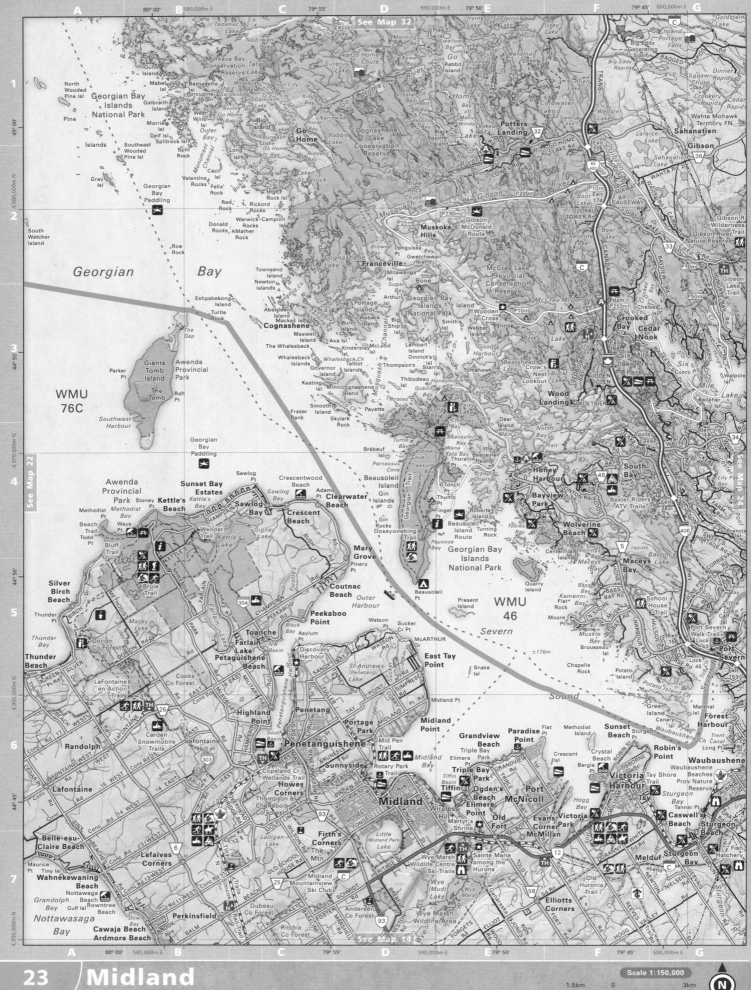

Midland

© Mussio Ventures Ltd.

Scale 1:150,000

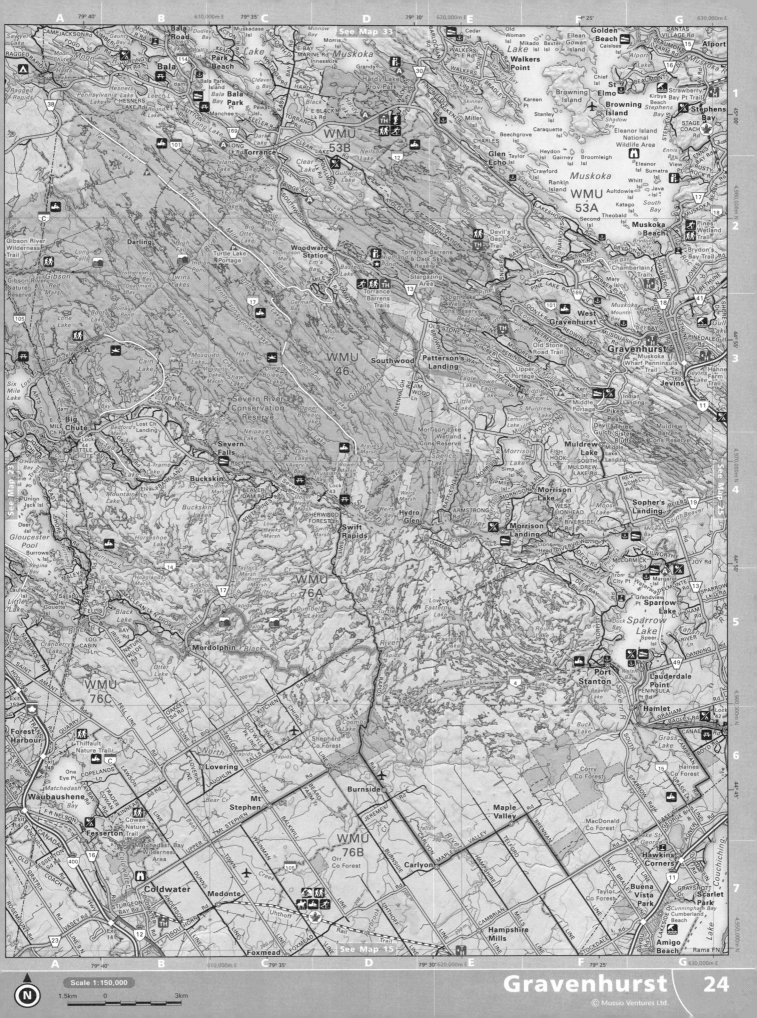

Muskoka Falls

© Mussio Ventures Ltd.

Scale 1:150,000

1.5km 0 3km

N

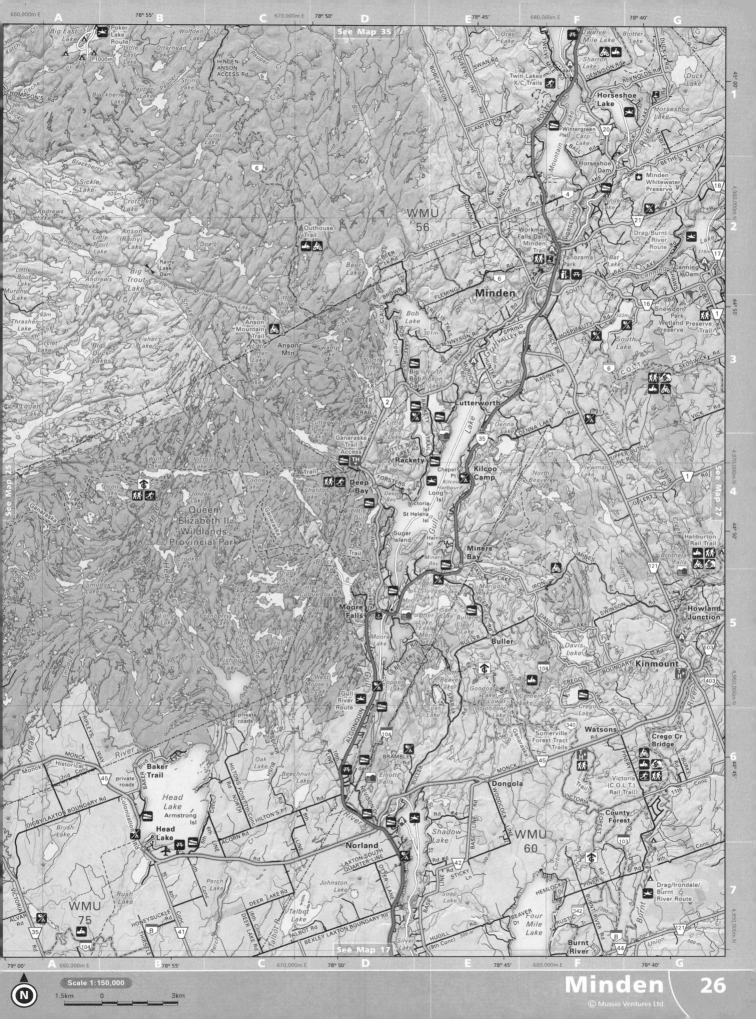

Minden

26

Scale 1:150,000

N

1.5km 0 3km

© Mussio Ventures Ltd.

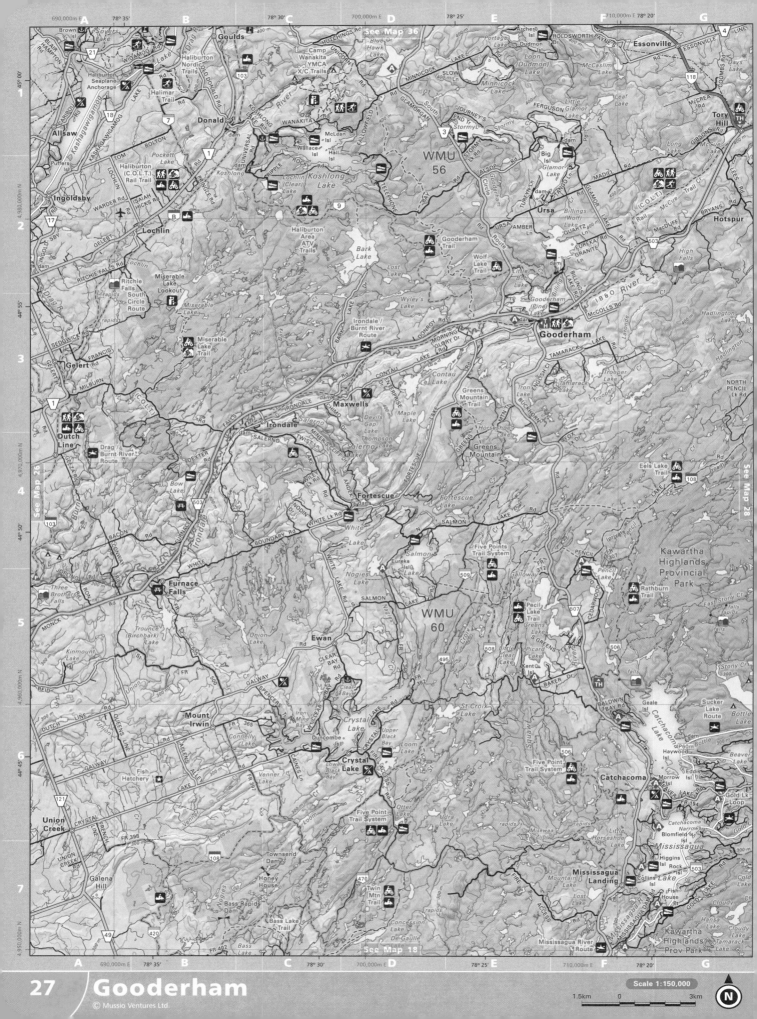

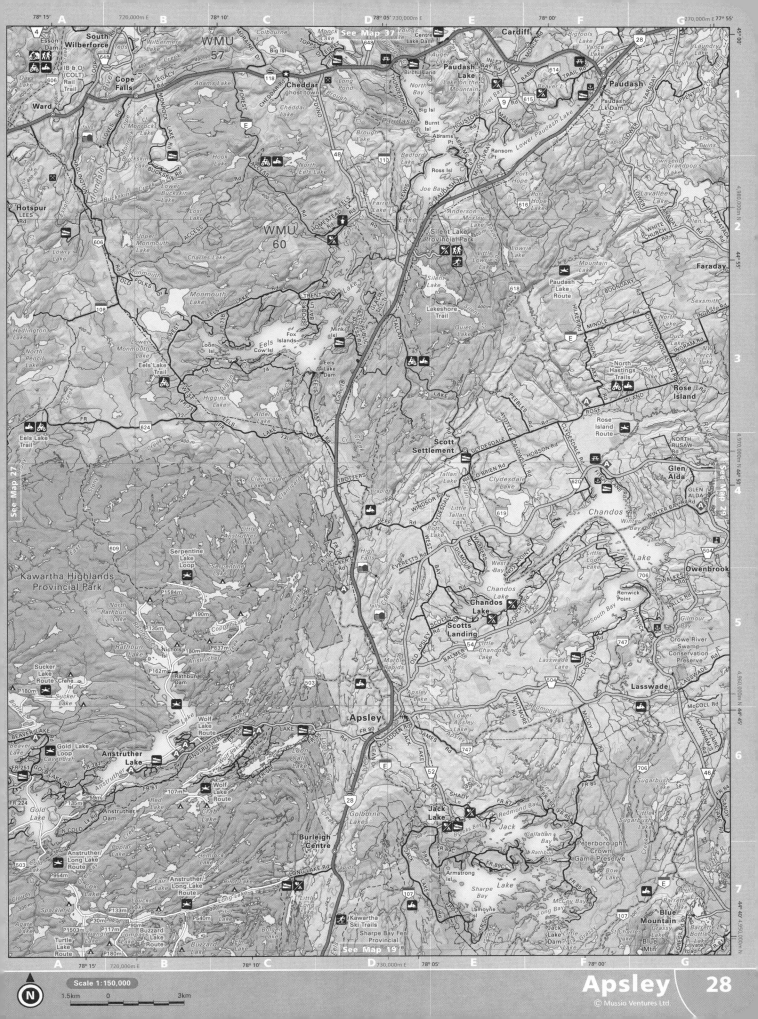

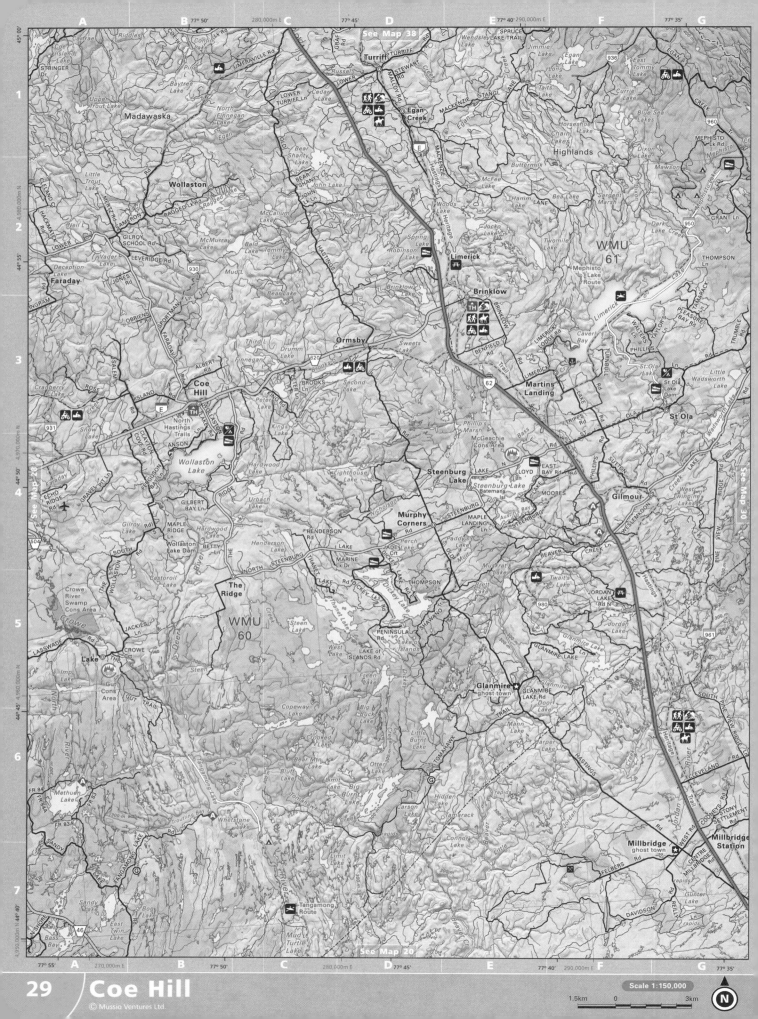

Coe Hill

© Mussio Ventures Ltd.

Scale 1:150,000

1.5km 0 3km

N

WMU 63A

Massanoga

Bon Echo Provincial Park

Bon Echo

WMU 61

Lingham Lake Cons Reserve

Lingham Lake

Mount Moriah Cons Reserve

Mt Moriah

Upper Black River Route

Deerock Conservation Area

Elzevir Peatlands Cons Reserve

Flinton

Cooper

See Map 29

See Eastern Ontario Mapbook

See Map 21

Scale 1:150,000

1.5km 0 3km

N

Lingham Lake

30

© Mussio Ventures Ltd.

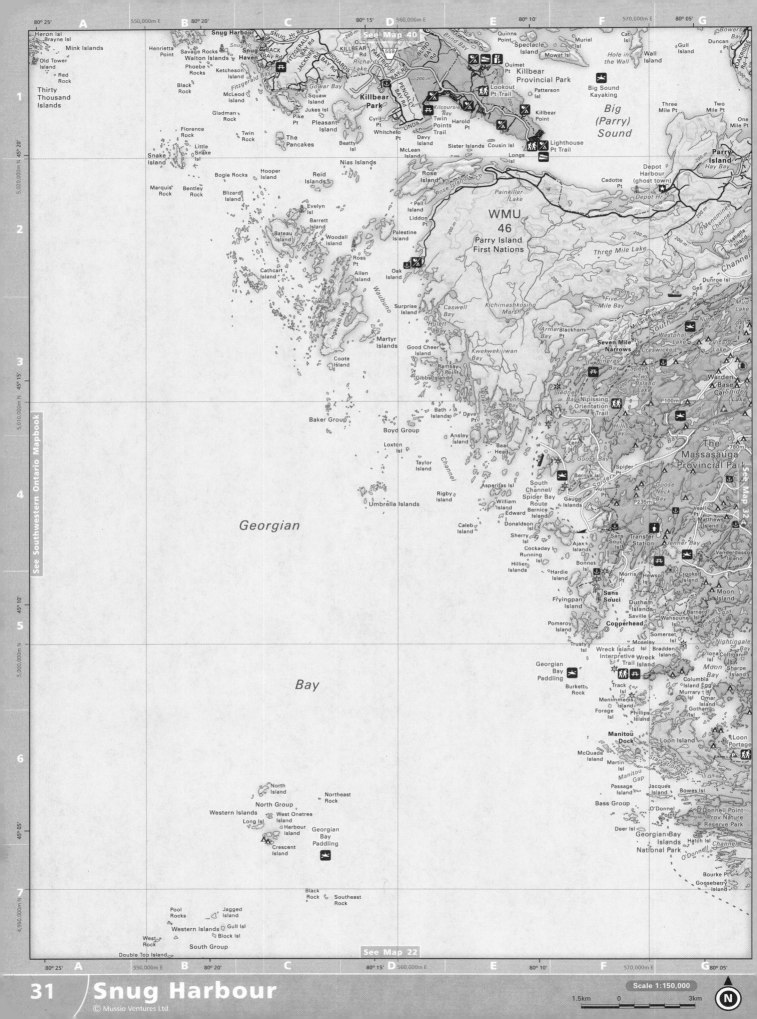

Scale 1:150,000

1.5km   0   3km

Scale 1:150,000

1.5km   0   3km

© Mussio Ventures Ltd.

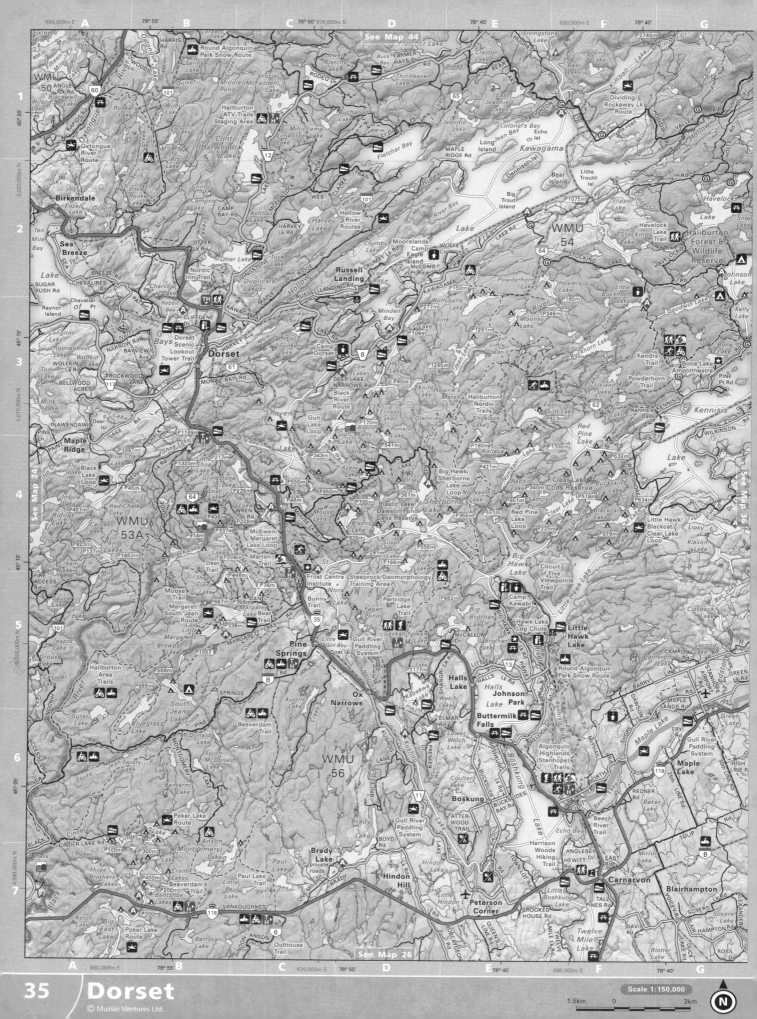

35 Dorset

© Mussio Ventures Ltd.

Scale 1:150,000

1,5km 0 3km

N

Algonquin Provincial Park

WMU 54

WMU 56

Haliburton Forest & Wildlife Reserve

Kennisis Lake

Redstone Lake

Fort Irwin

Eagle Lake

West Guilford

Harburn

Haliburton

Gould's

Madawaska Lake Route

Round Algonquin Park Snow Route

P780m Expect low water conditions in Spring from Cauliflower Lake to Billings Lake

Scale 1:150,000
1.5km 0 3km

N

Haliburton

36

© Mussio Ventures Ltd.

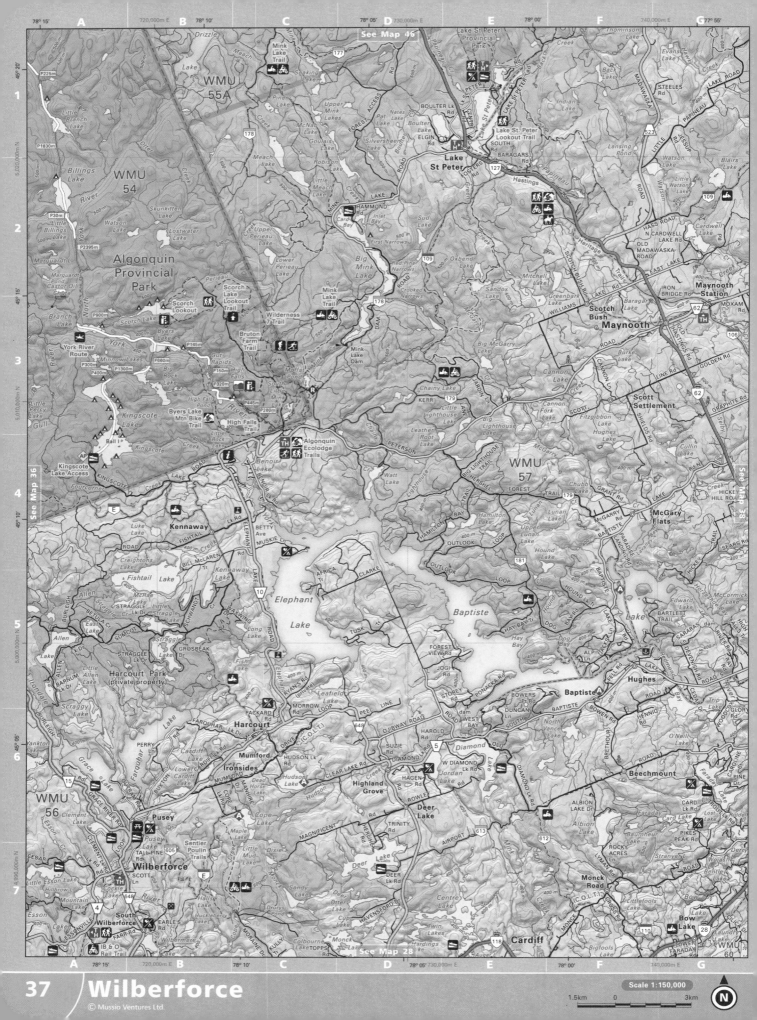

Wilberforce

© Mussio Ventures Ltd

Scale 1:150,000

N

Scale 1:150,000

1.5km   0   3km

© Mussio Ventures Ltd.

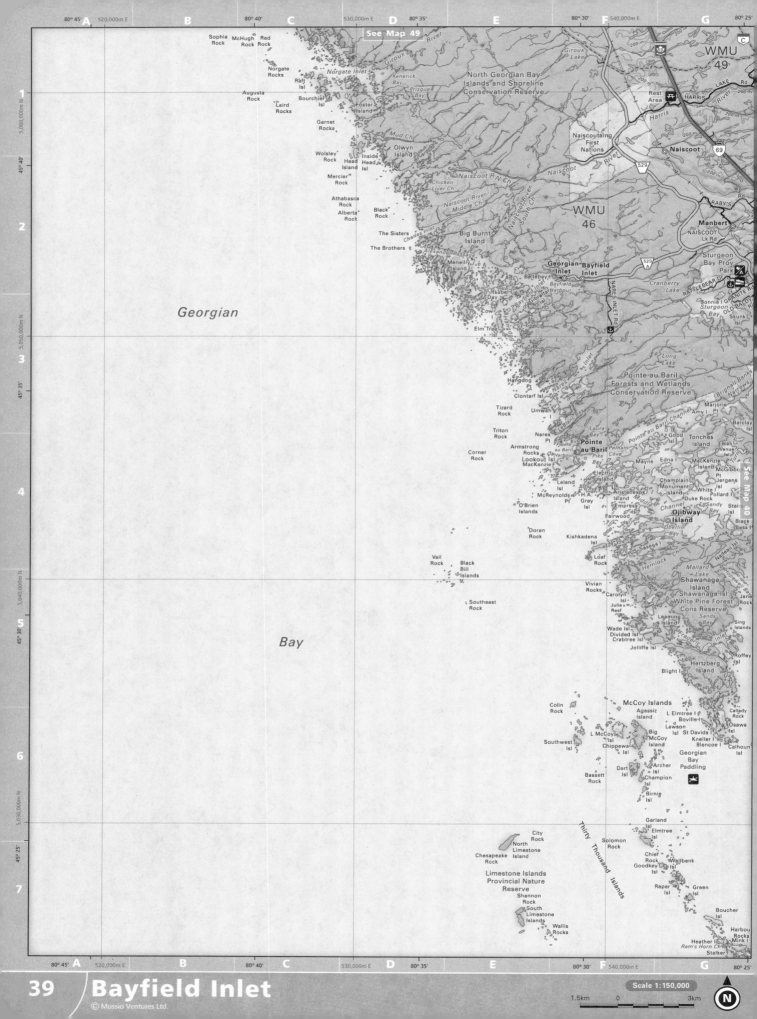

39 Bayfield Inlet

© Mussio Ventures Ltd.

Scale 1:150,000

1.5km   0   3km

N

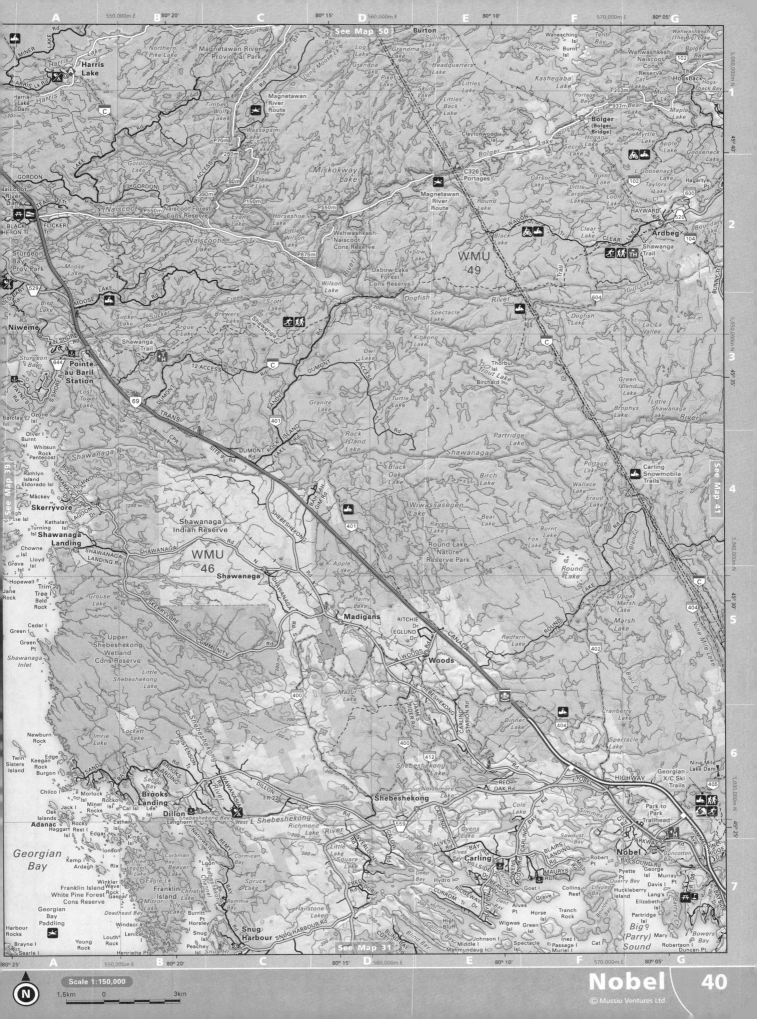

© Mussio Ventures Ltd.

Scale 1:150,000

1.5km   0   3km

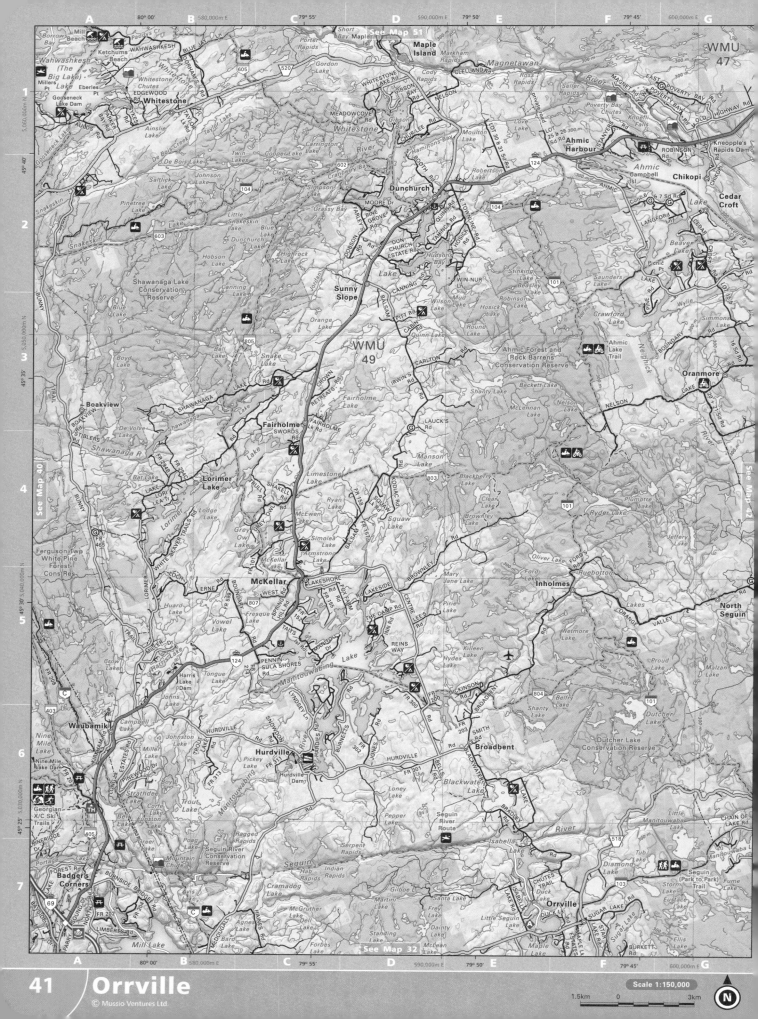

© Mussio Ventures Ltd.

Scale 1:150,000

WMU 47

WMU 49

See Map 40

See Map 42

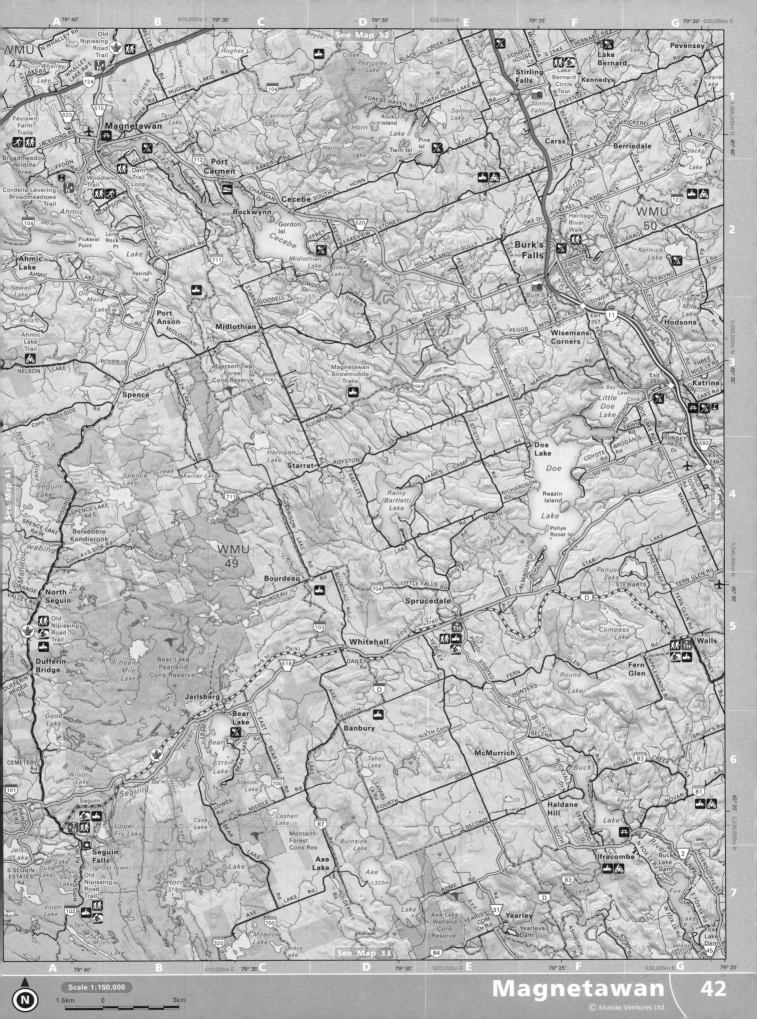

Scale 1:150,000

1.5km   0   3km

© Mussio Ventures Ltd.

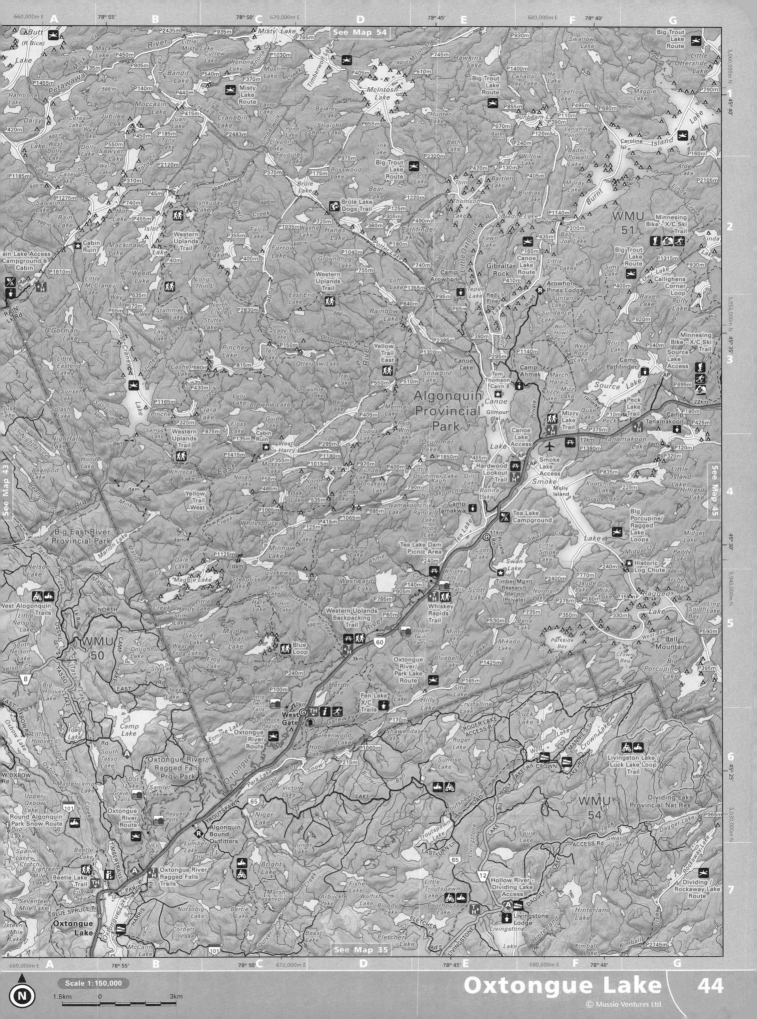

Algonquin
Provincial
Park

WMU 51

WMU 50

WMU 54

Big East River
Provincial Park

Oxtongue River
Ragged Falls
Prov Park

Scale 1:150,000
1.5km   0   3km
N

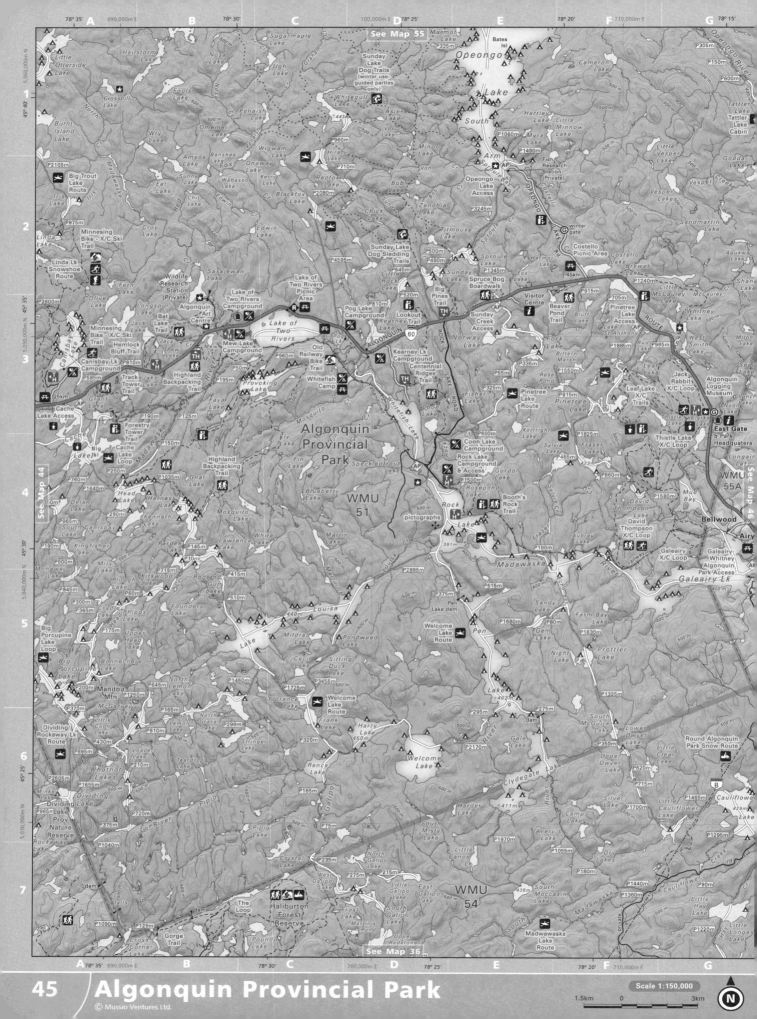

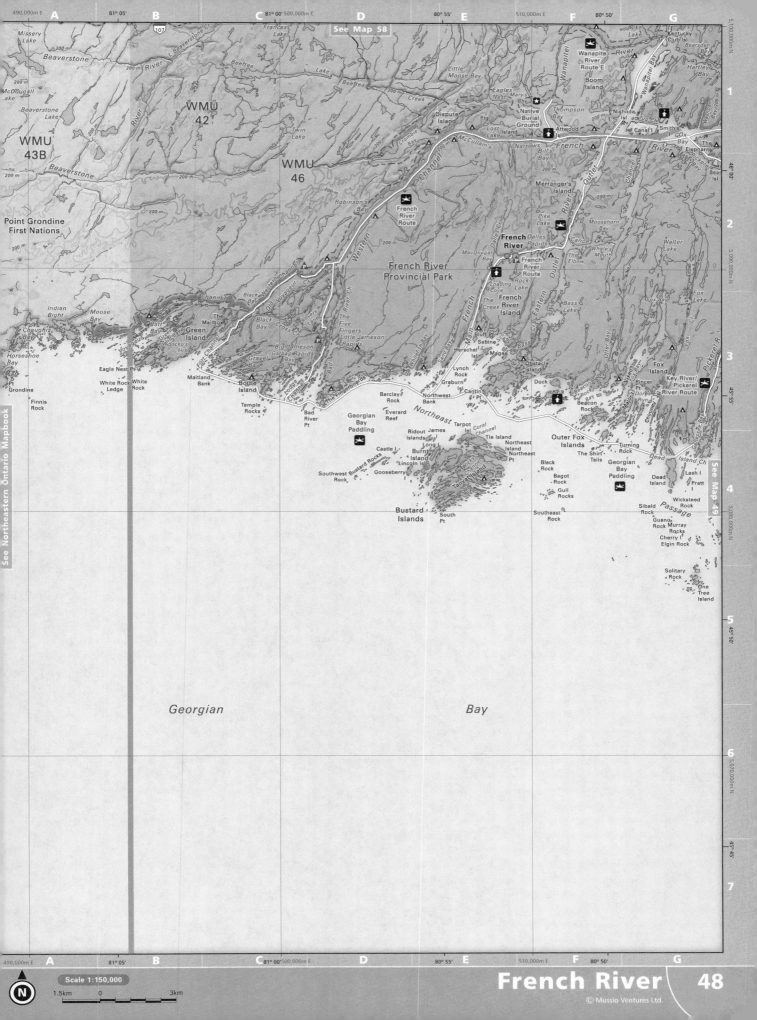

French River

48

Scale 1:150,000

1.5km 0 3km

© Mussio Ventures Ltd.

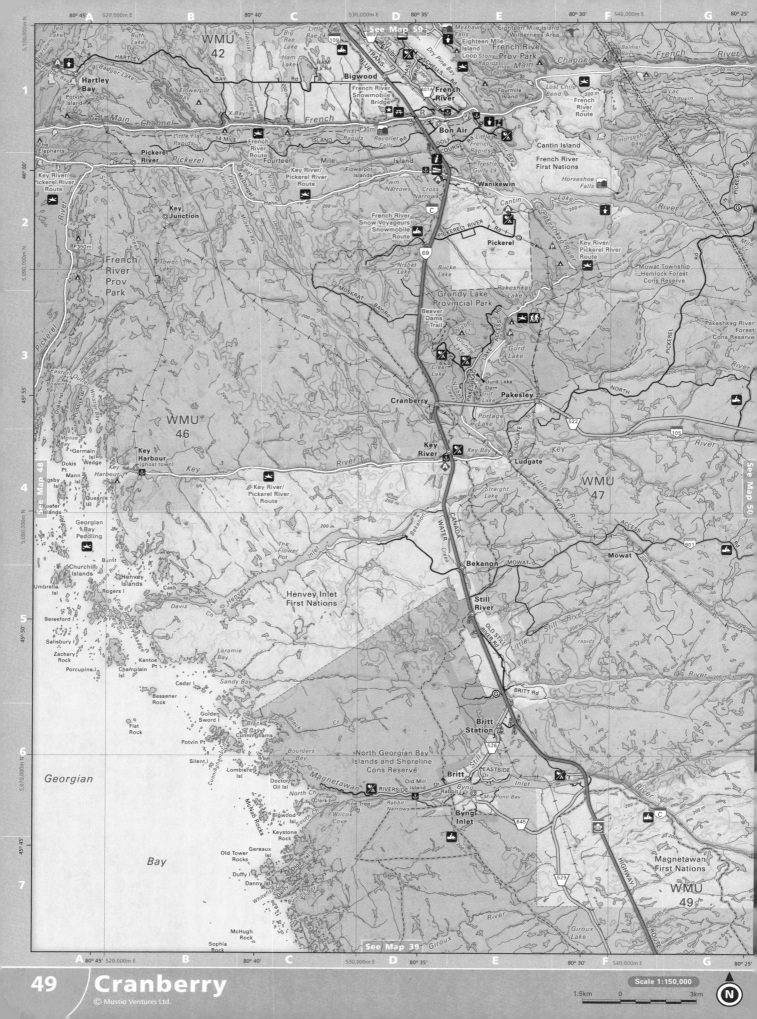

Scale 1:150,000

1.5km 0 3km

Scale 1:150,000

1.5km   0   3km

© Mussio Ventures Ltd.

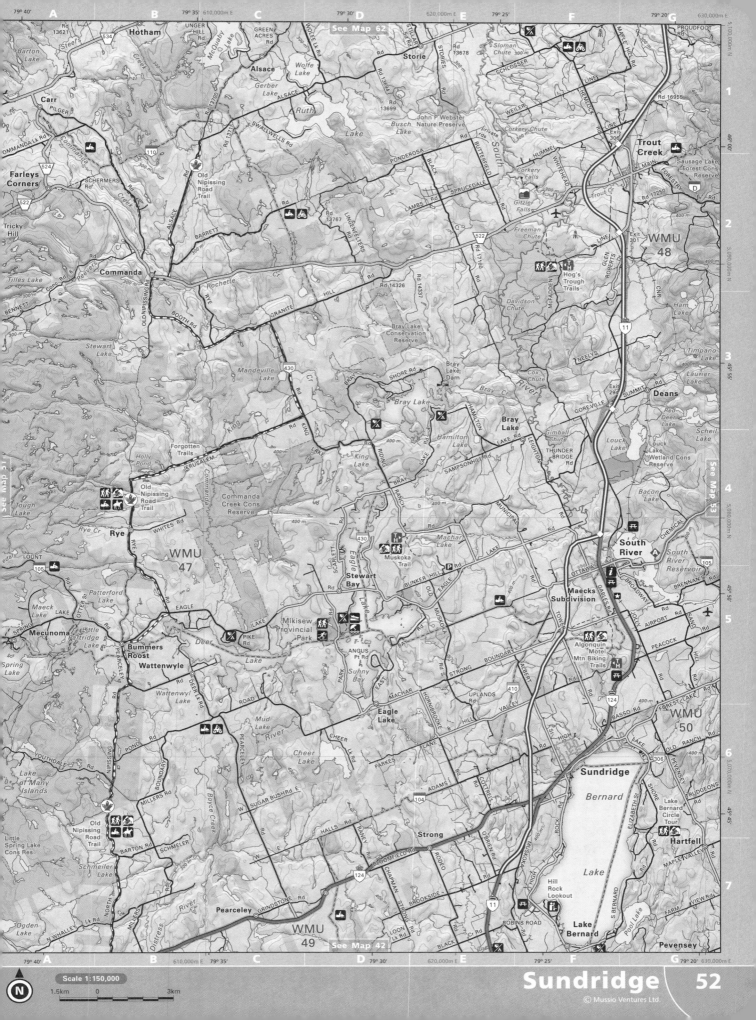

See Map 62
See Map 53
See Map 51
See Map 42

Scale 1 : 150,000

1.5km   0   3km

© Mussio Ventures Ltd

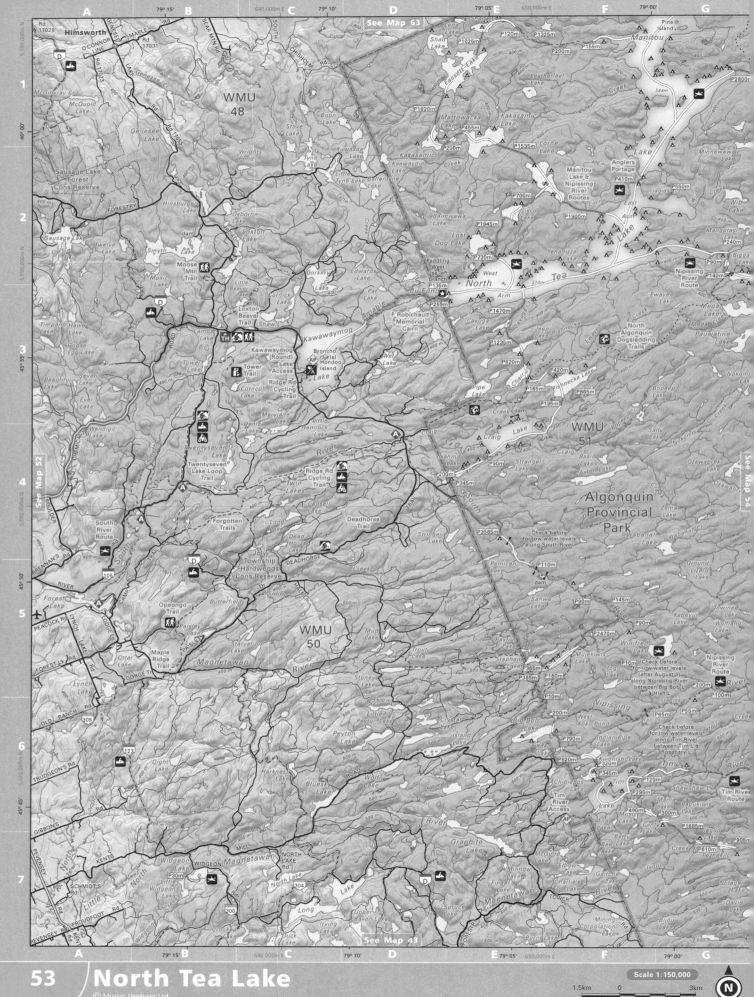

See Map 43

Scale 1:150,000

1.5km   0   3km

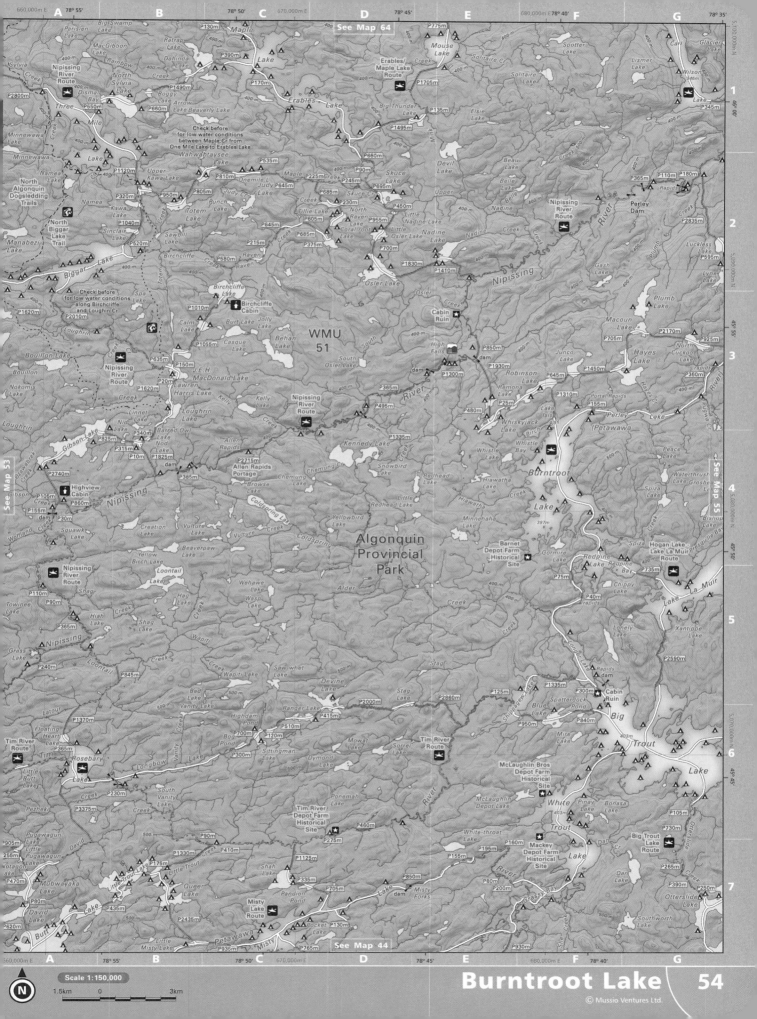

WMU 51

Algonquin
Provincial
Park

1.5km   0   3km

Burntroot Lake   54

© Mussio Ventures Ltd.

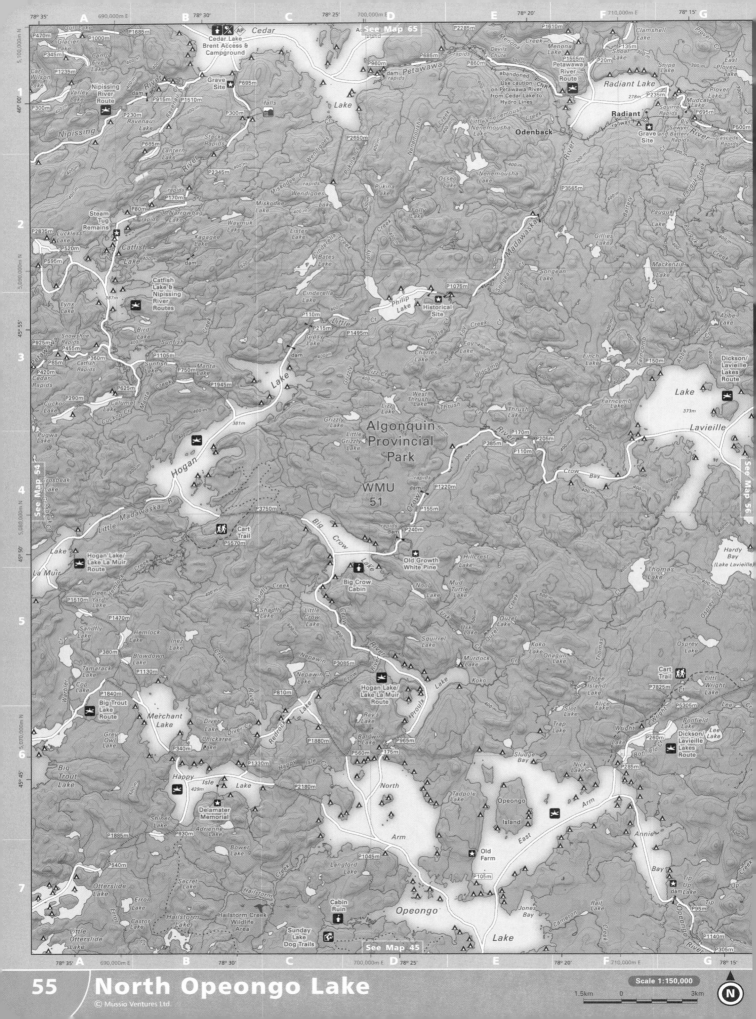

North Opeongo Lake

Scale 1:150,000

1.5km   0   3km

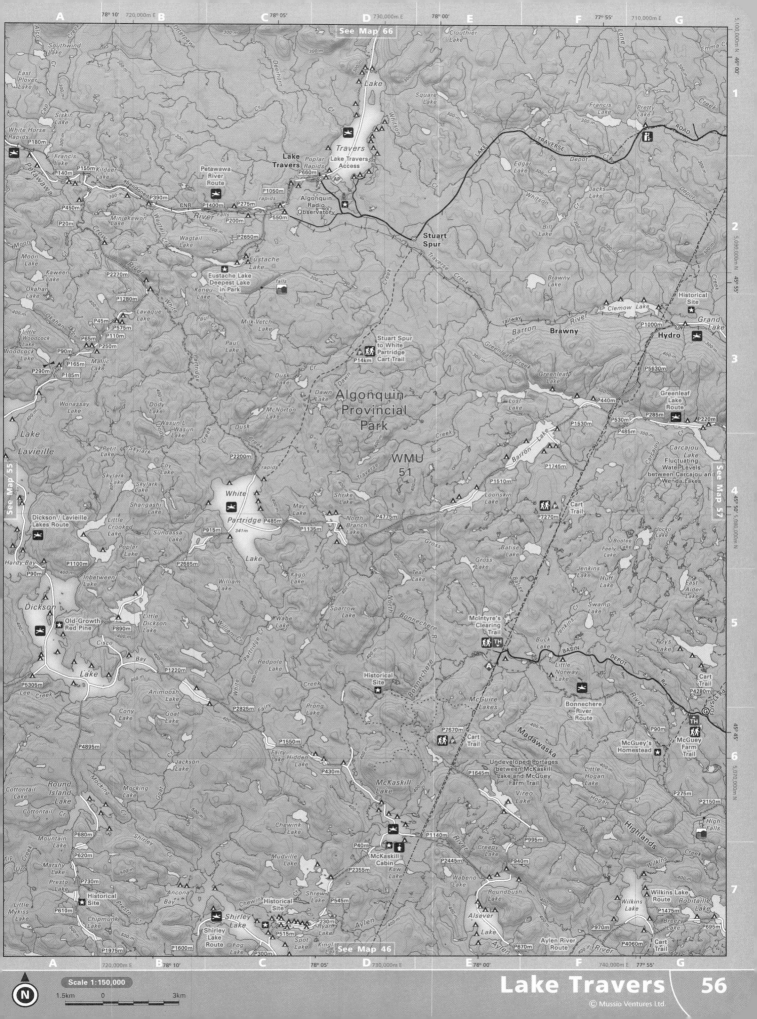

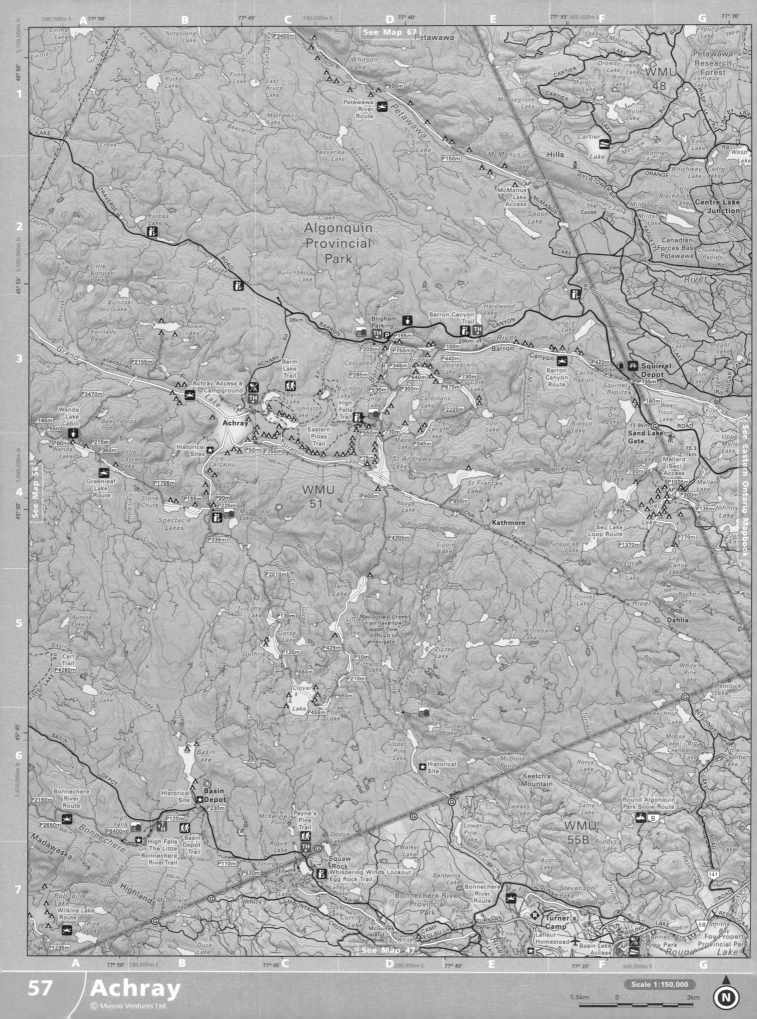

Scale 1:150,000

1.5km   0   3km

N

Burwash 58

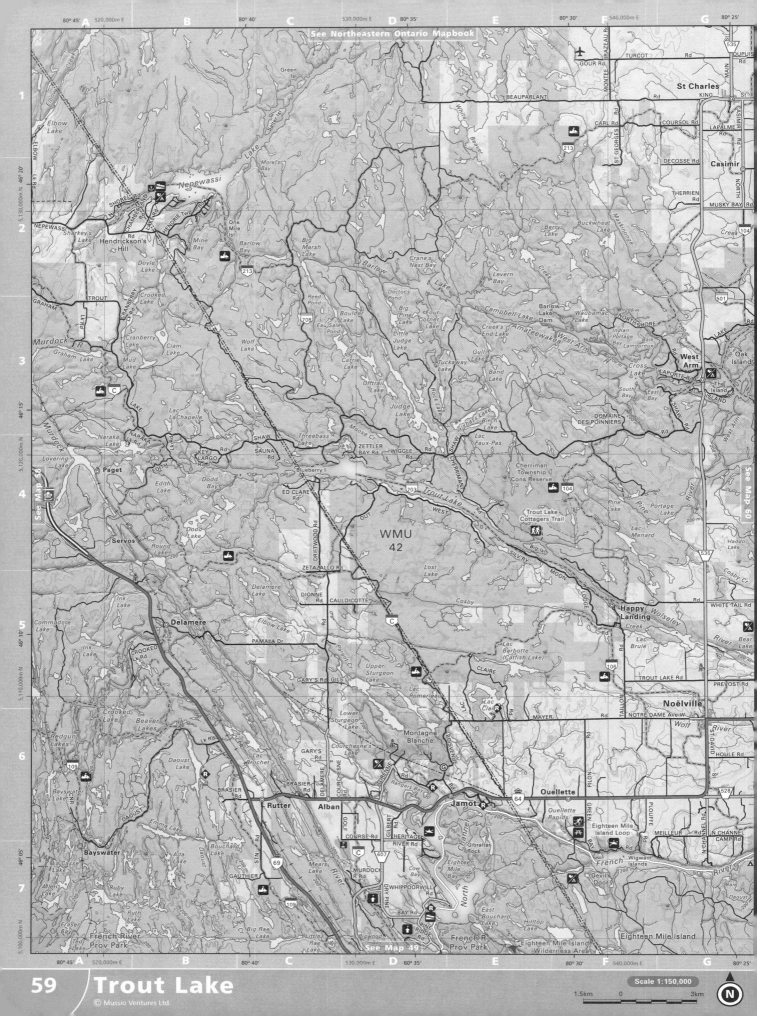

59 **Trout Lake**

© Mussio Ventures Ltd.

Scale 1:150,000

1.5km   0   3km

N

Scale 1:150,000

1.5km   0   3km

See Map 59

See Map 61

See Map 50

Caderette

Cache Bay

One Mile Point

Cache Bay Wetlands Cons Res

Ferris Pt

Theodore Fouriezos Wetlands Trail

Cranberry Marsh

McLeod Islands

Goulais

Point

Dalaire's Island

Garden Island

Little Oak Island

Sturgeon Falls

Nipissing First Nations

W Nipissing Nordic Trails

Marleau

Dutrisac's Bay

Mousseau Point

Sturgeon Falls Seaplane Base

Garden Village

Dokis Point

Moose Bay

Toba's Little Islands

Jocko Point Islands

Great North Bay

Burritt Island

Meadowside

Lake

Nipissing

Iron Island

Little Iron Island

Duck Island

Goose Islands

Mercer Lake/ Little French River Route

West Sandy Island Provincial Nature Reserve

Wigwam Island

Jennings Isl

Sandy Island

Little Sandy Island

Target Island

Fishermans Island

Coté Island

Coté Bay

Obashking Lake

Wigwam Bay

Wigwam Pt

Forestry Island

Burnt Island

Blueberry Island

Campbell's Point

Campbell's Bay

Boyer Point

Cross Point

Atkin Bay

BERTRAM

Redpine Lake

Redpine

Marsh Bay

Canoe Pass

Tiescher Island

Keystone Camps

Frank's

Frank Bay

Meadow Creek

French River Provincial Park

Twilight Bay

Bass Bay

Drunken Isl

Cleland Isl

Doolittle Isl

Sumner Isl

Elliot Isl

Partridge Island

River

Restoule / French River Route

Lunge Lodge

Hunt Isl

Concord Island

Wright Island

Sand Isl

Hardy Bay

Satchels

Satchels Bay

Creek

Sand

Shoal Lake

SAND LAKE

Dokis First Nations

Dokis Bay

Dokis

Chaudière Dam

WMU 47

Satchels Lake

Bass lake

Scud Lake

Beaudry Lake

Chaudière Rapids

falls

Hardy Creek

Dishaw Lake

Spruce L

Smallpox Lake

Clear Lake

Stinking Bay

Sand Lake

Restoule Bay

Limbo Lost Lake

Bruce Lake

Jinx Lake

Little Perch Lake

rapids

Restoule Provincial Park

Stinking Lake

Little Clear Lake

Burnt Lk

La France Pond

Dokis First Nations

MacArthur's Rapids

Lennon Lake

Creek

Restoule / French River Route

Scott's Dam

River

Patterson (Stormy) Lake

Hazel Lake Fire Tower Trail

Brimson L

Crowbar Bay

Hicks Lake

Restoule River Trail

Crawbarger's Rapids

DANIEL Dr

Ibbitson Lake

Woodcock Lake

Migisi Lake

Robin Lake

Woodcock Lake

Portage Lake

Dokis & Restoule/ French River Routes

Dry Island

Simms Bay

Green Isl

Restoule

Arthurs Pt

Porter Isl

PORTERS LANDING

Crooked Lake

Woodcock Lake

Lake

© Mussio Ventures Ltd.

Scale 1:150,000

1.5km   0   3km

N

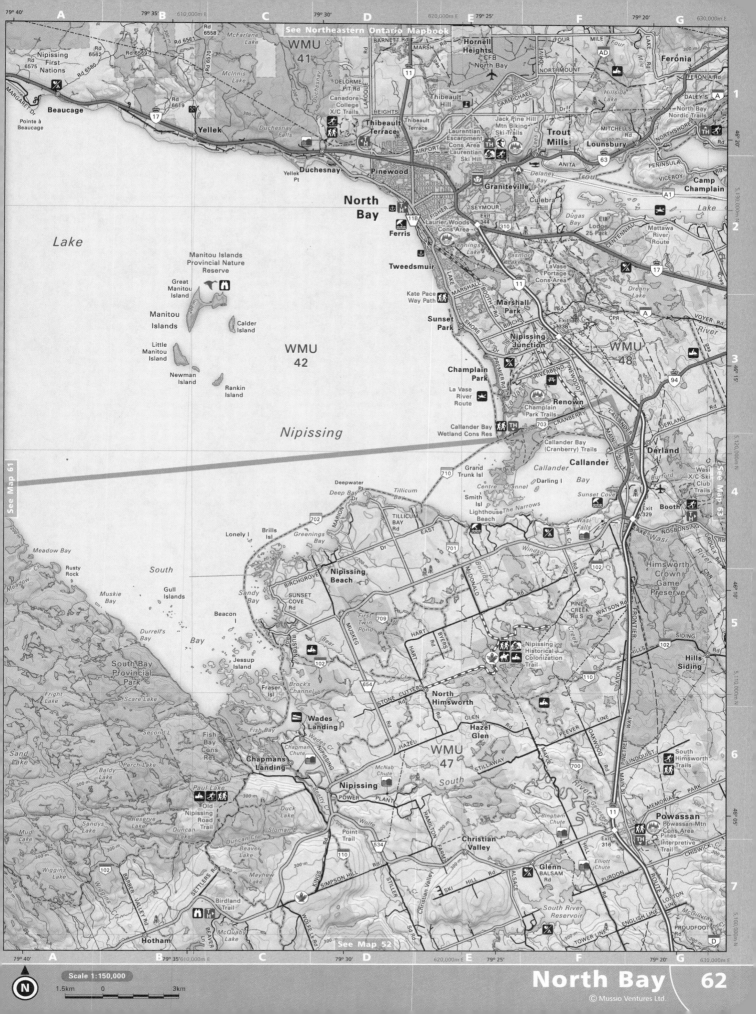

WMU 41

WMU 42

WMU 48

WMU 47

Lake

Nipissing

South

Bay

North Bay

Ferris

Tweedsmuir

Sunset Park

Marshall Park

Nipissing Junction

Champlain Park

Renown

Callander

Derland

Booth

Wades Landing

Chapmans Landing

Nipissing

North Himsworth

Hazel Glen

Christian Valley

Glenn

Powassan

Hills Siding

Hotham

See Map 61

See Map 52

See Map 63

Beaucage

Yellek

Duchesnay

Pinewood

Thibeault Terrace

Hornell Heights

Trout Mills

Lounsbury

Feronia

Camp Champlain

Graniteville

Manitou Islands Provincial Nature Reserve

Great Manitou Island

Manitou Islands

Calder Island

Little Manitou Island

Newman Island

Rankin Island

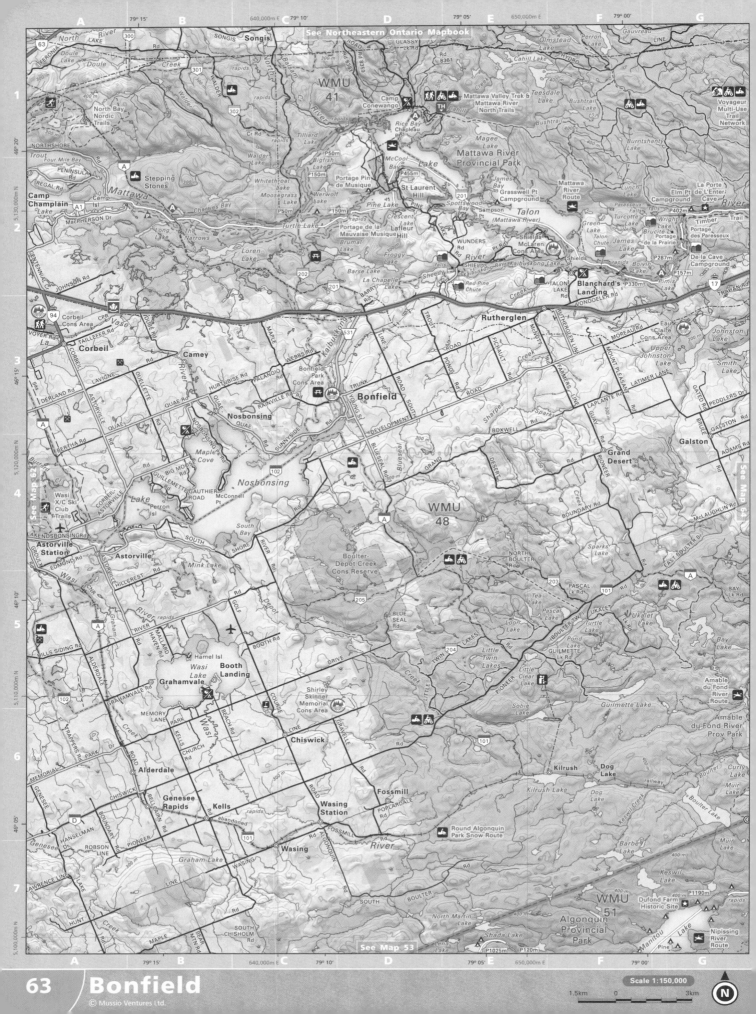

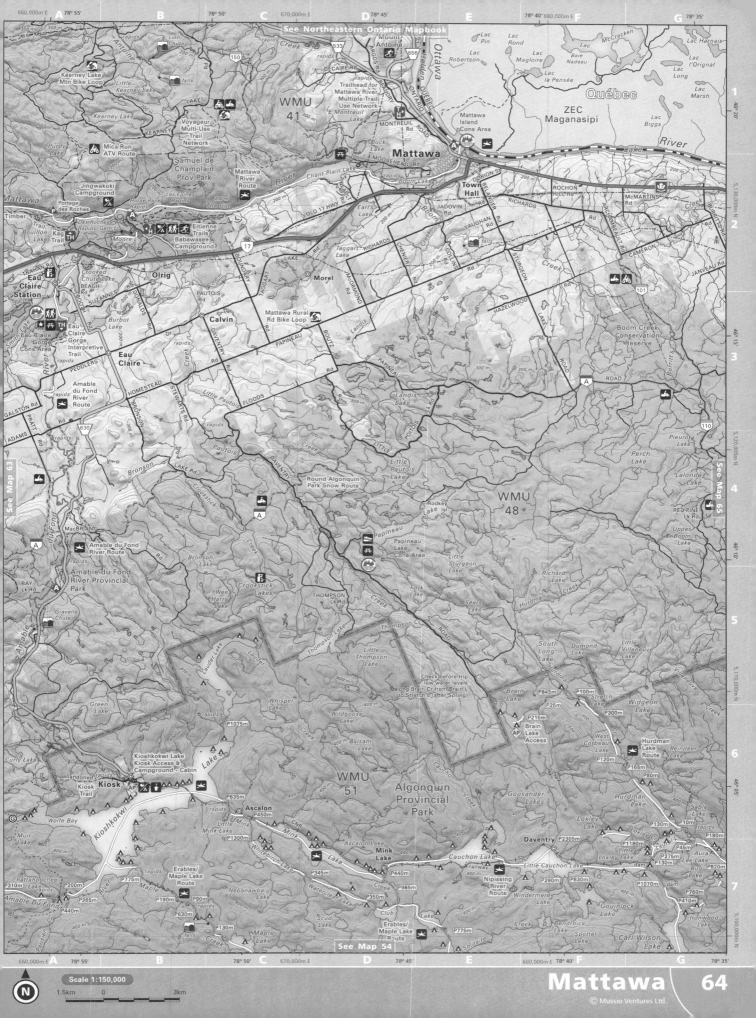

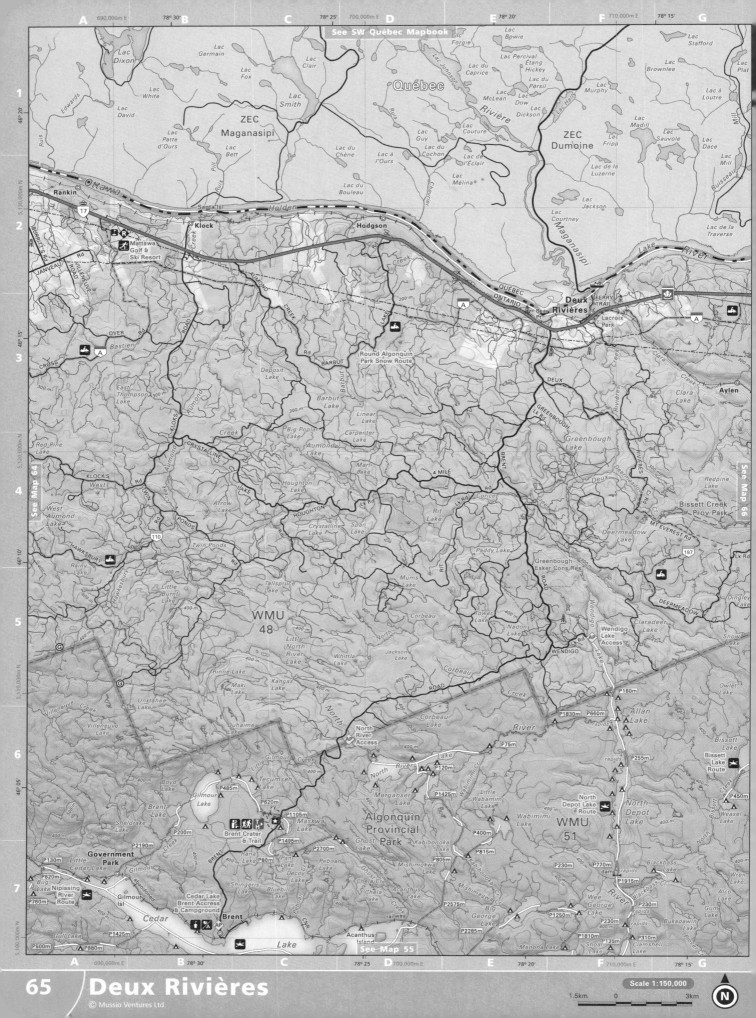

Scale 1:150,000

1.5km 0 3km

See Map 55

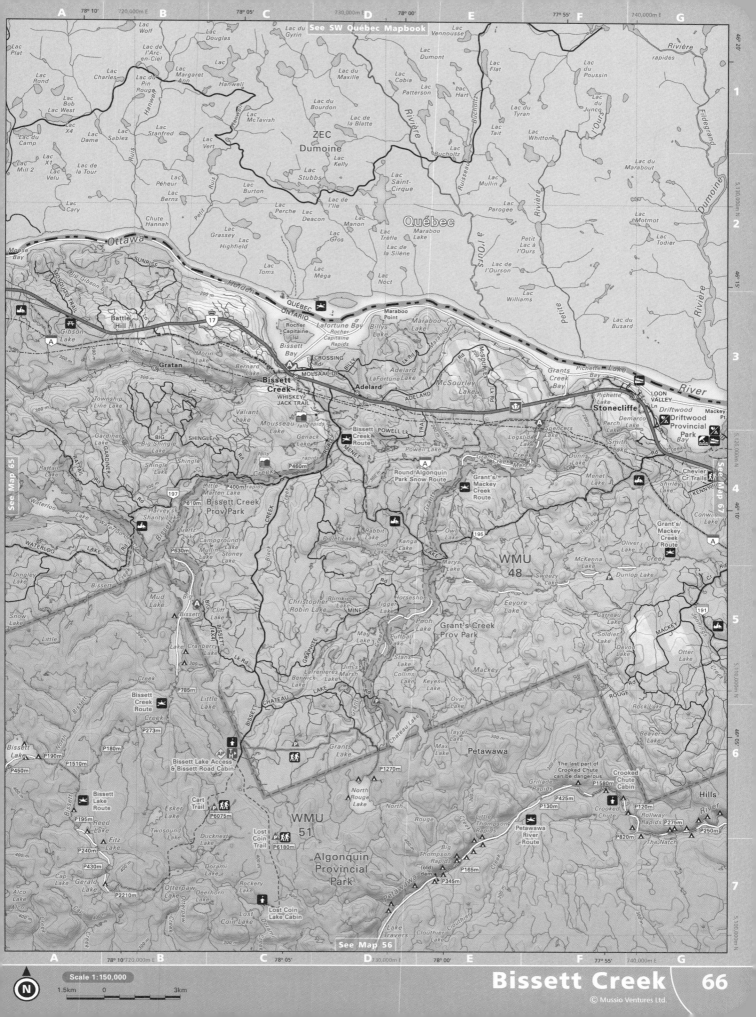

See SW Québec Mapbook

See Map 56

Scale 1:150,000

1.5km   0   3km

Bissett Creek   66

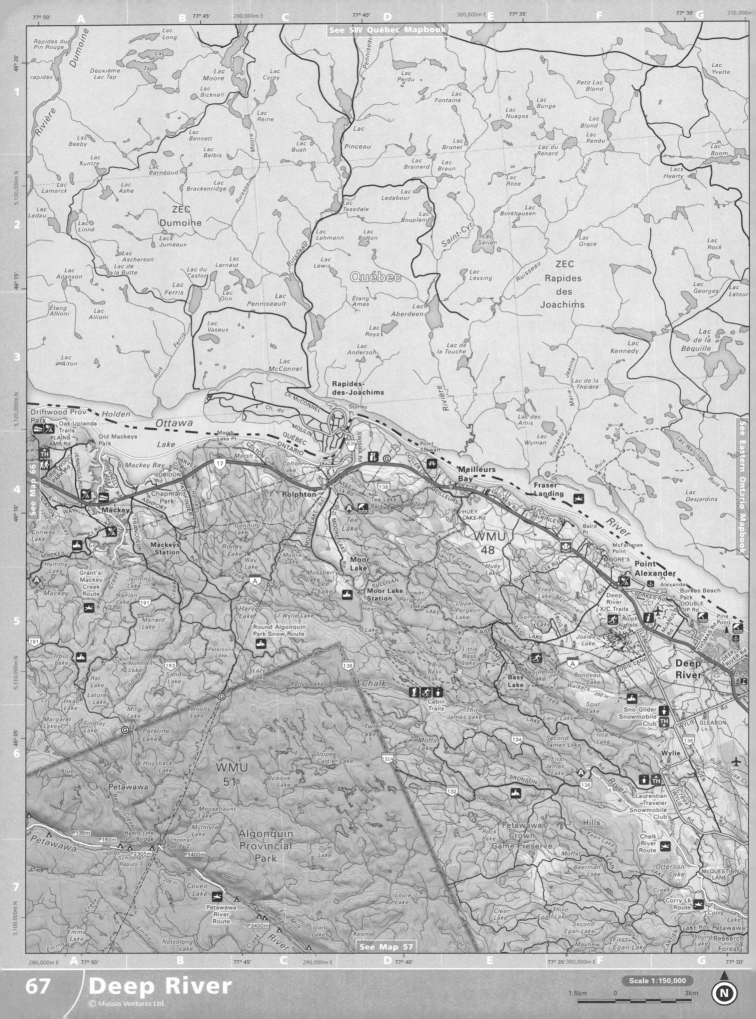

Rapides du Pin Rouge
rapides

Rivière

Dumoine

Lac Beeby
Lac Kuntze
Lac Lamarck
Lac Ladau
Lac Linné

Deuxième Lac Tap
Lac Tap

Lac Moore
Lac Bicknell

Lac Long

Lac Carey
Lac Reine

Lac Bennett
Lac Balbis
Lac Barnéaud
Lac Ashe
Lac Brackenridge

Moore

Ruisseau

Lac
Pinceau

Lac Fontaine
Lac Brainerd
Lac Braun
Lac Teasdale

Lac Perdu

Lac Nuages
Lac Bunge
Lac Brunet

Petit Lac Blond
Lac Blond
Lac Pendu
Lac Boom

Lac Yvette
Lacs Hearty

ZEC
Dumoine

Lacs Jumeaux
Lac Ascherson
Lac Adanson
Lac de la Butte
Lac Allioni
Étang Allioni

Lac Lernaut
Lac du Castor
Lac Ferris
Lac Olin

Ruisseau

Lac Lehmann
Lac Lewis
Étang Ames

Lac Ledebour
Lac Bolton

Québec

Lac Boupland

Lac Rose
Lac Sérien
Lac Borkhausen

Lac Léssing
Lac Grace
Lac Rock

Saint-Cyr

ZEC
Rapides
des
Joachims

Lac Georges
Lac Latour

Lac Ferris
Lac Vaseux
Lac Penniseault
Lac McConnel

Lac Roys
Lac Anderson
Lac de la Touche
Lac Aberdeen

Lac de la Béquille

Ruisseau

Lac Kennedy
Lac de la Théière

Marie
Jeanne

Lac des Amis
Lac Wyman

Lac Welghes
Lac Desjardins

Rapides-des-Joachims
Ch McConnel
Stoney Pt

Rivière

Lac Aiton

Ruis

Holden

Ottawa
Lake

Ch du
MOULIN
QUÉBEC
ONTARIO

635

Point Stewart

CUTLER Rd

'Meilleurs Bay'

Fraser Landing

River

Driftwood Prov Park
Oak Uplands Trails
PLAINS CAMP Rd
Old Mackeys Park

Mackey Bay
Marsh Lake Pt
Marsh Lake

COLTON Cr Rd
Colton Lake

SWISHA Rd

TEE Lk Rd

Tee Lake Park

MEILLEURS...

McKINLEY Dr
Baird Pt

McFarlanes Point
MOORE'S Rd
Point Alexander
Alexander Pt
Burkes Beach Park

JENNINGS Rd
DRIFTWOOD Park Rd
NATION Conway
WAY

HARVEY Rd
JOBIDON Rd
Chapman Park
ASHPORT
PATHFINDER

Rolphton
Gunning Lake

17

138

Tee Lake

HUEY LAKE Rd

Huey Creek
Huey Lake

WMU 48

SULLIVAN Lk Rd

Deep River X/C Trails
DOUBLE DIP Rd
Pine Pt

Mackey
Conway Lake
MACKEY
Hammy Lake

Mackeys Station

FRANCOEUR Rd
ROAD

Roney Lake
Way Lake
Moore Lake
Mossberry Lake
Lee Lake
Heart

Moor Lake

Moor Lake Station

Lower Pergeon Lake
Upper Pergeon Lake

WYLIE LAKE

BASS
Sullivan Lake

Freds Lake
McConnel

Josies Lake

BURKES Rd
McANUL

THOMAS Rd
DEEP RIVER Rd

Deep River

Grant's/Mackey Creek Route
Hanlan Lake
Jennings Lake
Manard Lake

191

Harvey Lake
Patersons Lake

Round Algonquin Park Snow Route

Wylie Lake

Kellys Lake
Lazy Lake

Chalk

Little Bass Lake
Big Bass Lake

Sidetrack Lake

A

Rondeau Lake
Walkers

Sno-Glider Snowmobile Club

GLEASON Ln

136

Trout Lake
Rat Lake
Lature Lakes
Head Lake
Margaret Lake
Findlay Lake

193

Norman Lake
Sand Lake
Mills Lake

Woods Lake

136

Cabin Trails
Third James Lake

Long Lake
Spur Lake

Iota Lake

Wylie

G

Parkline Lake

Blue

Hogsback Lake

WMU 51

Opaque Lake

Upper Cartier Lake
Twin Lakes
Moffat Lake

132A

132

Second James Lake
First James Lake

BRONSON

Laurentian Traveler Snowmobile Club

LEADER Rd

Petawawa

McIntyre Lake
Moosehaunt Lake
Schooner Rapids 2
Schooner Rapids 1
Hydro Line Bridge

Algonquin Provincial Park

Duff Lake

134

Petawawa Crown Game Preserve

Rock Lake
Moffat Lake
Beerman Lake

Hills

Chalk River Route

Petawawa

P135m
P160m
P2305m
P1400m

Coveo Lake

Petawawa River Route
P3400m

Five Mile
Rapids

River

Sloan Lake
Keon Lake

Louie Lake

Clear Lake

Kean Lake

KEAN Rd

Third Egan Lake
Second Egan Lake
Mayhew L
First Egan Lake

Otterson Lake

Corry Lk Route

McQUESTION LANE

Young Petawawa Research Forest

Emma Lake
Notsolong Lake

Creek
Emma

Scale 1:150,000

1.5km   0   3km

N

Image © David Lee (Just Outside Algonquin Park)

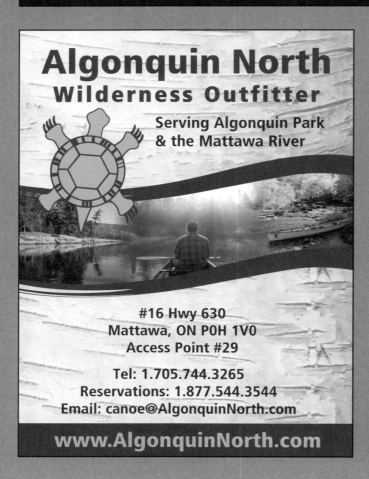
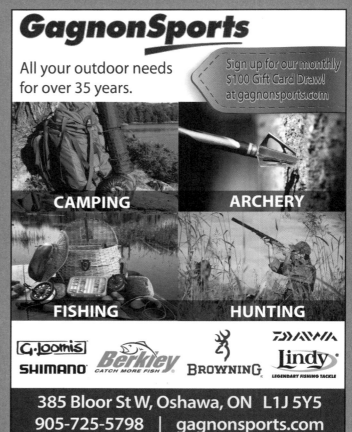

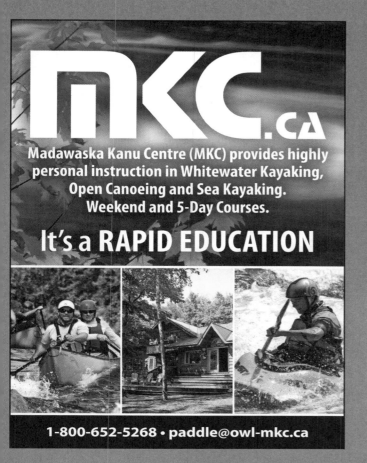

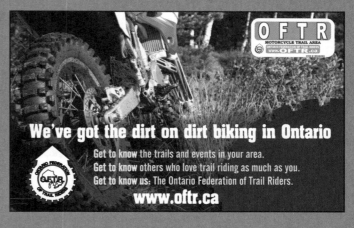

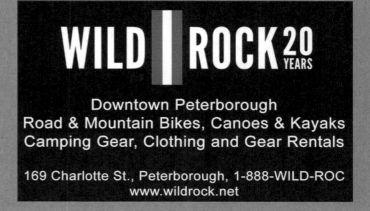

Service Directory

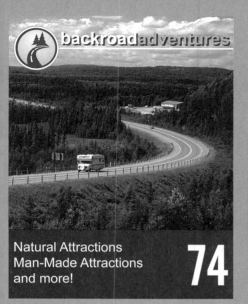
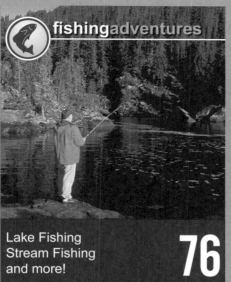

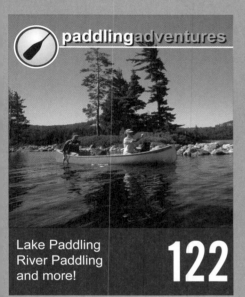
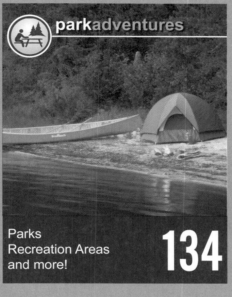
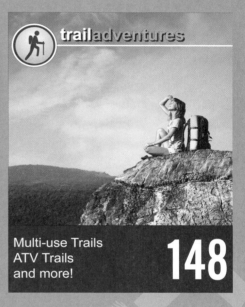

Information Wanted:

Send us your notes page or GPS tracks and win prizes and free stuff! Any information on road conditions or places you visit is invaluable in helping us make a better guidebook. We are also looking for GPS tracks to help increase the accuracy of trail locations and those out of way places few ever get to. Visit our website to find out more on prizes we are offering readers.

Email: updates@backroadmapbooks.com   toll free 1-877-520-5670   www.backroadmapbooks.com

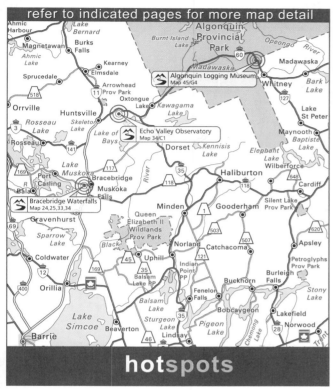

refer to indicated pages for more map detail

hotspots

For some, an adventurous outing is getting out of the city and onto one of the many secondary highways that knit together the hundreds of smaller communities that litter Cottage Country. For others, it isn't a backroad unless you need to break out the winch. Fortunately, there are plenty of backroads and bush roads to satisfy all manner of traveller.

Because this is such a heavily populated area, it features a number of main highways that serve as major arteries. One of the biggest and most travelled is Highway 400. Originally known as the Toronto-Barrie Highway, the 400 serves as the main access to Cottage Country. Other major highways include Highways 69, 115, 11, 12, 401, 17 and Highway 60, which is the main access into Algonquin Provincial Park. From these main routes, a number of secondary routes weave and wend their way through scenic but rocky Canadian shield.

For some people, exploring these backroads is the definition of a perfect Sunday afternoon. Passing through towns and villages with names like Siloam and Zephyr and Victoria Corners always seems to reveal something interesting.

As you move farther north, the number of paved roads falls off, while the number of bush roads pick up. While not all these bush roads lead anywhere interesting, many of the area's best fishing lakes are found alongside these roads. And 4wd/ATV enthusiasts will head out onto these roads simply for the challenge of driving.

Some of the roads in this area have been in use for over a century and were even used in part as ancient trading routes for Aboriginal peoples. In the mid-1800s, the province began building colonization roads to encourage residents to settle across the province. While some of these old roads have been turned into provincial highways (like Highway 62, which was originally the Hastings Colonization Road), many of these old routes are now county roads or township roads. Folks looking to explore the history of Ontario will enjoy finding and following these historic routes. As you head north, rugged terrain and isolation made new road construction difficult. Here, the logging companies maintain most of the existing bush road network, while farmers maintain a small percentage of the roads where the industry exists.

Even though Cottage Country abuts one of the most densely populated regions in the country, you don't have to go too far to find new roads to follow or new places to explore. From towns that you've never heard of to lakes that few have ever seen, the backroads of Cottage Country will take you there.

Algonquin Art Centre (Map 45/B3)
Originally the park museum, this unique stone sculpture is now the Algonquin Arts Centre. Here you can take part in a variety of arts programs and crafts, view the displays and learn more about the history of art in Algonquin.

Algonquin Logging Museum (Map 45/G4)
Located just inside the East Gate, this museum tells the story of the history of logging in the Algonquin area from the early square timber days to the last of the great river drives. There are video presentations, exhibits and a short trail.

Algonquin Visitor Centre (Map 45/E3)
Located at km 43 of Highway 60, the Algonquin Visitor Centre is home to world-class exhibits on the Park's natural and cultural history, a bookstore and the Algonquin Room, featuring ongoing exhibits of Algonquin art. There is a theatrical presentation and some great views out over the park from the viewing deck.

Barron Canyon (Map 57/E3)
Considered one of Algonquin Park's most spectacular sights, the canyon was formed 10,000 years ago as raging water from melting glaciers made its way to the Champlain Sea. Today, the Barron River gently courses through the impressive canyon. A 1.5 km long interpretative trail passes through pine forest to the rim of a 100 metre (328 foot) deep canyon. Canoeists also frequent the waterway.

Bethune Memorial House (Map 24/F3)
Designated to commemorate the life and achievements of Dr. Henry Norman Bethune, this attraction is found in Gravenhurst. The noted humanitarian spent the last years of his life serving as a surgeon and teacher in China, while the Memorial House is actually the manse of Knox Presbyterian Church, where Norman's father Malcolm was serving as minster when Norman was born. Bethune was intrigued by the social factors of disease and served in Spain during the Spanish Civil War before going to China.

Bracebridge Waterfalls (Maps 24, 25, 33, 34)
There are 22 waterfalls around the Bracebridge area. Rather than pick and choose between the falls, we recommend getting a copy of the Waterfalls of Bracebridge map (online at www.tourismbracebridge.com) and spend a day or two visiting them. Some of the showcase falls include the Bracebridge Falls and High Falls, both located within Bracebridge itself. Most of the waterfalls are located near roads, but the South Branch Falls are only accessible by paddling the South Branch of the Muskoka River.

Brent Crater (Map 65/C6)
This larger meteor crater near Cedar Lake is about 4 km (2.4 mile) wide and can be seen from an observation tower as well as on foot. The 2 km (1.2 mile) interpretive loop makes for an interesting walk.

Buckhorn Observatory (Map 18/F1)
The Buckhorn Observatory is located north of the town of Buckhorn, off Country Road 507. It features two main telescopes; one with an 11 inch aperture and one with a 6 inch aperture. The observatory is a popular destination with hardcore astronomy enthusiasts who often come for days at a time. However, the observatory is also open to the general public on clear nights when the observatory is open. Visit www.buckhornobservatory.com for more information.

Chedder (Map 28/C1)
Avid backroad explorers often have a love for deserted towns. Cheddar was home to a uranium mine from 1932 to 1942. The old road to the town is nearly impassable, except in winter on snowmobile and only the old boarding house still stands.

Depot Harbour (Map 31/G2)
Depot Harbour is the largest town in Ontario to become a ghost town. During the town's heyday, more than 1,600 people lived in the town, which was built on one of the deepest and most protected harbours on Parry Sound. At that time, this while was the most popular grain shipping port on Georgian Bay. However, in 1933, an ice floe destroyed a bridge in Algonquin Park and Highway 60 was completed and other ports, like Midland and Port McNicoll became more popular. In 1945, the elevators caught fire and burned, sealing the town's fate. Portions of many structures still remain, including the railway roundhouse.

Echo Valley Observatory (Map 34/C1)
Located just north of Huntsville in the near perfect darkness of the Echo Valley, this is the perfect destination for those with a love of star-gazing. Open year round, the observatory is run by the Nature Trails program out of the Delta Grandview Resort in Algonquin Park. Evenings that the observatory is open, the resort runs a two-hour presentation for guests, giving them the opportunity to view planets, nebulas and galaxies. The observatory is located on one of the highest points in Cottage Country, far from the city lights.

French and Mattawa Rivers (Maps 49, 50, 59–61; 62–64)
These rivers are popular canoeing and fishing destinations. They are also designated as Heritage Rivers, as 300 years ago Voyageurs travelled these rivers along the route from Montreal and Lake Superior. The 11 km (6.6 mile) La Vase Portage connects the Mattawa River system to Lake Superior.

Frost Centre Institute (Map 35/C5)
The Frost Centre Institute (formerly Leslie M. Frost Centre) is located in the Haliburton Highland and offers a variety of courses, camps and conferences designed to teach students and the public more about the environment. The centre sits on a beautiful parcel of land that is open to the public.

Huntsville (Map 34/C1)
The Muskoka region was a favoured hangout of the Group of Seven artists and the town of Huntsville has nearly a dozen recreated paintings from this famous group.

Muskoka Heritage Place (Map 34/C1)
Located in Huntsville, the Muskoka Heritage Place is home to the Muskoka Museum and the Muskoka Pioneer village, as well as Huntsville and Lake of Bays Railway Society's Portage Flyer Train Ride. Costumed narrators demonstrate life in the late 1800s using settlements from the Huntsville area.

Old Nipissing Road (Map 42/B1–62/D5)
One of a series of colonization trails built in the mid-1800s, this old road is a historian's dream. Along the road (which is part of the Trans Canada Trail) you will pass through a number of towns and past a number of empty cabins, barns and even old communities, like the ghost town of Ashdown near the south end of the trail. This town was settled around 1880 and prospered for a few years until two railroads were built, bypassing the town and drawing traffic away from the road. By 1908, the town was deserted. The road runs through the heart of the Parry Sound District and is crossed by a number of highways, including 141, 518, 520, 124 and 522. The road is 120 km (72 miles) long, varying between paved, graveled and rugged 4wd route and connects Rousseau to Nipissing.

Petroglyphs Provincial Park (Map 19/E2)
The Learning Place at Petroglyphs Provincial Park was built to communicate to visitors the spiritual significance that the "Teaching Rocks" had to the First nation's people of this region. The centre features information panels, paintings and videos. Of course, once people have visited the Learning Place, most continue on to see the Petroglyphs themselves, which are now housed in a protective building.

Seguin Falls (Map 42/A6)
Seguin Falls was already a thriving little town before J.R. Booth's railway arrived in town, built along the Nipissing Road. The railroad spared the town the same ignoble fate as many others along the road…at least for a few years. The town became a major lumber shipping station, but in 1933, an ice floe damaged a bridge in Algonquin Park. The bridge was never repaired and the town began its slow demise. The town was never fully abandoned and there are still a few old structures.

Tom Thomson Cairn (Map 44/E3)
Tom Thomson is one of Canada's most famous painters with paintings shown in art galleries across the country. He died mysteriously at the north end of Canoe Lake in 1917. Today, a cairn rests at his original burial site and is a popular attraction for area visitors.

Trent-Severn Waterway (Maps 10–13, 15–20, 23, 24)
This 386 km (240 mile) waterway has been called one of the finest interconnected systems of navigation in the world. It has beautiful scenery and history stretching back at least 9,000 years. In the 17th Century, the route was used by fur traders. The first lock was finished in 1833, but the entire route was not navigable until 1920, nearly 100 years later. There are 44 locks on the system, which will take about a week for boaters to complete.

Uxbridge (Map 8/E6)
Readers of Lucy Maud Montgomery's Anne of Green Gables flock to Prince Edward Island, where the book was set, but the hardcore fan knows that the place to go is Uxbridge. This is where Lucy Maud Montgomery actually lived between 1911 and 1926 and wrote a number of books, including the Avonlea Books, a couple Anne Books and Emily of New Moon. She lived at the Leaksdale Manse with her husband, Reverend Ewan MacDonald. One of the two churches he was in charge of, St. Paul's Presbyterian, is now the Uxbridge Historical Centre, where you can learn more about the heritage and history of the town and walk the Quaker Trail.

Wasaga Beach (Map 14/A4)
The 14 km (8.7 mile) Wasaga Beach is the longest freshwater beach in the world and is one of the most popular destinations from the Greater Toronto area. While Beach One next to Wasaga Beach is often thick with locals and visitors alike, the farther west you go, the less crowded the beach becomes. Nottawasaga Bay features shallow, warm water, making it a great destination for families with kids.

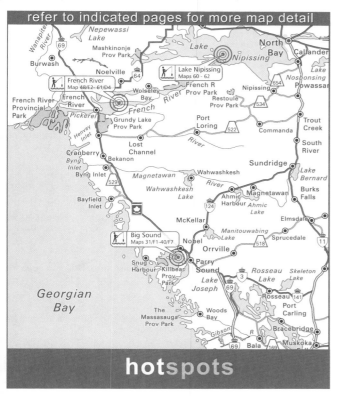

refer to indicated pages for more map detail

hotspots

Ontario is home to over 300,000 freshwater lakes and streams. To put that in perspective, if you were to fish a lake or river a day every day it would take over 800 years to fish every lake in Ontario. If you were to limit yourself to fishing just the lakes found in Algonquin Provincial Park alone, it would still take you more than three years to fish the thousand or so fish-bearing lakes at a lake a day.

Algonquin Park remains one of the most popular fishing destinations in the region. The higher elevation lakes support a colder environment, making the lakes more suitable for brook and lake trout. Further south and in shallower lakes, warm water species such as northern pike, smallmouth and largemouth bass, walleye and yellow perch are more common.

An impressive stocking program for a variety of sportfish including brook trout, lake trout, rainbow trout, splake and more recently walleye helps maintain the good fishery. We have noted the stocked lakes with a 🐟. As a general rule of thumb, trout lakes are good locations to try earlier in the year. As summer approaches, it is best to look for lakes that hold bass or other warm water species.

Stream fishing in Ontario boomed in popularity with the establishment of Great Lakes rainbow trout in the early 1970s. Salmon runs are also found on many of the larger streams in the province and continue to attract a lot of anglers. Today, a number of Ontario streams are noted as among the best trout and salmon fishing areas in North America.

The most common species you will find in Cottage Country rivers and streams is the brook trout. The cool, clear streams that are prevalent throughout Ontario provide ideal habitat for brook trout. Rainbow and brown trout can also be found. The murkier rivers of the region offer a whole different experience for the angler with warm water species such as bass, panfish and even smaller pike creating most of the action. A number of these rivers are also prime spawning habitat for walleye and muskellunge.

Before heading out, be sure to check the Ontario Recreational Fishing Regulations Summary. Many lakes listed below have special restrictions, from catch-and-release only to seasonal and gear restrictions to catch size limitations. In order to fit in more lakes and because every year the regulations change, we haven't listed specific regulations in the write-ups below. It is your responsibility to know what the regulations are on any lake you're planning on fishing.

LAKE FISHING

Described below are the majority of fish bearing lakes in the area with an emphasis on what species they offer anglers. The number and variety of lakes in the region is truly impressive. We have separated out the Algonquin Park lakes due to the fact you need a park permit to fish there and they truly are a unique fishery.

Abes and Essens Lakes (Map 30/F2)
Accessed by the Abes and Essens Hiking Trail of Bon Echo Provincial Park, these small lakes offer good fishing for smallmouth and largemouth bass as well as panfish. Northern pike are also present. Interior campsites are available on both lakes.

Acorn Lake (Map 57/E7) 🐟
This is a small lake that can be accessed on foot from the bush road that follows the Bonnechere River. The lake is stocked annually with brook trout.

Ada, Bouchard, Daoust and Emma Lakes (Map 59/B7)
West of Highway 69, these four lakes offer good fishing for smallmouth bass to 1.5 kg (3.5 lbs) and fair fishing for decent sized northern pike. Bouchard Lake also has a small natural population of lake trout.

fishingadventures

Adams Lake (Map 27/B1)
Adams Lake is stocked every couple of years with brook trout. It offers fair to good fishing at times through the ice and in the spring for brook trout that can exceed 35 cm (14 in). Live fish may not be used as bait in this lake.

Adams Lake (Map 32/F7)
This lake can be found by canoe and portage up a small feeder creek from the Moon River. The secluded lake is rumoured to produce fair sized largemouth bass.

Adelaird and Billys Lakes (Map 66/D3)
Located north of Highway 17 near the village of Bissett Creek, both lakes offer generally slow fishing for brook trout. Adelaird Lake has been stocked in the past with brook trout and usually has better fishing.

Ahmic Lake, Beaver and Crawford Lakes (Map 41/G2)
Three of the larger lakes in the area, these lakes continue to offer decent fishing opportunities despite increased fishing pressure. Fishing can be good at times for smallmouth and largemouth bass to 2 kg (4.5 lbs) in size. Walleye and northern pike are also found in the lakes, although fishing can be quite slow at times.

Albion Lake (Map 37/F7)
Found west of Bancroft, Albion offers fair fishing for smallmouth bass and decent sized splake. Splake are stocked in the lake every few years and are best found through the ice in winter or in early spring just after ice off.

Amable Lakes (Map 46/C7)
The Amable Lake can be found via a 4wd road and provide good fishing at times for largemouth bass. The lakes are surrounded by Crown land and there are no maintained access areas to the lakes.

Andrews and Browns Lake (Map 25/G2–26/A2)
These are two larger lakes that can only be accessed by a private road which you must have permission to travel on to enter the area. The lakes provide good fishing for smallmouth and largemouth bass to 1.5 kg (3.5 lbs).

Anson [Montgomery] Lake (Map 35/B7)
Anson is stocked about every two years with the fast growing hybrid, splake. Fishing is slow during warmer months, although it can be good through the ice or in the spring.

Anson [Rainy] Lake (Map 26/B2)
Also known as Rainy Lake, this Anson is stocked periodically with lake trout and holds smallmouth bass. The remote lake is most accessed by snowmobile in winter.

Anstruther Lake (Map 28/B6)
Anstruther Lake is the starting point to a few Kawartha Highland Provincial Park canoe routes and can be accessed from the public boat launch off Anstruther Lake Road. The lake offers good fishing at times for large and smallmouth bass. The lake is also home to a naturally reproducing strain of lake trout.

Arbuckle and Fisher Lakes (Map 44/D7)
These two secluded lakes can be accessed via rough 4wd roads/trails and provide fair to good fishing at times in winter and spring for average sized brook trout. Many access these lakes in winter by snowmobile.

Arnolds and Moon River Bay (Map 32/C6)
Walleye congregate in these bays as they move out to deeper water in the spring. Fall is also good for migratory walleye and fishing for bass is good throughout the season. Bass can be caught up to 3 kg (6.5 lbs) and are predominantly found near islands and in weedy bays.

Arrowhead Lakes (Map 43/C7)
Arrowhead Lake is a heavily used lake that offers fair fishing for smallmouth bass that average 0.5–1 kg (1–2 lbs) and slow fishing for small brook trout. Little Arrowhead Lake provides fair fishing for generally small lake trout and brook trout and is best fished through the ice. Further west, Mayflower Lake is a small lake that offers stocked rainbow trout.

Ashball Lake (Map 35/C2)
Ashball Lake is a small lake found off County Road 12 not far from Highway 35. The lake offers fair fishing for small northern pike. Spinner baits, top water lures/flies or a minnow imitation can be productive.

Atkins Lake (Map 34/C6)
Atkins Lake offers fair to good fishing at times for smallmouth bass to 1.5 kg (3.5 lbs). The lake can be accessed just off County Road 117, northeast of Bracebridge.

Austin Lake (Map 35/C6)
Austin Lake can be found just off Highway 35 via a 2wd road. The lake has fair fishing for average sized smallmouth and largemouth bass.

Avery Lake (Map 42/D7)
Stocked every couple years with the brook trout/lake trout hybrid, splake, Avery Lake remains a decent fishery. Look for the lake to the north of Sherborne Lake Road in the Frost Centre area.

Axe Lake (Map 42/D7)
Axe Lake is a fairly large lake that is a well-known largemouth bass hot spot. The lake can be accessed via a rough 2wd road.

Aylen Lake (Map 46/G1–47/B2)
Providing an access point to Algonquin Park, fishing can be good for smallmouth bass to 2 kg (4.5 lbs). There is also a natural strain of lake trout present, but fishing is slow most of the year. In summer, jigging off Big Green Island can be productive for smallmouth bass. Watch for special regulations on the lake.

Bain Lake and Seagull Lake (Map 51/C3)
Straddling Highway 522, both these lakes offer good fishing for smallmouth and largemouth bass as well as the odd northern pike.

Baldcoot and Littlecoot Lake (Map 38/E1)
Baldcoot Lake has a naturally reproducing strain of brook trout, while Littlecoot is stocked every few years with splake. Splake can be found in Littlecoot Lake in the 35 cm (14 in) range.

Balfour Lake (Map 46/G1)
Balfour can be accessed by a bush road west of Aylen Lake. Fishing is good for smallmouth bass to 2 kg (4.5 lbs) and fair for lake trout to 3 kg (6.5 lbs) in size.

Ball and Sinclair Lakes (Map 50/E6)
These remote lakes can be accessed off rough bush roads. Fishing can be quite good for smallmouth bass. Sinclair Lake also hosts a good population of northern pike, while largemouth bass are found in Ball Lake.

Balsam Lake (Map 17/D3)
Balsam Lake is home to two provincial parks, has many access points and the ever popular Trent Severn Waterway runs through the lake. Needless to say, this can be a busy place during the fishing season. Despite this, the large lake offers good fishing for bass, walleye, muskellunge and panfish.

Ban [Band] Lake (Map 36/A2)
Ban Lake is a small, secluded lake found in the Haliburton Forest and offers good fishing for small brook trout. The lake is mainly fished in the winter through the ice.

Banner Lake (Map 38/A7)
Banner Lake is found south of Bancroft off the Jeffrey Lake Road. It is stocked annually with rainbow trout allowing for a decent fishery for these acrobatic sportfish.

Baptiste Lake (Map 37/E5)
Baptiste is one of the larger lakes in the area and is a popular summer cottage destination. The big lake has two public access points and offers good fishing for smallmouth and largemouth bass as well as panfish. Bass up to 2 kg (4.5 lbs) are possible. However, most come here for walleye or lake trout despite the fact the fishing is much slower for these popular sportfish. Baptiste Lake is also home to a quality muskellunge fishery. Watch for restrictions.

Bark Lake (Map 27/D2)
Accessible by a gravel 2wd road, Bark Lake has a few cottages along its shoreline. Fishing is slow to fair for under average sized smallmouth bass. When action is slow, try working a tube jig along bottom structure.

Bark Lake (Map 46/G4–47/B6)
Bark Lake is a large scenic lake with surprisingly little development. Fishing can be good for smallmouth bass and rather slow for lake trout. Bass in the 2 kg (4.5 lbs) class are caught regularly.

Barlow Lake (Map 59/D2)
This secluded lake lies to the north of Trout Lake and is accessed by canoe or rough 4wd bush roads. Anglers will find the odd smallmouth bass and walleye.

Barns Lake (Map 46/C2)
Found west of Major Lake Road, Barns Lake can be accessed by ATV, snowmobile or on foot. It is with brook trout every other year. Nearby Major Lake was formerly stocked, but is no longer.

Barnum Lake (Map 36/B7)
This lake is found just south of the town of Haliburton and has fair fishing for smallmouth and largemouth bass. There are a few cottages on the lake and plenty of weed structure for bass to hide in. Recently the lake is being stocked with walleye to help establish the fishery. Rock bass and yellow perch are also present.

Barre & Ink Lakes (Map 43/F3) 🎣
Barre Lake is a small, secluded lake that can be reached by trail. The lake has been stocked in the past with rainbow trout. Nearby Ink Lake is stocked periodically with rainbow.

Bass Lake (Map 15/E2)
Found just west of Orillia, this lake can be quite busy in the summer months as it is home to a provincial park complete with boat launch. The lake offers good fishing for yellow perch, smallmouth and largemouth bass. Bass can reach up to 2 kg (4.5 lbs) in size.

Bass Lake (Map 18/C1–27/C7)
One of many Bass Lakes, this one offers fair fishing for smallmouth and largemouth bass to 2 kg (4.5 lbs) in size. Muskellunge are also present in the lake, although fishing is slow for muskie in the 4–5 kg (9–11 lb) range.

Bass Lake (Map 25/C4)
Bass Lake is a smaller lake that has a number of cottages along its shoreline. Smallmouth bass are the main species and can reach up to 2 kg (4.5 lbs), although there is a rumoured resident population of brook trout that remain in the lake.

Bass Lake (Map 61/E6)
Part of the Restoule/French River Canoe Route, it is also possible to access this lake via 4wd logging roads. The main access to the lake is via a portage from Stormy Lake to the south. Fishing in Bass Lake is good for smallmouth bass that average 1 kg (2 lbs), but can be found bigger. Northern pike and walleye are also present in the lake.

Basshaunt and Bushwolf Lakes (Map 36/D5) 🎣
The two lakes can be accessed via rough backroads and offer fair to good fishing for smallmouth bass to 1.5 kg (3.5 lbs). Anglers will also find a natural population of lake trout on Basshaunt Lake, which is part of the winter fishing sanctuary. There is also a boat launch on the lake.

Bat Lake (Map 26/F2)
Located just east of Minden, Bat Lake offers fair fishing for smallmouth bass. Crayfish imitation lures and flies fished slowly near bottom can be productive.

Bat Lake (Map 35/G5) 🎣
This Bat Lake is located north of Maple Lake and is best reached via canoe since the road into the lake is private. Anglers will find stocked splake, along with the much smaller pumpkinseed sunfish and yellow perch.

Baxter Lake (Map 23/F4) 🎣
Found just off Highway 400, Baxter Lake provides fair fishing for smallmouth and largemouth bass. Fishing for slightly bigger northern pike is also fair.

Bay Lake (Map 38/A7) 🎣
Located south of Bancroft, Bay Lake has recently benefited from a stocking program for lake trout. Anglers will also find smallmouth bass, pumpkinseed sunfish and yellow perch. Watch for special restrictions.

Bay Lake (Map 43/C5) 🎣
East of Highway 11 near Emsdale, this Bay Lake offers a host of species to try for. Notably, the lake is stocked with lake trout, there are also brook trout, smallmouth bass, pumpkinseed sunfish and whitefish.

Bay and Ukalet Lakes (Map 63/G5) 🎣
Accessed mainly by snowmobile, these remote lakes are rumoured to offer up brook trout to 35 cm (14 in). Ukalet is also stocked with splake every other year.

Bay of Quinte [Lake Ontario] (Map 13/A5–G4)
One of the most famous walleye areas in North America, fishing can be quite good once the underlying structure is understood. However, the fishery is susceptible to over fishing and the practice catch and release is encouraged. Anglers will also find smallmouth and largemouth bass that can easily exceed 2 kg (4.5 lbs) as well as good sized northern pike cruising the shallows of the bay. Other species include rainbow trout, crappie, muskellunge, perch and salmon. Big Bay and Muscote Bay are other popular destinations in the area.

Beanpole Lake (Map 36/E2) 🎣
This small lake south of Algonquin Park holds small numbers of periodically stoked rainbow trout.

Bear and Livingstone Lakes (Map 35/F1–44/E7)
Fishing for smallmouth bass to 2 kg (4.5 lbs) is good at times on these busy lakes. Both lakes were once stocked with lake trout, however, they now rely on natural regeneration. Fishing for lakers is slow to fair through the ice or by trolling in spring. There is also a small population of brook trout in the lakes.

Bear Lake (Map 42/C6)
Bear Lake provides fair fishing for smallmouth and largemouth bass to 1.5 kg (3.5 lbs) and northern pike to 3.5 kg (8 lbs). There is also a small population of walleye available in the lake. Ice fishing for perch is popular.

Bear Lake (Map 46/G4) 🎣
Stocked regularly with splake, this Bear Lake is found south of Highway 60 to the west of Barry's Bay. Fishing is fair throughout the winter months and into spring.

Beautiful and Seven Lakes (Map 53/A3) 🎣
Part of a series of secluded brook trout lakes, Beautiful Lake is stocked with brook trout every few years. Seven Lake supports a natural brook trout fishery.

Beaver and Gold Lakes (Map 27/G4–28/A6)
Good numbers of smallmouth and largemouth bass can be found in these lakes, with a good holding area found off the small island found in the eastern end of Beaver Lake. A small natural population of lake trout is also present in both lakes.

Beaver and Otter Lakes (Map 66/G6) 🎣
These lakes can be found via bush roads off the Mackey Creek Road and provide fair fishing for natural brook trout. Brookies can reach 35 cm (14 in) in size, although winter angling pressure often hinders the growth of the trout in these lakes.

Beech Lake (Map 35/F6) 🎣
Beech Lake offers good fishing at times for smallmouth bass to 1.5 kg (3.5 lbs) as well as the odd stocked lake trout. A small population of muskellunge that grow to 3.5 kg (8 lbs) also roam the lake. A public boat launch exists at this lake.

Beechnut Lake (Map 57/G6) 🎣
Found off the Beechnut Lake Road to the north of Round Lake, Beechnut Lake is annually with brook trout. The B Trunk snowmobile trail also runs through the area allowing for year round access.

Beer Lake (Map 26/D2)
Surrounded mostly by Crown land, this popular lake sees its fair share of anglers. There is fair to good fishing at times for smallmouth and largemouth bass.

Beetle and Martencamp Lakes (Map 44/B7) 🎣
Martencamp Lake is stocked every few years with brook trout and offers fair to good fishing for average sized brookies. Beetle Lake also holds a population of brook trout and fishing is fair in the spring.

Bell and Snake Lakes (Map 41/B3)
Found just south of the large Ahmic Lake, these lakes offer fair fishing for smallmouth bass in the 0.5–1 kg (1–2 lbs) range. A few camps and cottages lie along the shorelines of both lakes.

Bella and Rebecca Lakes (Map 43/F6) 🎣
These two cottage destination lakes offer good fishing at times for smallmouth bass to 2 kg (4.5 lbs) and fair fishing for lake trout to 70 cm (28 in). Bella Lake contains a naturally reproducing strain of lake trout and has slot size and ice fishing restrictions on lakers to help maintain stocks. Rebecca Lake is stocked periodically with lake trout to reinforce the fishery.

Bells and Newell Lakes (Map 42/A3)
Found just south of the large Ahmic Lake, these lakes offer fair fishing for smallmouth bass in the 0.5–1 kg (1–2 lbs) range. Larger bass can be found, although they can be quite challenging to catch. A few camps and cottages lie along the shorelines of both lakes.

Belmont Lake (Map 20/C4)
Part of the Crowe River system, Belmont Lake has good fishing for smallmouth and largemouth bass, walleye and northern pike. The shallow, weedy lake has fantastic habitat. Try fishing the shoal just off the northeast side of Big Island.

Bennett and Rintoul Lakes (Map 32/B2)
These small secluded lakes can be accessed via a 4wd road and offer fair to good fishing for largemouth bass in the 0.5–1 kg (1–2 lb) range. Minnow imitation lures and flies can be productive.

Benoir Lake (Map 37/B4)
Located just outside the southern tip of Algonquin Park, Benoir has a number of camps and cottages along its shoreline. It can be accessed via Elephant Lake Road (County Road 10) and provides fair fishing for walleye and muskellunge, as well as good fishing for smallmouth and largemouth bass.

Bernard Lake (Map 52/F7)
Resting next to Highway 11 & Sundridge, Bernard Lake can be a busy place. Lake trout can be caught to 70 cm (28 in), while smallmouth bass in the 1.5 kg (3.5 lb) range are also found in fair numbers. There is also a productive whitefish fishery along with a small population of brook trout in the lake.

Big Bald and Little Bald Lakes (Map 18/F3)

These are shallow connecting lakes that are really an extension of the northeast side of Pigeon Lake. Fishing in these lakes can be good for walleye. The narrows between the two lakes is a good spot for walleye. However, the most predominant sportfish are smallmouth and largemouth bass. A fair population of muskellunge is also found in the lakes and average 3–6 kg (6.5–13 lbs). One of the hotspots is the mouth of the Squaw River during spring.

Big Bissett Lake (Map 66/B5)

Stocked every other year with brook, this lake lies partially in Algonquin Provincial Park and is accessible by canoe or 4wd road. Yellow perch are also reported here, while older sources say there are smallmouth bass in the lake. Be sure to fish the head of the Bissett Creek for better brookie results.

Big Brother and Little Brother Lakes (Map 35/E5)

These two popular Frost Centre lakes can be found just off Highway 35. They provide fair fishing for average sized smallmouth and largemouth bass.

Big Caribou Lake (Map 50/G3)

Found north of Highway 522 west of Port Loring, this 529 hectare lake is home to lake trout, smallmouth bass and walleye, along with pumpkinseed sunfish, rock bass and yellow perch. The lake trout are stocked. Watch for special regulations.

Big Cedar Lake (Map 19/C2)

Found off Highway 28, there is a boat launch at the south side of Big Cedar Lake. The lake provides fair fishing for muskellunge to 7 kg (15.5 lbs) and fair to good fishing for smallmouth bass to 3 kg (6.5 lbs).

Big East and Little East Lakes (Map 26/B1–35/A7)

Big East Lake is part of the Poker Lake System Canoe Route and can be accessed by a short portage from the parking area on Highway 118. Little East Lake requires a rough portage from the southeast end of Big East Lake. The lakes offer good fishing at times for smallmouth and largemouth bass that average about 0.5 kg (1 lb) in size. Both lakes are also stocked with splake.

Big Gibson and Gibson Lakes (Map 66/A2)

Gibson Lake offers fair fishing for smallmouth bass, while Big Gibson Lake offers fair fishing for northern pike and smallmouth bass. Lake trout are stocked in Big Gibson every few years helping make this the more popular fishery.

Big Hawk and Little Hawk Lakes (Map 35/E5)

The Hawk Lakes offer slow to fair fishing for lake trout to 75 cm (30 in) and good fishing at times for decent sized smallmouth bass. Watch for slot size restrictions and other regulations imposed to aid lake trout stocks. A small population of muskellunge also inhabits the lakes.

Big Hoover Lake (Map 44/A6)

This fairly remote lake can be located by an old logging road/trail near the south end of Oxbow Lake. The lake offers good fishing at times for stocked brook trout. Pumpkinseed sunfish are also reported in the lake.

Big Lighthouse and Big McGarry Lakes (Map 37/E3)

Southwest of Maynooth off Peterson Road, a good forest road leads to Big Lighthouse Lake. The lake is stocked annually with splake, but also holds brook trout and rock bass. Nearby Big McGarry is also stocked with splake, but also offers largemouth bass, rainbow trout and yellow perch

Big Mink Lake (Map 37/C2)

This long, thin lake is found west of Highway 127 and Maynooth. Fishing for lake trout is fair in winter and spring and good for smallmouth bass to 2 kg (4.5 lbs). The lake is surrounded by Crown land, which makes for a nice wilderness setting.

Big Poplar Lake (Map 65/C4)

This remote walleye lake can be found with a snowmobile or on foot through some thick bush. Due to the access, the lake is most often fished in winter.

Big Shingle and Shingle Lakes (Map 66/B4)

These two secluded lakes hold natural strains of brook trout. Fishing can be good at times in winter and early spring. Be sure to limit your catch.

Big Sound (Map 31/F1–40/F7)

Big Sound is known for its large northern pike, which can be found in the 12 kg (26 lb) range. The best time to find big pike feeding in shallow bays and inlets is springtime. Some huge muskie can also be found in the sound. Adding to the fishery are lake trout, smallmouth and largemouth bass to 2.5 kg (5.5 lbs) and walleye that can reach 3.5 kg (8 lbs) in size.

Big Trout Lakes (Map 26/B2)

Big Trout Lake is connected to Anson Lake to the north, Millward Lake to the east and Fisher Lake to the south. Big Trout holds some nice sized lake trout, along with smallmouth and largemouth bass as well as muskellunge. South Anson Lake

is stocked with lake trout, while Fisher and Millward Lakes offer good fishing for smallmouth and largemouth bass. Millward and Anson also hold a fair population of nice sized muskellunge that are best fished for in the fall.

Bigfish, Moosegrass and Werewolf Lakes (Map 63/C2)

The only access to these lakes is by canoe on the Mattawa River. Small northern pike and walleye are found in all three lakes, while muskellunge are also found in both Moosegrass and Werewolf Lakes. Bass anglers will find smallmouth bass in Bigfish and Werewolf Lakes, while largemouth bass inhabit Moosegrass Lake.

Bigwind Lake (Map 34/F7)

Surrounded for the most part by parkland, Bigwind Lake is currently being stocked biennially with lake trout with the odd laker reaching up to 65 cm (26 in) in size. The lake is also home to smallmouth bass, pumpkinseed sunfish and yellow perch.

Billings and Gooderham [Pine] Lakes (Map 27/E2)

These lakes are popular cottage destination lakes with public boat launches. The lakes provide fair to good fishing for smallmouth bass that average 1 kg (2 lbs) and slow to fair success for average sized walleye.

Birchy Lake (Map 36/A3)

Birchy Lake is a small, secluded lake found just south of Kennisis Lake that offers small brook trout. Ice fishing or fishing in spring is the most productive.

Bird Lake (Map 34/F7)

Found just outside of Bigwind Provincial Park, Bird Lake offers good fishing for largemouth bass to 2.5 kg (5 lbs). Try the west end for these lunkers.

Bird Lake (Map 40/A3)

Fishing is fair in this lake for largemouth bass to 1 kg (2 lb). Despite its proximity to Highway 69, the lake is surrounded by Crown land.

Bird Lake (Map 58/D7)

This remote lake is accessible by a 4wd road south off Highway 637. Fishing is good at times for smallmouth bass to 1.5 kg (3.5 lbs) in size.

Bivouac Lake (Map 36/B1)

Accessed from North Road in the Haliburton Forest, Bivouac Lake is stocked every few years with splake. It also offers brook trout along with a few rustic campsites.

Black [Eyre] Lakes, Clean and MacDonald Lakes (Map 36/B3)

These lakes are home to a unique strain of lake trout. Although they are a smaller strain of lake trout, they are also much more numerous. MacDonald Lake is the most productive lake with good fishing at times for lakers to 40 cm (16 in). Smallmouth and largemouth bass are also present. In addition to respecting the size restrictions, please practice catch and release whenever possible to help preserve the Haliburton Forest Lake Trout.

Black Cat and Cat Lakes (Map 35/F4)

These lakes rest west of the larger Kennisis Lake are accessible by portage only and are stocked with brook trout. Pumpkinseed sunfish are also found in Blackcat. There are rustic campsites available for use on both lakes.

Black Lake (Map 24/B5)

Black Lake is a small lake that provides fishing for largemouth bass. The lake has plenty of natural structure for bass to hide in and your best bet to find active bass is to locate some structure and work a jig or tube bait.

Black Lake (Map 26/D5)

Despite bordering Queen Elizabeth II Provincial Park, this Black Lake has limited access to the public. Most hike or portage at the north end. Anglers will find fair fishing for smallmouth and largemouth bass.

Black Lake (Map 35/B4)

West of the Frost Centre, this Black Lake is stocked every few years with splake. There is also a good population of smallmouth and largemouth bass in the lake that can reach up to 2 kg (4.5 lbs) in size.

Black Lake (Map 36/E7)

Found off Highway 118 east of Haliburton, this small lake receives significant fishing pressure through the year. Walleye were recently stocked in the lake that is best known for its smallmouth bass fishing. A small population of muskellunge is also known to remain in the lake.

Blackstone Harbour (Map 32/B5)

Ontario's largest muskellunge, which weighed a whopping 30.5 kg (67 lbs) was caught here. Muskies in the 15 kg (33 lb) range have been caught in the bay and are best fished in the fall when they move into shallower waters such as Blackstone Harbour. Big northern pike can also be found in the harbour in the 9 kg (20 lb) range, although they are generally much smaller. Fishing for smallmouth and largemouth bass can be very good as can fishing for small perch.

Blackstone Lake (Map 32/D3)
Anglers can expect to find fair fishing for walleye and good fishing at times for smallmouth and largemouth bass. Bass can be found in one of the many bays and inlets of the lake and off almost any of the islands. The lake is also stocked with lake trout every few years and provides fair fishing for small lakers through the ice or in the spring by trolling. However, the largest sportfish found in the lake are northern pike and muskellunge. There are also panfish in the lake.

Blotter Lake (Map 26/G1)
Blotter Lake offers fair fishing for decent sized smallmouth bass. A crayfish lure or fly worked slowly near the bottom can be productive or try a type of minnow imitation such as a Rapala or crank bait.

Blue Chalk and Red Chalk Lakes (Map 35/A4)
Blue Chalk Lake now relies on natural reproduction for it lake trout fishery. Anglers can expect slow to fair fishing for lakers to 70 cm (28 in). Red Chalk Lake has a good population of largemouth bass in the 0.5–1 kg (1–2 lbs) range.

Blue Hawk Lake (Map 27/D1)
Blue Hawk Lake can be accessed by foot off the Glamorgan Road (County Road 3) just outside of Haliburton. The lake offers smallmouth and largemouth bass as well as muskellunge and walleye.

Blue Lake (Map 32/B2)
Found off Blue Lake Road and stocked biennially with splake, fishing here can be good through the ice or in spring just after ice off. There is also a small population of lake trout remaining in the lake, although catches are rare.

Blue Lake (Map 36/C5)
Splake are stocked in Blue Lake every two years and provide for fair fishing during the winter. A population of smallmouth bass are also found in the lake.

Blue Lake (Map 53/D3)
This small lake is found just south of the much larger Kawawaymog Lake. The lake supports a population of natural brook trout.

Bob Lake (Map 26/E3)
Smallmouth and largemouth bass to 2 kg (4.5 lbs) are available in fair numbers and can be found off any of the small islands found around the lake. A small population of lake trout also exists in the lake, although fishing is generally slow.

Boleau and Woodland Lakes (Map 24/D3)
Although referred to as Upper and Lower Boleau Lakes, there is no real separation of the two water bodies. The lakes can only be accessed on foot, by canoe or snowmobile. Fishing for largemouth bass to 1.5 kg (3.5 lbs) can be very good at times. To the northeast, Woodland Lake offers a similar fishery.

Bolger Lake (Map 40/E1)
Bolger Lake is part of the Magnetawan River Canoe Route and offers good fishing at times for smallmouth and largemouth bass. Walleye and northern pike can also be found in the lake, although in lower numbers.

Bon Echo Lake (Map 30/G2)
This lake is reached via Joeperry Road within the western section of Bon Echo Provincial Park. Good fishing is offered at times for smallmouth and largemouth bass. Northern pike and panfish are also found in the lake.

Bone Lake (Map 35/G3)
Bone Lake lies off the North Kennisis Drive and offers fair fishing for generally smaller smallmouth bass. Try a spinner bait or minnow imitation for better results.

Bonnie Lake (Map 34/B5)
Home to a municipal campground, this small, popular lake has good fishing at times for smallmouth bass. The lake once had a healthy population of lake trout, although heavy fishing throughout the years has made lake trout catches a rarity.

Boshkung Lakes (Map 35/E7)
Boshkung and Little Boshkung Lakes are accessed from the public launch found off Highway 118 between the lakes. Anglers will find slow fishing for lake trout to 75 cm (30 in), while smallmouth bass fishing can be good at times for bass to 1.5 kg (3.5 lbs).

Bottle Lake (Map 27/G6–28/A6)
As part of the Kawartha Highlands Provincial Park, Bottle Lake can be accessed by canoe down Bottle Creek from Catchacoma Lake. The lake has a good population of large and smallmouth bass to 2 kg (4.5 lbs) and lake trout.

Boullion [Papaud] and Moore Lake (Map 64/A2)
Part of the Mattawa River system, Moore Lake lies within Samuel De Champlain Provincial Park, while Boullion Lake is in nearby Mattawa River Provincial Park. Both lakes offer decent fishing for smallmouth bass, panfish and northern pike.

The odd big pike can be found. Walleye and muskellunge fishing is generally slow for under average sized fish. 2wd roads easily access both lakes.

Bow Lake (Map 27/B4)
Twenty years ago lake trout fishing in this lake was excellent, but pressure on the stock has slowed fishing dramatically. The lake is now part of the winter/spring sanctuary and with more catch and release fishing, the trout population may increase. Smallmouth bass are also present in the lake.

Bow Lake (Map 28/F7)
Bow Lake in the Peterborough Crown Game Preserve offers fishing for stocked splake as well as pumpkinseed and yellow perch.

Boy and Bell Lakes (Map 41/B6)
These lakes offer fair fishing for smallmouth and largemouth bass to 1.5 kg (3.5 lbs). Both lakes were stocked in the past with rainbow trout, but only Boy Lake is still stocked regularly. It is also stocked every few years with splake.

Brady Lake (Map 35/D7)
Brady Lake is a summer destination lake that has a number of cottages along its shoreline. There is fair fishing for smallmouth and largemouth bass to 1.5 kg (3.5 lbs). A small population of muskellunge is also present in the lake.

Brandy Lake (Map 33/D6)
There are a number of cottages along the shoreline of Brandy Lake and fishing for small walleye and northern pike is slow throughout the year due to heavy seasonal fishing pressure. The lake does offer fair fishing for smallmouth and largemouth bass to 1.5 kg (3.5 lbs).

Bray Lake (Map 52/E3)
This popular cottage destination lake offers fair fishing for smallmouth bass in the 0.5–1 kg (1–2 lb) range. The lake is located north of Eagle Lake, off Bray Lake Road. Be sure to fish near the dam at the north end of the lake.

Bright Lake (Map 44/C7)
Accessed via snowmobile or a rustic portage from Niger Lake to the north, Bright Lake is stocked with brook trout. Fishing for brook trout to 30 cm (12 in) can be good through the ice or in spring just after ice off.

Brush Lake (Map 32/F3)
Brush Lake has cottages along its shoreline and is located just north of Lake Joseph. Fishing for smallmouth bass is fair.

Buck Lake (Map 23/F3)
Anglers visiting this lake can expect largemouth bass that can reach up to 2 kg (4.5 lbs) in size. While fishing for bass, you may be surprised by a big northern pike that average 2–4 kg (4.5–9 lbs).

Buck Lake (Map 25/B3)
Found north of Kahshe Lake this peaceful Cottage Country lake offers fair fishing for smallmouth and largemouth bass that average 1 kg (2.2 lbs). The lake is generally surrounded by private property and can be accessed off County Road 6 to the east of Gravenhurst.

Buck Lake (Map 38/C1)
Northern pike reside in the lake in good numbers and are regularly found roaming the shoreline as evening approaches. The lake is also part of the winter/spring fishing sanctuary in order to aid lake trout populations. Watch for slot size restrictions.

Buck Lake (Map 42/F6)
Easily accessed via Ravenscliffe Road, there is good fishing for smallmouth and largemouth bass that average 1 kg (2 lbs), but have been found to 2 kg (6.5 lbs). There is also fair to good fishing for northern pike to 3.5 kg (8 lb). Spinners with bait or any minnow imitation lure or fly can be productive for both pike and bass.

Buck, Lower Raven and Upper Raven Lakes (43/D1)
Lower and Upper Raven Lakes are stocked with splake, which reach 75 cm (30 in) in size. Neighbouring Buck Lake continues to host a natural lake trout population. Lake trout average 45 cm (18 in), although can be found to 60 cm (24 in).

Bucke Lake (Map 49/D2)
Fishing is fair for small northern pike and largemouth bass. Walleye also inhabit the lake, although fishing is generally slow. The lake can be seen from Highway 69.

Buckhorn [Powderhorn] and Island Lakes (Map 35/F3)
Found within the Haliburton Forest and only accessible by trail or canoe, Buckhorn Lake is a shallow lake that offers fair fishing for smallmouth bass. Island Lake provides slow fishing for brook trout that have been stocked in the past.

Buckhorn Lakes (Map 18/E5)
Buckhorn and Lower Buckhorn lakes are connected by locks on the Trent Severn Waterway and see an abundance of anglers throughout the season. Buckhorn Lake is very shallow and angling success is best for smallmouth and largemouth bass. The lake also offers good walleye fishing at times for walleye that average 1–2 kg (2–4.5 lbs). Muskellunge is the largest fish in Buckhorn Lake and can reach up to 9 kg (20 lbs) in size. One of the hotspots for walleye and muskie is Gannon's Bay. As with most of the Kawartha area lakes, there are plenty of perch and other small sportfish available. Lower Buckhorn Lake is deeper and connected to Lovesick Lake. These lakes provide a similar fishery to Buckhorn.

Buckskin and Monrock Lakes (Map 28/B2)
Buckskin and Monrock Lakes can be found south of Highway 118. Monrock is home to smallmouth bass and perch, while Buckskin Lake is better known as a trout lake with stocked lake trout and stocked rainbow along with perch. There is a rough boat launch at Buckskin Lake.

Buller [Clear] Lake (Map 26/E5)
Buller Lake has many cottages scattered along its shore. It is stocked every two years with splake. Although, fishing for small splake is fair in the spring, in summer they are more difficult to locate. Also, the lake has a fair population of bass.

Bunn Lake (Map 33/D4)
This small hidden lake is located between County Road 24 and Three Mile Lake. The lake hosts a small population of brook trout that are generally small.

Burdock Lake (Map 36/A4)
This small lake is found just off County Road 7 south of Kennisis Lake and is stocked regularly with brook trout. Live baitfish is not permitted in Burdock Lake.

Burns and Docker Lakes (Map 34/G1–43/G7)
These two small hidden lakes are difficult to access and offer fishing opportunities for average sized brook trout. Docker Lake can be accessed via a rough 4wd road, while Burns Lake can only be walked to. Both lakes provide fair to good brook trout fishing in winter and spring.

Burnt Lake (Map 43/E1–53/E7)
Found south of the Forestry Tower Road, snowmobile trails in the area allow year round access. The 8 hectare lake is stocked biannually with brook trout. If fishing is slow, the unnamed lake to the north offers yellow perch.

Burnt and Horseshoe Lakes (Map 58/D2)
Fishing in Burnt Lake is generally slow for walleye and northern pike, although it improves for smallmouth bass. Horseshoe Lake is inhabited by northern pike as well as stocked rainbow trout.

Burnt Lake (Map 26/B2)
Limited access has kept this lake a good fishing spot. Anglers will find aggressive smallmouth and largemouth bass as well as muskellunge that can reach good sizes. There is also a larger unnamed lake that can be accessed from the south end of Burnt Lake that is as good or better than Burnt Lake for bass fishing.

Burrows Lake (Map 24/A4)
Burrows Lake is a little off the beaten path and offers a fair population of smallmouth bass. There is also a small population of walleye present in the lake, although heavy fishing has reduced their numbers.

Butterfield and Paisley Lakes (Map 53/B5)
Butterfield Lake has a small population of brook trout, while Paisley Lake is augmented by stocking. Much of the shoreline of both lakes is private land.

Buzzard Lake (Map 19/B1)
This favourite camping/canoeing destination continues to support lake trout. Anglers will also find smallmouth and largemouth bass in the weed beds and other cover. The lake is accessible by portage from the west end of Long Lake and offers rustic Crown land camping. Vixen Lake to the south is another popular stop for smallmouth bass.

Byng Inlet (Map 49/E6)
The inlet can be a busy boating area during summer months for boaters travelling to and from the Georgian Bay. Smallmouth bass and walleye are found all year in the inlet, although the mighty muskellunge is more commonly found in the fall. Musky in the 20 kg (44 lb) range have been hooked into in the Byng Inlet.

Cahill, Olmstead and Teesdale Lake (Map 63/E1)
Cahill and Olmstead Lakes are stocked annually with splake, while Teesdale Lake is stocked with brook trout.

Camel Lake (Map 33/F5)
Anglers can find Camel Lake off County Road 4 south of Three Mile Lake. The lake provides fair fishing for smallmouth bass and slow fishing for small walleye.

Cameron Lake (Map 17/E3)
Cameron Lake offers good fishing for bass to 2 kg (4.5 lbs) along with small yellow perch. Largemouth bass can be found in the weedy areas of the lake and smallmouth bass often hang near the many rocky shoals. A fair population of muskellunge also exists, which can be found in the 3–5 kg (6.5–11 lb) range. However, it is the walleye that attract the most fishing attention on this lake.

Cameron Lake (Map 35/G5)
Cameron Lake can be accessed to the north of Highway 118 and has fair fishing for smallmouth bass. Minnow imitation lures or flies can create a little better action.

Camp and Flossie Lakes (Map 44/B6)
Camp Lake and Flossie Lake are connected lakes that provide slow to fair fishing for lake trout to 70 cm (28 in) and brook trout to 35 cm (14 in).

Campbell Lake (Map 41/B6)
Campbell Lake is found just off Highway 124 and provides fair fishing for smallmouth bass and northern pike. Larger pike are available, but are harder to come by.

Campstool Lake (Map 34/G5)
Campstool Lake is a small fishing lake that offers largemouth bass. The lake can provide some good action at times.

Canal Lake (Map 16/G3)
Canal Lake is part of a chain of Kawartha walleye hotspots, with good fishing at times for small walleye. In addition, bass can literally be found almost anywhere in this shallow lake, while the odd northern pike is caught as well. Muskellunge to 10 kg (22 lbs) are also found occasion.

Canning Lake (Map 26/G2)
Canning Lake has many cottages along its shoreline making it a popular summer destination. Fishing is fair to good at times for smallmouth bass to 1.5 kg (3.5 lbs). There is a fair number of whitefish and a few of walleye, lake trout and muskellunge in the lake.

Cantin Lake (Map 49/E2)
Park of the Pickerel River system, Cantin offers fair fishing for smallmouth bass, panfish and northern pike. Muskellunge are also found in the lake and surrounding waters, although musky can be hard to find for the inexperienced fisher. Much of Cantin Lake's shoreline is First Nations land, please respect private property.

Capsell and Long Lakes (Map 53/C4)
These lakes can be accessed via a rough bush road off the Deadhorse Trail or by snowmobile in winter. Capsell is stocked with brook trout, while Long Lake holds stocked brook trout and rainbow.

Card Lake (Map 37/G7)
Card Lake is found west of Bancroft and offers slow to fair fishing for smallmouth bass. The bass in the lake are not very big, although the odd 1 kg (2 lbs) bass can be found.

Cardiff Lakes (Map 37/B6)
The Cardiff Lakes are found off Highway 648 and are both regularly stocked with rainbow trout. Fishing in both lakes for rainbow that average 30 cm (12 in) is fair, with the best action in the spring just after ice off.

Cardwell Lake (Map 37/G2)
Both smallmouth and largemouth bass are found in the lake in fair numbers. The lake is also stocked biennially with rainbow trout, although fishing is fair.

Carfrae Lake (Map 38/A7)
Found south of Bancroft on a series of bush roads, Carfrae Lake was last stocked in 2007 with a few hundred rainbow trout.

Carp Lake (Map 26/F1)
This is a small lake nestled between Horseshoe and Mountain Lakes. Anglers can expect fair fishing for marginal sized smallmouth bass.

Carson and Trout [Stubbs] Lakes (Map 47/C4)
Carson Lake is a deep, clear lake that supports a natural lake trout population along with a decent smallmouth bass fishery. On the other side of Highway 60, Trout Lake is stocked with lake trout. Both lakes are connected by a canal with the boat launch resting on the Trout Lake side of the highway.

Cassidy Lake (Map 32/G6)
Cassidy Lake is not far from Myers and Hoggart Lakes and offers fair fishing for largemouth bass. The lake also holds stocked splake.

Catchacoma Lake (Map 27/G6)
This beautiful cottage lake has a good population of smallmouth and largemouth bass in the 1 kg (2 lbs) range. Anglers can also expect some sporadic action in areas for lake trout to 4 kg (9 lbs).

Catfish Lake [Lac Barbotte] (Map 59/E5)
Catfish Lake lies west of the town of Noelville and offers fair fishing for small-mouth bass and northern pike. Try spinner patterns to find both pike and bass.

Cedar and Cooper Lakes (Map 26/D5)
Cedar Lake is found southeast of Gull Lake along Highway 35 in the Moore Falls area. The small lake offers fair fishing for stocked rainbow trout. Cooper Lake is found southeast of Moore Lake and offers stocked splake along with a few smallmouth bass.

Centre Lake (Map 37/E7)
Stocked in the past with splake, Centre Lake has more recently benefited from brook trout stockings. The lake is easily accessed off Highway 118 southwest of Bancroft and is also home to smallmouth bass and panfish.

Centre [Pivet] Lake (Map 36/B5)
Centre Lake is stocked with splake and fishing can be good during ice fishing season and in spring. A population of whitefish is also available.

Chain Lakes and Spruce Lake (Map 38/F7)
Despite their proximity to Bancroft to the west, some surprisingly decent sized splake can be found in these small, stocked lakes.

Chainy and Leather Root Lakes (Map 37/D4)
Southwest of Maynooth, Kerr Lane branches north from Peterson Road and leads by Chainy Lake, which is stocked with brook trout. To the south, Leather Root Lake also holds stocked brook trout.

Chandos Lake (Map 28/E5)
This bigger lake is found east of Highway 28. A boat launch is found off the 620 allowing anglers to test their luck for lake trout, northern pike, smallmouth and largemouth bass as well as pumpkinseed sunfish, rock bass and yellow perch.

Charcoal Lake (Map 35/B2)
Charcoal Lake is a hidden lake located near Highway 35 just past Dorset. Stocked every few years with brook trout, fishing is decent.

Chateau and Grants Lakes (Map 66/D6)
Found near Algonquin Park's northern border, fishing is good at times for small-mouth bass, which have taken over as the primary sportfish species in Chateau Lake. Both lakes also hold brook trout.

Chemong Lakes (Map 10/E1–18/G4)
These popular Kawartha area lakes are shallow lakes that can be found off the Trent Severn Waterway system north of Peterborough. Fishing for walleye is usu-ally fair for walleye but usually a bit more productive for smallmouth and large-mouth that can be found throughout the lake. The more weedy southern part of Chemong is a known holding area for big largemouth bass. Muskellunge can be found to 10 kg (22 lbs) in the deeper waters along weedlines and off Kelly Island. Panfish are another popular catch.

Cherry Lake (Map 19/A1)
Accessed by canoe in Kawarthas Highlands Provincial Park, Cherry Lake is home to lake trout.

Christopher Robin Lake (Map 66/D5)
Christopher Robin is a brook trout lake that is accessed by foot off the series of logging roads to the east of the Bissett Creek Road.

Circular Lake (Map 34/G5–35/A5)
This small lake can be found off a 2wd access road and offers slow to fair fishing for small brook trout. Due to the easy access to the lake, the lake does receive significant angling pressure.

Clanricarde Lake (Map 28/C4)
Clanricarde Lake can be very good at times for smallmouth bass. The lake is difficult to get to, as the only real means of access is by foot through heavy bush.

Clara Lake (Map 65/G3)
Accessed by snowmobile or on foot through some thick bush, Clara Lake holds stocked brook trout. Reports of good size brookies have surfaced here.

Claradeer and Deermeadow Lakes (Map 65/F5)
Short trails take anglers to the lakes, which are inhabited by natural brook trout. Ice fishing is productive as well as spring and fall fishing for brookies to 40 cm (16 in). Try a silver spoon or a streamer pattern in spring.

Clark and Palette Lakes (Map 43/B6)
Clark and Palette Lakes are two smaller lakes found to the west and east of Wa-seosa Lake. There is cottage development on both lakes and anglers will find fair to good fishing at times for smallmouth bass.

Clark Lake (Map 38/B6)
Found just off Highway 28, northeast of Bancroft, this lake offers fair fishing for smallmouth bass.

Clear and Little Leech Lakes (Map 34/G7)
Found just south of Bigwind Provincial Park, Clear Lake was once stocked with lake trout. The current status of the lake trout fishing quality is unknown; however, there remains a good population of smallmouth bass. Little Leech offers good fishing at times for largemouth bass.

Clear and Little Whitefish Lakes (Map 32/F3)
These lakes receive heavy fishing pressure throughout the year and therefore fish-ing success can be challenging at times. Fishing for smallmouth bass to 1.5 kg (3.5 lbs) is fair, while angling for natural lake trout is often slow. A fair population of whitefish is also available in the lakes. There are slot size restrictions in place for lake trout as well as special ice fishing regulations.

Clear and Loon Lakes (Map 40/F2)
Clear Lake can be accessed west of the settlement of Ardbeg, while Loon Lake can be accessed via portage from Clear Lake. Both lakes offer good fishing at times for bass, although Loon Lake is usually more productive.

Clear Lake (Map 19/B4)
Part of the Trent Severn Waterway and connected to the bigger Stony Lake, Clear Lake offers good fishing at times for walleye and good fishing for bass. The larger muskel-lunge are also prevalent throughout the lake. While most anglers have a tough time finding muskie, ardent muskie hunters boast of some good catches on Clear Lake.

Clear Lake (Map 24/C2)
Clear Lake is a popular Cottage Country lake. Fishing for smaller stocked rain-bow is fair with the best action during the spring just after ice off. This lake also holds smallmouth bass, largemouth bass and northern pike.

Clear Lake (Map 32/A4)
Clear Lake is one of the larger lakes in The Blackstone Harbour Provincial Park. The lake offers a few rustic camping sites and good fishing for smallmouth and largemouth bass. Fishing for northern pike is also good for smaller pike. A small population of walleye and lake trout also inhabit the lake.

Clear Lake (Map 35/F4)
This Frost Centre lake can only be accessed via portage. The lake offers fair fish-ing for natural lake trout and has a number of rustic campsites.

Clear Lake (Map 43/B5)
Clear Lake offers fair fishing for smallmouth bass and northern pike. The lake is also stocked with splake every few years, while rainbow where stocked here in the past.

Clear Lake (Map 67/E7)
Clear Lake is stocked with lake trout and is most heavily fished in the winter when access can be easily obtained by snowmobile. There is also an unnamed lake northeast of Clear Lake that is stocked with brook trout.

Clear [Watt] Lake (Map 61/F6)
Most visitors get to this lake by canoe from Stormy Lake. The lake holds stocked lake trout that provide for fair fishing, especially during the winter. Smallmouth bass, large-mouth bass, brook trout, muskellunge, northern pike and walleye are also found here.

Clearwater Lake (Map 25/C5)
Like so many other cottage lakes, this Clearwater Lake has limited public access since the roads to the south are private. The lake does offer good fishing for smallmouth and largemouth bass to 1.5 kg (3.5 lbs) as well as the odd lake trout.

Clearwater Lake (Map 34/C4)
Clearwater Lake provides fair fishing for smallmouth bass in the 0.5–1 kg (1–2 lb) range. There are a number of cottages along the shoreline.

Clement and Little Esson Lakes (Map 37/A7)
Your best bet for action on these lakes is for their resident smallmouth bass, although they hold stocked rainbow as well. Fishing is regarded as fair to good for smallmouth bass in the 1 kg (2 lb) range, while fishing for rainbow is slow.

Cliff and Cranberry Lakes (Map 66/C5)
These secluded lakes offer slow to fair fishing for small brook trout. Cranberry Lake can be accessed by a dirt road, while Cliff Lake must be walked to. Due to the more remote access, Cliff Lake usually has better action.

Clinto [Hardwood] and Crozier [McFadden] Lakes (Map 35/C2)
These cottage lakes are both found off County Road 12 and offer fair fishing for natural lake trout to 65 cm (26 in) in size. Rainbow trout were once stocked in both lakes, although the species is now extinct. It is believed that a small popula-tion of brook trout remains in Crozier Lake.

Clubbe Lake (Map 32/G3)
This small, secluded lake is located near the northern portion of Lake Joseph. There is a population of largemouth bass in the lake and fishing is good at times.

Clydesdale Lake (Map 28/E4)
Off Highway 620 north of Chandos Lake, this shallow, weedy lake offers ideal habitat for smallmouth bass. There are also sunfish and perch. Watch for private property.

Cod and Wilbur Lakes (Map 35/B1)
These lakes can be accessed via a rough 2wd road/ATV from either Highway 35 or Highway 60. Stocked every two years with brook trout, fishing for brookies to 30 cm (12 in) is good through the ice or in spring just after ice off.

Coe (Island) Lake (Map 28/G1–29/A1)
This lake east of Paudash is often stocked with splake. Smallmouth bass are also present. There is a boat launch located on the southeastern shore.

Coghlan Lake (Map 46/F6)
Coghlan Lake is stocked with splake and also has lake and brook trout present. Access is by secondary roads or by a short portage from Cross Lake.

Colbourne Lake (Map 28/C1)
Colbourne Lake is stocked regularly with rainbow trout, which provide fair to good fishing at times. The most productive period for rainbow is in spring after ice off. Try small spinners or nymph fly patterns.

Cold and Cloudy Lakes (Map 27/G7–28/A7)
These lakes can be accessed by a short portage from Gold Lake or a longer portage from Cox Lake. Once on Cold Lake, a rustic portage can take you into the smaller Cloudy Lake. Both lakes offer good fishing at times for small and largemouth bass to 2 kg, although Cloudy Lake can be more productive due to its difficult access. There is rustic camping available at both lakes.

Cole Lake (Map 50/B3)
This lake lies just off the north side of Highway 522 and has a few cottages along its shoreline. Fishing in the lake is fair for small northern pike and bass.

Coleman Lake (Map 36/B5)
Anglers can expect fair fishing for average sized smallmouth bass at this lake. Top water flies or lures such as poppers can create exciting action.

Commanda Lake (Map 51/G1)
Smallmouth and largemouth bass to 1.5 kg (3.5 lbs) make up the bulk of the action, although northern pike and walleye also inhabit the lake. Commanda Lake rests on the west side of Highway 534.

Compass Lake (Map 42/F5)
Accessed via the Seguin Trail or a rough 4wd road from the highway, most of the lake is surrounded by private land. Fishing can be good at times for smallmouth bass that can be found to 1.5 kg (3.5 lbs) in size.

Concession Lake (Map 27/D7)
There is no real road access to this lake, although snowmobiles can access it in the winter. Ice fishing for stocked lake trout can be good for trout that can reach up to 2 kg (4.5 lbs). Smallmouth and largemouth bass fishing can also be quite good at times for bass to 2 kg (4.5 lbs).

Conger [Pine] and LaForce Lakes (Map 32/C5)
Found off the north side of Healy Lake Road, Conger Lake offers largemouth bass and northern pike. LaForce Lake is the next lake to the west and offers generally slow fishing for small northern pike and panfish.

Connelly Lake (Map 27/B6)
This small lake is found just west of Crystal Lake and holds a small population of smallmouth and largemouth bass. Fishing is generally slow, although it picks up in the evening and during overcast periods.

Consecon Lake (Map 13/C7)
Found south of Trenton, off Highway 33, this bigger lake offers fair fishing at times for smallmouth and largemouth bass to 2 kg (4.5 lbs). Fishing is slow for walleye and fair at times for nice sized northern pike.

Contau Lake (Map 27/D3)
This shallow lake has a few cottages along its shoreline and offers fair to good fishing at times for smallmouth bass that average 0.5 kg (1 lb) in size. Fishing for walleye to 2.5 kg (5.5 lbs) is slow to fair throughout the season as is the fishing for muskellunge in the 4–6 kg (9–13 lb) range.

Coon Lake (Map 19/B2)
Coon Lake is home to a number of cottages and offers fair fishing for bass and slow to fair fishing for muskellunge.

Cope and Hudson Lakes (Map 37/C6)
These lakes can be found via backroads off Highway 648. Both have boat launches available. Cope Lake is stocked periodically with rainbow trout, while Hudson Lake offers fair fishing for lake trout and smallmouth bass. Lakers average 40 cm (16 in) and smallmouth average 1 kg (2 lbs).

Copper Lake (Map 28/C5)
Copper Lake is a part of the Serpentine Lake Canoe Route and can be accessed from nearby Rathbun Lake. There is rustic camping available at the lake and good fishing at times for largemouth bass to 1.5 kg (3.5 lbs). Largemouth tend to stick along shoreline structure. Walleye also inhabit the lake, although fishing is quite slow.

Cooper Lake (Map 34/G1)
This lake is located just to the north of the village of Dwight and Highway 60. Anglers will find fair fishing for smallmouth bass.

Corben Lake (Map 26/E6)
Corben Lake is set amid a beautifully forested area. Smallmouth and largemouth bass to 2 kg (4.5 lbs) provide fair to good fishing.

Cordova Lake (Map 20/C2)
Cordova Lake holds good number of walleye, bass and northern pike. The latter like to hang just off the lake's many drop offs and weedlines, while walleye are found near the Crowe River inlet. Bass can be found throughout the lake, but prefer hiding in the weeds.

Corkery Lake (Map 53/C2)
Corkery Lake rests just north of Kawawaymog Lake and is stocked every few years with splake. Pumpkinseed sunfish and yellow perch are also present.

Cornall Lake (Map 25/A4)
This lake is regulated by a dam on its southern end and remains very beautiful since it is surrounded by Crown land. A fair population of largemouth bass that can reach up to 2 kg (4.5 lbs) are often found along structure in the quiet bays.

Corncob and Tower Lakes (Map 53/B3)
A series of bush roads and trails access this area. Known as brook trout fisheries, the lakes are no longer stocked, but still offer up the odd brookie to 30 cm (12 in).

Cornick and Shaw Lakes (Map 53/C3)
Shaw Lake has been stocked with rainbow trout and fishing can be good at times for rainbow to 35 cm (14 in). Cornick Lake also supports a brook trout fishery.

Cox Lake (Map 28/A7)
As part of the Anstruther/Long Lake Canoe Route, Cox Lake can be accessed by portage from either Cold or Loucks Lakes. Anglers can find smallmouth and largemouth bass and stocked lake trout. There is rustic camping available at the lake.

Crab Lake (Map 28/B6)
The scenic Crab Lake is located just south of Wolf Lake via a short portage. There are a few secluded campsites that are frequented by canoeists and anglers alike. Fishing enthusiasts can look forward to fair to good fishing for smallmouth bass to 1.5 kg (3 lbs).

Cranberry and Lower Digby [Redboat] Lakes (Map 26/C5)
These lakes lies close together and are a part of a chain of lakes that offer good fishing at times for smallmouth and largemouth bass to 2 kg (4.5 lbs).

Cranberry Lake (Map 25/F6)
Cranberry Lake is privately owned and permission must be obtained to enter the area. The lake does offers good fishing for large and smallmouth bass that can grow to 2.5 kg (5.5 lbs) as well as a few walleye.

Cranberry Lake (Map 36/B5)
Off the north side of Eagle Lake Road (County Road 6) Cranberry Lake has a number of cottages scattered along its shoreline. It was stocked in 2008 with walleye, but the fishing remains more consistent for smallmouth and largemouth bass. There are also a few muskellunge for patient anglers, while rock bass and yellow perch are also found here.

Cranberry Lake (Map 40/G6)
Cranberry Lake is a secluded lake that is rarely visited by anglers. The lake offers very good fishing at times for largemouth bass.

Crane Lake (Map 18/G1)
Crane Lake offers good fishing for smallmouth and largemouth bass. Access is via a rough 4wd road off the north side of Highway 36.

Crane Lake (Map 32/C4)
West of Blackstone Lake, the best action on Crane Lake is for smallmouth and largemouth bass. However, the lake is stocked regularly with lake trout and holds a few walleye and northern pike.

Crawford Lake (Map 41/F3)
Crawford offers fair fishing for smallmouth and largemouth bass as well as a few walleye and northern pike.

Crego Lake (Map 26/F5)
Crego Lake has cottages along its shoreline along with a boat launch. Anglers can expect fair fishing for smallmouth and largemouth bass to 1.5 kg (3.5 lbs). A small population of muskellunge is present in the lake, but fishing is quite slow.

Creightons and McRae Lakes (Map 37/B5)
These two small, secluded lakes offer good fishing for brook trout to 35 cm (14 in). McRae Lake lies partially within the private Harcourt Park and can only be found via trail from East Lake.

Crevice and Moonbeam Lakes (Map 46/C2)
These brook trout lakes are found off a bush road that follows the powerline. Moonbeam and North Moonbeam are stocked every couple of years with brook trout, while Crevice Lake is stocked every couple of years with splake.

Crochet Lake (Map 26/B2)
Crotchet Lake is one of the larger lakes in the area and offers slow to fair fishing for lake trout and good fishing for smallmouth bass.

Crooked and Tea Lake (Map 43/B1)
These lakes are stocked with brook trout but are governed by special regulations and restrictions.

Crooked Chute and Burbot Lakes (Map 64/A3)
Fishing is fair at these lakes for generally small northern pike. Try a floating Rapala for active northerns. Crooked Chute Lake also hosts populations of muskellunge and walleye.

Crooked Lake (Map 53/C7)
Crooked Lake is stocked almost annually with lake trout, which provide for fair fishing, especially through the ice in winter. However, smallmouth bass provide the best fishing opportunities here.

Crooked [North Fishog] Lake (Map 26/B4)
Crooked Lake can be accessed from Fishog Lake by canoe down the Head River. Fishing for smallmouth and largemouth bass to 2 kg (4.5 lbs) is usually pretty good here.

Cross Lake (Map 46/F6)
Easily accessed off the west side of the Cross Lake Road (Highway 523), fishing remains productive for nice sized smallmouth bass here. Lake trout also inhabit this lake with some decent sized fish caught annually.

Crosson Lake (Map 34/G6)
Crosson Lake lies within Bigwind Provincial Park and provides good fishing at times for stocked rainbow trout. Fly-fishing with small nymphs or casting small spinners or spoons can be productive for fish in the 30 cm (12 in) range.

Crowe Lake (Map 20/E4)
North of Highway 7 near Marmora, Crowe Lake is a bigger lake with lots of structure for predatory largemouth bass, muskellunge northern pike and walleye to hang out in. Unsuspecting smaller fish, such as the black crappie and bluegill, are often the victims. The most active fishery is for the largemouth, but walleye fingerlings were stocked in the lake to help aide that fishery.

Crow Lake (Map 41/A5)
Crow Lake is a small lake found just west of the larger Harris Lake. Crow Lake provides good fishing at times for average sized largemouth bass.

Crown Lake (Map 44/F6)
Crown Lake can be accessed via a 4wd road and is located only a few kilometres from Algonquin Park. The lake offers fair fishing opportunities for brook trout.

Crystal, Island and Wolf Lakes (Map 53/D6)
These lakes can only be accessed by snowmobile or on foot by trail, which can be picked up off the road, near Wolf Lake. The two lakes found due north from Crystal Lake are unnamed, however, offer similar fishing. All of the lakes' inaccessibility has helped maintain a good natural brook trout fishery.

Crystal Lake (Map 27/D6)
Crystal Lake is stocked with lake trout to supplement natural populations that grow to 2 kg (4.5 lbs) in size on occasion. Walleye are also present in the lake and fishing pressure on the prized sportfish is heavy, resulting in fair fishing success at the best of times. Fishing for smallmouth bass is fair to good at times, with smallmouth reaching 1.5 kg (3.5 lbs) in size. There are even reports that the odd largemouth bass is caught periodically.

Crystalline, Roger and Sunrise Lakes (Map 44/E6)
These three out of the way lakes offer decent brook trout fishing. Crystalline Lake is the only lake that cannot be accessed by road and must be portaged to from one of the other lakes, while Roger Lake is stocked periodically with brook trout.

Curly Lake (Map 64/A6)
Most often visited in the winter, fishing can be steady for nice sized brook trout.

Dalrymple Lake (Map 16/E2)
Lower Dalrymple and Upper Dalrymple Lakes are well developed cottage lakes that are heavily fished throughout the season. Anglers can still find smallmouth bass to 2 kg (4.5 lbs) and the odd small walleye. Muskellunge were once abundant in the lake, although are now a rarity due to the introduction of pike many years ago. Fishing for pike does produce the occasional pike in the 6 kg (13 lbs) range.

Dan, McEwen and Horse Lakes (Map 35/C5)
Stocked with splake, fishing is most productive through the ice or in spring just after ice off. Small spoons or jigs can be productive during ice fishing season. In spring, both spoons or jigs and streamer flies or nymphs work well.

Darlington's Lake (Map 32/A1)
Found just north of Parry Sound, Darlington Lake offers fair fishing for smallmouth bass and stocked lake trout. Lakers are best caught through the ice or in spring.

Davis Lake (Map 26/F5)
Davis Lake was stocked with lakers in the past and the odd trout in the 2 kg (4.5 lb) range is caught annually. The lake also supports a fair smallmouth bass population.

Davis Pond (Map 38/B1)
Stocked every few years with brook trout, fishing for small brookies is fair throughout the year. A bush road leads right to the pond south of the much bigger Papineau Lake, but most of the fishing pressure occurs during winter.

De Gaulle Lake (Map 18/D1–27/D7)
This secluded lake offers a fair to good smallmouth and largemouth bass fishery. Bass up to 2 kg (4.5 lbs) can be a lot of fun to catch on popper presentations during calm evenings.

Deadhorse and Twin Lakes (Map 53/C4)
These lakes can only be accessed by trail from a bush road. The lakes support populations of natural brook trout and fishing can be good in both lakes, especially in spring.

Deep Bay (Map 40/E7)
Deep Bay is a popular bay found off Big Sound that offers good fishing for smallmouth bass that can be found to 2 kg (4.5 lbs) and northern pike. Pike in the bay can be quite large, although they average about 2–3 kg (4.5–6.5 lbs).

Deer Lake (Map 37/D7)
Deer Lake provides for fair fishing for smallmouth bass and lake trout. There is a boat launch onto the lake.

Deer Lake (Map 43/A3)
This popular cottage country lake offers fair fishing for walleye to 3 kg (6.5 lbs), as well as smallmouth bass that average 1 kg (2 lbs).

Deer Lake (Map 52/C5)
Fishing is generally fair for northern pike, smallmouth bass and largemouth bass in this cottage lake. Bass can be found to 1.5 kg (3.5 lbs).

Deerock Lake (Map 30/F6)
A dirt road provides access to this large, yet shallow lake. The lake is surrounded by mainly Crown land and offers good fishing periodically for smallmouth and largemouth bass to 2 kg (4.5 lbs) in size. Northern pike are also found in fair numbers.

Denna Lake (Map 26/E4)
This popular cottage destination lake provides fair fishing for smallmouth and largemouth bass.

Devil's Gap Lake (Map 27/D3)
Devil's Gap Lake is a small, secluded bass lake that is found south of Highway 503. It holds a fair number of smallmouth and largemouth bass in the 0.5–1 kg (1–2 lb) range. The lake was also stocked in 2003 with brown trout, but there are few reports on the success of that stocking.

Devine, Dunn and Fleming Lakes (Map 34/D4)
Although these are some of the smaller lakes in the area, they provide fair fishing for smallmouth bass. Devine Lake also has a population of largemouth bass that can be aggressive for topwater lures and flies.

De Volve and Bell Lakes (Map 41/B3)
Found in the Shawanaga Lake area, these remote lakes are best known for their bass fishery. De Volve Lake only holds smallmouth bass, while Bell also holds largemouth and northern pike.

Devon and Garreau Lakes (Map 66/G5)
Devon Lake is stocked with brook trout and offers good fishing in the winter and spring. Garreau Lake relies on natural reproduction but heavy fishing pressure has affected the brook trout fishery.

Diamond Lake (Map 37/E6)
This lake offers fair fishing for smallmouth bass in the 0.5–1 kg (1–2 lb) range and fair to good fishing at times for lake trout. Lakers are stocked in the lake annually.

Diamond Lake (Map 41/F7)
Next to Highway 518, this cottage lake offers fair fishing for smallmouth bass. Crayfish imitations worked slowly near bottom can be productive for bass. Rainbow trout were previously stocked but none are reported now.

Diamond Lake (Map 47/G6)
This easily accessed road is found off of Rockingham Road (County Road 68) east of Combermere. Previously stocked with lake trout, the lake also holds brook and rainbow trout as well as smallmouth and largemouth bass.

Dickey Lake (Map 29/D5)
Found west of Highway 62 and Steenburg Lake, Dickey Lake is home to lots of bass (both smallmouth and largemouth) and a few lake trout. The elusive lake trout are best fished for in the winter or early in spring before the waters warm.

Dick Lake (Map 43/G1)
Found near Algonquin Park's western border, half the challenge of fishing here is finding the lake. Fishing can be good at times for brook trout for trout that have been caught over 35 cm (14 in) in size.

Dickie Lake (Map 34/E5)
Found east of the town of Baysville, Dickie Lake is a popular summer cottage destination. Anglers can expect fair fishing for smallmouth bass to 1.5 kg (3.5 lbs), although bass are generally average sized.

Digby [Scrabble], Trawler [Clear] and Coburn Lakes (Map 26/C5)
This small chain of bass lakes is linked by rustic portages. Smallmouth and largemouth bass can grow fairly big in these seldom visited lakes. Coburn holds stocked rainbow, while Trawler or Clear Lake has recently been stocked with splake. Perch and pumpkinseed sunfish are also found in the area.

Dividing Lake (Map 45/A6)
Dividing Lake takes quite a bit of work to get to, but rewards anglers with nice sized brook trout. The scenic lake is also home to rustic campsites as well as a stand of beautiful old growth white pine trees.

Dixie Lake (Map 37/C7)
This small, secluded lake can be accessed via a rough 4wd road from the end of Magnificent Road. The small lake is stocked every two years with brook trout, which are best caught during ice fishing season or in spring after ice off.

Dodd and Round Lakes (Map 59/B4)
These two lakes offer fair fishing for small northern pike. Round Lake is also inhabited by walleye, while Dodd Lake also offers fair fishing for smallmouth bass.

Doe and Fawn Lakes (Map 25/B3)
These lakes can be found off County Road 6 east of Gravenhurst and offer good fishing at times for largemouth bass. Top water flies and lures or any minnow imitation can work well.

Doe and Little Doe Lakes (Map 42/F4)
Fishing is fair for walleye that can be found up to 3 kg (6.5 lbs) in size. Smallmouth bass and northern pike also inhabit the lakes. Try along the shallows in evening for bigger northerns.

Doe Lake (Map 26/B2)
Doe Lake is a secluded lake east of South Anson Lake and has good fishing for stocked brook trout. Ice fishing is popular on the lake.

Dog and West Deer Lakes (Map 51/B4)
These remote lakes are found south of Port Loring and offer some decent smallmouth bass fishing.

Dog, Duck and Little Birchy Lakes (Map 36/C3)
Located just south of the Haliburton Forest Reserve, the lakes can be accessed via rough 2wd roads and then by short trails. The lakes are stocked every few years with brook trout and brookies average 25–35 cm (10–14 in) in size.

Dogfish Lake, Gull Lake and Lac La Vallee (Map 40/F3)
These remote lakes can only be found via rough 4wd roads or trails. All three lakes are surrounded by Crown land where rustic campsites have been established. There is good fishing for smallmouth bass to 1.5 kg (3.5 lbs).

Dollars Lake (Map 50/D3)
Both smallmouth and largemouth bass are found in good numbers and can reach up to 2 kg (4.5 lbs) in size. Northern pike and walleye inhabit the lake in fair numbers, while a small muskellunge population is also present in the lake.

Dotty and Oxbow Lakes (Map 43/G5–44/A6)
Anglers can expect good fishing for smallmouth bass, fair fishing for lake trout and slow success for brook trout. Lake trout are stocked periodically in both lakes and can be found to 65 cm (26 in) in size.

Doughnut Lake (Map 44/B5)
This small brook trout lake can be reached via a short trail off the North Camp Lake Road to the east of Tasso Lake. Brook trout are stocked every couple years to help enhance the fishery.

Drag and Spruce Lakes (Map 36/E6)
These connected lakes are located east of Haliburton and are popular cottage destination lakes. There are a couple of boat launches on the lakes and fishing for smallmouth bass to 1.5 kg (3.5 lbs) is good. A natural population of lake trout is also present with the odd trout reaching 65 cm (26 in) in size.

Duck and Blotter Lakes (Map 26/G1)
These two lakes offer fair fishing for decent sized smallmouth bass. A crayfish lure or fly worked slowly near the bottom can be productive or try a type of minnow imitation such as a Rapala or crank bait.

Duck Lake (Map 17/A1)
Duck Lake still has the odd muskellunge resident in the lake, although fishing is much better for smallmouth and largemouth bass. There is a private campground near the lake.

Duck Lake (Map 41/E7)
This small lake along the Seguin River Paddling Route is stocked periodically with lake trout. Northern pike, smallmouth and largemouth bass are also found.

Duck Lake (Map 50/F6)
Accessed by rough bush roads, fishing here can be quite good for smallmouth bass to 2 kg (4.5 lbs) along with the odd walleye.

Duck Lake (Map 51/A4)
An extension of the bigger Lake Wauquimakog, this Duck Lake offers fishing for stocked rainbow. Smallmouth bass and walleye are also present. Access is by Duck Lake Road just east of Port Loring.

Dummer Lake (Map 19/D3)
Located south of the much larger Stoney Lake, Dummer Lake is accessible off a small access road on the south side of County Road 6. There is a marina at the north end of the lake and cottages occupy most of the shoreline. The lake has good sized smallmouth and largemouth bass. The other main sportfish is walleye. Try working weedlines and along the drop off at the south end of the lake. Another place to try is around an underwater point that reaches out into the middle of the lake.

Dunchurch and Hobson Lakes (Map 41/C2)
A good population of small brook trout inhabits Dunchurch Lake, while Hobson Lake holds smallmouth bass. The difficult access limits visitors to these remote lakes.

Dunlop, McKenna and Sweezy Lakes (Map 66/F5)
These secluded brook trout lakes offer fair fishing in the winter and spring. A bush road leads to McKenna Lake and short trails join the other lakes from there.

Durrell Lake (Map 51/D2)
Fishing in Durrell Lake can be good at times for nice sized smallmouth bass and northern pike. Try a top water lure or fly at dusk to find feeding pike and bass.

Dutcher Lake (Map 41/F6)
Dutcher Lake is a remote hike or ATV access lake that sees very few anglers throughout the year. Anglers can expect good to very good fishing at the lake for smallmouth bass that average 1 kg (2 lbs).

Dyson Lake (Map 33/A4)
Located southwest of Lake Rosseau, Dyson Lake received constant fishing pressure throughout the year. There are a number of cottages on the lake and fishing is fair for smallmouth bass. There also remains a small population of lake trout in the lake, although fishing is quite slow.

Eagle and Moose Lakes (Map 36/C5)
Located off Eagle Lake Road (County Road 14) these lakes have a number of cottages along their shoreline. There is a public boat launch on the southern shore of Eagle Lake. Both lakes offer fair fishing for lake trout that average 40 cm (16 in) in size and fair to good fishing for smallmouth bass to 1.5 kg (3.5 lbs). Anglers will also find a fair population of whitefish. Watch for slot size restrictions on lake trout and special ice fishing regulations.

Eagle Lake (Map 52/D5)
Eagle Lake is a popular cottage lake that is home to Mikisew Provincial Park. Fishing in the lake is fair to good at times for panfish and smallmouth bass that are rumoured to reach 2 kg (4.5 lbs) in size. Walleye and northern pike are also found in smaller numbers. Recently, rainbow trout have been stocked into the lake.

Earl's and Taggart Lakes (Map 64/D2)
Off Highway 17 west of Mattawa, Earl's Lake receives a lot of local angling pressure and fishing is often slow for walleye. Largemouth bass are a little more plentiful in the lake. Nearby Taggart Lake also holds largemouth bass caught to 1.5 kg (3.5 lbs).

East and Boundary [Martin] Lakes (Map 36/F2)
Access into this area is limited by private and 4wd roads. Those that do visit the lakes will find decent brook trout fishing. Boundary Lake is stocked, while East Lake contains a self-sustaining population of brook trout.

East Jeannie Lakes (Map 35/E1)
These two lakes are located off the Bear Lake Road south of County Road 12. Stocked every few years with brook trout, fishing for brookies can be a challenge at times.

East Paint Lake (Map 35/E3)
East Paint Lake is one of the lesser-visited lakes in the Frost Centre due to the 1,300 m (4,265 ft) portage from Red Pine Lake that is the primary access route. The lake is stocked every few years with splake and offers good fishing through the ice and in spring. Splake average 30 cm (12 in) and can be found much bigger. There is a beautiful island campsite at this lake.

Eastell Lake (Map 43/F7)
A portage is available from the much larger Solitaire Lake found southeast of Eastell Lake. The lake contains a natural population of brook trout and fishing can be good in the spring just after ice off or through the ice in winter. Live baitfish are not allowed.

Echo Lake (Map 24/D2)
Found near County Road 13, this lake offers fair to good fishing for smallmouth and largemouth bass to 2 kg (4.5 lbs). A large portion of the shoreline is within the Torrence Barrens Conservation Reserve, which has helped the lake remain undeveloped.

Echo Lake (Map 34/F4)
Echo Lake is one of the larger lakes in the area and can be found near County Road 117 south of Lake of Bays. Anglers can expect fair to good fishing for smallmouth bass to 1.5 kg (3.5 lbs) in size. There are a number of cottages along the shoreline that have dock structures that can be good hiding areas for bass.

Eels Lake (Map 28/C3)
Eels Lake is one of the larger lakes in the area and has a number of cottages along with few boat launches along its shoreline. The most sought after sportfish in the big lake are lake trout, which have recently been stocked. There is also good fishing at times for smallmouth and largemouth bass along with perch. Eels Lake is part of the winter/spring fishing sanctuary and there are slot size restrictions for lake trout.

Eeyore Lake (Map 66/E5)
Eeyore Lake, on the Grant's Creek Paddling Route, is stocked yearly with splake and holds perch, pumpkinseed sunfish and whitefish.

Egan, Jimmie, Long, East Tommy and Currie Lakes (Map 29/F1)
Found off of bush roads to the east of Highway 62 south of Bancroft, Egan Lake is the biggest of the bunch. It offers stocked rainbow trout along with largemouth bass and yellow perch. To the south is Long Lake, which is also stocked with rainbow and home to perch. Further east is East Tommy and Currie Lake, which both offer stocked brook trout. Jimmie Lake is northwest of Egan and also offers stocked brookies.

Eighteen, Seventeen, Sixteen and Fifteen Mile Lakes (Map 44/A7)
These lakes can each be accessed west of Highway 60 and offer good fishing for smallmouth bass to 1.5 kg (3.5 lbs) as well as lake trout to 70 cm (28 in). Fifteen Mile Lake is part of a winter fish sanctuary to protect natural lake trout stocks.

Eiler Lake (Map 44/A7)
Stocked with brook trout, this lake is found west of Highway 60 and Oxtongue Lake off of Blue Spruce Road.

Elbow Lake (Map 58/G1–59/A1)
This lake is accessible by rough 2wd road off Highway 69 and offers fair fishing for smallmouth bass.

Elephant Lake (Map 37/C5)
This is one of the larger lakes in the area and is a popular cottage destination. Anglers can expect good fishing for smallmouth and largemouth bass. Walleye averaging 1 kg (2 lbs) and nice sized muskellunge also inhabit the lake. Winter is one of the better periods for walleye, while muskellunge fishing is more productive in the fall.

Elzevir Lake (Map 30/E6)
This secluded lake sees most of its company during the winter months, when it can be accessed by snowmobile. It is stocked annually with splake, which provide for good fishing, especially through the ice in winter and in early spring.

Emily Lake (Map 18/B5)
This small extension of Sturgeon Lake offers good fishing for smallmouth and largemouth bass to 2 kg (4.5 lbs). A small boat or canoe from Sturgeon Lake down Emily Creek can access the lake.

Emsdale Lake (Map 43/C4)
Emsdale Lake offers good fishing at times for average sized smallmouth bass, while lake trout are being stocked to help supplement that fishery. There are some nice sized lakers here.

Esson Lake (Map 36/G7–37/A7)
Esson Lake has a number of cottages along its shoreline and offers good fishing at times for smallmouth bass to 1.5 kg (3.5 lbs). The lake is also stocked annually with lake trout to help maintain the trout fishery.

Fair Lake (Map 32/G4)
Fair Lake offers very good fishing at times for smallmouth bass to 2 kg (4.5 lbs). Access is difficult and can be done by rustic portage or following the creek from Cox Lake.

Fairholme Lake (Map 41/C3)
Found on the east side of Highway 124, Fairholme Lake is stocked with lake trout every few years. This lake also holds smallmouth and largemouth bass.

Fairy Lake (Map 34/D1)
As a beautiful backdrop to the town of Huntsville, Fairy Lake is a busy lake year round. Fishing is fair at times for bass that can reach up to 2.5 kg (5.5 lbs) and the lake is stocked periodically with lake trout, which provide for slow fishing for trout to 70 cm (28 in). Ice fishing and trolling are the preferred methods of angling for lake trout in Fairy Lake. A few northern pike also exists in the lake.

Faraday Lake (Map 37/G6)
Located just outside of the town of Bancroft, Faraday Lake is inhabited by a natural population of lake trout. Fishing for lakers is slow and there are a number of special restrictions to help the ailing trout stocks.

Faris, Long and Plate Lakes (Map 32/D1)
These three small lakes are located near Highway 518 and offer slow to fair fishing for average sized bass. All three lakes contain smallmouth bass, while Plate Lake is also home to largemouth bass.

Farlain Lake (Map 23/B5)
Farlain Lake is located just before Awenda Provincial Park north of the town of Penetanguishene. The lake has cottages scattered along its shoreline and offers slow fishing for smallmouth and largemouth bass.

Farquhar Lake (Map 37/B6)
Your best bet for action on this lake is for its resident smallmouth bass. The popular lake also provides slow fishing for lake trout that average 40 cm (16 in). There are special regulations in place to help the lake trout fishery.

Fawn Lake (Map 34/B5)
Fawn Lake sees heavy fishing pressure in the summer, but still offers fair fishing for smallmouth bass to 1.5 kg (3.5 lbs) and largemouth bass to 2.5 kg (5.5 lbs). Look for weed structure, which is prominent around the lake, as the main holding areas for bass.

Fifteen and Fourteen Lakes (Map 43/D3)
Both of these lakes have been stocked in the past with rainbow trout. Fishing is generally slow, but picks up in spring.

Findlay, Mill and Parkline Lakes (Map 67/A6)
Located near Algonquin Park's boundary, all three lakes offer brook trout. Mill and Parkline are stocked regularly and have produced trout in the 35 cm (14 in) range. Findlay is stocked with rainbow trout on a regular basis.

Finger Lake (Map 47/B2)
This hidden trout lake can be found off the southwest bay of Aylen Lake. Stocked every other year with brook trout, fishing can be decent here in the spring and through the ice in winter.

Finger Lake (Map 53/E7)
Similar to most of the small lakes in the area, this lake is stocked with brook trout. However, it also holds northern pike. The 3 hectare lake is found north of the Forestry Tower Road on the way to the Tim River Algonquin Park access point.

First, Second and Third James Lakes (Map 67/F6)
These lakes offer good fishing for smallmouth bass that can be found to 1.5 kg (3.5 lbs) as well as panfish. Northern pike are found in fair numbers, while muskellunge also inhabit the lakes. There is a public access point located at the southern end of First James Lake. .

First, Second and Third Lakes (Map 32/D3)
Accessed by backroads southeast of Parry Sound, these lakes offer fair to good fishing for smallmouth bass, largemouth bass and northern pike. Pike in the lakes are generally small, while bass can be found to 1.5 kg (3.5 lbs). These lakes do not receive as much attention as some of the larger, more populated lakes in the area.

Fish and Long Lakes (Map 37/C5)
Fish and Long Lakes are two small, secluded lakes found west of Elephant Lake. Long Lake offers good fishing for small rainbow and slow fishing for brook trout. Fish Lake provides fair to good fishing for small brook trout.

Fish Lake (Map 47/A3)
This small, hidden lake is found near the Aylen Lake/Highway 60 junction. Stocked every other year with brook trout, fishing is fair for brook trout to 25 cm (10 in).

Fish [Perch] and Oudaze Lakes (Map 43/C6)
These lakes can be found to the east of Highway 11 and offer slow to fair fishing for brook trout to 35 cm (14 in). Oudaze Lake also provides good fishing at times for smallmouth bass to 1.5 kg (3.5 lbs), while Fish Lake does indeed have a few perch to look for.

Fishog Lake (Map 26/C5)
Your best bet for fishing success here is for smallmouth and largemouth bass. There is also a small resident population of muskellunge in the lake.

Fishtail Lake (Map 37/B5)
Originally named Trout Lake in 1855, Fishtail Lake was once well known for its lake trout. Today, fishing is fair at times for lakers that average 40 cm (16 in) in size. The better action comes from smallmouth bass, which average 1 kg (2 lbs). The lake is part of a fall to spring fish sanctuary to protect the fragile lake trout population in the lake.

Flaxman Lake (Map 32/E1)
Flaxman Lake can be found via a rough 2wd road and offers fair to good fishing for smallmouth bass. The lake has been stocked in the past with lake trout; however, it now relies on natural reproduction. Angles can expect slow to fair fishing for lake trout throughout the season. There are special restrictions on this lake to help protect lake trout.

Fletcher Lakes (Map 35/C1–44/D7)
The Fletcher Lakes can both be accessed off County Road 12 northeast of Dorset. The popular cottage destination lakes are stocked every few years with lake trout.

Fogal Lake (Map 32/D4)
Fogal Lake can be found not far from the north side of Healy Lake Road. The lake holds a fair number of largemouth bass that can be quite active during overcast periods or in the evening.

Foote Lake (Map 43/D5)
Visitors will find that there are a number of cottages along the shoreline and fair fishing for small smallmouth bass. The shallow nature of the lake is a haven for aquatic weed growth, providing good structure for bass.

Forest Lake (Map 53/A5)
Forest Lake is part of the South River system and has many cottages along its shoreline. Fishing is slow for brook trout that were stocked in the lake in the past.

Forget Lake (Map 32/D3)
Forget Lake is stocked every few years with lake trout and provides good fishing for lakers through the ice and in spring after ice off. As summer approaches, the smallmouth bass become the targeted species.

Fork and Sears Lakes (Map 64/E5)
Fork Lake is accessed off the Brain Lake access road and is stocked biennially with brook trout. Sears Lake is a lot more difficult to find and holds naturally reproducing brook trout. Fishing can be good through the ice or in spring for brookies..

Fortescue Lake (Map 27/D4)
While this lake is stocked annually with lake trout, the main sportfish species available is smallmouth bass. Smallmouth fishing can be good at times for bass that reach up to 2.5 kg (5.5 lbs). A small population of muskellunge also exists in the lake and they can be found in the 2–3 kg (4.5–6.5 lb) range on occasion.

Foster's [Stringer] Lake (Map 38/E2)
Much of Foster's Lake is surrounded by private land, although there is a public access area on the lake's north shore. Fishing is fair for small walleye and northern pike.

Four Mile Lake (Map 17/F1–26/E7)
This scenic Kawartha area lake is a popular lake that holds a fair population of smallmouth and largemouth bass that are known to grow quite big, up to 2.5 kg (5.5 lbs). A good holding area for largemouth is the northern portion of the lake. Walleye and muskellunge are also available in the lake with fair fishing available for good sized walleye. There is also slow to fair fishing for muskellunge that average 3–4 kg (6.5–9 lbs). A public boat launch lies on the east side of the lake.

Fourcorner Lake (Map 36/G4)
Stocked lake trout provide for good fishing in the winter and spring for lakers that average 40 cm (16 in). Try small spoons and streamer patterns in spring or small jigs and spoons through the ice. Although a portion of the lake is within Algonquin Park, the lake is open all year for fishing.

Fox and Willie Lake (Map 43/E4)
The rough bush road access helps reduce angling pressure. As a result, the action for smallmouth bass is usually pretty steady.

Fox Lake (Map 42/G7)
North of Lake Vernon, this lake provides good fishing for smallmouth and largemouth bass to 3 kg (6.5 lbs) and fair to good fishing for northern pike in the 3.5 kg (8 lb) range. Spinner baits or any minnow imitation lure or fly can be productive.

Fraser Lake (Map 38/F3)
Fraser Lake offers fair fishing for smallmouth bass in the 0.5–1 kg (1–2 lb) range and for northern pike to 60 cm (24 in). Walleye can also be found up to 70 cm (28 in), although fishing is generally slow. The narrow, around Welsh Island, can be a productive spot. A public access point is located on the lake's eastern shore.

Freen Lake (Map 29/D6)
Stocked regularly with lake trout and brook trout, Freen Lake is a remote access lake found south of Dickey Lake. The lake is also home to smallmouth and largemouth bass, along with panfish.

Froggy Lake (Map 63/D2)
This small, stocked lake is found north of Highway 17, just west of Pine Lake Road. Fishing is fair in spring or during the winter for brook trout. There are also pumpkinseed sunfish in the 11 hectare lake. .

Fry Lakes (Map 42/A7)
The Fry Lakes can be accessed by the Seguin Trail or off Highway 518. Upper Fry Lake provides fair fishing for marginal sized northern pike and Lower Fry Lake offers fair to good fishing for smallmouth and largemouth bass.

Galloway and Greens Lakes (Map 27/E5)
These lakes are hidden off the west side of Highway 507 and are productive smallmouth and largemouth bass as well as panfish waters. Bass do not grow big but you can expect plenty of action on overcast days. There is also a fair muskellunge population in both lakes.

Gardiner and Township Line Lakes (Map 66/A4)
A bush road branching west from the Bissett Creek Road leads to Gardiner Lake, which is stocked with brook trout and also holds largemouth bass. To the north, Township Line Lake offers a stocked brook trout fishery.

Genak [Ignace] Lake (Map 66/C4)
Located close to Highway 17, Genak receives heavy winter angling pressure. Fishing on the lake is usually slow for small brook trout.

Genesee Lake (Map 53/B1)
Fishing can be good for brook trout to 35 cm (14 in). Try a small spoon through the ice or mayfly patterns in early spring.

Georgian Bay (Map 22, 23, 31, 39, 40, 48, 49)
This large bay, itself larger than most lakes in the province and almost as large as Lake Ontario, is a nearly self-contained offshoot of Lake Huron. The bay holds bass, pike, walleye, muskellunge, brook, brown, lake and rainbow trout, Chinook salmon and several species of panfish, such as black crappie, pumpkinseed sunfish and yellow perch. There are dozens of bays and thousands of islands, making this an angling paradise. While there are too many hot spots to name (many of the best spots already have their own listing in this section), a popular place to try for Chinook are around Christian, Hope and Beckwith Islands (Map 23), as well as the hole, which is midway between Sawlog Point and Beausoliel Island (Map 24/D5).

Georgian Bay [French River Outlet] (Map 48/E3)
Some of the best fishing in this region happens where the French River flows into Georgian Bay. Walleye are found in the area in good numbers in the 3 kg (6.5 lb) range, while some big northern pike and muskellunge also provide for good fishing at times. Anglers can also find smallmouth bass with the odd largemouth bass in the 2 kg (4.5 lb) range.

Gibson Lake (Map 23/G2)
Gibson Lake is part of the Gibson-McDonald Canoe Route and can be accessed by vehicle from a few different areas off Highway 69/400 or Muskoka Road 33. The lake holds a fair population of walleye and northern pike that can reach 3.5 kg (7 lbs) in size. Fishing for smallmouth and largemouth bass to 2 kg (4.5 lbs) can also be good at times.

Gignac Lake (Map 23/C4)
This lake is found on the eastern side of Awenda Provincial Park and offers fair to good fishing for smallmouth and largemouth bass that can reach sizes of up to 2 kg (4.5 lbs).

Gin Lake (Map 38/G6)
Gin Lake offers good fishing for average sized smallmouth and largemouth bass. The lake can be reached by a short portage from the bush access road to Mayo Lake and receives surprisingly little pressure compared to neighbouring Mayo Lake.

Giroux Lake (Map 39/F1–49/F7)
Giroux Lake offers fair fishing for smallmouth bass and generally slow fishing for smaller sized walleye and northern pike. The lake is surrounded mainly by Crown land but still receives heavy fishing pressure.

Glamor and Little Glamor Lakes (Map 27/F2)
Both of these lakes are popular cottage destination lakes and offer good fishing for smallmouth bass to 1.5 kg (3.5 lbs). Glamor Lake is stocked regularly with rainbow trout and also holds a few natural lake trout that average 45 cm (18 in). Little Glamor Lake also has a population of largemouth bass.

Gliskning and Lobster Lake (Map 46/A3)
North of Whitney, Lobster Lake can be accessed via bush road and provides good fishing at times for nice sized smallmouth bass and the odd lake trout. Gliskning Lake continues to support a small natural lake trout population. Watch for slot size restrictions.

Gloucester Pool and Little Lake (Map 23/G4–24/A5)
These water bodies see a lot of boating traffic throughout the summer months since they are on the Trent Severn Waterway and are home to many cottages, lodges and marinas. The northern portion of the Gloucester Pool is a hotbed for bass action and one of the better areas to look for walleye. Walleye action is at its peak just after the season opens and slows considerably as the water warms. Some large northern pike and muskellunge also roam these waters. Fishing for pike is usually fair throughout the season with muskie fishing peaking in the fall.

Go Home Lake (Map 23/E1)
Many islands and small bays are scattered throughout this lake, which make for great holding areas for bass, northern pike and walleye. Bass can be found in almost every bay around the lake, while walleye and pike are more readily found along one of the many shoal areas located around the lake.

Goodwin [Loon], Johnson and Kelly Lakes (Map 35/G3–36/A3)
Lake trout and bass inhabit each of these Haliburton Forest Reserve lakes. All three lakes have smallmouth bass and Johnson Lake also hosts a small population of largemouth bass. Goodwin Lake and Kelly Lake are part of the winter/spring fishing sanctuary and there are slot size restrictions for lake trout on Johnson Lake.

Gooseneck Lake (Map 40/G2)
Gooseneck offers generally fair for smallmouth bass or northern pike. Walleye also inhabit the lake, although they are often harder to find.

Gordon Lake (Map 40/B2)
This remote lake can be portaged to from Harris Lake or accessed by a rough, old 4wd road system. Fishing on the lake can be quite good for smallmouth bass in the 1 kg (2 lb) range. Northern pike exist in the lake in good numbers and average about 2 kg (4.5 lbs) in size.

Grace and Pusey Lakes (Map 37/B6)
These popular lakes provide slow fishing for lake trout that average 40 cm (16 in). However, your best bet for action on these lakes is for their resident smallmouth bass. There are special regulations in place to help the lake trout fishery.

Graham Lake (Map 63/B7)
Graham Lake can be accessed by bush road and offers good fishing for northern pike and bass. Northerns can be caught in the 4 kg (9 lb) range, while smallmouth and largemouth bass reach sizes of up to 2 kg (4.5 lbs). Try a floating Rapala for great pike and bass top water action.

Grandview Lake (Map 34/F4) 🐟
Grandview Lake is a smaller lake found near the south end of Lake of Bays. Grandview provides fair fishing for average sized smallmouth bass and stocked splake.

Graphite Lake (Map 38/A3)
Graphite Lake offers fair fishing for small northern pike. Although the lake is surrounded by private property, a public boat launch is found on the lake's northern shore.

Graphite Lake (Map 53/E7)
This long, thin lake lies near the western border of Algonquin Provincial Park. The lake offers fair fishing for lake trout and unconfirmed reports of brook trout. Lakers can be found to 60 cm (24 in).

Grass, Island and Loon Lake (Map 43/B1)
Fishing for trout can be good at times on all three lakes. Grass Lake continues to sustain a natural lake trout and brook trout population, while lake trout are the name of the game on Loon and Island Lakes.

Grass Lake (Map 36/B7)
Linking the larger Kashagawigamog Lake with Head Lake and Haliburton, Grass Lake offers fair fishing for smallmouth bass and walleye. A small population of muskellunge is also present in the lake, although fishing for muskie is generally slow.

Grassy and V Lakes (Map 38/F7) 🐟
These two lakes are stocked every few years. Grassy Lake offers good fishing for splake, while V Lake provides fair to good fishing for rainbow trout.

Green Canoe Lake and Ike's Pond (Map 36/C4) 🐟
These small lakes can be found via a 4wd road and are stocked every few years with brook trout. Fishing for brookies to 35 cm (14 in) can be good at times in the winter and spring.

Green Lake (Map 35/G6–36/A5)
Green Lake is a popular cottage destination lake that can be found off Highway 118. There is a boat launch at the eastern side of the lake and fishing is fair for average sized smallmouth bass. Muskellunge also inhabit the lake in small numbers.

Green Lake (Map 46/F5) 🐟
South of the village of Madawaska, Green Lake is accessed by trail. The lake stocked every few years with brook trout.

Greenbough Lake (Map 65/F4)
Often overlooked because only small smallmouth bass are found here, this lake can be accessed by bush road south of the village of Deux-Rivieres. Smallmouth have been found to 2.5 kg (5.5 lbs) here.

Greengrass and McFee Lakes (Map 46/C4) 🐟
These two secluded lakes can only be accessed by snowmobile or on foot through sometimes-dense bush. Greengrass Lake is stocked with splake, while McFee Lake is stocked with brook trout.

Grey Owl, Limestone and McKellar Lakes (Map 41/C4)
These three easily accessed cottage lakes all lie to the west of Highway 124. Fishing in the lakes is fair for smallmouth and largemouth bass, while a small population of walleye also inhabits Grey Owl and McKellar Lakes.

Grimsthorpe Lake (Map 30/D3)
A very rough bush road located west of Bon Echo Provincial Park provides access to this lake. The lake offers fair to good fishing for smallmouth bass to 1.5 kg (3.5 lbs) and slow to fair fishing for natural lake trout. Be sure to practice catch and release and watch for slot size restrictions for lakers.

Grundy, Bucke and Gurd Lakes (Map 49/E3)

Found in Grundy Lake Provincial Park, these lakes offer slow to fair fishing for generally small northern pike and panfish. Largemouth bass are also found in Gurd and Bucke Lakes, while Grundy Lake supports a hard to find population of walleye. Grundy and Gurd Lakes also hold smallmouth bass.

Guilford Lake (Map 36/C4)

Found east of Redstone Lake, Guildford is stocked every other year with splake. Pumpkinseed sunfish and yellow perch are also found in the lake.

Guilmette Lake (Map 63/G6)

Stocked splake provide the bulk of the action here and are most active in winter and spring. Lake trout are also present.

Gull Lake (Map 24/G3–25/A3)

This is in Gravenhurst and is stocked every two years with rainbow trout. Fishing success for rainbow trout is usually slow, although fishing for smallmouth and largemouth bass is a bit better. A crayfish imitation lure or fly can work quite well on this lake, especially off drop-off areas along bottom structure.

Gull Lake (Map 26/E4)

Originally named Kinashingiquash Lake, Gull Lake is a fairly large waterbody with many cottages scattered along its shoreline. The lake has a small natural lake trout population and a good number of smallmouth and largemouth bass and panfish. Fishing for lake trout to 2 kg (4.5 lbs) can also be productive in early spring. The odd bass tops 3 kg (6.5 lbs) in size here.

Gullwing Lake (Map 24/D2)

Gullwing Lake has cottages along its shoreline and is located just east of Clear Lake. The lake offers fair fishing for smallmouth and largemouth bass.

Gun Lake (Map 47/F5)

Gun Lake is a scenic 28 hectare lake that is home to a few cottages and a popular trail system to the southeast of Barry's Bay. Stocked yearly with splake, anglers can expect some good fishing opportunities.

Gun, Ernest and Herb Lakes (Map 35/D3)

Part of the Gun Lake Canoe Route, these connected lakes provide good fishing for smallmouth bass and the odd largemouth bass. There are rustic campsites available on each of the three lakes.

Gunter Lake (Map 29/G7)

Accessed by rough roads, anglers can expect fair to good fishing for largemouth bass in the 1 kg (2 lb) range. Larger bass are caught in the lake quite regularly.

Haas Lakes (Map 36/D7)

Found off Highway 118 just east of Haliburton, Haas Lake holds a few smallmouth and largemouth bass. There are also rumours of the odd muskellunge and walleye in the popular lake.

Hadlington Lake (Map 27/G3–28/A3)

Hadlington Lake is a secluded fishing lake that can be accessed via a rough 4wd road and offers fishing opportunities for smallmouth bass. Much of the lake is surrounded by Crown land.

Haines and McNutt Lakes (Map 32/C1)

These two lakes offer fair to good fishing for average sized smallmouth and largemouth bass as well as northern pike. Try near weed beds and other structure at dusk for feeding bass and pike. There is also a small population of walleye in the lakes.

Halfway Lake (Map 47/F6)

Running next to the Old Barry's Bay Road, this lake is stocked yearly with splake offering good fishing through the ice and in spring. Northern pike, walleye and smallmouth and largemouth bass are also present.

Haliburton and Oblong Lakes (Map 36/E4)

Both of these lakes are popular cottage destinations with a few lake trout. Fishing for lakers is fair, although can be quite slow at times. However, fishing for smallmouth bass is often better. Oblong Lake is part of the winter/spring fishing sanctuary to help preserve natural lake trout stocks.

Halls Lake (Map 35/E5)

A fair population of smallmouth bass to 1.5 kg (3.5 lbs) is present in the lake, while the natural population of lake trout are not as abundant. There are public boat launches on either side of the lake.

Halls Lake (Map 37/B7)

This small, secluded lake is stocked with brook trout every few years. There is a live fish bait ban on the lake.

Harburn Lakes (Map 36/D3)

The Harburn Lakes can be accessed via rough bush roads. Harburn is stocked every other year and also holds pumpkinseed sunfish, while Little Harburn is exclusive to brook trout. Winter and spring are the most productive periods for brookies.

Hardings and Twin Lakes (Map 37/D7)

These two secluded brook trout lakes offer fair to good fishing for stocked brook trout. Some decent sized trout are caught here.

Hardtack Lake (Map 46/A3)

Hardtack is stocked every few years with rainbow trout. Fishing is usually good through the ice or in spring, just after ice off.

Harp and Walker Lakes (Map 43/D7)

Found to the north of Highway 60 east of Huntsville, these lakes provide fair fishing for smallmouth bass to 1.5 kg (3.5 lbs). Harp Lake is also stocked every few years with lake trout, while Walker Lake is stocked with rainbow trout. The trout fishery is better earlier in the year.

Harris Lake (Map 40/A1)

One of the main access points to the Magnetawan River Canoe Route, Harris has a few cottages and camps along its shoreline, although a good portion of its shoreline is crown land. Fishing in Harris Lake can be good at times for decent sized smallmouth bass. Walleye and northern pike also inhabit the lake in fair numbers.

Harris Lake (Map 41/B5)

Harris Lake is a popular summer cottage lake that can be found off Highway 124. The lake offers fair fishing for smallmouth and largemouth bass to 1.5 kg (3.5 lbs) and average sized northern pike. Any good minnow imitation will work well for bass and pike.

Hart Lake (Map 43/E4)

Hart Lake is a secluded lake that provides fair fishing for brook trout. The small, unnamed lake directly to the east of Hart Lake also hosts a population of brook trout.

Harvey's Shanty, Little Marten and Rattail Lakes (Map 66/B4)

A bush roads branching west from the Bissett Creek Road leads past Little Marten, Harvey's Shanty and eventually Rattail Lake. Little Marten and Rattail are home to largemouth bass and yellow perch, while Harvey's Shanty Lake offers smallmouth and largemouth bass along with yellow perch.

Harvey and Wylie Lakes (Map 67/C5)

Both of these hold previously stocked, now naturally reproducing brook trout. The lakes are popular ice fishing lakes.

Harvey Lake (Map 35/C2)

Harvey Lake has a few cottages along its shoreline, although the majority of the shore is Crown land. The lake is stocked with splake and fishing is generally fair for average sized splake through the ice in winter and in the spring just after ice off.

Haskin Lake (Map 47/B2)

Best accessed by snowmobile in winter, there is a rough bush road leading to the southwest bay of Haskins Lake. The lake holds a fair population of lake trout.

Hassard Lake (Map 43/C3)

Hassard is inhabited by smallmouth bass and provides fair fishing at times for smallmouth to 1.5 kg (2.5 lbs).

Havelock Lake (Map 35/G2)

Set within the Haliburton Forest Reserve, Havelock Lake can be accessed by trail or via a rough road. The deep lake holds lake trout. Please check your fishing regulations before heading out, as there are special ice fishing and slot size restrictions in place to help maintain lake trout populations.

Hawe and Timpano Lake (Map 53/A3)

A 4wd road can access Hawe Lake, although much of the lake is surrounded by private property. Nearby Timpano Lake can only be accessed by snowmobile or on foot. As a result the brook trout is often better on Timpano.

Hawk Lake (Map 46/G7)

This secluded lake can be accessed by walking through dense bush from Cross Lake Road (Highway 523). Fishing for average sized brookies is fair throughout the year.

Hay Lake (Map 46/B6)

Home to an Algonquin Park access point, Hay Lake is a big lake holding brook trout, lake trout, smallmouth bass and walleye. There are also pumpkinseed sunfish and yellow perch. To the north, separated by a large channel of Otter Creek, Lower Hay Lake holds lake trout, smallmouth bass and pumpkinseed sunfish and yellow perch. Most anglers test their luck for the lake trout.

Head Lake (Map 26/B6)
Head Lake is a very shallow lake with a lot of bottom structure that is a magnet for attracting sportfish. The lake is known for its muskellunge that can reach up to 5 kg (11 lbs) in size. Smallmouth and largemouth bass are also present in fair to good numbers with bass to 2 kg (4.5 lbs) caught annually. The odd walleye also surfaces. A public boat launch is available.

Head Lake (Map 36/C7)
Set in the town of Haliburton, Head Lake has recently been stocked with walleye to re-establish that fishery. There are also muskellunge and smallmouth bass along with the ever popular pumpkinseed sunfish and yellow perch.

Head and Trout Lakes (Map 67/A6)
Rough bush roads lead from Mackey Creek Road to these lakes near the northern boundary of Algonquin Park. The 19 hectare Head Lake is stocked annually with brook trout, while the bigger Trout Lake offers stocked brook and lake trout.

Headstone and West Headstone Lakes (Map 46/A3)
Found close to Algonquin Park, road access is limited in the area. Headstone Lake is inhabited by smallmouth bass to 1.5 kg (3.5 lbs), while West Headstone Lake is stocked with brook trout.

Healey Lake (Map 34/D6)
A few cottages are scattered along the shorelines of this shallow lake. Fishing remains fair for smallmouth bass but the rainbow trout that were once stocked seemed to have disappeared.

Healy Lake (Map 33/C5)
This is one of the larger lakes in the area and can be found off Healy Lake Road just before reaching The Blackstone Harbour/Massasagua Provincial Park. There are a few boat launches at the eastern side of the lake and a number of cottages along the shoreline. The lake holds good populations of smallmouth and largemouth bass that can be found up to 2 kg (4.5 lbs). There is also a fair number of northern pike and panfish available.

Heeney Lake (Map 34/E5)
This small lake is situated just south of the town of Baysville. Anglers can expect fair to good fishing at times for smallmouth bass that can be found up to 1.5 kg (3.5 lbs) in size. The lake is fairly shallow, therefore bass can almost be found anywhere in the lake.

Henshaw Lake (Map 33/C6)
Set amid the heart of Muskoka, Henshaw Lake is a small lake that can be found off County Road 118 near Port Carling. The lake received regular fishing pressure throughout the season and anglers should only expect slow fishing for largemouth bass. While most bass are small in Henshaw Lake, the odd bucketmouth to 1.5 kg (3.5 lbs) is available.

Henvey Inlet (Map 49/C5)
Accessed via boat from the Key River or Byng Inlet, fishing here can be very good at times for nice sized smallmouth bass and northern pike. Pike can reach sizes in excess of 10 kg (22 lbs) throughout the area. Fair numbers of good sized walleye and muskellunge are also found in the inlet.

Hicks and Potash Lake (Map 47/B7)
These two brook trout lakes are rather difficult to find off the south side of Harris Bay of the much bigger Bark Lake. Hicks is stocked every other year with brook trout and also holds lake trout. Potash is also stocked with brookies.

High Lake (Map 33/E3)
Much smaller than its neighbour Skelton Lake, High Lake is stocked with rainbow trout. There are also smallmouth bass here.

Hindon Lakes (Map 35/E7)
Found between Kushog Lake and Highway 118, the Hindon Lakes provide fair fishing for smallmouth and largemouth bass.

Hogart and Toronto Lakes (Map 32/F6)
These small cottage lakes are found off Highway 69. Both offer fair fishing for smallmouth and largemouth bass. A small population of walleye is also available in Hogart Lake.

Holland and Kennibik Lakes (Map 36/G6)
These lakes can be accessed via Kenneway Road and provide for good fishing for smallmouth bass in the 0.5–1 kg (1–2 lb) range. Minnow imitation lures and flies as well as crayfish patterns are productive.

Holland Lake (Map 38/B6)
Holland Lake sees significant angling pressure and fishing for lake trout can be quite slow. Watch for restrictions on the lake.

Home and Neville Lakes (Map 32/C1)
These are two small Cottage Country lakes that can be accessed by rough 2wd roads. The lakes offer fair to good fishing at times for largemouth bass.

Horn Lake (Map 42/C7)
Horn Lake is found off the West Bear Lake Road after you pass Bear Lake. The lake has many bays and inlets that provide perfect habitat for largemouth bass. Bass fishing can be good at times for average sized bass that can reach lunker sizes.

Horn Lake (Map 42/D1)
Horn Lake is easily accessed to the west of Highway 11. Anglers will find good fishing at times for smallmouth bass to 1.5 kg (3.5 lbs). A natural population of lake trout also inhabits Horn Lake and fishing is generally fair.

Horseshoe and Marys Lakes (Map 66/E5)
These two natural brook trout lakes receive a lot of pressure in winter. They are easily accessed on snowmobile, while in the spring and summer they can be hiked to.

Horseshoe Lake (Map 24/B5)
Horseshoe Lake can be accessed via a rough 2wd road south of Severn Park and offers good fishing at times for largemouth bass to 1.5 kg (3.5 lbs).

Horseshoe Lake (Map 26/F1)
This popular cottage lake north of Minden offers fair fishing for smallmouth bass as well as stocked rainbow trout. There is also a population of whitefish in the lake.

Horseshoe Lake (Map 32/D2)
Located off Highway 69 southeast of Parry Sound, Horseshoe Lake is a very popular summer cottage destination lake. Although the lake receives heavy pressure throughout the year, there are countless bays on the lake that provide opportunities for good fishing. Fishing for smallmouth and largemouth bass to 2 kg (4.5 lbs) and northern pike is usually fair. It is rumoured that a small natural population of lake trout remains in the lake. There is a marina and boat launch access available off the highway at the outlet of the Blackstone River.

Horseshoe Lake (Map 40/C2)
Horseshoe Lake offers good fishing at times for decent sized smallmouth bass and northern pike. A fair walleye population is also present in the lake and are often fished for through the ice.

Howland Lake (Map 26/F4)
Howland Lake is not far from County Road 121 and offers decent fishing for smallmouth and largemouth bass. Top water lures such as Rapalas and top water flies, such as poppers and Muddler minnows can be productive and exciting.

Hudson Lake (Map 37/C6)
Best accessed from an old road off Clear Lake Road, Hudson Lake offers decent fishing for smallmouth bass. The odd lake trout, along with pumpkinseed sunfish and rock bass are also found in the lake.

Hunter [Attlee] Lake (Map 58/C6)
South of Highway 637, this long lake provides fair fishing for average sized smallmouth bass and northern pike.

Hurst Lake (Map 32/G3)
Found hidden east of Lake Joseph, Hurst Lake is stocked every few years with brook trout. Fishing for brook trout to 30 cm (12 in) can be good during ice fishing season or in spring just after ice off.

Index Lake (Map 50/C4)
Index Lake can only be accessed by portage from Kawigamog Lake and offers quite good fishing at times for smallmouth bass. Fishing can also be good at times for generally small northern pike.

Inright, Johnson and Yuill Lakes (Map 47/A7)
Accessed by snowmobile or on foot through heavy bush, a small stream flows out of Inright Lake into Harris Bay on Bark Lake. The lake is stocked biennially with brook trout. Similarly, Johnson and Yuill Lakes to the south are also stocked regularly with brook trout.

Iron Lake (Map 27/F3)
Iron Lake can be found off Highway 507 and surprisingly still has a small resident population of muskellunge available. The small lake is surrounded by Crown land and is a scenic spot, but fishing for the great muskellunge is slow.

Irwin Lake (Map 50/F5)
One can expect nice sized northern pike, which feed on the limited minnow population in this small, seldom-fished lake.

Isabella Lake (Map 41/E7)
Isabella Lake can be accessed via the Blackwater Lake Road or the Seguin River Canoe Route north of Highway 518. Walleye were recently stocked here, while decent size largemouth bass and northern pike are caught annually. Whitefish, pumpkinseed sunfish and rock bass are much easier to catch, but not the preferred sportfish here.

Island Lake (Map 43/B1)
With a snowmobile trail on the north side and a good road on the south side, this Island Lake is found east of Pickerel Lake. Fishing remains fair for stocked lake trout and smallmouth bass.

Island Lake (Map 50/C6)
Island Lake lies along the Magnetawan River Canoe Route. Fishing is good for smallmouth bass in the 1 kg (2 lb) range and for northern pike that average 3 kg (6.5 lbs) in size. Walleye are also found in the lake.

Island Lake (Map 50/G6–51/A6)
This Island Lake boasts very good fishing at times for both smallmouth and largemouth bass to 2 kg (4.5 lbs) in size. Access is mainly via canoe or fly-in.

Island Lake (Map 60/B7)
Fishing is good in Island Lake for smallmouth bass, which are rumoured to reach 2 kg (4.5 lbs) in size.

Jack and McCoy Lakes (Map 32/A2)
These two secluded lakes can only be accessed by portage. McCoy Lake has good fishing for nice sized smallmouth and largemouth bass, while Jack Lake offers good fishing for smallmouth bass and northern pike. Fishing for small lakers can also be good through the ice and in spring on McCoy.

Jack Lake (Map 28/E7)
Mostly protected by the Peterborough Crown Game Preserve, Jack Lake is a very scenic destination with countless islands and bays for the fish to hide in. Anglers can spend days here searching for the elusive muskellunge, smallmouth and largemouth bass and walleye. Pumpkinseed sunfish and yellow perch are also found here and are often easier to catch.

Jacks Lake (Map 42/G2)
Found just outside of Burk's Falls, Jacks Lake also offers fair fishing for nice sized walleye that can be found up to 2 kg (4.5 lbs). However, the action is usually a bit faster for the smallmouth bass in the lake.

Jack's Lake (Map 51/D3)
Home to many pocket bays, Jack's Lake offers fair to good fishing for smallmouth bass and slower fishing for northern pike and walleye.

James Lake (Map 47/D7) d
James Lake is a small lake that is located just north of Purdy Lake, which is stocked every other year with brook trout.

James and Wright Lakes (Map 63/G2)
These two hidden lakes lie north of Pimsi Bay on the Mattawa River. Fishing can be good in both lakes. Smallmouth bass are found in James Lake and largemouth bass in Wright Lake.

Jeffrey Lake (Map 38/A7)
Located south of Bancroft, this picturesque lake holds a few smallmouth bass and lake trout. Younger anglers can also try casting for the more aggressive pumpkinseed sunfish and yellow perch. Watch for special restrictions.

Jevins Lake (Map 24/G3)
Jevins Lake can be found off Highway 11 south of the town of Gravenhurst. The small lake offers fair fishing for smallmouth and largemouth bass.

Johnston Lakes (Map 63/G3)
These out of the way lakes take a bit of effort to get to. As a result they offer some good fishing. Smallmouth bass are the most active. Northern pike and largemouth bass are also found in Upper Johnston Lake, while the odd brook trout also surfaces in Johnston Lake.

Johnstone Lake (Map 26/D7)
Johnstone Lake is a small hidden lake just south of Norland. The lake offers good fishing for smallmouth bass.

Jordan Lake (Map 37/D6)
This small lake southwest of Baptiste Lake is stocked annually with rainbow trout. Brook trout are also present.

Julian Lake (Map 19/C2)
Julian Lake is a popular cottage lake that can be found off Highway 28. Some good sized muskellunge and smallmouth bass roam the lake. There is a boat launch on the lake.

Kabakwa Lake (Map 35/D6)
Kabakwa Lake lies in the southern end of the Frost Centre and is stocked almost annually with lake trout and periodically with rainbow trout. Fishing for lakers and rainbow is fair throughout the year and can be good through the ice or in the spring. In spring, trolling spoons or minnow imitations can be effective. Smallmouth bass also inhabit the lake and fishing for smallmouth is generally fair.

Kahshe Lake (Map 25/B4)
This odd shaped lake can be accessed off Highway 11 and is a popular summer destination lake. Fishing can be surprisingly good throughout the year with smallmouth and largemouth bass that can reach up to 2.5 kg (5.5 lbs) in size and the ever popular walleye tipping the scales in the 4.5 kg (10 lb) range occasionally. Muskellunge also roam the waters of Kahshe Lake. To aid walleye spawning, there is a special no fishing sanctuary area around the Kahshe River.

Kakakiwaganda Lake (Map 58/G4)
Located just south of the junction of Highway 69 and Highway 637, fishing in this lake is fair for marginal sized smallmouth bass and northern pike. Walleye also inhabit the lake, although fishing is usually slow.

Kamaniskeg Lake (Map 47/D4–7)
Forming the backdrop to Barry's Bay, this beautiful lake is home to several cottages and public access points. Fishing is good for smallmouth bass in the 1–2 kg (2–4.5 lb) range with larger bass to 3 kg (6.5 lbs) caught annually. Lake trout can be found to 80 cm (31 in) and are best found through the ice in winter. Watch for slot size restrictions for lake trout as well as special winter regulations. Northern pike and walleye are also found in fair numbers in the big lake.

Kapikog Lake (Map 32/D5)
A good population of smallmouth and largemouth bass inhabit Kapikog Lake with the odd bass caught up to 2 kg (4.5 lbs) annually. Pike can be found in the 3–6 kg (6.5–13 lb) range, although smaller hammerheads are more common. Kapikog Lake has also been stocked with rainbow trout regularly, which can provide fair fishing throughout the season.

Kashagawigamog Lake (Map 27/A1–36/B7)
Kashagawigamog Lake is one of the larger lakes in the Haliburton area and can be quite busy with boat traffic. Anglers have a variety of sportfish to focus on including bass, lake trout, walleye and muskellunge. Lake trout and walleye attract the most attention from anglers and fisheries now supplement the lake trout population with stocking. There is also a small population of muskellunge and a fair number of whitefish in the lake.

Kashegaba and Maple Lakes (Map 40/F1)
Angling can be good here for smallmouth and largemouth bass to 2 kg (4.5 lbs) in these fairly remote lakes. Kashegaba Lake also offers fair populations of walleye and northern pike to add diversity to the angler's pursuit.

Kasshabog Lake (Map 19/G1–29/A7)
This large, sprawling lake has many islands and bays, making a great place to fish for largemouth bass, muskellunge and smallmouth bass. The lake also contains rock bass, perch and walleye.

Katchewanooka Lake (Map 19/A5)
Katchewanooka Lake is a relatively shallow lake that is a southern extension of Clear Lake. Similar to the nearby Trent Severn lakes, smallmouth and largemouth bass are found in the lake in fair numbers and can reach up to 2 kg (4.5 lbs). Walleye and muskellunge are also present in the lake in fair numbers with muskie averaging 3–5 kg (6.5–11 lbs). Be sure to check the regulations before heading out, as there is a sanctuary period to aid walleye and muskellunge spawning. Ice fishing is not allowed.

Kawagama Lake (Map 35/E2)
Kawagama Lake is one of the largest lakes in the region covering 3,150 hectares. Your best bet for consistent action is to try for its resident smallmouth bass that can reach 2 kg (4.5 lbs) in size. However, most anglers visit this lake in search of its more elusive lake trout. The lake was recently stocked with brook trout to try to establish that fishery and is also home to pumpkinseed sunfish, rock bass and yellow perch.

Kawasda, Little Tyne and Tyne Lakes (Map 53/D2)
There are a few camps on Tyne and Little Tyne Lakes; however, Kawasda Lake is surrounded by Crown land. Tyne Lake is stocked with splake and provides good fishing to 50 cm (20 in). Little Tyne Lake continues to support a natural brook trout population and is stocked with splake. Kawasda Lake is stocked with brook trout.

Kawawaymog Lake (Map 53/C3)

Kawawaymog serves as one of the western access points to Algonquin Provincial Park and is mostly surrounded by Crown land. Despite constant pressure, the lake still produces some good sized brook trout.

Kawigamog Lake (Map 50/C4)

Fishing here is fair for average sized walleye and generally small northern pike. Good populations of smallmouth bass can also provide for a great day of action.

Kearney Lake (Map 64/B1)

The scenic Kearney Lake is inhabited by lake trout, although fishing is usually slow after spring.

Kennisis Lakes (Map 35/G4–36/A3)

Accessed through the Haliburton Forest Reserve, Kennisis and Little Kennisis lakes offer fair fishing for lake trout to 75 cm (30 in) and fair fishing for smallmouth bass. The bigger, more developed Kennisis also offers good fishing for stocked brook trout and largemouth bass. Be sure to check the regulations for these lakes before heading out.

Kernick Lake (Map 42/G2)

Kernick is a small lake found just outside of Burk's Falls. The lake provides fair fishing for smallmouth bass in the 0.5 kg (1 lb) range. There is a private campsite on the lake.

Ketch Lake (Map 35/A7)

This lake is stocked almost annually with brook trout that provide for good fishing through the ice and in the spring. In spring small spinners or spoons work well or try nymph and bead head fly patterns.

Kettle's Lake (Map 23/B4)

Kettle's Lake is located in Awenda Provincial Park and offers fair fishing for smallmouth and largemouth bass as well as panfish.

Keyhole Lake (Map 34/G7)

This small, secluded lake is hidden in the interior of Bigwind Provincial Park. The difficult access ensures a good largemouth bass fishery. Top water lures and flies can be particularly productive.

Kimball Lake (Map 35/F1)

Visitors will find a few camps along the shoreline of Kimball Lake but it is mostly surrounded by Crown land. The lake is part of the Rockaway Lake Canoe Route and anglers can expect good fishing for smallmouth bass to 2.5 kg (5.5 lbs) and fair fishing for lake trout that average 40–45 cm (16–18 in) in size. There is also a fair population of brook trout in the lake that can reach up to 40 cm (16 in) in size.

Kingshot Lake (Map 32/B3)

Kingshot Lake can be accessed via backroad south of Parry Sound and offers fair fishing for largemouth bass. Fish near weed beds and other structure with a spinner or minnow imitation for increased action.

Kinmount Lake (Map 27/A5)

Visitors can find this lake via a rough 2wd road. The lake has a few smaller smallmouth and largemouth bass.

Klaxon and Lipsy Lakes (Map 35/G4)

Lake trout are stocked almost annually in these fairly remote lakes. There is an access point on Lipsy, while Klaxon to the south is mainly accessed by canoe.

Koshlong Lake (Map 27/C1)

Originally, Koshlong Lake was inhabited with only smallmouth bass, however stocking of lake trout has proven successful. Lake trout action is best during ice fishing season and in the spring just after ice off for fish to 75 cm (30 in). Watch for slot size restrictions on lake trout. Good numbers of smallmouth bass to 1.5 kg (3.5 lbs) continue to thrive in the lake. There are boat launches on the lake.

Kuwasda Lake (Map 53/C2)

Bordering Algonquin Park to the northwest of North Tea Lake, this fairly remote lake offers stocked brook trout.

Kushog Lake (Map 35/D6)

This long lake has cottages scattered along its shoreline and offers fishing opportunities for lake trout and smallmouth bass. While lake trout are more often found in the northern end of the lake, smallmouth bass can be found almost anywhere near shore structure. Watch for slot size and other restrictions.

La Brash Lake (Map 51/D7)

Fishing at La Brash is generally fair for smallmouth bass and northern pike. Walleye also inhabit the lake, although fishing is often slower.

La Casse Lake (Map 59/A7)

La Casse Lake sits just north of French River Provincial Park and provides for fair fishing for small sized walleye. A forest trail or canoe can access the lake.

La Chapelle and Sheedy Lakes (Map 63/D2)

Accessed west of Pine Lake Road, these lakes hold smallmouth bass, northern pike and walleye. Smallmouth bass, in particular, can be very active and provide good action for anglers.

L'Amable Lake (Map 38/A7)

Located south of Bancroft, this picturesque lake offer slow fishing for smallmouth bass and lake trout. Watch for special restrictions on the lake.

Lake Cecebe (Map 42/C2)

On the doorsteps of the town of Magnetawan, Lake Cecebe is part of the river system by the same name. Fishing can be fair for nice sized smallmouth bass and northern pike. Walleye also inhabit the lake in fair numbers.

Lake Couchiching (Map 16/G2–25/A7)

The two most abundant sportfish in Lake Couchiching are smallmouth and largemouth bass. Northern pike and walleye also inhabit the lake. Northern pike can reach up to 6.5 kg (14 lbs) and are often found along the more weedy southern section of the lake near Orillia. Fishing for walleye is usually slow, although catches to 4.5 kg (10 lbs) are reported annually.

Lake Joseph (Map 32/F3–33/B6)

Lake Joseph is a large cottage destination lake that can be bustling with boat traffic during the summer months. Anglers will find a number of boat launches and descent action for smallmouth and largemouth bass. Lake trout can be found to 70 cm (28 in), while walleye also offer fair fishing through the ice and in late spring. Anglers will also find a few muskellunge.

Lake Muskoka (Map 24/F2–33/C6)

Despite its popularity with boaters, this lake receives surprisingly limited fishing pressure. Most of the action comes from the bass, panfish and pike. Lunker largemouth bass can be found in the many weedy, log infested bays whereas big smallmouth bass can be found near sharp drop-offs along islands on the lake. For big pike action try Bala Bay, near the Moon River outflow or at the Muskoka River mouth near Bracebridge. Other sportfish in the lake include stocked lake trout that reach 70 cm (28 in) and walleye to 3.5 kg (8 lbs).

Lake Nipissing (Map 60–62)

Lake Nipissing is the second largest freshwater lake in Ontario. There are numerous public boat launches in the lakeside towns. Walleye up to 4 kg (9 lbs) and northern pike to 8 kg (18 lb) provide for fair to good fishing opportunities near river mouths and in most of the shallower, calmer bays of the lake. Muskellunge are often difficult to catch, while smallmouth bass offer the best fishing in Lake Nipissing. Success for these scrappy fish can be good at times around the larger islands.

Lake Nosbonsing (Map 63/B4)

Fishing on this large lake is fair for walleye to 3 kg (6.5 lbs) and northern pike in the 2–3 kg (4.5–6.5 lb) range. A good holding area for walleye, sauger and pike is near the mouth of the Kaibuskong River. Fishing can be good at times for smallmouth and largemouth bass as well as panfish and the odd muskellunge is caught too. Be sure to check the special regulations for this lake.

Lake of Bays (Map 34/E4–35/B3)

Lake of Bays is synonymous with Cottage Country and is a busy water body during the summer months. Bass fishing is good for smallmouth or largemouth bass to 2.5 kg (5.5 lbs) off points and near islands. The lake currently relies on natural reproduction for lake trout that reach 75 cm (30 in). It is also rumoured that a small population of natural brook trout remains in the lake.

Lake of Many Islands (Map 51/G6–52/A6)

This lake offers good fishing at times for smallmouth bass to 1.5 kg (3.5 lbs) and fair fishing at times for walleye in the 1–2 kg (2–4.5 lb) range. There are a few different access points to the lake, although some roads pass through private land.

Lake Ontario (Map 2–5, 12, 13)

Lake Ontario is the smallest of the five Great Lakes of North America. The lake has made a remarkable recovery since the 1970s, when algae blooms and rampant pollution killed off many of the fish in the lake. Today, the lake holds nearly every species of fish that is fished for recreationally in Cottage Country. This includes bass, pike, walleye, muskellunge, brown, lake and rainbow trout, Chinook and Coho salmon and several species of panfish, such as black crappie, pumpkinseed sunfish and yellow perch. The trout and salmon fisheries are the most popular and aided by regular stocking. Most of the fishing happens offshore from May to end of September and if you don't have your own boat, there are plenty of charters. It is also possible to fish at the mouth of rivers when the salmon spawn in late summer.

Lake Rosseau (Map 33/B3-D6)

Even though the lake receives a lot of attention, there remains a good sport fishery. Muskellunge fishing is good especially in the fall. Lake trout to 70 cm (28 in) are found in the lake in fair numbers and the odd walleye still surfaces. Fishing is best through the ice or in spring for both species. Smallmouth and largemouth bass as well as panfish are often overlooked with fishing for bass to 2.5 kg (5.5 lbs) generally good.

Lake Scugog (Map 9/D5)

The large, weedy lake has good fishing for panfish as well as smallmouth and largemouth bass that average 1–2 kg (2–4.5 lbs). Largemouth are more abundant in the southerly portion of the lake, whereas smallmouth bass can be located in deeper water around structure or drop-offs. Lake Scugog is also renowned for its muskellunge fishing, which can be good at times. They average 3–4 kg (6.5–9 lbs), although every year a fair number of 10 kg (22 lbs) muskie are caught. Walleye average 1–2 kg (2–4.5 lbs). Lake Scugog is one of the few Kawartha area lakes where ice fishing is permitted.

Lake Simcoe (Map 7, 8, 15, 16)

Lake Simcoe is the largest lake in the Trent Severn Waterway system covering 72,500 hectares. It remains fairly productive and offers a host of sportfish including bass, pike, walleye, muskellunge, brook, brown, lake and rainbow trout and several species of panfish, such as black crappie and yellow perch. The lake also has an extensive lake whitefish stocking program, which provide for decent fishing throughout the season. Shoals and island areas offer good smallmouth bass fishing during summer, while some of the best locations for walleye is around the mouth of the Talbot River. For northern pike and largemouth bass the shallow, weedy Cook's Bay offers good fishing at times. In winter, the lake becomes an ice hut shantytown, but some of the best lake trout action comes through the ice.

Lake St. John (Map 16/A1–25/A7)

Lake St. John is located just east of Lake Couchiching and is a popular destination. There is plenty of weed structure available, which provides prime holding areas for both bass species as well as pike. Fishing is best for averaged sized smallmouth and largemouth bass, although pike in the 4.5 kg (10 lb) range are not uncommon. Walleye are the main targeted species in this lake with fair fishing for smaller walleye.

Lake St. Peter (Map 37/E1)

Fishing on the lake is fair throughout the year for average sized smallmouth bass. The lake also supports a natural strain of lake trout up to 80 cm (31 in) in size, therefore it is imperative to practice catch and release whenever possible. Watch for slot size restrictions and winter regulations.

Lake Talon (Map 63/E2)

Part of the Mattawa River system, there are a number of park campsites and cottages located on the lake. Laker trout can reach sizes in excess of 65 cm (26 in), while walleye can be found to 4 kg (9 lbs). Smallmouth and largemouth bass as well as panfish are often overlooked by anglers, but can also provide for some good fishing. Good sized northern pike can be found in quiet bays of the lake during dusk periods, while the larger muskellunge are much more elusive.

Lake Vernon (Map 33/G1–34/B1)

Fishing for smallmouth and largemouth bass can be good at times for bass that reach up to 1.5 kg (3.5 lbs). Northern pike also roam the lake and provide for slow to fair fishing for pike in the 3.5 kg (8 lb) range. In order to sustain angling pressure, lake trout are now stocked every few years. Anglers will find lake trout up to 75 cm (30 in) in size.

Lake Wauquimakog (Map 51/B3)

The scenic town of Port Loring is found on the shores of this Pickerel River system lake. As a result, it can be a busy lake during summer months. Fishing on the lake is fair for smallmouth and largemouth bass and often slow for northern pike and walleye.

Lambs and Little Beaver Lakes (Map 53/B2)

Lambs Lake lies at an intersection of bush roads, while Little Beaver Lake can only be accessed by trail. Lamb Lake supports a natural brook trout, while Little Beaver Lake is stocked with brook trout.

Langford Lake (Map 43/A6)

Langford Lake is found just outside the village of Novar off Long Lake Road. Featuring average sized brook trout, the best time to visit is winter or spring. Rainbow trout are also stocked into this lake.

Lasseter and Lee Lakes (Map 43/F7)

These two small, hidden lakes contain the elusive brook trout. Lee Lake is much more difficult to get to, as it is accessed by a rough 4wd road. The lake provides good fishing at times for brook trout to 35 cm (14 in) in size.

Lasswade Lake (Map 28/F5)

This lake just south of Chandos Lake is stocked annually with rainbow trout; largemouth and smallmouth bass are also present. A boat launch can be found on the access road off of McCauley's Road.

Last Lake (Map 50/E5)

Last Lake offers good fishing at times for smallmouth and largemouth bass to 2 kg (4.5 lbs). Northern pike also roam this long lake in good numbers and average 3–4 kg (6.5–9 lbs) in size. They are often found much bigger.

Laurier Lake (Map 52/G3)

Found off Summit Road, which branches east from Highway 11 between Sundridge and Trout Creek, Laurier Lake offers stocked brook trout. There are also yellow perch in the 14 hectare lake.

Lavallée Lake (Map 28/G2)

Lavallée Lake was previously stocked with lake trout and still holds a population of these fish, as well as smallmouth bass.

Lavery Lake (Map 18/D1)

Lavery Lake is another secluded bass lake. Fishing for smallmouth and largemouth bass to 2.5 kg (5.5 lbs) can be very good at times.

Lee and Mossberry Lakes (Map 67/C5)

These two lakes receive significant angling pressure in the winter. As a result the brook trout fishing is usually slow.

Leech Lake (Map 24/B1)

Visitors will find that there are a number of cottages along the shore of Leech Lake, although there is public access at the northern end of the lake. The lake is home to a fair number of smallmouth bass that average 0.5–1 kg (1–2 lbs) and was once stocked with rainbow trout.

Leonard Lake (Map 33/E7)

Leonard Lake has many cottages along its shoreline and provides a couple boat launches. The lake is stocked with rainbow trout, which provide for fair fishing at times for average sized rainbow. There is also a small population of walleye in the lake as well as fair fishing for smallmouth bass to 1.5 kg (3.5 lbs).

Liebeck, Mohan and Spectacle Lakes (Map 32/E1)

These lakes are best accessed by the Seguin Trail and are beautiful wilderness lakes. Mohan Lake offers good fishing for average sized largemouth bass that can be quite active at times. Liebeck & Mohan have been regularly stocked with splake and fishing is generally fair and best in the spring just after ice off. Spectacle provides good fishing for average sized smallmouth bass.

Limburner Lake (Map 35/C1)

Limburner Lake is a small lake found just off County Road 12 between Clinto and Crozier Lakes. It is stocked every two years with brook trout.

Limerick Lake (Map 29/F3)

Nestled in the rocky, rolling hills of the lower Madawaska Highlands, this scenic lake is home to several camps and cottages. Despite the development, fishing remains steady for smallmouth and largemouth bass. There are lake trout here as well, but fishing is usually slow for those elusive lakers.

Lingham Lake (Map 30/C5)

At one time, Lingham Lake was perhaps the best bass lake in Eastern Ontario. Recently, however, media publicity on the lake has literally turned it into a water circus, especially on weekends. The lake is man-made by the damming of the Black River and can be accessed by trail from the north or from near the dam on the south end. Today, 2 kg (4.5 lbs) bass are uncommon and it may take a good day of fishing to catch six bass. Be sure to check the regulations for sanctuary periods.

Lioness and Pender Lakes (Map 32/D2)

These two small lakes that can be accessed north of Highway 400 via 2wd roads. They provide fair fishing for smallmouth and largemouth bass.

Little Anstruther Lake (Map 28/C4)

Best accessed by snowmobile, the lake is stocked periodically with lake trout, which provide fair fishing during winter. If you do access the lake in the summer, there is also a good population of smallmouth and largemouth bass available.

Little Blackstone Lake (Map 32/B4)

This remote lake can be accessed by portage from Blackstone Harbour. The lake provides good fishing for largemouth bass and fair fishing for small walleye. There is also a small population of northern pike in the lake.

Little Bob Lake (Map 27/E2)

Little Bob Lake is found just off the 2wd road to Gooderham Lake. The lake has been stocked with brook trout, although fishing is fair.

Little Clear, Pond and Turtle Lakes (Map 63/E5)
Found off the south side of Pioneer Road south of Bonfield, Little Clear Lake and Turtle Lake are stocked annually with brook trout. Between the two small lakes rests Pond Lake, which is stocked annually with splake and also holds brook trout.

Little Dudman Lake (Map 36/F7)
Heavy fishing pressure has affected this former trout fishery. Lake trout are no longer and the rainbow stocking program was suspended in the 1990s. Anglers can still find smallmouth and largemouth bass.

Little Gull Lake (Map 26/D4)
This lake can be accessed from the public boat launch off County Road 2. The lake has fair fishing for large and smallmouth bass.

Little Horseshoe Lake (Map 27/F7)
This lake is rarely noticed off the west side of Highway 507, although it supports a fair population of smallmouth and largemouth bass.

Little Lake (Map 15/B6)
This shallow lake is heavily fished due to its close proximity to Barrie and Toronto. However anglers can expect fair fishing for yellow perch, bass and decent sized walleye. Look for underwater irregularities such as humps, weeds and rock piles to improve success.

Little Lake (Map 23/D7)
Located near the town of Midland, Little Lake once was a pretty good fishing lake. Unfortunately heavy pressure and lack of environmental awareness has reduced the fishing quality substantially. Smallmouth and largemouth bass are still found on occasion.

Little Lake (Map 24/E4)
Little Lake is another heavily used Cottage Country lake that hosts a marginal population of smallmouth and largemouth bass.

Little Lake (Map 66/B6)
Found along the Algonquin Park border, splake are stocked in Little Lake annually. Fishing is good through the ice and in spring for fish in the 30–35 cm (12–14 in) range.

Little Lake Joseph (Map 33/A4)
This small lake is actually a part of the much larger Lake Joseph. Anglers can expect good fishing at times for both smallmouth and largemouth bass. There are a number of prime bays with plenty of structure for bass to hide under. The lake is also home to a population of walleye and lake trout; however, fishing success for both species is usually slow. Watch for sanctuary periods.

Little Long, Toad and Duck Lakes (Map 50/G4–51/B4)
These popular lakes lie along the Pickerel River and are fished heavily during the open seasons. Anglers will find generally small walleye and northern pike along with average sized smallmouth bass. All three lakes are accessible via rough 2wd roads and offer ample Crown land camping opportunities.

Little Mayo and Whyte Lakes (Map 38/G6)
The lakes are surrounded by Crown land and are stocked annually with lake trout. Fishing for lakers is generally fair through the ice and in the spring just after ice off.

Little North River Lake (Map 65/C5)
Access to the lake is by travelling up river from the North River Access Point into Algonquin Park. Fishing is good during the spring for nice sized brook trout.

Little Otter Lake (Map 24/C2)
Little Otter Lake can be found via a rough 4wd road and offers good fishing through the ice and in the spring for stocked brook trout. The lake is stocked about every two years and the brookies are quite aggressive after ice off and can be found to 30 cm (12 in) in size.

Little Papineau Lake (Map 38/A1–47/A7)
This lake offers fair fishing for small northern pike with some fish caught in the 2–3 kg (4–6.5 lb) range. Smallmouth bass can also be aggressive feeders during overcast periods and are found to 2 kg (4.5 lbs).

Little Patterson and Wilkins Lake (Map 43/E2)
These two lakes continue to support a fair number of natural brook trout. This is partly due to the rough bush road access into the area.

Little Seguin Lake (Map 41/E7)
Linking Maple with Isabella, Little Seguin Lake is a busy Cottage Country lake in the summer. The lake offers fair fishing for smallmouth and largemouth bass and a few lake trout. There is also a fair population of whitefish in the lake.

Little West Lake (Map 36/D4)
Little West Lake offers fair to good fishing for smallmouth bass, especially during overcast periods or at dusk.

Lochlin Lake (Map 27/C2)
Lochlin Lake is a secluded Crown land lake that offers good fishing for smallmouth bass in the 1 kg (2 lb) range. There is a rough car top boat launch at the northern end of the lake.

Logan and Big Duck Lakes (Map 26/A3)
These lakes have limited access since they are surrounded by private property. Those that ask for permission will find good fishing for smallmouth and largemouth bass to 2 kg (4.5 lbs).

Lone Lake (Map 58/A6)
Accessed by portage from the eastern side of Tyson Lake, Lone Lake offers good fishing at times for smallmouth bass. Try just off the small islands in the middle of the lake for the best action.

Long and Loren Lake (Map 63/B2)
Accessed by a long portage from the south shore of the Mattawa River, fishing is usually good in both lakes. Smallmouth and largemouth bass are found in Long Lake, while smallmouth bass and northern pike inhabit Loren Lake.

Long and Louks Lakes (Map 28/C7)
These two lakes are part of a fine canoe route and offer fair fishing for smallmouth bass. A small, self-sustaining population of lake trout also exists from past stocking programs but fishing is poor throughout the year.

Long and Miskwabi Lakes (Map 36/F7)
Anglers can expect good fishing for smallmouth and largemouth bass to 1.5 kg (3.5 lbs). Miskwabi Lake is also stocked with lake trout, which provide for fair fishing throughout the season. Watch for special restrictions on these lakes.

Long and Mud Lakes (Map 51/A4)
Both lakes offer fair to good fishing for smallmouth bass, largemouth bass and northern pike. Long Lake also offers angling opportunities for walleye.

Long Lake (Map 24/B1)
Highway 169 passes by the eastern end of the 124 hectare Long Lake. The lake is stocked with brook trout, lake trout and rainbow trout and also holds smallmouth and largemouth bass along with pumpkinseed sunfish, rock bass and yellow perch. The variety of sportfish and good access allows for a good year round fishery.

Long Lake (Map 25/E2)
This Long Lake can be accessed via a rough 2wd road and offers slow fishing for small brook trout. Fishing is most productive during ice fishing season and in spring just after ice off.

Long Lake (Map 29/F1)
Southeast of Bancroft, this Madawaska Highland lake is stocked annually with rainbow trout.

Long Lake (Map 33/D1)
Long Lake can be found via backroad north of Skeleton Lake and has a few cottages along its shoreline A population of smallmouth bass and whitefish are present in the lake.

Long Lake (Map 64/B2)
Found within Samuel De Champlain Provincial Park, this small lake is stocked with brook trout and splake to help offset the fishing pressure.

Longairy Lake (Map 45/G4)
This lake, on the eastern border of Algonquin Park, is stocked annually with splake.

Longline Lake (Map 34/G3–35/A3)
Longline Lake can be easily accessed off Highway 117 and is stocked with splake every few years. Fishing for splake is fair through the ice during spring. There is also a rumoured population of brook trout in the lake.

Longs and Mainhood Lakes (Map 33/G4)
These smaller Cottage Country lakes provide fair to good fishing for average sized smallmouth bass. Longs Lake also has a small population of brook trout available, although fishing is generally slow.

Loom Lake (Map 27/D6)
Loom Lake can be found south of Crystal Lake offer a fire access road. Recently stocked with walleye, the better fishing here is often for smallmouth and largemouth bass. Pumpkinseed sunfish and yellow perch are also readily caught. There is a rough boat launch on the lake.

Loon [Dudman] Lake (Map 36/E7)
Loon Lake offers fair fishing for stocked lake trout to 55 cm (22 in) and fair to good fishing for walleye to 2.5 kg (5.5 lbs). While most anglers visiting Loon Lake are after its resident trout and walleye, the best action is often for its smallmouth bass. Fishing for smallmouth bass to 1.5 kg (3.5 lb) can be good at times and is best during overcast periods. A small population of muskellunge also inhabits the lake.

Loon and Partridge Lakes (Map 51/A5)
With limited access, ardent anglers will find very good populations of largemouth bass can be found in both lakes. Smallmouth bass are also found in Loon Lake.

Loon and Windy Lakes (Map 50/E4)
Both lakes offer quite good fishing for smallmouth and largemouth bass. Windy Lake is much larger than Loon Lake and is also inhabited by a fair population of northern pike.

Loon Lake (Map 43/C1)
Loon Lake is found east of Pickerel Lake and has been stocked in the past with lake trout. There are also smallmouth bass here.

Loon Call Lake (Map 28/C6)
Stocked every few years with splake, the lake also hosts small and largemouth bass to 1.5 kg (3.5 lbs).

Lorimer Lake (Map 41/B4)
Smallmouth and largemouth bass is the most productive fishery, although some decent sized northern pike are also found in the big lake. To help offset the heavy fishing pressure, Lorimer Lake is stocked every two years with lake trout.

Lost and Little Shoe Lakes (Map 35/B4)
These are small, secluded lakes offer good fishing for small brook trout. Little Shoe Lake can be accessed by about a short portage from the marsh area west of Wheeler Lake. Lost Lake requires bushwhacking from the end of an old logging road and is stocked with brook trout.

Lost and Mountain Lakes (Map 27/F7)
These two secluded fishing lakes can be accessed via a fire access road, which leads to Lost Lake. Mountain Lake can be found by orienteering north from Lost Lake. Lost Lake has been stocked in the past with rainbow trout, although fishing success is sketchy. Fishing in Mountain Lake for natural brook trout is good for small but numerous brookies.

Lost Lake (Map 19/G4)
This is a secluded bass lake that can only be accessed via rustic portage or on foot. Fishing for smallmouth and largemouth bass can be quite good at times. Bass can be found up to 2 kg (4.5 lbs) in size on occasion.

Lost Lake (Map 28/B2)
Lost Lake can be accessed by foot and offers good fishing at times for smallmouth bass to 1.5 kg (3.5 lbs). Plastic crayfish or flies worked slowly near the bottom can produce well.

Lost, Nugget and Sprucehen Lakes (Map 36/C1)
This collection of lakes is accessible by a 2wd road or short trail within the Haliburton Forest. All three lakes have small brook trout populations, while smallmouth bass can also be found in Lost Lake.

Louie Lakes (Map 44/E7)
The Louie Lakes are accessed off County Road 12 and offer slow fishing for brook trout. The larger Louie Lake is also stocked every few years with splake and fishing for splake can be good at times through the ice or in spring.

Lovesick Lake (Map 19/B3)
Found east of Lower Buckhorn Lake over the Trent Severn Waterway lock, Lovesick Lake offers fair fishing for walleye and bass. The mighty muskellunge can also be found in much smaller numbers.

Lower Fletcher Lake (Map 35/C1)
North of Dorset along the Livingstone Lake Road (County Road r), Lower Fletcher Lake is stocked periodically with lake trout.

Lower Pine Lake (Map 57/E6)
Lower Pine Lake can be found via bush road and offers good fishing at times for small northern pike that usually do not exceed 2.5 kg (5.5 lbs).

Lowry Lake (Map 28/A2)
Lowry Lake can be accessed via a rough 2wd road and has a boat launch. The lake is stocked biennially with brook trout and offers fair to good fishing for brookies that can reach 35 cm (14 in) in size. There is a live fish bait ban on the lake.

Loxton Lake (Map 53/B2)
Mostly surrounded by Crown land, Loxton Lake is found off the west side of the aptly named Forestry Road. The lake supports a natural brook trout population and has recently been stocked with lake trout.

Luck and Wolf Lakes (Map 44/F6)
These lakes rest to the south of Algonquin Park and provide fair fishing for brook trout to 40 cm (16 in). Luck Lake is the more secluded of the two and has been stocked in the past with brook trout to supplement natural stocks.

Lumber and Thumb Lakes (Map 44/B7)
These two secluded lakes are mostly fished in the winter. Thumb Lake is stocked with brook trout and both lakes offer fair to good fishing for average sized brookies.

Lutterworth [Devil's] Lake (Map 26/C4)
Accessed off County Road 2 at the public boat launch, the lake has been stocked almost annually with lake trout. The lake also holds a fair population of smallmouth and largemouth bass.

Lynch Lake (Map 54/A6)
There are cottages along the shoreline of Lynch, however, the eastern side of the lake remains Crown land. Rainbow trout are stocked in the lake and provide fair fishing opportunities in spring and late fall.

MacDonald Lake (Map 36/A3)
This lake is home to a strain of lake trout found only in a few Haliburton Lakes. They are generally smaller than other lake trout, but more numerous. Unfortunately, smallmouth and largemouth bass have invaded. Although they provide a decent fishery, they could wipe out this unique strain of lake trout.

Mag Lake (Map 66/D5)
A short hike takes anglers to this often overlooked lake where fishing is good for small, but plentiful, brook trout. Fly anglers can have great success on this lake.

Magee Lake (Map 63/E1)
Magee Lake is accessible via rough 4wd/ATV road and offers good fishing for smallmouth bass. Top water lures and flies can be a lot of fun on this remote lake.

Manitouwabing Lake (Map 41/C5)
This large lake is home to a variety of sportfish. Perhaps the best fishery is for decent sized smallmouth bass and northern pike. However, the lake also boasts largemouth bass to 2 kg (4.5 lbs) and walleye to 3 kg (6.5 lbs) as well as a whitefish.

Manson, McEwen and Squaw Lakes (Map 41/D4)
These three lakes provide good fishing for smallmouth bass and northern pike. Manson and Squaw Lakes also provide a decent walleye fishery in the winter or late spring.

Maple and Sugar Lakes (Map 32/F1–41/F7)
These lakes are found near the town of Orrville and provide fair fishing for smallmouth bass. Try during overcast periods and at dusk for increased bass activity. Maple Lake was stocked at one time with lake trout and more recently with splake. A fair population of whitefish is also present in Maple Lake, while Sugar Lake is stocked with rainbow trout. The marginal fishing in the lakes is due to the heavy pressure they receive during the year.

Maple Lake (Map 27/D4)
Maple Lake is a small, hidden fishing lake that has a good population of smallmouth and largemouth bass, as well as a fair population of smaller walleye.

Maple Lake (Map 35/G6)
Maple Lake is stocked occasionally with lake trout to help maintain this fishery. The lake also holds a fair number of average sized smallmouth bass and a small number of muskellunge. Whitefish can also be found in fair numbers.

Margaret Lakes (Map 35/B5)
The Margaret Lakes are two beautiful semi-wilderness lakes. Margaret Lake has a boat launch and offers slow fishing for natural lake trout, while Little Margaret Lake offers good fishing at times for stocked splake. Margaret Lake is part of the winter/spring fish sanctuary in order to protect its heavily depleted lake trout stocks. Practicing catch and release on these lakers will aid in the regeneration of the fragile species.

Marigold and Sam's Lakes (Map 26/E5)
These lakes can be found not far off Highway 35. They offer fair fishing for good sized smallmouth and largemouth bass.

Marsh [Marsden] and Upper Pelaw Lakes (Map 36/B3)
Upper Pelaw Lake has a number of cottages along its shoreline and offers fair fishing for smallmouth bass, with the odd lake and brook trout periodically caught. Marsh Lake can be accessed via portage from Upper Pelaw Lake and provides fair fishing for natural lake trout and slow fishing for smallmouth bass and brook trout. Watch for special restrictions on these lakes.

Marshal and Mercer Lakes (Map 60/D5)
These lakes provide for good fishing at times for smallmouth bass in the 1 kg (2 lb) range and fair fishing for northern pike in the 1–2 kg (2–4.5 lb) range. Walleye are also found in both lakes.

Martin and Insula Lakes (Map 34/G4–35/A4)
These are two semi-wilderness lakes that are surrounded mainly by Crown land. Martin Lake can be accessed via a rough 4wd road and a short portage found at the south side of Martin Lake can take you to Insula Lake. Both lakes offer fair fishing at times for small brook trout while Martin Lake also provides steady fishing for largemouth bass.

Martin and McLean Lakes (Map 32/D1)
Both lakes offer fishing for smallmouth and largemouth bass, with Martin Lake providing the most consistent action and the biggest fish. Bass can reach 2 kg (4.5 lbs) in Martin Lake.

Mary Jane Lake (Map 41/D5)
East of Highway 124, fishing is fair to good at times for smallmouth bass in Mary Jane Lake. There is also a small northern pike population in the lake.

Mary Lake (Map 34/B3)
Located south of Huntsville, Mary Lake is a busy cottage destination lake year round. Anglers can expect good fishing at times for smallmouth and largemouth bass to 1.5 kg (3.5 lbs). Bass anglers should try off any rocky drop-off areas or nearby one of the small islands. The lake now relies on stocking for its lake trout fishery. Ice fishing season is the most productive time for lakers. A population of northern pike also makes Mary Lake home.

Mason and Himbury Lakes (Map 43/C2)
These lakes offer fair fishing for smallmouth bass that average 1 kg (2 lbs). Mason Lake is surrounded by private land, while the north shore of Himbury Lake is Crown land.

Mayo Lake (Map 38/G7)
Mayo Lake is part of a winter/spring fishing sanctuary in order to help pressured lake trout stocks. Fishing is fair for smallmouth bass and quite slow for lakers. But, fishing for lakers might pick up in the future as they are now beginning to stock lake trout.

McCan Lake (Map 33/A2)
Located just north of the town of Rosseau, McCan Lake still contains small brook trout. Fishing is generally slow and spring just after ice off is the best time to find aggressive brookies.

McCauley Lake (Map 46/C3)
There are a few cottages along the shoreline of McCauley Lake, but fishing is still good at times for smallmouth bass in the 1 kg (2 lb) range. Brook and lake trout are also found in the lake, but can be hard to find. Watch for special restrictions on the lake, including slot size regulations.

McCormick Lake (Map 47/B7)
Accessed by snowmobile or on foot, McCormick Lake is stocked with brook trout. These trout can be finicky at times.

McCrae Lake (Map 23/F3)
McCrae Lake is a part of the popular Gibson-McDonald Canoe Route, which can be quite busy during summer weekends. There are many campsites at the lake, which offers fair fishing for smallmouth and largemouth bass. There is also a small population of northern pike in the lake.

McCue Lake (Map 27/G1)
McCue Lake is located near the intersection of Highways 118 and 503. There is a fair population of average sized smallmouth bass in the lake. Try minnow imitation lures or flies for added success.

McGee Lake (Map 19/C1)
McGee Lake is stocked with lake trout regularly and is fairly productive for small lakers during ice fishing season. The only real access to the lake is by snowmobile or by bushwhacking.

McKay Lake (Map 34/D7)
This is a popular summer destination lake located just off County Road 14 outside the town of Bracebridge. There is a fair population of smallmouth bass and

fishing can be good at times. Try a jig or spinner near the deeper sections off the larger island for best results.

McKenzie Lake (Map 46/E7)
A good gravel road leads to the public access point on the lake's northern point. Fishing for smallmouth bass can be quite good. Many larger bass are caught yearly. Lake trout are caught up to 60 cm (24 in) in length. Watch for slot size restrictions and winter regulations.

McMaster and White Lakes (Map 32/F7)
McMaster Lake is surrounded by Crown land and takes a hike or portage to locate. It is one of the better bass lakes in the area since it is more secluded. White Lake to the east is easier to access and also provides a decent largemouth bass fishery.

McMaster Lake (Map 47/C5)
McMaster Lake, along Siberia Road southwest of Barry's Bay, is stocked annually with splake. There are also smallmouth bass in the lake.

McNevin and Sea Lakes (Map 46/E2)
Access to these lakes is along a series of rough bush roads. Bass are found to 2 kg (4.5 lbs) in both lakes.

McQuaby Lake (Map 52/C1–62/C7)
South of Highway 534, you can expect fair to good fishing at times for smallmouth bass and walleye here.

McQuillan Lake (Map 32/D4)
This can be accessed by a short rustic portage and offers fair to good fishing for smallmouth and largemouth bass. In the past few years, the lake has also been stocked with rainbow trout.

McSourley Lake (Map 66/E3)
Stocked annually with lake trout, McSourley is found north of Highway 17 to the west of Driftwood Provincial Park. Fishing is fair in winter and spring for trout to 45 cm (18 in).

Meach Lakes (Map 37/C1)
These are two average sized brook trout lakes that can be accessed via a 4wd road or snowmobile. Fishing in the lakes can be good through the ice or in spring for brook trout to 40 cm (16 in) in size.

Meadow Lake (Map 33/C1–42/C7)
Meadow Lake is found between Highway 141 and 518 via a 2wd road. Surrounded by Crown land, fishing can be good at times for largemouth that can reach 3 kg (6.5 lbs) in size.

Medora Lake (Map 33/A7)
This lake can be found not far from County Road 169 north of Bala. Fishing at the lake is fair for largemouth bass.

Memesagamesing and Playfair Lakes (Map 50/G1–51/A1)
These picturesque lakes provide good fishing. Smallmouth bass to 2 kg (4.5 lbs) are most prevalent, although decent numbers of walleye and northern pike are also found. Pike and walleye can both be found exceeding 4 kg (9 lbs). During the cooler periods, fishing for lake trout is also available.

Menet Lake (Map 66/G4)
Menet Lake is stocked annually with splake, which provides for fair to good fishing for splake to 40 cm (16 in). White jigs through the ice can be effective.

Mephisto Lake (Map 29/G2)
Found northwest of Gilmour, this lake holds a natural population of lake trout, which are most frequently found in the winter. However, anglers will have better luck fishing for smallmouth and largemouth bass throughout the open water season.

Merrill Lakes (Map 30/D2)
A rough bush road allows access to these two remote lakes. Both lakes are inhabited by smallmouth bass and provide fair to good fishing for smaller bass. Little Merrill Lake is also stocked every few years with splake. Fishing can be fair for splake through the ice.

Middle Shanty and Pine Lakes (Map 43/F1)
Pine Lake provide good fishing for stocked brook trout in the 20–35 cm (8–14 in) range, while Middle Shanty is stocked with splake. Across the road from Middle Shanty Lake rests another small, unnamed lake that also has a good population of brookies in it.

Mill Lake (Map 32/B1–41/B7)
Mill Lake is a main drainage of the Seguin River on the outskirts of Parry Sound. The lake has a number of cottages and some homes along its shoreline and offers fair to good fishing at times for smallmouth bass to 1.5 kg (3.5 lbs) and fair fishing for walleye to 2 kg (4.5 lbs). There is also a fair population of northern pike in the lake that are generally small. In 2004, the lake had a few thousand splake stocked as a one-time event.

Millichamp Lake (Map 35/C1)
This fairly remote access lake is stocked periodically with brook trout, which provide for fair fishing for generally small brookies.

Milton Lake (Map 51/D3)
This small lake lies just off the south side of Highway 522. Fishing in the lake is fair for smallmouth bass and slow at times for small northern pike and walleye.

Minden Lake (Map 26/F2)
Minden Lake is a reservoir created by the damming of the Gull River. Stocked almost annually with rainbow trout, anglers will find the best action in the spring after ice off. Try a leech pattern or spinner for rainbow. There is also a fair population of smallmouth bass to 1.5 kg (3.5 lbs) in the lake.

Miner Lake (Map 50/A7)
Part of the Magnetawan River system, fishing is good here for decent sized smallmouth bass and northern pike. Walleye can also be found in the lake in fair numbers.

Mink Lake (Map 35/A3)
Mink Lake is a secluded lake that is most often visited by snowmobilers. It offers a few small brook trout through the ice or in spring just after ice off.

Mink Lake (Map 46/G5)
The easiest access to Mink Lake is by following the outflow stream from Bark Lake. Fishing is fair for small brook trout.

Mink Lake (Map 63/B5)
Largemouth bass inhabit the lake in fair numbers. Fishing is best during overcast periods or during dusk.

Minnicock and Portage Lakes (Map 27/E1)
These lakes have a number of cottages along their shore, but still offer fair to good fishing for smallmouth bass in the 1 kg (2 lb) range.

Mirror Lake (Map 33/C6)
Mirror Lake is a branch off Lake Muskoka outside of the town of Port Carling. Fishing for smallmouth and largemouth bass is fair at times for bass in the 0.5–1.5 kg (1–3.5 lb) range. Northern pike and walleye can be found in the lake, although fishing success is generally slow.

Miserable Lake (Map 27/B3)
This secluded, Crown land lake can provide fair to good fishing at times for smallmouth bass.

Miskokway Lake (Map 40/D2)
Fishing can be quite good here for smallmouth and largemouth bass to 1.5 kg (3.5 lbs). Lake trout are also found in the lake in fair numbers, partly due to the winter/spring sanctuary period to help preserve stocks.

Mississagua Lake (Map 27/G7)
Mississagua Lake is a beautifully scenic cottage lake in the heart of the Kawarthas. The lake has good fishing for smallmouth and largemouth bass to 1 kg (2 lbs). Lake trout populations have dwindled over the years, but they can still be found.

Mitchell Lake (Map 17/B3)
This man-made lake is very weedy providing inviting habitat for sportfish. Good numbers of smallmouth and largemouth bass to 2 kg (4.5 lbs) are available, however heavy boating traffic the Trent Severn Waterway can make the bass finicky at times. Fishing for walleye is slow to fair with walleye, while fair fishing for the mighty muskellunge is also available. There are boat launches available off Highway 48.

Mitchell Lake (Map 37/F2)
Mitchell Lake's northern shore borders Crown land; however most of the lake is surrounded by private property. The lake is stocked every few years with brook trout and also holds a few rainbow.

Moira Lake (Map 21/C4)
Located to the south of Madoc, this is a popular summer destination. Fishing for walleye and northern pike is considered fair, while fishing for smallmouth and largemouth bass can be quite good at times. A fair population of muskellunge is also found here. Watch for special restrictions.

Monck Lake (Map 28/D1–37/D7)
Found north of Highway 118, this is a popular summer cottage lake. There is fair fishing for smallmouth bass and the lake is stocked periodically with splake. Fishing for average sized splake is fair with increased action through the ice or in the spring. There is a boat launch at the lake.

Monkshood Lake (Map 46/F2)
Found via a long trail from Aylen Lake Road, this lake is stocked with splake and provides good fishing through the ice and in spring for nice sized fish.

Monmouth Lakes (Map 28/B3)
The Monmouth Lakes can be accessed via a 4wd road and provide good fishing for smallmouth and largemouth bass. The larger Monmouth Lake is also stocked yearly with lake trout and offers good fishing at times for average sized lakers. Lake trout action is best through the ice or by trolling in spring.

Moore Lakes (Map 26/D5)
Although the lakes are really only one waterbody, some people still distinguish the waterbody as Moore and East Moore Lake. The lake trout here are supplemented with some stocking, while the action heats up with smallmouth and largemouth bass that are more active in the summer. Whitefish also provide a good opportunity to test your skills. Check the regulations for ice fishing restrictions and lake trout slot size limits.

Moot Lake (Map 34/D5)
Being a cottage lake, Moot Lake is fished regularly throughout the season. Fishing success for smallmouth and largemouth bass is fair for bass averaging 0.5–1 kg (1–2 lbs). One of the prime holding areas for largemouth bass is the northeast corner of the lake.

Morgan's Lake (Map 43/F4)
This out of the way lake offers a variety of sportfish. The most active fish are the smallmouth bass, although whitefish can provide for some good action as well. Brook trout are also found in the lake, but in smaller numbers.

Morin Lake (Map 66/B3)
This small lake that can be found by snowmobile from Highway 17 or on foot through some dense bush. Small brook trout inhabit the lake.

Morrison Lake (Map 24/F4)
This popular lake has many cottages scattered along its shoreline. Smallmouth bass are the predominant bass species in the lake and can be found as big as 2.5 kg (5.5 lbs), with average catches in the 0.5–1 kg range. Fishing is usually slow with greatest success being in the fall or during overcast periods.

Mountain Lake (Map 26/F1)
Located off Highway 35 north of Minden, Mountain Lake is a fairly busy lake in the summer. Anglers can expect fair to good fishing for smallmouth bass to 2 kg (4.5 lbs) and slow to fair fishing for natural lake trout to 65 cm (26 in). There is also a fair population of whitefish in the lake. A boat launch is found on the northwest shore. Watch for slot size restrictions on lake trout and special ice fishing regulations.

Mouse Lake (Map 35/C4)
This lake can be accessed via a rough 2wd road off the Sherborne Access Road, although the road is regularly gated. The lake has been stocked in the past with rainbow trout; however, reports of success have been limited.

Mousseau and Valiant Lakes (Map 66/C4)
Mousseau Lake is stocked every few years with brook trout that can be found in the 40 cm (16 in) range. Valiant Lake has fishing for lakers in the 40–50 cm (16–20 in) range.

Mud, Trout and Stoney Lakes (Map 53/D5)
Natural brook trout are found in all three lakes as well as in a few of the small, unnamed, surrounding lakes.

Mug and Jill Lakes (Map 35/A5)
Increased logging activity in the area has made most of the area lakes accessible by vehicle and this once fabulous cane route is all but obsolete. Regardless, good fishing is still available at times for largemouth bass to 2 kg (4.5 lbs).

Mutton Lake (Map 32/F1)
Mutton Lake is a popular Cottage Country lake that provides fair fishing for generally small smallmouth and largemouth bass as well as northern pike. Minnow imitations lures and flies can create better action for both pike and bass.

Myers Lake (Map 32/G6)
Located just south of Toronto Lake, Myers Lake has many cottages along its shoreline. Fishing for largemouth bass is slow, although bass can be found to 1.5 kg (3.5 lbs).

Naraka Lake (Map 59/A4)
Naraka Lake is home to few cottages and camps and offers fair to good fishing for smallmouth bass. Northern pike are also found in the lake.

Negeek Lake (Map 47/G7)
Negeek Lake is part of the Madawaska River system and has a number of cottages along its shoreline as well as a public access point near McPhees Bay, on the east side of the lake. Fishing is fair for average sized smallmouth and large-mouth bass. Northern Pike also inhabit the lake in fair numbers and range in size from small hammer handles to about the 70 cm (28 in) range.

Nelson and Little Nelson Lakes (Map 44/A5)
Northwest of Tasso Lake, Nelson Lake offers fair fishing for brook trout, while Little Nelson Lake is stocked every other year with brook trout.

Nepewassi Lake (Map 59/B2-C1)
Fishing in this big lake can be good at times for panfish as well as smallmouth bass and northern pike in the 2 kg (4.5 lb) range. Walleye are also found in the lake, although fishing is usually slow.

Niger Lake (Map 44/C7)
Located near the West Gate of Algonquin Park off the Troutspawn Lake Road, this lake is stocked with brook trout. There are also pumpkinseed sunfish and yellow perch in 34 hectare Niger Lake.

Nine Mile Lake (Map 24/C2)
This long Cottage Country lake can be accessed via a 2wd road off County Road 13. Fishing for largemouth bass can be good at times for fish that average 0.5 kg (1 lb). Try along any structure near shore for good action.

Nine Mile Lake (Map 40/G5–41/A6)
This is a long lake created by the Nine Mile Lake Dam. The lake has a few cottages at the southern end and can be accessed off Highway 124. Anglers will find smallmouth and largemouth bass to 2 kg (4.5 lbs) and northern pike that can be found to 5 kg (11 lbs). Action in the northern half of the lake can be exceptionally good at dawn and dusk.

Noganosh Lake (Map 50/C5)
The odd shaped Noganosh Lake has good fishing for smallmouth and large-mouth bass that average 1–1.5 kg (2–3.4 lbs) in size. Good populations of nice sized northern pike also inhabit the lake and can be caught to the 5 kg (11 lb) range.

Nogies Lake (Map 27/D5)
The shallow nature of the lake is ideal habitat for bass and anglers can expect fair to good fishing at times for bass to 2 kg (4.5 lbs). Try a popper in the shallows for lunker largemouth or a jig in deeper areas for active smallmouth.

Noname Lake (Map 45/B7)
At the north end of the Haliburton Forest, Noname Lake offers fair fishing for stocked brook trout. It has also been stocked in the distant past with rainbow trout.

North and South Muldrew Lakes (Map 24/F3)
These lakes are two beautiful Cottage Country lakes that can be accessed east of the town of Gravenhurst. The lakes join each other to form a 'U' shape and offer fair to good fishing for smallmouth and largemouth bass to 2 kg (4.5 lbs). Fishing for walleye is fair during the year with the most productive period being ice fishing season.

North Beaver Lake (Map 26/F4)
Surrounded by Crown land, this lake does not see as much action as other lakes in the area. Fishing for smallmouth and largemouth bass can be exciting during the right conditions.

North Chainy Lake (Map 46/E7)
It is a rough 400 m (1,312 ft) bushwhack to get to this lake, but it is worth the effort. The lake offers good fishing for smallmouth bass and stocked brook trout. Bass average 1.5 kg (3 lbs), but can be found larger.

North Eels Lake (Map 28/C1)
This lake can be found via a 4wd road and provides for good to very good fishing at times for smallmouth bass that average 1 kg (2 lbs). Action on the lake is fairly consistent, although picks up during overcast periods and at dusk.

North Lake (Map 28/G3)
Accessed off Ingram Road near the community of Faraday, North Lake is often stocked with splake. There are also smallmouth bass in the lake.

North Lake (Map 53/C7)
The western half of the lake is private land, while the eastern half is Crown land. Fishing is fair for average sized brook trout and lake trout.

North Lake (Map 36/E3)
North Lake was stocked with lake trout at one time to supplement natural stocks, although now is part of the winter/spring fishing sanctuary to help preserve these fragile fish. In the summer months anglers can expect fair fishing for smallmouth bass.

North Otter Lake (Map 26/D3)
It offers fair to good fishing at times for large and smallmouth bass to 2 kg (4.5 lbs).

North Pigeon and Little Bob Lakes (Map 26/E3)
These two popular lakes are stocked with lake trout. The trout are best caught in the spring, but do not grow very big due to the heavy fishing pressure. Both lakes also have fair fishing for smallmouth and largemouth bass.

Nottawasaga Bay (Map 14/A4–22/A6)
The Nottawasaga Bay is a part of Georgian Bay and is renowned for its recreation opportunities. Fishing near the many river and creek outflows can be quite productive for Chinook salmon, rainbow trout and the odd brown trout. The bay also holds good populations of yellow perch along with the odd pink and Coho salmon, lake trout and splake reported annually.

Number One Lake (Map 60/F4)
Number One Lake lies just south of the western shore of Lake Nipissing and offers northern pike in the 2 kg (4.5 lb) range. Walleye are also found in the lake in fair numbers.

Nutt Lake (Map 33/E4)
Nutt Lake is a small cottage destination lake found off Highway 141 and offers slow fishing for marginal sized smallmouth bass.

Oak and Beechnut Lakes (Map 20/A2)
These are two beautiful cottage lakes that offer fair to good fishing for smallmouth and largemouth bass to 2 kg (4.5 lbs). Try a floating Rapala or popper near structure for some good breakwater action.

Oastler Lake (Map 32/B2)
Home to a provincial park, which offers camping, the lake can be a busy place on weekends. Anglers will still find fair fishing for smallmouth and largemouth bass to 1.5 kg (3.5 lbs) and some decent sized northern pike. The lake was last stocked with rainbow trout in 2005, but the fishery never really did well.

Obashking and Redpine Lakes (Map 61/B4)
Remote lakes south of Lake Nipissing, Obashking Lake offers good fishing for smallmouth and largemouth bass. Both lakes support a fair population of northern pike.

Oliver Lake (Map 66/F5)
Oliver is a small, secluded lake that is stocked every few years with brook trout. Fishing is often good for small trout.

Oneside and Otherside Lakes (Map 46/D3)
There is a short trail from Oneside to the Otherside. Oneside is stocked with splake, while Otherside is stocked with brook trout. Fishing is good at times in both lakes in winter or early spring.

Orr Lake (Map 14/F2)
Orr Lake offers slow fishing for northern pike to 4 kg (9 lbs) and fair fishing for largemouth bass to 2 kg (4.5 lbs). The lake's shoreline is dotted with cottages and homes, although there are a few private campgrounds located off Highway 93 near the lake.

Otter Lake (Map 27/D6)
There is a boat launch at this lake and anglers can expect fair fishing for smallmouth and largemouth bass to 1.5 kg (3.5 lbs). Fishing for muskellunge is slow, although the odd 5 kg (11 lb) muskie is caught yearly.

Otter Lake (Map 32/B2)
Otter Lake has fair to good fishing at times for smallmouth and largemouth bass to 2 kg (4.5 lbs). Small northern pike are also available in good numbers throughout the lake and lunkers in the 6 kg (13 lb) range are caught yearly. The lake has been stocked in the past with lake and rainbow trout, but no longer.

Otter Lake (Map 35/C2)
Otter Lake is a popular cottage destination lake that has a boat launch. Anglers will find fair numbers of smallmouth bass and a few northern pike. There is also rumoured to host a small population of brook trout.

Otterhead Lake (Map 26/B1)
Otterhead Lake has been stocked every few years with splake and is mainly fished in the winter due to the remoteness of the lake. Access is easiest by snowmobile.

Oval Lake (Map 66/E6)
Stocked annually with brook trout, this out of the way lake can produce steady results. Old bush roads lead past the northeast side of the lake.

Owl Lake (Map 66/E4)
This small, secluded lake is stocked biennially with brook trout. Fishing is quite good, especially in spring.

Oxbend and Sandox Lakes (Map 37/E2)
Both lakes are stocked periodically with splake. Fishing is fair through the ice and in spring, just after ice off.

Oxtongue Lake (Map 44/B7)
Located west of Algonquin Park, Oxtongue Lake is accessible via Highway 60. The lake can be busy during the summer but fishing is usually good. Smallmouth bass to 2 kg (4.5 lbs) are plentiful, while lake trout to 70 cm (28 in) are more difficult to find. Brook trout are found in the small pond, which can be accessed by a short trail at the southernmost tip of the big lake.

Paint [Deer] and Chub Lakes (Map 34/G3–35/A3)
Chub and Paint Lakes are two easily accessed lakes off Paint Lake Road and provide fair fishing for smallmouth bass in the 0.5–1 kg (1–2 lb) range and slow fishing for brook trout. Paint Lake has been stocked with splake, which provide fair fishing through the ice and in the spring.

Pairo Lakes (Map 35/A4)
The Pairo Lakes are two small, secluded fishing lakes that are turning into bass lakes. The introduction of largemouth bass to the lakes has seriously hindered brook trout populations. A rough 4wd road leads to the Lower Pairo Lake.

Pakeshkag Lake (Map 49/E3)
Found in Grundy Lake Provincial Park, smallmouth bass and northern pike inhabit Pakeshkag in fair numbers, although fishing success is sporadic. Walleye are an even rarer find.

Papineau Lake (Map 38/B1–47/B7)
This popular summer destination lake is home to several cottages. Largemouth bass to 2 kg (4.5 lbs) are found in good numbers throughout the lake, while fishing for average sized northern pike is fair. Lake trout are found to 70 cm (28 in) in the lake and fishing is fair through the ice or in spring, after ice off. There are two public boat launches onto the lake: one on the north side and one on the south side of the lake. Check regulations for slot size and winter restrictions.

Papineau Lake (Map 64/D4)
A stocked species of lake trout inhabits this lake. Fishing can be good at times in winter and spring. Whitefish are also a good catch and are often more plentiful than lake trout. Lakers and whitefish reach sizes of 65 cm (26 in). The Papineau Lake conservation area also lies on the lake and provides camping opportunities for visitors.

Park Lake (Map 44/C6)
Park Lake is located near the western entrance to Algonquin Park and can be accessed by canoe and low maintenance portage. The lake offers fair fishing for smallmouth bass in the 1 kg (2 lb) range.

Partridge and Wallace Lakes (Map 40/F4)
Part of the Shawanaga River system, northern pike and walleye can be found in both lakes in fair numbers. Fishing can also be quite good for smallmouth and largemouth bass up to 2 kg (4.5 lbs).

Partridge Lake (Map 35/D5)
Brook trout are stocked in this lake every few years and fishing is good at times for generally small brookies. Try ice fishing or casting small spoons or spinners in the spring.

Pascal Lake (Map 63/F5)
Found off the north side of Pioneer Road south of Bonfield, this small lake offers fair fishing for stocked splake.

Pat and Silversheen Lake (Map 37/D1)
These two small brook trout lakes found southwest of Lake St. Peter Provincial Park. Stocked every few years with brook trout, fishing can be good through the ice and in the spring.

Pat Lake (Map 53/D2)
This is a small, secluded natural brook trout lake. There is barely a trail, which helps keep it hidden and maintains the quality of the fishery.

Patersons, Sand and Woods Lakes (Map 67/B6)
Found near Algonquin Park's boundary, these three lakes are accessible by foot. They are quite small and fishing is fair for brook trout to 30 cm (12 in).

Paudash Lakes (Map 28/E1)
Accessed from either Highway 28 or Highway 118, these lakes are popular cottage lakes. Most of the fishing action is for smallmouth and largemouth bass, but there are also lake trout, walleye and panfish including the perennial favourite yellow perch.

Paugh Lake (Map 47/D2)
Paugh Lake has a few cottages along its shoreline and offers fair fishing for lake trout and walleye. Lakers can be found to 70 cm (28 in), while walleye average 1–1.5 kg (2–3.5 lbs). Much of the lake remains Crown land and there is a public access point on the lake's eastern shore.

Paul Lake (Map 35/C7)
Accessed by a 4wd road, this secluded lake offers good fishing for smallmouth and largemouth bass to 1.5 kg (3.5 lbs). Rapalas and jigs can be productive as can Muddler minnow fly patterns.

Pauper Lake (Map 26/B1)
Pauper Lake is a secluded fishing lake that offers good fishing for smallmouth bass to 2 kg (4.5 lbs). The lake sees very little fishing pressure throughout the year due to its remoteness.

Pearceley Lake (Map 42/D1)
This small lake that lies just south of Highway 124 and is stocked every two years with splake.

Pencil Lake (Map 27/F5)
Pencil Lake offers fair fishing for stocked lake trout to 2 kg (4.5 lbs) and good fishing for smallmouth bass to 2 kg (4.5 lbs). Ice fishing for lake trout is sometimes productive. There is a public boat launch at the north end of the lake.

Peninsula Lake (Map 34/E1)
Although the most prized sportfish in this lake are stocked lake trout, your best bet for fishing success on this lake is to try for bass. Smallmouth and largemouth bass provide good fishing at times for bass to 2 kg (4.5 lbs). Try working presentations along drop-off areas, near Hills Island or even near manmade structures such as boat docks. A population of northern pike also exists in the lake.

Perch and Smith Lakes (Map 66/G4)
Perch Lake is stocked with splake and provides for fair fishing. Smiths Lake is stocked with rainbow trout, which can be elusive.

Perch Lake (Map 26/B7)
Perch Lake is a small bass lake that provides fair to good fishing for small smallmouth and largemouth bass.

Percy Lake (Map 36/E3)
Since 1964 lake trout have been stocked every other year in Percy Lake. Fishing for lakers to 75 cm (30 in) is fair and can be good by trolling in spring or ice fishing in winter. Smallmouth bass to 2 kg (4.5lbs) are also found in the lake in good numbers. The action for these aggressive fish usually picks up at dusk and during overcast periods.

Peyton Lakes (Map 53/D6)
Found in the Almaguin Highlands, the limited access helps maintain the quality brook trout fishery. Almost all of the fishing on these lakes is done through the ice in winter.

Picard Lake (Map 27/E5)
Accessed from a public boat launch at the south end, Picard Lake holds a good number of smallmouth bass. The lake was once stocked with rainbow trout, however success is sporadic.

Pickerel Lake (Map 42/G1–43/A1)
As you might expect from the name, walleye can be found here in excess of 2.5 kg (5.5 lbs). Northern pike can top 3.5 kg (7.5 lbs), while smallmouth bass are also found in the lake in fair numbers and fishing can be good at times.

Pigeon Lake (Map 18/C7–D3)
Pigeon Lake is known for its prolific weed growth and inviting shoals that provide ideal conditions for a quality fishery. It produces many big sportfish with walleye up to 4.5 kg (10 lbs) and muskellunge to 12 kg (26.5 lbs). Popular hot spots include Gannon's Narrows and the bay leading to Nogies Creek. However, the resident smallmouth and largemouth bass provide most of the action on the lake.

Piglet Lake (Map 66/D5)
Access by rough bush road or snowmobile in winter, Piglet Lake is stocked with brook trout. There are also lake trout, whitefish as well as pumpkinseed sunfish and yellow perch. Lake trout are protected through a winter/spring fishing sanctuary.

Pine Lake (Map 34/F7)
Pine Lake is found just outside the western border of Bigwind Provincial Park and has some cottages along its shoreline. Lakers can be found up to 75 cm (30 in), although average 30 cm (12 in). The lake was also once stocked with rainbow trout, although fishing for rainbow is slow.

Pine Lake (Map 36/A5)
Found north off the Eagle Lake Road (County Road 6) outside of Haliburton, there is a boat launch on Pine Lake. The lake was stocked with walleye in 2003 and is also home to a small population of muskellunge, yellow perch and whitefish.

Pine Lake (Map 51/F2)
On the north side of Highway 522, Pine Lake is a decent bass lake. Both smallmouth and largemouth are found in good numbers, while a small population of walleye also roams the lake.

Pine Lake (Map 63/D2)
Found in Mattawa River Provincial Park, fishing is fair for small northern pike and even slower for the mighty muskellunge. Most of the fishing action is for smallmouth bass and panfish.

Playfair Lake (Map 50/G1)
Part of the Memesagamesing River system, fishing in the lake is good at times for smallmouth bass and generally fair for northern pike and walleye.

Plewman Lake (Map 26/F4)
Plewman Lake is a small Cottage Country lake found not far off from County Road 121. The lake offers fair fishing for smallmouth and largemouth bass to 1.5 kg (3.5 lbs).

Poker, Bentshoe, Cinder and Crane Lakes (Map 35/B7)
These three scenic lakes are part of the popular Poker Lake Canoe Route and offer good fishing for smallmouth and largemouth bass. Bentshoe Lake can be accessed via a short portage from the parking area off Highway 118 and short portages link the remaining lakes. Scenic rustic camping sites are available on all the lakes. Upper Crane Lake is stocked every other year with splake.

Ponsford Lake (Map 32/G1–33/A1)
Ponsford Lake is a secluded lake that is surrounded by Crown land. The lake is rarely visited and offers good fishing for smallmouth bass in the 0.5–1 kg (1–2 lb).

Pooh, Puffball and Tigger Lakes (Map 66/E5)
These three lakes have all been stocked with rainbow trout, although Pooh is no longer being stocked. Fishing can be good for small rainbow, especially when using flies or small lures.

Pool Lake (Map 52/G7)
Pool Lake is a smaller lake that is found to the southeast of Bernard Lake. Smallmouth bass fishing is fair for generally smaller bass.

Poorhouse Lake (Map 44/E7)
Poorhouse Lake can be found north off County Road 12 and offers fair fishing for brook trout.

Poplar Lake (Map 28/A7)
This lake has a fair population of stocked splake that are best fished in the winter. The hybrid fish is quite active in winter and can grow up to 4 kg (9 lbs) on occasion. It is possible to access the lake via a rustic portage or on foot from Cox Lake.

Poplar Pond (Map 47/B7)
Access to this small pond is limited to snowmobile or foot. It is about a 300 metre walk from the road to the pond, which is stocked every few years with brook trout.

Porcupine Lake (Map 34/G5)
Porcupine Lake is found just south of Ril Lake and was once stocked with rainbow trout to supplement natural brook trout populations.

Port Rawson Bay (Map 32/A5)
Port Rawson Bay is a semi-wilderness bay. Northern pike are one of the more abundant species, which average 2–4 kg (4.5–9 lbs), but can also be found in the 10 kg (22 lbs) range. Fishing for smallmouth and largemouth bass can be very good at times for bass that average 0.5–1.5 kg (1–3.5 kg). Walleye are found in fair numbers averaging 0.5–1 kg (1–2 lbs) and muskellunge can be caught in the 15 kg (33 lbs) range.

Portage and Silver Lakes (Map 32/E4)
These lakes reside beside Highway 69 and offer fair fishing for smallmouth and largemouth bass as well as slow fishing for lake trout. Lake trout are stocked periodically, although not enough to make a great fishery.

Portage Lake (Map 41/A7)
Portage Lake is part of the Seguin River drainage and has a number of cottages along its shoreline. There is fair to good fishing for smallmouth bass to 1.5 kg (3.5 lbs) and average sized northern pike. If you are using flies, try a larger Muddler minnow or large streamers for pike.

Portage Lake (Map 27/E1–36/E7)
Portage Lake can be accessed via bush roads and has a number of cottages along the shore. The lake offers fair to good fishing for smallmouth bass in the 1 kg (2 lb) range.

Portage Lake (Map 49/E4)
A fair population of walleye and northern pike can be found in the lake, although the fishing for smallmouth and largemouth bass is usually better. Overcast or dusk periods can produce some bigger fish.

Pot and Frying Pan Lakes (Map 36/C5)
These two small lakes are located off the Eagle Lake Road and offer fair fishing for smallmouth bass. A short portage will take you between the two lakes.

Poverty Lake (Map 46/A5)
Found just outside of Whitney, fishing for largemouth bass is fair for bass in the 0.5–1 kg (1–2 lb) range.

Prospect Lake (Map 25/E1)
Smallmouth and largemouth bass are the main species found in Prospect Lake. Fishing can be fair to good for bass to 1.5 kg (3.5 lbs).

Purdy Lake (Map 47/D7)
Purdy Lake is a popular cottage destination lake that has been stocked with lake trout in the past. Lakers can be found up to 65 cm (26 in) and are best caught through the ice. Purdy Lake also has a fair population of smallmouth bass, which can be found up to 2 kg (4.5 lb) in size.

Rabbit Lake (Map 35/E4)
Rabbit Lake is a small hidden lake that is accessed by a short portage from the south end of Nunikani Lake. There is a rustic campsite available and the lake is stocked every two years with brook trout.

Rainbow Lake (Map 36/D1)
Rainbow Lake lies partially within Algonquin Park and is accessed through the Haliburton Forest Reserve. There is a fair population of smallmouth bass in the lake.

Rainy Lake (Map 25/E6)
Rainy Lake is a secluded bass fishing lake that can be accessed by canoeing or lining up the Cranberry River. The lake has a good population of smallmouth and largemouth bass that can create nonstop action at times. Bass grow to 2 kg (4.5 lbs) and are readily taken with a spinner, top water popper or minnow imitation.

Rainy Lake (Map 40/D5)
Found off Shebeshekong Road, fishing is fair for generally small northern pike and good at times for both smallmouth and largemouth bass. A number of cottages lie on the west side of the lake, although much of the lake's eastern shoreline is Crown land.

Rankin Lake (Map 32/C2)
Rankin Lake can be found not far off Highway 69/400 and provides fair fishing for smallmouth and largemouth bass as well as northern pike. There are a number of cottages on the lake, which can be quite busy during summer months. In the past the lake was stocked with splake and rainbow trout and a few trout still roam the lake.

Rapid Lake (Map 46/A4)
Rapid Lake is really a widening of the Madawaska River, found downstream from Whitney. Smallmouth bass and walleye are found in the lake.

Rathbun Lakes (Map 28/B5)
These lakes can be accessed by canoe from Anstruther Lake. Rathbun Lake offers fair fishing for walleye and stocked lake trout. Small smallmouth and largemouth bass are also available in fair numbers. North Rathbun is a little more secluded and offers good fishing at times for larger smallmouth bass and stocked splake.

Rausch [Long] Lake (Map 51/F2)
Accessed by rough bush road, largemouth are the predominant bass species in Rausch Lake. Anglers will also find a small population of northern pike in the lake.

Raven Lake (Map 17/B2)
Raven Lake contains some nice smallmouth and largemouth bass. The lake can be a good spot for finding larger fish on overcast days.

Raven Lake (Map 35/C4)
Raven Lake is one of the larger lakes in the area and has many cottages along the shoreline. Fishing for natural lake trout to 75 cm (30 in) is slow, while success can be good at times for smallmouth bass to 2.5 kg (5.5 lbs). Watch for slot size restrictions on lake trout and any other special regulations. A few rustic campsites are available for overnight use.

Red Deer and Scheil Lakes (Map 52/G4)
These remote trout lakes are found not far from Highway 11 between Sundridge and Trout Creek. They were stocked in the past with brook trout.

Red Pine and Nunikani Lakes (Map 35/E4)
Red Pine Lake has a number of cottages and camps along its shoreline, while Nunikani Lake is accessible by portage only and has no development. Both lakes offer rustic campsites, including a few beautiful island sites. Anglers will find good fishing at times for smallmouth bass that average 0.5 kg (1 lb) and fair fishing for natural lake trout to 65 cm (26 in). There are slot size restrictions for lake trout on both lakes.

Redpine Lake (Map 65/G4)
Access into this remote lake northwest of Waterloo Lake and the Bissett Creek Provincial Park is a challenge. As a result, the fishing for stocked brook trout should be good.

Redstone Lakes (Map 36/B4)
Redstone Lake and Little Redstone Lake are connected by a shallow channel and are popular cottage destinations. Visitors can expect fair fishing at times for lake trout to 75 cm (30 in) and good fishing for smallmouth bass in the 0.5–1 kg (1–2 lb) range. Redstone Lake is stocked biennially with lake trout.

Restoule Lake (Map 51/G1–61/E7)
This big, semi-remote lake offers many prime holding areas for a variety of sportfish. Fishing can be good for smallmouth bass and northern pike, while walleye and muskellunge are a little more difficult to find. There is also a small population of lake trout in the deep lake.

Rice Lake (Map 10/G5–11/E2)
Rice Lake is a part of the Trent Severn Waterway. Resident walleye are the main attraction of the lake, with fish reaching up to 3 kg (6.5 lbs). Try around the mouth of the Otonabee River. Smallmouth and largemouth bass fishing can also be good for fish to 2 kg (4.5 lbs). The great muskellunge is present in Rice Lake and average around 3.5–4.5 kg (8–10 lbs). Yellow perch and other panfish are also found throughout the lake.

Richard Lake (Map 46/B2)
Just south of Algonquin Park, this lake stocked is splake every other year and also holds brook trout. Access to this lake is by ATV/snowmobile trails from McCauley Lake Road north of Whitney.

Richmond and McGowan Lakes (Map 32/B1)
These lakes are found just off Highway 69/400 south of Parry Sound and offer fair fishing for average sized smallmouth bass and small northern pike. Richmond Lake also has a fair population of average sized largemouth bass in the lake. Both lakes see heavy fishing pressure due to their easy access.

Riddell Lake (Map 37/G7–38/A7)
Fishing in this small lake is generally fair for stocked splake. Smallmouth bass can also be found in the lake.

Ridout Lake (Map 34/G4–35/A4)
This beautiful Crown land lake offers lake offers fair fishing for natural brook trout to 30 cm (12 in). Fishing is most productive in the spring after ice off, however the fall period just before the season closes can also be productive.

Ril Lake (Map 34/G5)
Cottages and camps line the shore of the odd shaped Ril Lake. The many shallow bays are ideal hideouts for smallmouth bass that reach 1.5 kg (3.5 lbs) in size. Look for weed beds or even try off manmade shore structure, such as docks, to find big smallmouth. Brook trout are thought to still exist in the lake as well.

Riley Lake (Map 25/D4)
Located just off County Road 6, the lake provides for fair to good smallmouth and largemouth bass fishing. Largemouth tend to frequent the numerous shallow, weedy bays around the lake, while smallmouth bass are often found along the shore areas of the deeper east end.

Ritchie Lake (Map 36/E5)
Ritchie Lake can be found via the Carroll Road and provides good fishing at

times for smallmouth bass to 1.5 kg (3.5 lbs). Minnow and crayfish imitations can be very productive.

Robinson and Spring Lakes (Map 29/D2)
These lakes rest are easily accessed from Highway 62 south of Bancroft. Robinson is often stocked with lake trout and holds smallmouth bass. Spring Lake is stocked with splake and also holds smallmouth as well as largemouth bass.

Roberts, McKechnie and Burnt Lakes (Map 32/E3)
These are three smaller lakes that can all be accessed via 2wd roads and offer fair to good fishing at times for average sized bass. Largemouth bass inhabit each of the lakes, while smallmouth bass can be found in McKechnie Lake only.

Rock Island and Black Oak Lakes (Map 40/D4)
Rock Island Lake offers fair fishing for largemouth bass in the 1 kg (2 lbs) range. Small populations of walleye, smallmouth bass and northern pike are known to also inhabit the lake. If you find success too slow in Rock Island Lake, Black Oak Lake can be easily accessed by a short portage to the east. Fishing in Black Oak can be very good at times for smallmouth and largemouth bass, while success for northern pike and walleye is generally fair.

Rockaway Lake (Map 44/G7)
Rockaway Lake can be accessed by a gruelling 2,745 m (9,005 ft) portage from Kimball Lake. The northern shore of Rockaway Lake is part of the Dividing Lake Provincial Nature Park. The lake offers fair fishing for brook trout to 45 cm (18 in) and is part of the Rockaway Lake Canoe Route. An Algonquin Park permit is required for the rustic campsite available at the north end of the lake.

Roderick Lake (Map 32/G7)
Roderick Lake can be reached via a rough 2wd road or by canoe from Cassidy Lake. There is fair fishing for smaller largemouth bass at the lake. Try along the shoreline near any type of structure for largemouth holding areas.

Ronald and Nehemiah Lakes (Map 35/D4)
These are two small secluded lakes found in the Frost Centre and are stocked on opposing years with brook trout. Nehemiah Lake can be accessed via the Sherborn access road and a 455 m (1,493 ft) portage can take you to Ronald Lake. There are rustic campsites available on both lakes.

Roney Lake (Map 67/C4)
This small lake holds a good population of smallmouth bass. Spinners or minnow imitation lures work well.

Rose Lake (Map 33/G3)
Rose Lake can be found via a 2wd road off Old Muskoka Road and offers good fishing at times for smallmouth bass that average 0.5–1 kg (1–2 lbs). Any minnow imitation lure or fly can be productive.

Ross and Morrow Lakes (Map 36/D3)
These are stocked in offsetting years with splake and provide fair to good fishing at times for average sized splake. Ross Lake also has a fair population of smallmouth bass. Ice fishing for splake is popular on both lakes.

Round Lake (Map 20/B4)
Located north of Havelock, this popular summer destination holds good numbers of smallmouth and largemouth bass along with a smaller population of walleye. Walleye are the more popular catch. In the early season, look for walleye around the inflow and outflow of the North River.

Round Lake (Map 42/F5)
This lake can be accessed off Fern Glen Road and is often busy in the summer. The lake provides good fishing at times for smallmouth and largemouth bass to 1.5 kg (3.5 lbs) and fair to good fishing for average sized northern pike. Anglers will also find a small population of brook trout, whitefish and perch in the lake.

Round Lake (Map 43/G2)
Found off Rain Lake Road en route to the Rain Lake Campground in Algonquin Park, fishing is generally slow here, but does pick up in spring and fall. The brook trout are usually quite small.

Round Lake (Map 47/G1–57/G7)
One of the bigger lakes on the east side of Algonquin Park, fishing in Round Lake can produce some big fish. Northern pike are the biggest and known to reach 5 kg (11 lbs) in size. Walleye and lake trout offer fish in the 3.5 kg (8 lb) class, while smallmouth and largemouth bass are known to top 2.5 kg (5.5 lbs). Unfortunately, the bigger fish are few and far between.

Ruby and Ruth Lakes (Map 59/A7)
These secluded lakes offer fair fishing for smallmouth bass and walleye. Northern pike are also found in Ruth Lake.

Ruebottom, Oliver and Ryder Lakes (Map 41/E5)
These lakes are accessible by rough bush roads. Fishing is fair to good at times for smallmouth bass in Oliver Lake and is generally slow for small northern pike in all three lakes.

Rush Lake (Map 26/B7)
This lake has cottage development along its shoreline and is easily accessed off County Road 45. At times the lake can be good for smallmouth and largemouth bass. A small population of muskellunge is still present in the lake.

Ruth and Wolfe Lakes (Map 52/C1)
Separated by the Trans Canada Trail, there is also good road access to these lakes. You can expect fair fishing for smallmouth bass and walleye.

Salerno Lake (Map 27/C4)
This shallow lake was once home to a fantastic fishery, however shoreline development has taken its toll on the lake. Anglers can expect fair fishing for smallmouth bass to 1.5 kg (3.5 lbs) and slow success for walleye to 2.5 kg (5.5 lbs). Muskellunge fishing is also slow for muskie that average 4–6 kg (9- 13 lbs).

Salmon Lake (Map 27/D5)
Salmon Lake offers fair fishing for smallmouth bass in the 0.5–1 kg (1–2 lb) range. The lake was stocked in the past with lake trout that now relies on natural regeneration. Fishing is usually slow for trout that average 0.5–1 kg (1–2 lbs).

Salmon Lake (Map 32/B3)
Salmon Lake provides for good fishing for smallmouth and largemouth bass in the 1 kg (2 lb) range. Bass are readily caught using standard bass gear such as spinners, jigs and topwater lures or flies. Generally, small northern pike also inhabit the lake in fair numbers, with a few lunkers caught annually.

Salmon Trout Lake (Map 38/B3)
This lake offers fair fishing for smallmouth bass and slower fishing for walleye. Much of the lake is surrounded by private land, although there is a public boat access on the lake's eastern shore.

Sampson Pond (Map 35/E4) d
The Sampson Pond is hidden at the end of a 340 m (1,116 ft) portage found at the south end of Red Pine Lake. The lake offers good fishing at times for smallmouth bass and stocked splake.

Sand Lake (Map 43/C2)
Interrupting the Magnetawan River, anglers will find stocked lake trout and a few smallmouth bass in Sand Lake. Ice fishing for lakers is the most productive method to catch the elusive fish.

Sand Lake (Map 62/A6)
Sand Lake is found north of the settlement of Restoule and is accessible by bush roads. The lake is surrounded by Crown land and offers food fishing for smallmouth bass that can reach 2 kg (4.5 lbs) in size.

Sandy Bay (Map 43/B6)
Fishing can be quite good at times here for smallmouth bass to 2 kg (4.5 lbs) and decent sized northern pike. Muskellunge also cruise the bay and can be found more predominantly in the fall. Both muskie and pike can reach sizes in excess of 10 kg (22 lbs).

Sandy Lake (Map 18/E3)
Sandy Lake is quite shallow in areas, with plenty of bottom structure, the perfect habitat for warm water sportfish. Anglers can expect fair to good fishing for bass and slow to fair fishing for walleye and muskie.

Saskatchewan Lake (Map 35/D5)
Saskatchewan Lake is a small, easily accessed lake with a boat launch at the southeast side of the lake. There are smallmouth and largemouth bass in the 1.5 kg (3.5 lbs) range. Fishing is the best in the evening before sundown.

Scott Lake (Map 32/B3)
Scott Lake is a small lake that can be found off Three Legged Lake Road. It offers fair to good fishing at times for smallmouth bass. Try near drop-offs or rocky points for better results.

Secret Lake (Map 40/F2)
Secret Lake offers good fishing at times for brook trout. This lake is mainly accessed by snowmobile during winter.

Seesaw Lake (Map 46/A3)
Seesaw is another remote lake that is stocked with brook trout. Brookies are small and can be quite active in late winter or early spring.

Seguin and Spence Lakes (Map 42/A4)
Found off Nipissing Road, these lakes are mostly surrounded by private land. Fishing on the lakes is fair to good at times for smallmouth bass in the 1 kg (2 lbs) range.

Serpentine Lake (Map 28/B5)
Serpentine Lake is the furthest lake in a chain of lakes that make up the Serpentine Lake Canoe Route. It offers good fishing for largemouth bass to 1.5 kg (3.5 lbs). Rustic campsites can be found along the shoreline.

Severn Sound (Map 23/F5)
The stretch of Severn Sound from Midland to Port Severn is renowned for its walleye that can grow to 5 kg (11 lbs). Northern pike are caught in the 13 kg (28.5 lb) range annually, while muskellunge have been found in the 20 kg (44 lb) range. Smallmouth and largemouth bass fishing can be very good in areas, with the bass reaching up to 3 kg (6.5 lbs). The odd lake trout, splake and Pacific salmon can also be found in the Severn Sound area.

Shadow and Silver Lakes (Map 26/D7)
These lakes are a part of the Gull River system and offer fair to good fishing for smallmouth and largemouth bass. However, most anglers visiting the lakes are fishing for walleye. The odd muskellunge also inhabit the lakes.

Shark Lake (Map 19/B1)
Although splake are stocked in Shark Lake every few years, your best bet for fishing fun is for its resident smallmouth and largemouth bass. The lake can be accessed by canoe along the Buzzard Lake Canoe Route and is home to a few user maintained rustic campsites. The natural sandy beaches make this lake a worthwhile visit.

Sharron Lake (Map 26/F1)
Sharron Lake is a small lake that can be accessed off the east side of Highway 35 north of Horseshoe Lake. There is a fair population of smallmouth bass in the lake.

Shawanaga Lake (Map 41/B3)
Smallmouth bass and small northern pike can be found in some of the more secluded, shallower bays. There also remains a fair population of walleye in the lake.

Shebeshekong Lake (Map 40/E6)
This popular cottage destination lake has good fishing for average sized smallmouth bass and northern pike. Some big fish are reported annually.

Sheldon Lake (Map 26/C4)
Sheldon Lake is stocked almost annually with lake trout and offers good fishing for small lakers after ice off in the spring. Smallmouth bass are also found in the lake in good numbers and average 0.5–1 kg (1–2 lbs).

Sheldrake Lake (Map 30/F4)
Fishing can be quite good at times here for smallmouth and largemouth bass. Fair populations of northern pike and walleye are also found in the lake, which lies to the south of the larger Skootamatta Lake and is mainly surrounded by Crown land.

Sherborne Lake (Map 35/D4)
Sherborne Lake is one of the main lakes in the Frost Centre and has a few private camps, rustic campsites and even a public boat launch available. The main attraction is the fishing for natural lake trout to 65 cm (26 in). A population of smallmouth bass is also present in the lake and fishing is generally good for bass in the 1 kg (2 lb) range.

Shoal Lake (Map 61/F5)
Part of the Restoule/French River Canoe Route, access to the lake is mainly by canoe. Fishing in the lake is good for smallmouth bass to 1.5 kg (3.5 lbs) and fair to good for northern pike. Walleye are also present in the lake in fair numbers and are best caught at dusk or during early evening periods.

Shoe Lake (Map 35/B4)
Lake trout are stocked in Shoe Lake periodically and provide generally small fish. Action is best through the ice in winter or in the spring just after ice off.

Shoelace Lake, Glennies and Wallace Ponds (Map 35/E4)
These three secluded portage access lakes have been stocked, Shoelace and Glennies with brook trout, Wallace with splake. They offer good fishing through the ice and in the spring, just after ice off. There are rustic campsites available at Shoelace Lake and Glennies Pond.

Silver Buck and Silver Doe Lakes (Map 35/D5)
Found on Frost Centre lands, these are two portage accessible lakes that offer fair to good fishing for stocked brook trout. Brook trout can be found in the 30 cm (12 in) range.

Silver Lake (Map 33/C6)
This small Muskoka area lake is home to several cottages and is easily accessible. Found just outside of Port Carling, the lake offers sporadic fishing for lake trout.

Silver Lake (Map 36/B5)
This small lake is found off County Road 7 and offers fair fishing for average sized smallmouth bass.

Silver Sand Lake (Map 32/F6)
This small lake rests south of Highway 69 and MacTier. The lake is stocked with lake trout and was stocked in the past with rainbow. Smallmouth bass are also present in the lake.

Six Mile Lake (Map 23/G3–24/A3)
Six Mile Lake is a popular lake that is home to a provincial park. The most dominant sportfish species found in the lake is smallmouth and largemouth bass. Fishing success is fair to good for bass to 2.5 kg (5.5 lbs) in size. Walleye offer fair fishing, while northern pike, panfish and even muskellunge are also present in the lake.

Six Mile Lake (Map 40/B2)
Six Mile Lake is part of the Magnetawan River Canoe Route and offers fair fishing for smallmouth and largemouth bass to 1.5 kg (3.5 lbs). Northern pike and walleye are also present in the lake, although in smaller numbers. Pike can be found up to 5 kg (11 lbs), while walleye are usually in the 1 kg (2 lb) range.

Skeleton Lake (Map 33/E3)
Some of the best fishing in Skeleton Lake is for its smallmouth bass. The many rocky bays and islands make for ideal smallmouth habitat. However walleye and lake trout receive the majority of the fishing pressure. Lakers can be found to 75 cm (30 in) in size and walleye to 3.5 kg (8 lbs).

Skootamatta Lake (Map 30/F3)
One of the bigger lakes in the area, fishing can be good for smallmouth and largemouth bass that can reach 2 kg (4.5 lbs) in size. Walleye and northern pike are also present, although fishing is often slower than for bass. Pike can reach 5 kg (11 lbs) in size, while walleye average about 1–2 kg (2–4.5 lbs). Rustic campsites can be found on the lake.

Slipper and Stocking Lakes (Map 35/F2)
Both lakes are inhabited by lake trout and brook trout. Anglers can expect fair to good fishing at times for both species. Lakers are generally small but brook trout can be found to 45 cm (18 in).

Sludge [Round] Lake (Map 26/D5)
Sludge Lake is stocked with rainbow trout and over the last decade, fishing for rainbow has picked up. There is also a fair population of large and smallmouth bass in the lake.

Smith Lake (Map 63/G3–64/A3)
The Eau Claire Gorge Conservation Area helps protect a portion of this lake's shoreline. Panfish, smallmouth bass, walleye and northern pike are all present. Fishing for walleye is usually slow, while fishing for northern pike and bass is often decent.

Smoky Lake (Map 50/D5)
Accessed by canoe and portage, fishing in Smoky Lake can be good at times for smallmouth and largemouth bass to 2 kg (4.5 lbs). There is also a good population of northern pike.

Smudge Lake (Map 26/A5)
Smudge Lake is stocked every two years with splake. A good population of smallmouth bass is also present in the lake.

Smyth and Twelve Lakes (Map 53/B2)
Smyth Lake is found south of Forestry Road and offers stocked rainbow trout, which provide for good fishing, especially in spring. Nearby Twelve Lake is stocked with brook trout.

Snake and Pine Lakes (Map 26/B3)
Snake and Pine Lakes are remote bass fishing lakes that can be accessed via a rough 4wd road and short trail. Both lakes provide good smallmouth and largemouth bass fishing. Bass can be found in the 2 kg (4.5 lb) range.

Snap Lake (Map 35/G2)
This small, secluded lake was stocked with rainbow trout at one time, however, it is currently unclear of the fishing quality available at the lake. Access is available via the Snap Lake Trail from Stocking Lake Road.

Snowshoe Lake (Map 35/E4)
This is a small hidden lake only accessible by canoe from Big Hawk Lake. There is a small natural brook trout population available in the lake and fishing can be good in the spring after ice off for small brookies. Be sure to limit your catch of this fragile natural strain.

Soaking Lake (Map 37/C1)
Soaking Lake is a small, secluded lake that can be found via a 4wd road. Ice fishing is popular and if you can get down the soggy roads in the spring, you should have fair to good success. The road to the lake may be difficult to find due to the maze of logging offshoot roads the area. The lake offers fair fishing for small brook trout.

Soldier Lake (Map 66/F5)
Stocked with brook trout, this remote access lake also holds yellow perch.

Solitaire Lake (Map 43/G7)
Resting next to a provincial park, it is no wonder the lake receives heavy fishing pressure. In order to maintain the preservation of the fragile lake trout stocks, the lake is part of a fall to spring fishing sanctuary. The odd smallmouth bass can also be found here.

South Beaver and Spar Lakes (Map 26/E5)
South Beaver has a few cottages along its shore and is home to a small resident muskellunge population. Both lakes offer average size smallmouth and largemouth bass.

South Jean Lake (Map 35/B6)
Located just off the Pine Springs Dump Road, South Jean Lake has fair to good fishing for smallmouth and largemouth bass to 2 kg (4.5 lbs). The shore structure of the lake provides great holding areas for good sized bass.

South Lake (Map 26/F3)
South Lake is a popular cottage destination lake that can be found off County Road 16 outside of Minden. Heavy fishing pressure has reduced fishing quality and anglers can expect slow fishing for small smallmouth bass.

South McDonald Lake (Map 35/B6)
South McDonald Lake can be found via a rough backroad and offers good fishing at times for smallmouth and largemouth bass. Larger bass are occasionally caught.

South Portage Lake (Map 36/E7)
South Portage Lake can be a busy lake but still offers fair to good fishing for smallmouth and largemouth bass to 2 kg (4.5 lbs). There is also a small muskellunge population in the lake.

South River Reservoir (Map 62/F7)
Next to Highway 11, this man-made lake still produces the odd brook trout. Anglers can find better action for smallmouth bass and panfish here.

Soyers and Little Soyers Lakes (Map 36/A7)
The larger Soyers Lake is a popular cottage destination lake that offers fair fishing for average sized lake trout and walleye. Anglers can also expect good fishing at times for smallmouth bass. Little Soyers Lake is more secluded and has good fishing for smallmouth bass in the 1 kg (2 lb) range.

Sparks Lake (Map 63/F4)
Sparks Lake is a fairly remote lake that offers a few stocked brook. Fly-fishing is often productive, but small spinners or spoons can also be effective.

Sparrow Lake (Map 24/G5)
There are a variety of sportfish species available in Sparrow Lake including smallmouth and largemouth bass, walleye, northern pike and muskellunge. Some nice sized fish are caught annually with walleye to 3 kg (6.5 lbs) and the odd pike reaching 6.5 kg (14 lbs).

Spectacle Lake (Map 47/A4)
Spectacle Lake is a resort lake near Barry's Bay. The stocked splake offer fair to good fishing at times.

Spence Lake (Map 25/B1)
Spence Lake is heavily used throughout the year and fishing has diminished continuously. Walleye can be caught in late spring with varied success. Fishing continues to be fair for smallmouth and largemouth bass.

Spider Lake (Map 31/G3)
Spider Lake is the largest lake within The Blackstone Harbour/Massasauga Wildlands Provincial Park and can be accessed via portage from Clear or Three Legged Lake. Fishing is very good for smallmouth and largemouth bass that can reach up to 2 kg (4.5 lbs). Northern pike are quite abundant in Spider Lake and provide good fishing opportunities for smaller pike, although larger fish in the 6 kg (13 lb) range are caught regularly. Natural lake trout also inhabit the lake but fishing is generally slow, except in the spring after ice off. Walleye are available in small numbers.

Sprat Lake (Map 35/A6)
Sprat Lake is a small, secluded lake that is stocked with rainbow trout. Fishing is fair to good at times for generally small rainbow.

Spring and Maeck Lakes (Map 51/G5–52/A5)
Found west of Eagle Lake, fishing in these lakes is usually fair for smallmouth bass. Lake trout are also found in Spring Lake, although heavy fishing has jeopardized this fishery.

Spruce Lake (Map 53/D7)
Found a good distance from any highway, Spruce Lake continues to be inhabited by a natural strain of brook trout.

Squaw Lake (Map 50/B2)
Part of the Pickerel River system, Squaw Lake offers good fishing for smallmouth bass to 1.5 kg (3.5 lbs) and fair fishing for walleye and northern pike. Walleye average 1–2 kg (2–4.5 lbs), while pike can be found in the 3 kg (6.5 lb) range.

St. Croix Lake (Map 27/D6)
This rustic, dark coloured Crown land lake can be accessed via a rough 4wd road . The lake provides good fishing at times for smallmouth and largemouth bass that can reach sizes of up to 2.5 kg (5.5 lbs). Muskellunge are also present in the lake in fair numbers and average 4–6 kg (9–13lbs). Muskellunge action is best in the fall.

St. Nora Lake (Map 35/C5)
Found just south of the village of Dorset, St. Nora Lake is the scenic backdrop for the Frost Centre. Fishing success is slow to fair for natural lake trout to 75 cm (30 in) and good for smallmouth bass to 1.5 kg (3.5 lbs). Ice fishing or trolling in the spring is best for lake trout success, while flipping jigs along rocky shoreline structure or working a crayfish imitation fly or lure off bottom can entice bass strikes.

Star Lake (Map 32/F1)
Star Lake receives heavy fishing pressure throughout the year and offers fair fishing for smallmouth and largemouth bass. Northern pike and lake trout fishing is slow for less than average sized fish. Lakers are stocked every few years and are best fished through the ice and in spring.

Starvation Lake (Map 53/C5)
This remote waterbody is home to some decent smallmouth bass fishing at times. The odd smallmouth reaches 2 kg (4.5 lbs) in size.

Steenburg Lake (Map 29/E4)
Easily accessed west of Highway 62, Steenburg Lake is stocked annually with splake. There is also good populations of smallmouth and largemouth bass at this cottage lake.

Stewart Lake (Map 32/F5)
Found off County Road 11, Stewart Lake is the scenic backdrop for the town of MacTier. There is slow fishing for small northern pike and fair fishing for smallmouth bass. The lake is also stocked every few years with splake, which provide for fair fishing throughout the year.

Stoco Lake (Map 21/F4)
Part of the Moira River system, Stoco Lake is located just outside of Tweed. Fishing is good for smallmouth and largemouth bass, while success for walleye and northern pike is generally fair. Muskellunge also reside here, but are difficult to find on most days.

Stoneleigh Lake (Map 34/C6)
Found just off County Road 117 east of the town of Bracebridge, Stoneleigh Lake experiences significant fishing pressure during the season. Fishing is fair for smallmouth bass.

Stony Lake (Map 19/D3)
Although a big lake, Stony (or Stoney) Lake receives a little less pressure than some of the other large Kawartha Lakes. The fabled muskellunge is one of the most sought after fish in Stony Lake and fishing is good at times, especially in the fall. Walleye fishing is regarded as good at times, while smallmouth and largemouth as well as panfish (bluegill, pumpkinseed sunfish and yellow perch) are also present in good numbers. A hotspot for largemouth and walleye is the weed beds north of Horseshoe Island.

Stoplog Lake (Map 19/B1)
Stoplog Lake was stocked at one time with lake trout and continues to support a small natural population. Fishing for lakers is slow during summer and the lake is part of a winter and spring sanctuary. Bass fishing, on the other hand, can be good at times with smallmouth and largemouth bass.

Storm and Tub Lakes (Map 41/G7)
These two small lakes are found along the Seguin Trail and offer fair to good fishing for bass. Both lakes contain largemouth bass while Tub Lake also has a population of smallmouth bass.

Stormy Lake (Map 27/E1)
There is a boat launch at Stormy Lake and anglers can expect fair fishing for smallmouth bass to 1.5 kg (3.5 lbs). A natural population of lake trout remains in the lake with the best action occurring in spring after ice off. The lake is part of the winter/spring fish sanctuary in order to protect the fragile lake trout population.

Stormy [Patterson] Lake (Map 61/F7)
Stormy Lake is stocked almost annually with lake trout, although fishing is usually a bit steadier for smallmouth bass and northern pike. Walleye and muskellunge are also present in the lake.

Stump Lake (Map 36/E7)
Part of the Burnt River system, Stump Lake can be found off Highway 118 east of Haliburton. The lake has a few smallmouth bass and even fewer muskellunge.

Sturgeon Bay (Map 23/G6)
The mouth of the Sturgeon River is a hot sport for big rainbow trout during the spring spawning run. Rainbow running up the river can be found as big as 13 kg (28.5 lbs). During summer many of the rainbow head for deeper water, although during fall they can be found again in the bay and around the river mouth. At other times, warm water species such as northern pike, bass and walleye can also be found in fair to good numbers. The occasional muskellunge is also caught

Sturgeon Lake (Map 17/E6–18/B4)
Walleye offer fair to good fishing at times for fish that average 2 kg (4.5 lbs). Below the dam in Fenelon Falls is a popular hotspot. Smallmouth and largemouth bass are the second biggest attraction with good fishing at times for bass to 2.5 kg (5.5 lbs). The Goose Bay area of the lake is a popular spot to find big bucket mouths. Small panfish and lunker muskellunge are also caught.

Sturgeon Lakes (Map 59/D6)
These lakes offer fair fishing for walleye, northern pike and bass. Access to Upper Sturgeon Lake is limited, although access is much easier on Lower Sturgeon Lake.

Sucker Lake (Map 28/A5)
As one of the most secluded lakes in the Kawartha Highlands Provincial Park, Sucker Lake can be accessed via a short portage from Bottle Lake. Visitors will find a few rustic user maintained campsites available. Fishing for smallmouth bass to 1.5 kg (3.5 lbs) can be good at times and a natural population of lake trout is present in the lake. Trout can grow as big as 3 kg (6.5 lbs), although angling success is usually quite slow. Watch for sanctuary periods.

Sucker Lake (Map 33/A3)
Sucker Lake is a busy summer cottage lake that offers fair to good fishing at times for smallmouth bass to 1.5 kg (3.5 lbs) and is stocked biennially with lake trout. Fishing for lakers is fair through the ice and by trolling in spring just after ice off. Watch for slot size restrictions on lake trout.

Sucker Lake (Map 40/B3)
Access to Sucker Lake is limited. Fishing success can be good at times for largemouth bass to 1.5 kg (3.5 lbs) or slow for generally small northern pike.

Sunken Lake (Map 35/C3)
Sunken Lake can be found off County Road 8 and has a number of cottages along its shoreline. The lake has been stocked with rainbow trout, which provide fast action in the spring. Brook trout are also thought to inhabit the lake, although fishing reports vary.

Sunny Lake (Map 25/B3)
The northern portion of Sunny Lake is developed, although the southern half is less busy. Fishing tends to be a little better in the southern half of the lake for smallmouth bass to 1.5 kg (3.5 lbs).

Surprise and Verner Lakes (Map 43/D5)
Verner and Surprise Lakes can be accessed via rough 4wd roads or on foot. The difficult access helps the brook trout fishery. Verner is stocked with brookies and also offers pumpkinseed sunfish if so desired.

Swamp Lake (Map 25/G1)
This small, secluded lake can be accessed by a 4wd road. The shallow lake has good fishing for smallmouth and largemouth bass in the 0.5–1 kg (1–2 lb) range.

Sward Lake (Map 44/G7)
This is a small, remote lake that can be accessed by a 4wd road. The 10 hectare lake offers fair fishing at times in the spring and fall for small brook trout. Brookies have been recently stocked, while pumpkinseed sunfish also roam the lake.

Talbot Lake (Map 26/C7)
Talbot Lake is a fair sized lake that can be good for bass at times. Generally the fishing is fair for average size smallmouth and largemouth bass, although some lunkers can be found along the islands.

Tamarack and Trooper Lakes (Map 27/F3)
Home to a few cottages, both lakes offer fair fishing for smallmouth and largemouth bass to 1.5 kg (3.5 lbs). For best results, try a spinner or a minnow imitation fly or lure.

Tangamong Lake (Map 29/B6)
Almost completely surrounded by private land, there is a public access point at the southwest end of the lake. The lake holds smallmouth and largemouth bass that can get to 1.5 kg (3 lbs). They are best fished in the weedy areas and along the rocky shoreline. One of the best places to try is where Tangamong and Whetstone Lake connect.

Tasso and Toad Lakes (Map 44/A5)
These lakes are found near the end of County Road 8 and offer fair fishing for smallmouth bass to 1.5 kg (3.5 lbs). The larger Tasso Lake also offers fishing for brook trout and lake trout to 80 cm (31 in). Brookies are becoming harder to find each year.

Tea Lake (Map 24/B4)
Tea Lake is home to a number of cottages along its shoreline and can be busy during the summer months. Fishing is fair for smallmouth bass, although success for walleye is usually limited.

Tea Lake (Map 43/B1)
Home to lake trout and stocked brook trout, this Tea Lake is found west of Island Lake Road. The 33 hectare lake is best fished in the winter or in spring just after ice off.

Teapot and Grouse Lakes (Map 34/G5–35/A5)
In the past these lakes were stocked with rainbow trout, however they have not been stocked in some time and the quality of the fishing in the lakes is unclear.

Ted Lake (Map 49/A1)
Found in French River Provincial Park, Ted Lake is mainly accessible by canoe. Fishing is good at times for panfish as well as nice sized smallmouth bass and northern pike.

Tedious and Bitter Lakes (Map 36/A4)
Located off Kennisis Lake Road (County Road 7), Bitter Lake is stocked with lake trout and also holds perch and rock bass. Tedious is stocked with rainbow trout along with naturally reproducing lake trout and walleye.

Ten Mile Lake (Map 33/A1–42/A7)
Ten Mile Lake is a fairly large secluded lake that can be accessed by a rough 2wd road. There is good fishing for smallmouth bass to 1.5 kg (3.5 lbs) at the lake. Top water flies and lures can create good action or a crayfish imitation worked slowly near bottom can be good.

Thrasher Murphy and Little Boot Lakes (Map 26/A3)
Accessed by a private road, these lakes offers good fishing for smallmouth and largemouth bass for those who ask permission to fish here. There is also a fair population of muskellunge in Thrasher Lake that can reach good sizes, while Little Boot Lake has also been stocked with rainbow trout in the past.

Three Legged Lake (Map 32/A3)
This is the northern access point for The Blackstone Harbour/Massasauga Wildlands Provincial Park. There is fair to good fishing at times for smallmouth bass in the 0.5–1 kg (1–2 lb) range and slow fishing for stocked rainbow trout.

Three Mile Lake (Map 31/F2)
Three Mile Lake is a fairly large lake found on Parry Island on Wasauksing First Nations land. Fishing for walleye to 2.5 kg (5.5 lbs) is fair, while the action for some nice sized smallmouth bass is generally good.

Three Mile Lake (Map 33/E4)
Fishing is generally fair for smallmouth and largemouth bass that average 0.5 kg (1 lb) in size. The best action for bass is often in the evenings at sundown. A small population of walleye is also in the lake that can be found to 2.5 kg (5.5 lbs).

Three Mile Lake (Map 43/A3)
East of Highway 11, Three Mile Lake Road provides decent access to this midsize lake. Recently stocked with walleye, Garden Island can be a good holding area for fish that can reach 3 kg (6.5 lbs) in size. Northern pike, smallmouth bass, rock bass and yellow perch also inhabit the lake.

Tilliard Lake (Map 63/C1)
Fishing in this small lake is often good for generally small largemouth bass and northern pike. Both of these sportfish species are quite aggressive top water feeders as they see little angler action throughout the year.

Tim Lake (Map 38/A5)
Off the west side of Highway 62 north of Bancroft, Tim Lake is stocked biennially with brook trout.

Too Good Pond (Map 2/B3)
The first full weekend past Canada Day, The Urban Fishing Festival hits this small, fishing pond, which holds brown bullhead, creek chub, goldfish, largemouth, northern pike, pumpkinseed and rock bass, as well as stocked rainbow trout.

Tory Lake (Map 28/A1)
Tory Lake can be found via a rough 2wd road and is stocked biennially with splake. Fishing for splake to 35 cm (14 in) can be good through the ice or in spring. There is also a fair population of smallmouth bass in the lake.

Traves Lake (Map 32/C3)
Traves Lake is tucked to the west of Blackstone Lake and offers good fishing at times for smallmouth bass. Much of the lake is surrounded by Crown land.

Triangle, Cherry and Turtle Lakes (Map 19/A1)
Triangle and Cherry lakes are stocked with lake trout, although Turtle Lake offers the best fishing opportunities with good action at times for smallmouth bass. Portages between the three lakes are short.

Trounce [Birchbark] Lake (Map 8/C5)
Trounce Lake holds a fair population of smallmouth and largemouth bass, although fishing can be slow at times. Try during the evening and overcast days for best action.

Trout and Long Lakes (Map 32/G2)
These two connected lakes are found off Highway 141. It is unknown whether there was ever trout in the lakes or not, although the lakes offer fair fishing for smallmouth and largemouth bass to 1.5 kg (3.5 lbs). There are a number of cottages on these lakes.

Trout Lake (Map 40/E3)
Home to a few lake trout, smallmouth bass are usually easier to catch. The average size of bass is about 1–1.5 kg (2–3.5 lb). Ice fishing is closed on the lake to protect the fragile natural lake trout fishery.

Trout Lake (Map 41/B6)
This lake can be accessed by a rough 2wd road and has a number of cottages along its shoreline. Anglers can expect fair to good fishing for smallmouth and largemouth bass to 1.5 kg (3.5 lbs) and fair fishing for lake trout. Lake trout are stocked regularly to offset the heavy winter and spring fishing pressure. Northern pike are also present here.

Trout Lake (Map 59/D4)
Trout Lake is a big, long lake to the west of Highway 535. Fishing in the lake is slow to fair at times for lake trout that can be found to 65 cm (26 in) in size. Walleye and northern pike are also found in the lake but your best bet for angling success is for smallmouth bass.

Trout Lake (Map 62/F2–63/A1)
Found east of North Bay, this is a very popular lake. Anglers will find a variety of sportfish including lake trout, muskellunge, northern pike and walleye. However, for more consistent action, it is best to target both smallmouth and largemouth bass. Try working the bays during dusk. For something different, anglers can even look for ouananiche, a strain of Atlantic salmon.

Troutspawn Lakes (Map 44/E7)
Troutspawn Lake can be found via a rough 2wd road, while Little Troutspawn Lake is accessible by bushwhacking from the bigger lake. The lakes have been stocked in the past with brook trout and it is believed that a self-sustaining population still exists in the lakes.

Turtle and Gilbank Lakes (Map 32/G2)
These two lakes have a number of cottages along their shorelines and provide fair fishing for nice sized bass. Both lakes have smallmouth bass, while Gilbank Lake also has a number of largemouth bass. Top water plugs, lures and flies can all be productive.

Turtle Lake (Map 63/C2)
Found in Mattawa River Provincial Park, this Turtle Lake offers fishing for stocked lake trout. This lake also holds good populations of northern pike, walleye, smallmouth and largemouth bass.

Tuya Lake (Map 46/B3)
Accessed by following the powerline access road, Tuya Lake is stocked with brook trout.

Twelve Mile Bay (Map 32/A7-C7)
Twelve Mile Bay juts inland over 10 km (6 mi) and offers good fishing for northern pike that can reach sizes of up to 13 kg (28.5 lbs). This is muskie country where big muskellunge can also be found roaming in the bay, especially in the fall. Smallmouth and largemouth bass as well as panfish fishing can be very good at times for bass, while walleye averaging 1 kg (2 lbs) can be also be caught in the bay.

Twelve Mile Lake (Map 26/F1–35/F7)
Twelve Mile Lake is one of the larger lakes in the area and has a boat launch on its northern shore off Highway 35. Anglers can expect slow to fair fishing for natural lake trout to 75 cm (30 in) and good fishing for smallmouth bass to 2 kg (4.5 lbs). Trolling with spoons in spring after ice off can produce some decent trout.

Twentyeight Lake (Map 43/E2)
Fishing at this hidden lake is good in the winter and spring for nice sized brook trout. Fly-fishing can be great in spring.

Twentyseven Lake (Map 53/B4)
Twentyseven Lake supports a natural brook trout fishery, which provides good fishing at times for nice sized trout.

Twinpine Lakes (Map 29/G4)
West Twinpine Lake is stocked biannually with brook trout and fishing can be good periodically through the ice or in spring, just after ice off. The Hastings Heritage Trail passes near this series of lakes, which are found just south of Gilmour.

Two Island Lake (Map 31/F3)
Two Island Lake is a secluded wilderness lake found in the heart of The Blackstone Harbour Provincial Park. The only access to the lake is by orienteering trail. As a result, the lake is rarely visited and fishing for largemouth bass is rumoured to be very good for bass to 2 kg (4.5 lbs).

Two Islands Lake (Map 36/E6)
Anglers visiting Two Islands Lake east of Drag Lake can expect fair fishing for lake trout and good fishing at times for smallmouth bass. Be sure to check for special regulations on this lake.

Tyson Lake (Map 58/A6)
Fishing on the large, complex lake is fair for northern pike in the 2 kg (4.5 lb) range and good at times for smallmouth bass in the 1 kg (2 lbs) range. Lake trout also inhabit the lake, although fishing can be frustrating at times.

Union Lake (Map 27/C5)
This lake is mainly surrounded by Crown land and has fair to good fishing for smallmouth and largemouth bass. Top water lures and flies can create a frenzy of action on this lake.

Upper Oxbow Lake (Map 44/A6)
This hidden lake provides fair to good fishing at times for small brook trout. The 16 hectare lake is stocked every other year and is best fished with small flies or worms.

Upper Raft Lake (Map 43/D5)
Upper Raft Lake is a hidden difficult to access lake that supposedly has been stocked in the past with rainbow trout. Fishing reports vary and the fishing quality is currently unknown.

Urbach Lake (Map 29/C4)
Found south of Highway 620 near Wollaston Lake, Urbach Lake stocked regularly with splake. It is also home to largemouth bass, pumpkinseed sunfish and yellow perch.

Venner Lake (Map 27/C6)
Venner Lake is located off Crystal Lake Road just before the bigger Lake. The lake is small and fishing for smallmouth and largemouth bass is often slow.

Vicary and Westphal Lakes (Map 31/G3)
These two small, secluded wilderness lakes can be reached via rustic trails or orienteering. Both are good bass lakes with Vicary offering smallmouth to 1.5 kg (3.5 lbs) and Westphal Lake offering largemouth bass to 2 kg (4.5 lbs).

Victoria and Wolf Lakes (Map 26/B4)
Accessed off the Ganaraska Trail in Queen Elizabeth II Provincial Park, Victoria Lake is home to smallmouth and largemouth bass, rainbow trout and pumpkinseed sunfish and yellow perch. Further west, Wolf Lake was stocked in the past with splake and also holds both bass species. Those willing to bushwhack south will find good fishing for smallmouth and largemouth bass in Jordan's Lake.

Victoria Lake (Map 46/E2)
Found near the boundary of Algonquin Park, there are several cottages along the shoreline. Fishing is good for smallmouth bass to 2 kg (4.5 lbs) and fair for lake trout to 70 cm (28 in). Watch for slot size restrictions and special winter regulations on the lakers.

Virtue Lake (Map 32/E2)
This small Cottage Country lake provides fair fishing for average sized smallmouth bass and northern pike. Heavy fishing pressure and settlement on the lake has reduced the quality of the fishery.

Wadsworth Lake (Map 47/F5)
Found off Old Barry's Bay Road, Wadsworth Lake is stocked annually with lake trout and offers fair fishing for lakers. In addition, this lake holds nice populations of walleye, northern pike, smallmouth and largemouth bass.

Wahwashkesh [The Big] Lake (Map 40/G1–51/A7)
Also known as The Big Lake in the south and The Top Lake in the north, Wahwashkesh Lake is indeed a big lake. Anglers will find good fishing at times for smallmouth and largemouth bass to 2 kg (4.5 lbs). Walleye, lake trout, northern pike and panfish are also found in the lake in fair numbers.

Walker Lake (Map 57/D7)
Fishing in Walker Lake is good for stocked brook trout, which can reach 35 cm (14 in) in size. Try ice fishing or fly fishing for good success.

Waseosa Lake (Map 43/B7)
Waseosa Lake has a number of cottages along its shoreline and can be accessed by a few different roads to the west of Highway 11. The lake provides fair fishing for smallmouth bass to 1.5 kg (3.5 lbs) and good fishing at times for stocked rainbow trout. Lake trout and brook trout were once natural inhabitants of the lake; however, these species are reported to be extinct from the lake.

Wasi Lake (Map 63/B6)
Wasi Lake is a popular cottage destination in summer and sees more than its fair share of anglers. Fishing is fair at times for walleye and can be good for smallmouth bass, which reach sizes of up to 2 kg (4.5 lbs) on the lake. Look for underwater rock structure for smallmouth bass and walleye.

Waterloo Lake (Map 66/A4)
Lake trout in Waterloo Lake can reach 45 cm (18 in) and brook trout average 25–35 cm (10–14 in). However, the trout population has shown signs of stress and it is imperative to practice catch and release to maintain a quality fishery.

Wee Trout Lake (Map 57/G3)
Wee Trout can be reached by trail from Barron Canyon Road about 1.2 km before the Sand Lake Gate and Algonquin Park. The lake is stocked with brook trout and provides good fishing in the spring for brookies to 30 cm (12 in).

Weeden Lake (Map 32/E1)
Weeden Lake is a short portage to the east of the bigger Flaxman Lake. Weeden is only 4 hectares in size and was recently stocked with brook trout.

Weeharry Lake (Map 64/C5)
This small, 15 hectare, lake is located just outside of Algonquin Park's northern boundary and can be accessed from Bronson Lake by trail. Stocked brook trout inhabit the lake and fishing is fair throughout the winter and in spring.

Weismuller Lake (Map 25/C2)
Weismuller Lake is a small, shallow lake east of Gravenhurst that contains a fair population of largemouth bass.

Welch Lakes (Map 35/D6)
Lower Welch Lake used to be stocked with rainbow trout. These days, anglers can expect to find only smallmouth bass. Welch Lake also offers fair fishing for smallmouth bass. There is a boat launch onto Lower Welch Lake.

Wellers Bay [Lake Ontario] (Map 13/B7)
Wellers Bay is protected from the big waters of Lake Ontario, by Becroft Point. Closer to the mainland, anglers can expect to find mostly northern pike and walleye. Further out onto the lake, on the west side of Becroft Point, Chinook salmon, largemouth bass and the odd muskellunge can be found.

Wendigo Lake (Map 53/A3)
Stocked with rainbow trout, Wendigo Lake has good fishing for rainbow up to 35 cm (14 in) in size. The lake is easily accessed from the Forestry Tower Road en route to Kawawaymog Lake and Algonquin Park.

Wendigo Lake (Map 65/F5)
Wendigo Lake is a quieter access point into Algonquin Park. The lake offers fair fishing for lake and brook trout. Lakers are caught in the 45–55 cm (18–22 in) range, while brookies average 25–35 cm (10–14 in).

West Aumond Lake (Map 65/A4)
This secluded walleye lake receives most of its pressure in winter by ice fishing anglers. Walleye average 0.5–1 kg (1–2 lbs).

West Lake (Map 36/D5)
West Lake is stocked with rainbow trout. There is also a good population of smallmouth bass in the lake.

Wet Lake (Map 53/D3)
Wet Lake offers good fishing at times for natural brook trout, especially in spring and late September. Brookies are also found in the unnamed lake to the east, just before the Algonquin Park border.

Whetstone Lakes (Map 43/D1)
These lakes offer fair to good fishing for brook trout. Whetstone Lake is stocked every few years with brookies. Just north of Whetstone Lake, there are two unnamed lakes that also offer decent fishing for nice sized brookies.

White Lake (Map 27/D4)
Visitors to White Lake can expect fair fishing for smallmouth and largemouth bass to 2.5 kg (5.5 lbs). Muskellunge fishing is usually slow for muskie in the 4–6 kg (9–13 lb) range, although fishing picks up in the fall.

Whiteduck Lake (Map 47/D7)
Fishing for stocked rainbows in the 25–30 cm (10–12 in) range can be good at times, especially in spring. The lake can be accessed off Highway 62.

Whitefish and Cosh Lakes (Map 32/F2)
Whitefish Lake can be found just off Highway 141 and is a popular lake. Anglers can expect fair fishing for smallmouth bass to 1.5 kg (3.5 lbs) and slow fishing for natural lake trout. Lake trout were stocked in the past. To the north, Cosh Lake is another smallmouth bass alternative.

Whitestone Lake (Map 41/D2)
Fishing at this lake is fair for smallmouth and largemouth bass as well as northern pike. Walleye are also found in the lake in fair numbers. Watch for special walleye restrictions.

Wicklow Lake (Map 46/F7)
Wicklow is an out of the way lake that is stocked every few years with brook trout.

Widgeon Lakes (Map 53/B7)
Widgeon Lake can be accessed by a dirt road and offers good fishing for stocked splake. Little Widgeon can be found via canoe and a short portage. The smaller lake hosts stocked brook trout.

Wilbermere Lake (Map 28/B1–37/B7)
Fishing for stocked lake trout that average 35 cm (14 in) is fair to good here. A fair population of smallmouth bass also inhabits the lake.

Wilcox Lake (Map 32/B4)
This small secluded lake lies partially within the boundary of the Blackstone Harbour Provincial Park. The difficult to access lake provides good fishing for largemouth bass.

Wildcat Lake (Map 34/F4)
This is a small lake that has a few cottages along its shoreline to the east of the larger Echo Lake. Wildcat has fair fishing for smallmouth bass.

Wildcat Lakes (Map 36/B1)
Wildcat Lake lies within the Haliburton Forest and is the easier of the two to access. South Wildcat Lake offers fair fishing for natural lake trout and is part of the winter/spring fishing sanctuary. Both lakes also have small populations of native brook trout.

Wilson Lakes (Map 40/C2)
These two remote access lakes offer good fishing at times for smallmouth bass and fair fishing for northern pike and walleye.

Wish Lake (Map 46/C2)
Wish Lake is a hidden lake found to the east of Major Lake Road. The lake holds stocked brook trout.

Wiwassasegen Lake (Map 40/D4)
Found in Round Lake Nature Reserve, Wiwassasegen Lake can only be accessed by foot or canoe in summer months or by snowmobile in winter. The lake offers very good fishing at times for smallmouth and largemouth bass to 2 kg (4.5 lbs).

Wolf Lake (Map 28/C6)
As part of the Wolf Lake Canoe Route, visitors can access the lake from Anstruther Lake Road. The lake offers fair fishing for smallmouth bass to 1.5 kg (3.5 lbs) and slow fishing for small muskellunge. There is a public boat launch at the north end of the lake.

Wolf Lake (Map 30/A7)
Located not far from the east side of Highway 62, this lake offers fair to good fishing for largemouth bass. Bass average about 0.5–1 kg (1–2 lb), although can be found bigger.

Wolf Lake (Map 36/B2)
Wolf Lake is found in the Haliburton Forest Reserve and is a nice place to wet a line. There is a fair population of smallmouth bass, which are best fished in the summer months, while fishing for stocked splake can be good through the ice or in spring. There are a few campsites available at the lake.

Wolf Lake (Map 44/F6)
North of Livingstone Lake, Wolf Lake had decent road access and a boat launch. The 69 hectare lake is stocked with splake and brook trout on occasion, but also offers smallmouth bass as well as pumpkinseed sunfish and yellow perch.

Wollaston Lake (Map 29/B4)
Like many of the lakes in this region, the main fish species here are smallmouth and largemouth bass. The lake also holds lake trout and northern pike, although fishing for these is usually slow.

Wood Lake (Map 25/F1)
North of Highway 118, Wood Lake is a mid-size lake that has recently been stocked with walleye. However, the fishing remains more consistent for bass or, if preferred, pumpkinseed sunfish. Smallmouth and largemouth bass can be found to 1.5 kg (3.5 lbs), while walleye can be found up to 3.5 kg (8 lbs).

Woods Bay (Map 32/B5)
Woods Bay is a part of the renowned Moon River basin and is a hotspot for migratory walleye in the spring and fall. The bay can be quite good for walleye averaging 1–1.5 kg (2–3 lbs). However, northern pike are the most abundant predatory fish in the area. Fishing can be very good at times for pike that can reach up to 10 kg (22 lbs). Fishing for monster muskie can be fair, especially in the fall. Fishing for smallmouth and largemouth bass to 3 kg (6.5 lbs) can also be very good at times.

Woods Lake (Map 33/B3)
Woods Lake is a small hidden lake found via a 4wd road and offers good fishing for smallmouth bass to 1.5 kg (3.5 lbs). Not many people know of this small Cottage Country lake.

Wren and Grindstone Lakes (Map 35/C4)
These Frost Centre Lakes can be found west of Highway 35. The lakes are stocked every two years with splake, while Wren Lake also has a fair population of smallmouth bass. Little Wren is another stocked splake lake in the area.

Wyley's Lake (Map 27/D3)
This small, hidden lake is located north of Highway 503 and was once stocked with rainbow trout. Current reports are sketchy.

Wylie Lake (Map 57/F1)
Located within the Petawawa Forest Reserve, Wylie Lake is stocked with splake, which are most active in winter and spring.

Yankton Lake (Map 36/G6–37/A6)
Found north of Wilberforce off of County Road 15, this lake offers good fishing for smallmouth bass in the 1 kg (2 lb) range.

Young Lake (Map 25/D7)
Young Lake provides fair fishing for smallmouth bass that average 0.5 kg (1 lb) and lake trout to 75 cm (30 in). Lake trout were once stocked in the lake.

Young Lake (Map 33/C4)
South of Highway 141 to the east of Rosseau, this Young Lake is stocked periodically with lake trout. Anglers can also find smallmouth bass.

Young Lake (Map 34/C4)
This lake offers fishing for a variety of species including northern pike, bass, muskellunge and walleye. The best action is usually for bass.

ALGONQUIN PROVINCIAL PARK LAKES

Algonquin Park remains one of the most popular fishing destinations in the region. Anglers should note the special regulations and all visitors require park permits when visiting these lakes.

Allan and North Depot Lakes (Map 65/F6)
Found south of the Wendigo Lake Access Point, lake and brook trout are found in both Allan and North Depot in decent numbers. There are reports of 60 cm (24 in) lake trout taken annually.

Alsever, Roundbush and Vireo Lakes (Map 56/E7)
All three lakes offer fair fishing for trout, especially in spring and late September. Alsever Lake is inhabited by lake and brook trout. Roundbush Lake houses brook trout. Vireo Lake is the most difficult lake to access with lake trout.

Animoosh, Alluring and Cat Lakes (Map 56/B5)
Animoosh Lake is the only one of these three lakes on an established canoe route. Cat Lake sits about 700 metres north of Animoosh Lake, and Alluring is about another 500 metres from Cat Lake. Fishing in all three lakes is good for brook trout in the 40 cm (16 in) range. Lake trout also inhabit Alluring Lake.

Aubrey Lake (Map 45/F4)
Found near the northwestern shore of Galeairy Lake across the old OA & PS railbed, Aubrey Lake is quite small. It does have a good population of smallmouth bass that can reach the 1 kg (2 lb) range.

Aura Lee and Bug Lakes (Map 64/G7–65/A7)
These lakes can both be found by portage from Cedar Lake's northeastern corner. Fishing is generally fair for brook trout in the 20–30 cm (8–12 in) range. There are two campsites located on each of these small lakes.

Bailey, Band and Boot Lakes (Map 46/A2)
These lakes are in a lower used area of Algonquin and fishing is decent, especially in spring. Bailey and Band Lake are inhabited by brook trout, while Boot Lake offers both brook and lake trout.

Barron Lake (Map 56/F4)
Six wilderness campsites are found on Barron Lake. Fishing for brook trout is fair for decent sized fish, while fishing for smallmouth bass can be very good at times. Brook trout have been caught in excess of 35 cm (14 in) and smallmouth bass can reach 2 kg (4.5 lbs) in size.

Basin Lake (Map 57/B6)
Found at the end of a rough road, Basin Lake has four charming campsites, including one on a small island. Fishing is fair for smallmouth bass to 1.5 kg (3.5 lbs). Northern pike are also found in the 1.5–2.5 kg (3.5–5.5 lb) range.

Big Bob Lake (Map 53/F6)
This remote Algonquin lake is rarely visited. There are three wilderness campsites and fishing can be good in spring or late September for brook trout.

Big Crow and Little Crow Lakes (Map 55/C5)
These lakes offer quite good fishing for trout, especially in spring. Brook trout reportedly caught in the 50 cm (20 in) range are found in both lakes and lake trout are also found in Big Crow Lake. There are 10 rustic campsites on Big Crow Lake and another three on Little Crow.

Big George Lake (Map 65/E7)
Found along a detour from the canoe route along the Petawawa River to Radiant Lake, Big George has two scenic campsites, including a beautiful island site. The lake holds brook trout, which are most active in spring, after ice off.

Big Porcupine and Bonnechere Lakes (Map 44/G6–45/A6)
There are a number of rustic campsites found on both lakes and fishing is fair for brook trout and lake trout in the spring and slows considerably as summer progresses. Brookies average 25–30 cm (10–12 in) and lake trout can be found to 55 cm (22 in).

Big Rock Lake (Map 37/B3)
This interior lake is located in the southern panhandle of Algonquin Park. The lake can be accessed via portage from Kingscote Lake to the west or from Byers Lake to the east. Fishing can be quite good in the spring for average sized lake trout.

Big Trout Lake (Map 54/G6–56/A6)
Found at least two days from the nearest access point, there are over 30 interior campsites on the lake. Both lake and brook trout inhabit the lake, but fishing is tough most of the time, due mainly to the size of the lake.

Biggar Lake (Map 54/A2)
Lake trout can be found in excess of 70 cm (28 in), while brook trout have been caught to 45 cm (18 in). Locating these trout can be a challenge.

Billings and Little Billings Lakes (Map 37/A1)
Due to the number and distance of the portages, these lakes are rarely visited. Brook trout to 35 cm (14 in) are possible.

Billy Lake (Map 46/C1)
Billy Lake is found off the Major Lake Road and offers six campsites. The lake has been stocked with splake that average 30–35 cm (12–14 in) in size.

Birchcliffe and Calm Lakes (Map 54/B3)
It will take at least two days to access these two lakes. There are two nice campsites on Birchcliffe Lake and an old ranger cabin to rent. Anglers will find good numbers of smallmouth bass, while Calm Lake is home to small brook trout.

Bissett and Weasel Lakes (Map 65/G6–66/A6)
Bissett Lake is much larger than Weasel Lake, although both lakes offer fair fishing for nice sized brook trout. Water levels on Bissett Creek can be very low during summer, which can make these lakes difficult to get to.

Blackfox Lake (Map 45/C2)
Blackfox Lake is stocked every few years with brook trout. There are also lake trout in this difficult to access Algonquin Park lake.

Blue and Longer Lakes (Map 54/F6)
Accessed by portage from Big Trout Lake, there are three campsites found on Longer Lake and one on Blue Lake. Both lakes offer good fishing in spring for average sized lake trout. Brook trout are also found in Longer Lake.

Bluebell and Hilly Lakes (Map 44/E6)
These lakes offer good fishing in the spring for small brook trout. The lakes can only be accessed by canoe and low maintenance portages. There is a rustic campsite available on Bluebell Lake.

Bluff and Brewer Lakes and Lake St. Anthony (Map 45/F2)
Accessed off Highway 60, Brewer Lake is the only lake that can be seen from the highway and is stocked with splake every few years. Lake St. Anthony is a small lake that can be accessed by portage from Brewer Lake. Bluff Lake is accessed by portage from Highway 60.

Booth Lake (Map 46/A1)
Booth Lake is a very scenic lake that makes a nice weekend destination with several beautiful campsites. Fishing can be decent for lake trout and brook trout, while smallmouth bass and northern pike are quite active as the waters warm. There are some large lake trout and pike landed here each year. Those looking for brook trout should try near the creek mouths and the inlet of the Opeongo around the dam.

Branch and Byers Lakes (Map 37/A3)
These lakes are somewhat connected and provide fishing opportunities for average sized lake trout and brook trout. There are a few rustic camping sites available on Byers Lake.

Bruce and Owl Lakes (Map 44/G3)
Bruce Lake is stocked with splake that can reach the 55 cm (22 in) range, while Owl Lake continues to support a small lake trout population.

Brule and Potter Lakes (Map 44/D2)
Found off the old OA&PS (Ottawa Arnprior & Parry Sound) railway, these lakes are inhabited by lake trout and smallmouth bass. Brook trout are reportedly still caught in Potter Lake, although the introduction of smallmouth bass reduced brook trout numbers dramatically.

Bud and Leaf Lakes (Map 45/G3)
Found off a trail from Highway 60 near the East Gate of Algonquin Park, Bud Lake is stocked every few years with splake. Fishing is fair for splake to 40 cm (19 in). Leaf Lake can be found by following a small creek from Pinetree Lake. The lake is stocked with brook trout and offers fair fishing for small brookies.

Burnt Island Lake (Map 44/G1)
Burnt Island is one of the bigger lakes in the park and has several spectacular campsites to choose from. There are also some big lake trout present in the deep lake. Smallmouth bass are often easier to find as they prefer the shallower bays.

Burntroot Lake (Map 54/F4)
This large lake offers over 25 great interior campsites, but fishing can be frustrating at times. The trout are hard to find, although perseverance is often rewarded, as lake trout have been caught exceeding 60 cm (24 in) and can be found to 70 cm (28 in). Brook trout are also found and often top 30–35 cm (12–14 in) in size.

Butt and Little Trout Lakes (Map 43/G1–54/B7)
These two lakes lie in a popular area. Butt Lake is the larger of the two and offers fair fishing for lake and brook trout. Lake trout can be found larger than 60 cm (24 in), while brook trout are in the 25–30 cm (10–12 in) range. The fishing in Little Trout Lake is generally better than in Butt Lake.

Cache Lake (Map 45/A3)
One of the most developed lakes in Algonquin Park, Cache Lake was once a good lake trout lake, but is not nearly the lake it once was. Special slot size restrictions are in place on the lakes, however, practicing catch and release can help greatly in the preservation of these great fish. Smallmouth bass were introduced many years ago and provide fair angling opportunities.

Calumet and Cuckoo Lakes (Map 55/A3)
Found northwest of Hogan Lake, Calumet Lake has two campsites along its shoreline, while Cuckoo Lake has one. Both lakes are inhabited by brook trout, although lake trout are also found in Calumet Lake. The trout found in these lakes may not be as big as in other larger interior lakes, but are plentiful in spring.

Canisbay Lake (Map 45/A3)
Found along the Algonquin Park Highway 60 Corridor, the busy campground and 15 paddle-in campsites ensure this is a busy place in summer. Lake trout are found in small numbers, while smallmouth bass are the most productive sport fish on the lake. Bucketmouths to 2 kg (4.5 lbs) are not out of the question.

Canoe Lake (Map 44/E4)
The access point and close proximity to Highway 60 keeps a steady flow of trippers running through here. Anglers can find a few lake trout and decent smallmouth bass fishing.

Carcajou Lake (Map 56/G4)
It is a challenging, marshy one-day trip from the Achray Access Point to this lake. Those that trek in will be rewarded with four scenic campsites on the north shore and good fishing in spring for lake and brook trout.

Carl Wilson Lake (Map 54/G1–64/G7)
Large portions of the lake's shoreline have been designated natural reserve areas. There are also seven wilderness campsites on the lake. Anglers can find good sized lake trout and brook trout. Try near the dam on the north end.

Casey Lake (Map 44/A2)
Found between Daisy and Rain Lakes, there are three beautiful campsites on Casey Lake and fishing is usually fair for small brook trout.

Catfish Lake (Map 55/A2)
Home to many intriguing arms, there are 12 rustic campsites on Catfish Lake, including many great island sites. Fishing can be good in spring or late September for lake and brook trout.

Cauchon, Cauchon Lakes (Map 64/E7)
Lake and brook trout inhabit the lakes in fair numbers and fishing can be decent at times during spring when trout cruise near the surface. Eleven interior campsites are found on Cauchon and another six on Little Cauchon.

Cauliflower Lake (Map 45/G7–46/A7)
Fishing for both lake trout and brook trout is fair at times in the spring just after ice off. There are also smallmouth here, too. The main access point to the lake is from Hay Lake to the east and there are four backcountry campsites available at Cauliflower Lake.

Cedar Lake (Map 55/D1–66/A7)
Cedar Lake is one of the largest lakes in Algonquin Park and is a designated interior access point. The village of Brent is located on the lake's north shore, along with the Brent Campground. In addition, there are also over 25 canoe access campsites scattered about the big lake. Fishing in the lake is generally slow for walleye and lake trout, while smallmouth bass offer the best opportunity at angling success. Fishing can be good at times for smallmouth that have been caught in the 2.5 kg (5.5 lb) range. Brook trout also inhabit the lake, although are tough to find.

Chickaree Lake (Map 55/B6)
This small lake has no designated campsites, although it makes a perfect day trip from Merchant Lake. Lake trout are found in decent numbers, although they are not as big as those found in the larger interior lakes.

Cinderella Lake (Map 55/C2)
Like a dream, Cinderella is out there. However, finding it takes real perseverance. Those that due will find good brook trout fishing.

Clarke Lake (Map 45/G3)
Clarke Lake was once a natural brook trout lake. Today, smallmouth bass can also be found and provide fair fishing for bass to 1.5 kg (3.5 lbs).

Claude and Grape Lakes (Map 44/F5)
Claude Lake is stocked every few years with splake, while the more remote Claude Lake and has been stocked in the past with brook trout.

Clemow Lake (Map 56/F3)
Found west of the much larger Grand Lake, fishing is good for smallmouth bass to 2 kg (4.5 lbs) and fair for lake trout to 60 cm (24 in) in size. Opposite the rail bed on the lake's northern shoreline are four interior campsites.

Clover Lake (Map 57/C6)
Clover Lake can be reached within a long day from the Achray Access Point, but an early start is needed. There are five campsites on the lake's shore and a number of smaller lakes can be reached within one or two portages. Fishing on the lake is rumoured to be good for nice sized brook trout.

Club and Waterclear Lakes (Map 64/D7)
These two interior brook trout lakes offer fair fishing for average sized brookies in spring. There are three wilderness campsites found on each lake.

Clydegate Lake (Map 45/E6)
This is a large lake by Algonquin standards and is a popular destination lake for southern interior canoe trippers. There are six rustic campsites available on the lake and fishing is fair for brook trout.

Coon Lake (Map 45/D3)
Coon Lake is home to vehicle accessible campground making it a popular fishery in the park. The lake is stocked with splake and also offers lake trout along with pumpkinseed sunfish and yellow perch for the younger anglers.

Cork Lake (Map 57/E3)
Part of a small series of lakes that are found south of the Barron Canyon, there are three wilderness campsites here. Fishing is good at times for smallmouth bass.

Costello Lake (Map 45/F3)
Costello Lake can be accessed from the Opeongo Lake Road and is home to a nice picnic site. The lake is stocked with splake.

Crotch, Farm and Shall Lakes (Map 46/C1)
All three of these lakes are easily accessed from the Shall Lake Access Point and home to interior campsites for those wishing to overnight. Fishing is fair for northern pike that are most predominantly found in the weedier sections. Smallmouth bass are also found in decent numbers, while lake trout remain a popular pursuit during the cooler spring months.

Daisy Lake (Map 44/A1)
There are seven rustic campsites on the lake, with two of the sites lying on the lake's large island. Fishing is slow throughout the year for both lake trout and brook trout.

David and Mubwayaka Lake (Map 54/A7)
These lakes offer fair fishing for brook trout in the 25–30 cm (10–12 in) range. The main access route to these lakes is from Butt Lake.

Delano and Hilliard Lakes (Map 44/G4–45/A4)
There is one rustic campsite at each lake. Hilliard Lake is stocked with splake every few years, which provides fair fishing for splake to 60 cm (24 in). Delano Lake continues to have a small population of lake trout; however, fishing is relatively slow.

Devine Lake (Map 54/D6)
Devine is rarely visited because of the difficult canoe route and long portages. The one exquisite island campsite is rumoured to be a favourite among poachers of days gone by. On average, brook trout in the lake are not very big, however, they can be found exceeding 30 cm (12 in).

Dickson and Little Dickson Lakes (Map 56/B5)
While outdoor writers may overstate their reputations at times, the Dickson Lakes are still quite productive. Brook trout have been found to 50 cm (20 in), while good sized lake trout are also found in Dickson Lake. The trout in Little Dickson Lake are somewhat smaller, however brook trout are caught in excess of 40 cm (16 in). Twelve wilderness campsites are located on Dickson Lake and another three can be found on Little Dickson.

Dividing Lake (Map 45/A7)
Fishing for average sized brook trout here is good in the spring and fall. There are two rustic campsites at the lake and the western shore is part of the Dividing Lake Provincial Park. The beautiful old growth stand of white pine trees is worthy of a look.

Erables and Maple Lakes (Map 54/C1)
Found within a day from the Kiosk Access Point, there are 12 interior campsites on scenic Erables Lake. In spring, lake trout and brook trout fishing can be good for decent sized trout.

Ermine Lake (Map 44/C6)
Ermine Lake is stocked with splake every couple of years, and supports a very small natural brook trout population. The out of the way lake is difficult to get to.

Eustache Lake (Map 56/C2)
The route to Eustache Lake entails travelling up the Petawawa River followed by a gruelling portage. It is the deepest lake in Algonquin Park and wonderfully clear. Adding to the scenery are magnificent cliffs that surround the lake. Fishing in the lake can be good at times in spring for nice sized brook and lake trout.

Farm Bay Lake (Map 45/F5)
This small lake can only be found by following a small stream from Purcell Cove on Galeairy Lake. Farm Bay has been stocked with brook trout.

Farncomb Lake (Map 55/F3)
Reached by a short portage near the north end of Lake Lavieille, there are no campsites on this lake. Fishing is reportedly good at times for brook trout to 40 cm (16 in).

Fassett and Shad Lakes (Map 53/E1)
It is at least a two day trip from the nearest access point to reach these lakes. The scenery is magnificent and the fishing is good. Both lakes are inhabited by brook trout, while Fassett Lake also has lake trout. There are two wilderness campsites on Shad Lake and another three on Fassett Lake.

Fisher and Cloud Lakes (Map 45/E4)
Fisher Lake rests next to the Rock Lake Road and offers stocked brook trout and lake trout. Nearby Cloud Lake is accessed by the Centennial Ridges Trail and is home to stocked brook trout along with lake trout and splake.

Fitz, Gerald and Reed Lakes (Map 66/A7)
Short portages separate all three lakes, making them easily accessible. Fishing is fair on all three lakes for decent sized brook trout. To keep these lakes as a quality fishery, be sure to limit your catch.

Florence and Frank Lakes (Map 45/B1)
These southern interior lakes are often passed through by canoeists en route to other destinations. Both lakes provide small brook trout.

Fools and Hailstorm Lakes (Map 45/A1–55/B7)
These remote lakes hold both lake and brook trout. Currently, there are no developed canoe routes or interior campsites in these Algonquin Park lakes.

Found Lake (Map 44/G3)
Tucked on the south side of Highway 60, to the north of Tanamakoon Lake, Found Lake is a 12 hectare lake. Stocked with splake and brook trout, there are also lake trout, rainbow trout, smallmouth bass and yellow perch.

Foys Lake (Map 56/G5)
The Basin Lake Road travels from Bonnechere Provincial Park, deep into the Algonquin interior. But it is still a long trek into Foys from the road. Brook trout can be found to 35 cm (14 in) and lake trout have been caught to 45 cm (18 in). There are three interior campsites found on the lake.

Francis Lake (Map 56/A2)
Part of the Petawawa River system, Francis sits down river from Radiant Lake. Brook trout are hard to find, but bass are plentiful.

Fraser and Sylvia Lakes (Map 45/F4)
Fraser Lake supports a small lake trout population that is most active in early spring. Sylvia Lake offers fishing for both brook and lake trout.

Galeairy Lake (Map 45/F5–46/A5)
One of the access points to Algonquin Park's southern panhandle, Galeairy is quite large and often busy. It is inhabited by lake trout, smallmouth and largemouth bass. Bass fishing is fair throughout the lake for fish to 2.5 kg (5.5 lbs). Fishing for lake trout is slow most of the year, although it picks up in late winter/early spring. Lakers can be found in excess of 75 cm (30 in).

Gem and Sandy Lakes (Map 45/F5)
These two small, southern Algonquin lakes are stocked with brook trout. There is an established portage to Gem Lake from Pen Lake. Fishing in Gem can be good at times for generally small brook trout. A rustic trail leads to Sandy Lake, where fishing is good at times for small brookies.

Ghost Lake (Map 65/C7)
Two secluded interior campsites are found on the lake and fishing can be good for small brook trout.

Gibson Lake (Map 54/A4)
There are four campsites and an old cabin on Gibson Lake, which is at least a two day trip to get to. Fishing is fair for brook trout to 30 cm (12 in).

Gilmour and Tecumseh Lakes (Map 65/B7)
These lakes rest in the bottom of the Brent Crater and have a heavy limestone base. The limestone is so rich that Gilmour Lake is the only lake in the park that is not affected by acid rain. Fishing in the lakes is fair for decent sized brook trout. Lake trout are also found in Gilmour Lake.

Glacier, Gull and Varley Lakes (Map 55/A1)
These three, small trout lakes are found en route from Cedar Lake to Carl Wilson Lake. All three lakes are a nice place to spend some time and there is a campsite on Gull and Varley Lakes. Fishing is often good in spring for brook trout.

Godda and Tattler Lakes (Map 45/G1–46/A1)
Godda Lake is a few portages away from Booth Lake and provides decent fishing for lake and brook trout. Lakers can be found to 55 cm (22 in), while brookies can be caught up to 40 cm (16 in). Tattler Lake is really an extension of Booth Lake's western side. Fishing for smallmouth bass is good throughout the season and the odd brook trout is still found.

Gordon and Rosepond Lakes (Map 45/E4)
Rosepond is a small lake that is stocked with a couple hundred splake every few years. In the last five years, it has been stocked with brook trout once. Gordon Lake is inhabited by smallmouth bass that can reach 2 kg (4.5 lbs) in size. Fishing for smallmouth can be good during overcast periods.

Gouinlock Lake (Map 64/F7)
Found via portage from the south shore of Little Cauchon Lake, there are two secluded campsites on this lake. Nice sized lake and brook trout are available.

Grand Lake (Map 56/G3–57/C3)
Home to a designated access point and the popular Achray Campground this lake can be a busy destination. There are 19 interior campsites, while the Eastern Pines Backpacking Trail and the old Canadian National Railway bed travel along the entire length of the lake to help spread the crowds. Fishing is generally slow for lake trout and is often good for smallmouth bass. Brook trout are also found in the lake, but fishing is spotty.

Grant and Jake Lakes (Map 45/A3)
Found just south of Highway 60, the Track and Tower Trail travels past Grant Lake, while Jake Lake can be walked to from the highway. Grant Lake is stocked with splake every few years and offers fair fishing in spring for splake to 40 cm (16 in). Smallmouth bass also inhabit the lake and provide fair fishing throughout the summer months. Jake Lake is stocked every few years with brook trout.

Greenleaf Lake (Map 56/F3)
Set in a designated nature reserve, visitors will find three picturesque campsites here. Lake trout and smallmouth bass are present.

Happy Isle Lake (Map 55/B6)
Located west of Opeongo Lake, you will indeed be happy once the gruelling portage is done. The lake offers lake trout and smallmouth bass fishing. Smallmouth bass fishing in good numbers to 2 kg (4.5 lbs). Lake trout fishing is good in spring for lakers that can reach 65 cm (26 in). Fourteen rustic campsites are found on Happy Isle, with three of the sites resting on an island in the middle of the lake.

Harry, Rence and Welcome Lakes (Map 45/D6)
The main access to these lakes is from Rock Lake, although there is at least one difficult portage in. Brook trout can be found in all three lakes and fishing is generally good. All three lakes are designated catch and release lakes and only artificial lures can be used as bait. Welcome and Rence Lakes also have size restrictions on brook trout.

Hartley, Little Minnow and Myra Lakes (Map 45/E1)
Accessed by long portage from the south end of Opeongo Lake, these lakes are rarely visited. Little Minnow is stocked with brook trout and also holds rainbow, splake and perch. Myra Lake was stocked in the past with brook trout, while Hartley Lake is stocked with splake.

Head and Kenneth Lakes (Map 45/A4)
These lakes continue to support a natural strain of lake trout, although fishing is generally slow. Kenneth is a good lake to find a little seclusion close to Highway 60, although it usually offers better angling success, especially in spring. Lakers can reach 55 cm (22 in) in these lakes.

Hemlock Lake (Map 55/A5)
There are no campsites here, but the fishing can be good for brook trout to 35 cm (14 in). It is recommended to set up camp at Merchant Lake to the south and travel to Hemlock Lake for a day trip.

Heron Lake (Map 44/C6)
Located within Algonquin Park near the western gate of the Highway 60 Corridor, this lake is stocked every few years with splake. Fishing for splake is fair, while fishing for smallmouth bass that average 0.5–1 kg (1–2 lbs) can be good at times.

Hogan Lake (Map 55/B4)
Both lake and brook trout are found in this big, beautiful lake. Patient anglers are often rewarded with nice sized trout, especially in spring. Parks Bay is a popular area for finding good numbers of trout. If you plan on visiting Hogan Lake in the spring by canoe, be prepared to see a number of power boats on the lake. The lake is accessible by road to native fishermen, which can make the long trek in by canoe less appealing for those looking for solitude.

Hot and Islet Lakes (Map 44/B2)
Smallmouth bass were introduced many years ago to these Algonquin lakes, providing good fishing opportunities for interior trippers. Bass average 0.5–1 kg (1–2 lbs) but can be found much larger.

Hurdman Lake (Map 64/G6)
This lake can be accessed within a day from either Cedar Lake or the Brain Lake Access Points. Two rarely used campsites are found on the lake's northern shore and fishing is good at times in spring for nice sized brook trout.

Ignace Lake (Map 57/F3)
Ignace is found just inside the park boarder en route to the Barron Canyon. Fishing can be good at times for smallmouth bass.

Iris Lake (Map 45/A2)
Iris Lake lies north of Linda Lake and offers fair fishing in spring for average sized brook trout. Try small spoons for cruising brookies.

Jack Lake (Map 45/B3)
Jack Lake is stocked every few years with splake. Brook trout and perch are also present. The Hemlock Bluff Trail off Highway 60 provides access to the lake.

Joe, Little Joe and Tepee Lakes (Map 44/E3)
There is fair fishing for smallmouth bass on all thereof these lakes. Joe Lake also offers slow fishing for average sized lake trout, while Little Joe Lake continues to support a small population of brook trout. Tepee Lake is inhabited by both lake and brook trout.

Kearney Lake (Map 45/D3)
Found along the Highway 60 Corridor, there is a campground on this lake. Fishing is generally slow for small lake trout. Smallmouth bass fishing can be productive at times for bass that average 0.5 kg (1 lb). Brook trout are also found in the lake in small numbers.

Kingscote Lake (Map 37/A3)
Kingscote is the access point for folks heading into the southern interior of Algonquin Park. Fishing for lake and brook trout is fair in the spring and slows significantly as summer progresses. The portage at the north end of the lake opens up a variety of interior tripping options.

Kioshkokwi Lake (Map 64/B7)
The lake's name in native Algonkin means 'lake of many gulls', which is recognizably true. From Highway 17, the 630 travels directly to the lake. The Kiosk Campground, an old ranger cabin and 25 interior campsites are found on the lake making it a busy place at times. Fishing is usually slow for brook and lake trout, but the odd laker is caught in excess of 70 cm (28 in).

Kirkwood and Phipps Lakes (Map 45/A5)
These southern interior lakes offer fair fishing for lake trout in the 35–45 cm (14–18 in) range. There are two wilderness campsites on each lake.

Kitty Lake (Map 46/B1)
Kitty Lake is a relatively short paddle and portage from the Shall Lake Access Point. In addition to two nice campsites, there is an old ranger cabin that can be rented. Although most of the fishing action is for smallmouth bass, the odd northern pike can take anglers by surprise. There are also unconfirmed rumours of brook trout here.

Lake La Muir (Map 54/G5–55/A5)
Deep in the heart of the park, fishing on the lake is good for both brook and lake trout during late September. Lake trout have often been caught in excess of 55 cm (22 in) and can reach sizes in excess of 70 cm (28 in). Brook trout average 30–40 cm (12–16 in) in size but are found bigger. There are eight wilderness campsites found on this picturesque lake.

Lake Lavieille (Map 55/F4–56/A4)
The trip to get to Lavieille Lake is challenging, but worthwhile as the lake has a long history as a great lake trout lake. Although it is a good fishing lake, the size of the lake also makes it challenging to fish. Even in spring, some days can be brutally slow, while others offer fierce activity. Brook trout are found to 40 cm (16 in) while lake trout can reach 60 cm (24 in) in size. Lavieille's reputation as 'the spot' brings many anglers after the spring thaw. There are 25 interior campsites on the lake.

Lake Louisa (Map 45/C5)
Lake Louisa is one of the larger lakes in Algonquin Park's southern interior and has a number of regularly used campsites. The scenic lake offers slow to fair fishing in the spring for lake trout to 55 cm (22 in). Trolling a spoon or streamer fly are productive methods for fishing.

Lake of Two Rivers and Pog Lake (Map 45/C3)
Campgrounds are found on both of these corridor lakes, which increases angling pressure. Fishing is often slow for lake trout and fair for smallmouth bass.

Lake Traverse (Map 56/D1–66/D7)
Warm water species are found in Lake Traverse, including smallmouth bass, walleye, catfish, panfish and muskellunge. Fishing for walleye and muskie is generally slow, while smallmouth bass action can be good at times. Smallmouth have been found in the lake to 2.5 kg (5.5 lbs). Access to the lake is by dirt road from the east side of the park and the Sand Lake Gate.

Langford and Marmot Lakes (Map 45/E1–55/D7)
Marmot Lake is a small lake that is stocked with brook trout. Langford Lake is located at the end of a 1 km (0.6 mi) portage from the North Arm of Opeongo Lake and is stocked with splake.

Lauder Lake (Map 64/B5)
Fishing here is fair for good sized lake and brook trout. The stream found at the southern part of the lake often has decent numbers of brookies. The lake can be easily accessed from Kioshkokwi Lake to the south.

Laurel and Loxley Lakes (Map 64/G7)
Laurel Lake has five wilderness campsites to choose from and offers generally slow fishing for lake trout and walleye. Loxley Lake is a little more secluded than Laurel Lake. The southern shore has been designated a nature reserve area and there are three campsites on the lake. Fishing is fair for lake trout and brook trout that have been caught in excess of 40 cm (16 in).

Length Lake (Map 57/D4)
Hidden to the south of the Barron Canyon, there are two interior campsites here. The lake has been stocked with brook trout.

Linda and Polly Lakes (Map 44/G2)
These lakes are found northwest of Canisbay Lake and the Minnesing Trail also travels around both lakes. Bass provide good fishing at times for smallmouth bass to 2 kg (4.5 lbs). Lake trout also inhabit Linda Lake. Fishing for lakers to 45 cm (18 in) is fair in early spring, just after ice off. Polly Lake has two rustic campsites available, while Linda Lake offers four.

Little Cauliflower Lake (Map 45/G7)
Access is by long portage only from the east or the west end of the lake, fishing for brook trout to 35 cm (14 in) is good, especially in the spring, just after ice off.

Little Coon Lake (Map 45/A6)
Fishing at this lake is fair for lake trout and small brook trout.

Little Crooked Lake (Map 56/A4)
Found at the end of a challenging portage, there are only two campsites on the lake, which is the home of some of the last remaining pure strains of Algonquin Park brook trout. The lake has been designated catch and release only.

Little Hay Lake (Map 45/G7)
Accessed via Hay Creek and a portage from Hay Lake, fishing for average sized smallmouth bass is good here. There are also rainbow trout in the 85 hectare lake.

Little McAuley Lake (Map 45/F3)
Little McCauley Lake lies along an old stretch of railway bed and can be hiked or portaged to from Highway 60. The 18 hectare lake is stocked with brook trout and also holds rainbow trout, pumpkinseed sunfish and yellow perch.

Loontail, Beaverpaw and Vulture Lakes (Map 54/B5)
Three of the most remote lakes in Algonquin Park, these lakes are set in a designated Algonquin nature reserve area. There is no direct access to the lakes and there are no designated campsites. Those that can make there and back in a day should find good brook trout fishing.

Lorne, Lost Dog and Sisco Lakes (Map 53/E2)
All three lakes are inhabited by lake trout, while Lorne and Lost Dog Lakes also host brook trout. Fishing can be good in spring, after ice off or in late September as the water begins to cool again. Lost Dog Lake is the easiest of the three to access, while Sisco offers the fewest fish.

Lost Coin and Otterpaw Lakes (Map 66/B7)
Accessed by long cart trails that lead from the Bissett Creek Access Point, the lakes are rarely visited. Of the two, Lost Coin is more popular due to the old ranger cabin that can be rented. Fishing for brook trout is spotty.

Luckless and Lynx Lakes (Map 54/G2–55/A2)
Brook trout are found in both lakes in good numbers and impressive sizes. Lynx Lake also features lake trout. Spring is the best time to fish these lakes.

Lunch and Milon Lakes (Map 45/G3)
The lakes along the park's eastern boundary are stocked with brook trout every few years. Access to the lakes is limited to snowmobile or on foot. Fishing can be good at times for brookies in the 25–35 cm (8–14 in) range.

Madawaska Lake (Map 36/E1)
Madawaska Lake lies within the southern Algonquin Park interior and is a good base for exploration of the South Madawaska River and the northern bog section of the lake where moose are often spotted. There are three rustic campsites available and fishing for lake trout to 65 cm (26 in) and average sized brook trout is generally fair in the spring just after ice off.

Magnetawan and Hambone Lakes (Map 43/G1)
Magnetawan Lake is one of the more popular western interior access points to the park. Hambone Lake is one portage east of Magnetawan Lake. Fishing in the lakes is slow, except in early spring. Both lakes are inhabited by brook trout, although Hambone Lake also has a population of lake trout.

Manitou Lake (Map 53/G1–63/G7)
There are over 45 designated campsites at the lake, including some beautiful island and beach sites. Similar to North Tea Lake, wind can be a major hindrance to travel and to fishing success. Lake trout in excess of 3.5 kg (8 lbs) have been caught, while brook trout have been found in the 40 cm (16 in) range.

Maple Lake (Map 54/C1–64/C7)
Maple Lake is a good day's paddle from the Kiosk Access Point and features seven interior campsites. It is a scenic lake that also offers good fishing for lake trout that can exceed 75 cm (30 in).

Maple Leaf Lake (Map 44/C5)
This lake is stocked every few years with splake. It can only be accessed via the Western Uplands Backpacking Trail and is home to several nice campsites.

Marie Lake (Map 57/D4)
Accessed by portage from St. Andrews Lake, Marie Lake is stocked biennially with brook trout. The 11 hectare lake also holds pumpkinseed sunfish.

Marmot Lake (Map 45/D1)
Hidden on the west side of the much bigger Opeongo Lake, Marmot Lake is only 3 hectares in size. It is stocked biennially with brook trout and also offers splake.

McCraney [Moose] Lake (Map 44/B3)
One of the bigger lakes in the area, it takes a bit of effort to get here. You are rewarded with fishing for lake trout averaging 40–50 cm (16–20 in) and brook trout to 30 cm (12 in) in size.

McIntosh and Timberwolf Lakes (Map 44/D1)
Found several portages from the nearest access point, some decent sized trout are found here. McIntosh Lake offers fishing for lakers in the 55–65 cm (22–26 in) range, as well as brook trout to 35 cm (14 in). Timberwolf Lake sports sizes of up to 70 cm (28 in) for lake trout.

McGarvey Lake (Map 45/A6)
McGarvey Lake offers fair fishing for lake trout to 75 cm (30 in) and is found in the southern Algonquin interior. There are three beautiful campsites at the lake with one being a nice island site.

McKaskill Lake (Map 56/D6)
Found a good distance from any access point, fishing can be good here for nice sized brook and lake trout. Spring is the most productive time of year; however the last few weeks of September can also be good.

McManus Lake (Map 57/E2)
One of the park's eastern interior access points, there are five rustic campsites to choose from here. Smallmouth bass, walleye and muskellunge are found in the lake and fishing is generally fair for all three species. Panfish are also found here in good numbers. Note: Be sure not to venture east from McManus Lake. This is Canadian Forces Base Petawawa territory and part of a live firing range!

McNorton Lake (Map 56/C4)
There was an old portage trail off White Partridge Creek that once provided access to the lake. Unfortunately, it is heavily overgrown and tough to find and follow. Brook trout inhabit the lake and there are no designated campsites.

Menona Lake (Map 55/F1)
Menona Lake is found in the transition area of the park, where the highland becomes lowland. Fishing can be quite good for brook trout, especially in spring.

Merchant Lake (Map 55/B6)
Seven rustic campsites are found well situated along the shore of this beautiful lake. It is a popular spring destination and fishing can be good at times for lake trout to 60 cm (24 in) and brook trout in the 30–35 cm (12–14 in) range.

Mink Lakes (Map 64/C7)
Lake and brook trout inhabit the lakes in fair numbers and fishing can be decent at times during spring when trout cruise near the surface. Ten rustic campsites are found on Mink Lake and the old Canadian National Railway bed passes along the north end of the lakes.

Minnow Lakes (Map 37/A3)
These two small lakes can only be accessed by portage from Kingscote Lake. There are no campsites on the lakes, but anglers can expect decent fishing for stocked brook trout, especially in the spring.

Misty Lake (Map 44/C1–54/C7)
Misty is a fair size lake with many nooks and crannies for the trout to hide. Brook trout up to 40 cm (16 in) in size are reported.

Moccasin Lake (Map 44/B1)
This small lake has two exquisite wilderness campsites along its shoreline. Smallmouth bass were introduced to the lake some time ago and provide good fishing opportunities to today's visitors.

Mole and Raja Lakes (Map 46/A1)
South from Booth, Mole Lake offers good fishing for smallmouth bass to 1.5 kg (3.5 lbs) as well as a few brook trout. Raja Lake has a healthy population of brook trout, which can grow to 35 cm (14 in).

Mouse [Moose] Lake (Map 54/E1)
Brook trout are found in good numbers to 35 cm (14 in) here. Of course, the heat of summer reduced success dramatically.

Nadine, Osler and Little Osler Lakes (Map 54/E2)
Springtime offers good fishing for nice sized brook trout, which reach 35 cm (14 in). There are four rustic campsites on Nadine and Osler Lakes and three more on Little Osler Lake. Each of the lakes is a short day trip from one another.

Namakootchie and Sam Lakes (Map 44/E4)
These lakes experience low use for being so close to Highway 60 and offer a great park experience. Sam Lake has been stocked with splake, offering fair fishing in spring. Namakootchie Lake offers slow fishing for generally small lake trout and fair fishing in spring for brook trout.

Narrowbag Lake (Map 55/B2)
Brook trout are found in decent numbers and have been caught to 35 cm (14 in) in this oddly named lake.

Norm's Lake (Map 57/G4)
This small, hidden lake borders the eastern side of the park. Small brook trout inhabit the lake in fair numbers and fishing can be good at times.

North Branch and Sundassa Lakes (Map 56/D4)
North Branch Lake lies to the east of White Partridge Lake, while Sundassa lies to the west. There are four interior campsites on North Branch Lake. Brook trout fishing can productive throughout the year.

North Cuckoo and Plumb Lakes (Map 54/G3)
Fishing is good for nice sized brook trout on these out of the way lakes. The trout are a little easier to find on North Cuckoo Lake, although they seem to be a little bigger in Plumb Lake.

North Grace Lake (Map 45/B6)
North Grace Lake is found in the southern Algonquin interior and offers fair to good fishing at times in the spring for average sized brook trout and lake trout.

North Raven Lake (Map 54/D2)
This lake is at least a two day trip from the nearest access point. There are four nice campsites on the lake and fishing is often good in spring for lake trout.

North River and Merganser Lakes (Map 65/D6)
Only a 90 m (295 ft) portage separates North River and Merganser Lake. Fishing on North River Lake is fair in spring for lake trout to 45 cm (18 in) and brook trout to 35 cm (14 in). The inflow and outflow areas of the North River often hold good numbers of feeding trout. Merganser Lake is inhabited by brook trout and the fishing quality is similar to the North River Lake.

North Rouge Lake (Map 66/D6)
This secluded lake offers slow fishing for brook trout due to the abundance of smallmouth bass that have infiltrated the lake's waters.

North Tea Lake (Map 53/F2)
One of the more popular lakes on the west side of Algonquin Park, there are over 70 interior campsites available, many on small, secluded islands. The lake can be easily accessed within a day from Kawawaymog Lake. Some good sized lake trout are pulled from North Tea each year, although the best time to try and fish for lakers is in the spring. Watch for afternoon winds.

O'Neill Lake (Map 46/G1)
Found on the boundary of the park, fishing is good in spring for stocked splake to 50 cm (20 in).

Opalescent Lake (Map 57/D3)
There are six campsites found along this popular lake's shoreline. Fishing is good at times for smallmouth bass that average 0.5–1.5 kg (1–3.5 lbs).

Opeongo Lake (Map 45/E1–55/D6)
The largest lake in Algonquin Provincial Park, there are over 135 interior campsites scattered on Opeongo Lake. On top of steady boating traffic, wind is often a problem here. Anglers will find lake trout, whitefish and smallmouth bass inhabit the lake. Lakers are found up to 80 cm (32 in) and smallmouth bass can be caught to 1.5 kg (3.5 lbs). Whitefish are quite aggressive at times and fishing is usually slow for lake trout and fair for smallmouth bass.

Otterslide and Little Otterslide Lakes (Map 44/G1–55/A7)
Fishing is good in spring for lake trout that can be found to 4 kg (9 lbs). Otterslide Lake is an ideal camping lake and has eleven wilderness campsites available. Little Otterslide is just as beautiful and provides ten campsites.

Peck and Ouse Lakes (Map 44/F3)
Found just off Highway 60 in Algonquin Park, these lakes are stocked with splake every few years. If you prefer panfish, they also hold feisty sunfish and perch.

Pen Lake (Map 45/E5)
Pen Lake is easily accessed via a 375 metre portage from the busy Rock Lake access point. There are a number of campsites available and fishing is fair at times in the spring just after ice off for lake trout and brook trout.

Perley and Hayes Lakes (Map 54/G3)
Hayes Lake is a small, out of the way lake, that does not see much traffic. Brook trout to 40 cm (16 in) are found in the lake. Perley Lake is part of the Petawawa River system, just before the river begins to quicken. There is one campsite on this elongated lake and fishing is generally fair for brook trout.

Philip Lake (Map 55/D3)
The damming of the Little Madawaska River created this lake. Good sized brook trout can be found congregating near the inflow and outflow areas of the river where fishing can be good, especially in spring. Four wilderness campsites are found on the remote lake.

Pinetree Lake (Map 45/F3)
Pinetree Lake can be found a few portages south of Highway 60 and is a picturesque lake with three superb wilderness campsites. The lake offers fair fishing for generally small lake trout.

Prottler Lake (Map 45/F1)
Prottler Lake is not as busy as most of the neighbouring lakes due to the 1,630 m (5,348 ft) portage to access the lake from Galeairy Lake. There are two rustic campsites available at the lake and fishing is fair for lake trout, brook trout and good at times for smallmouth bass. The decline of the trout fishery is due in part to the introduction of smallmouth bass into the lake.

Proulx Lake (Map 55/D6)
The north portion of the lake is quite marshy and leads to the Crow River, a known viewing area for Algonquin moose. Fishing in Proulx Lake can be quite good in spring with brook trout caught to 45 cm (18 in).

Provoking and Faya Lakes (Map 45/B3)
Provoking Lake has been stocked with splake and is also inhabited by smallmouth bass. Faya Lake is stocked with brook trout every few years. For trippers, there are 12 campsites on Provoking Lake and one on Faya Lake.

Queer Lake (Map 54/B7)
This lake has 13 rustic campsites and offers good fishing in spring for nice sized trout. Both brook trout and lake trout inhabit the lake.

Radiant [Trout] Lake (Map 55/F1)
Lake trout, brook trout, smallmouth bass and walleye are all found in Radiant Lake. Fishing is generally fair for lake trout and walleye while smallmouth bass fishing can be very good at times. Unfortunately, brook trout are often tough

to find. Walleye can reach 2.5 kg (5.5 lbs), while smallmouth bass have been caught to 2 kg (4.5 lbs).

Ragged Lake and Parkside Bay (Map 44/G5)
There are numerous campsites located on both of these water bodies, which can be quite busy all season long. Fishing is generally slow for brook trout and average sized lake trout. Smallmouth bass picks up in the warmer months.

Rain and Sawyer Lake (Map 44/A2)
Rain Lake is one of four western access points to the interior of Algonquin and is busy at times. There are 18 interior campsites on Rain Lake and another six on Sawyer Lake. Fishing in both lakes for lake trout is usually slow. Smallmouth bass fishing is usually a bit more active, while a small population of brook trout is also found in Sawyer Lake.

Rainbow, Groundhog and Loft Lakes (Map 44/D3)
These lakes are often overlooked by paddlers entering Canoe Lake. Fishing is fair in the spring for brook trout in the 25–30 cm (10–12 in) range. Rainbow Lake is usually the better of the three lakes.

Rana Lake (Map 65/C7)
Rana Lake can be found not far off the Brent Road. Fishing is slow to fair for small brook trout. Try a small bead head nymphs fly pattern or a shiny spinner.

Ravenau Lake (Map 55/B1)
There is a great campsite on Ravenau's shore or, alternatively, anglers can also stay at Lantern Lake to the south. Fishing at Ravenau is fair for brook trout in the 25–30 cm (10–12 in) range.

Redfox Lake (Map 45/C2)
Redfox Lake continues to support a natural brook and lake trout population along with yellow perch. The difficult to reach lake is often quieter than many others in the area.

Redrock and Nepawin Lakes (Map 55/C6)
Redrock Lake is much larger than Nepawin and offers seven rustic campsites. Nepawin Lake can be found via an 810 m (2,658 ft) portage from Redrock and makes an ideal day trip. Both lakes have good fishing for lake and brook trout. The trout are larger in Redrock, but more plentiful in Nepawin. The long narrow bay on Redrock Lake is a good area to find cruising trout.

Robinson and Whiskeyjack Lakes (Map 54/F3)
At least three days are needed to access these rarely visited lakes. There are two campsites on Robinson Lake and another four sites on Whiskeyjack Lake. Lake trout are found in both lakes and brook trout are also found in Whiskeyjack.

Robitaille and Wilkins Lakes (Map 56/G7–57/A7)
There are six wilderness campsites on both of these trout lakes. Robitaille Lake is also inhabited by brook trout, which can reach 35 cm (14 in).

Rock Lake (Map 45/D4)
This popular lake is easily accessed form the Highway 60 Corridor. In addition to the drive-in campsite, there are rustic interior sites as well as popular hiking/biking trails. Lake trout and smallmouth bass are found in the lake. Fishing for lake trout is slow, while smallmouth bass can be active at times.

Rosebary and Longbow Lakes (Map 54/B6)
Fishing is quite good in spring for decent sized brook and lake trout. Brookies average 25 cm (10 in) and are frequently found near creek mouths and the outflow area of the small dam on Longbow Lake, while lake trout are almost impossible to find in summer. Access to the lakes is via the Tim River, which can be quite difficult to navigate during summer months.

Rouge Lake (Map 57/E4)
There are no campsites on Rouge Lake, but the lake is worth visiting for its brook trout.

Round Island Lake (Map 56/A6)
Fishing is good here for lake trout that average 35–40 cm (14–16 in) in size, but can be found to 70 cm (28 in). This is no doubt due to the difficult access.

Rowan Lake (Map 57/B3)
This remote lake within Algonquin Provincial Park is a tough 2,155 meter portage from Grand Lake. Those that do haul their canoes up to this lake will find wilderness campsites along the shore and fishing for stocked splake.

Ryan Lake (Map 56/C7)
This tiny lake is stocked with splake that can be found to 50 cm (20 in). Similar to most trout species, spring is the prime time to fish for splake.

Scorch Lake (Map 37/B3)
This remote interior Algonquin Park lake can be found up a small creek from Branch Lake. There are a few campsites at the lake and if you do make the journey, you should be rewarded with good fishing for lake trout, especially in spring. Similar to many lake trout in this part of the park, these lake trout have a unique dark colouring.

Scott Lake (Map 44/E5)
Brook trout inhabit the isolated Scott Lake in decent numbers. Fishing can be fair for brookies that are 28–30 cm (10–12 in) in size.

Sec Lake (Map 57/G4)
Sec Lake can be busy during summer weekends, but is often deserted during the week. Fishing is slow for lake trout and brook trout, although the action for northern pike and smallmouth bass is often better. The majority of pike are small, but scrappy, while smallmouth bass can reach 2 kg (4.5 lbs).

Shawandasee Lake (Map 44/D6)
Shawandasee Lake can only be accessed by canoe and low maintenance portage. The lake offers fair to good fishing in spring for brook trout.

Shirley Lake (Map 46/C1–56/C7)
Another popular destination from the Shall Lake Access Point, fishing in Shirley is mainly for lake trout to 65 cm (26 in). The action picks up in early spring.

Smith and Whitson Lakes (Map 57/D1)
A total of fifteen campsites can be found on the lakes, with many sites set amidst beautiful stands of Silver Maple. Anglers will find decent numbers of generally small walleye. Muskellunge can also be found, although they too are small compared to most southern Ontario lakes.

Smoke Lake (Map 44/F4)
Easily accessed off Highway 60, Smoke Lake sees more than its fair share of anglers. As a result the lake trout fishing is slow. Smallmouth bass were introduced many years ago and provide fair angling opportunities.

Source Lake (Map 44/G3)
Lake trout are found in small numbers in Source Lake, while smallmouth bass are the most productive sport fish on the lake. Bucketmouths can be found to 2 kg (4.5 lbs) in size here.

South Little Mink Lake (Map 37/C3)
South Little Mink Lake is found within the southern boundary of Algonquin Park and can be accessed on foot down an old road into the park. The lake offers slow fishing for small lake trout and fair fishing for brook trout in the 25–35 cm (10–14 in) range.

Speckledtrout Lake (Map 45/D4)
Accessed by canoe from the Rock Lake Access Point or by foot, this lake is stocked with splake and offers fair fishing in spring for average sized fish. The lake is also occasionally stocked with brook trout.

St. Andrews Lake (Map 57/D4)
Easily accessed for a weekend trip, St Andrews Lake is a popular destination. Lake and brook trout inhabit the lake, although fishing is usually slow after the waters warm in spring.

St. Frances Lake (Map 57/E4)
Home to a lonely campsite, most visitors test their luck for brook trout in the early spring and smallmouth bass during warmer periods. The odd bass to 2 kg (4.5 lbs) is reported.

Stratton Lake (Map 57/D4)
A short portage from Grand Lake leads to Stratton. The popular lake is home to numerous interior campsites and can be accessed from the Eastern Pines Backpacking Trail. Anglers will find mostly smallmouth bass, although the odd lake trout surfaces in the spring.

Stringer Lake (Map 45/B6)
Unfortunately this lake is closed to fishing due to the near collapse of the brook trout. The lake may be opened in the next few years once stocks are back to acceptable levels. Please abide by all regulations when using natural resources in order to avoid similar abuse of other lakes.

Sunbeam Lake (Map 44/F1)
Home to several interior campsites, this is a gorgeous lake to visit. Fishing for lake trout that average 1–2 kg (2–4.5 lbs) and brook trout that can grow to about 30–35 cm (12–14 in) is fair. Brookies are stocked in this 81 hectare lake.

Sunday and Sproule Lakes (Map 45/E2)
There are three wilderness campsites on Sunday Lake and another five sites on Sproule Lake. Fishing is fair in spring and late September in both lakes for stocked splake in the 30–35 cm (12–14 in) range.

Tea Lake (Map 44/E4)
Next to Highway 60 and home to a drive-in campsite, Tea Lake can be a busy place. Anglers can find the odd lake trout and a few more smallmouth bass.

Three Mile Lake (Map 54/A1)
It takes about two days to get to this lake, where you will find lake and brook trout. The lake is fairly big and holding areas are difficult to locate, making fishing more challenging.

Tim Lake (Map 53/F6)
Found along one of the more popular western access routes to the interior of Algonquin Park, there are six nice wilderness campsites on the lake. Both brook and lake trout are found in fair numbers.

Tom Thomson and Little Doe Lakes (Map 44/E2)
These two fine Algonquin interior lakes offer fishing for smallmouth bass to 2 kg (4.5 lbs). There are some reports of brook trout still caught in Little Doe Lake; however, smallmouth have displaced the species. Lake trout are also found in Tom Thomson Lake in decent numbers.

Upper Pine Lake (Map 57/D6)
Upper Pine Lake falls can be accessed by travelling up the Pine River from Lower Pine Lake. It hosts small northern pike.

Wabamimi Lake (Map 65/E7)
This low-use lake can be accessed in a day and is home to two nice campsites. Fishing can be good for nice sized brook trout.

West Harry Lake (Map 44/C4)
West Harry only has one wilderness campsite available, on the lake's western shore. This is also the site of the dam on the Big East River and the best place to look for brook trout.

West Smith Lake (Map 45/G3)
Found off the east side of Highway 60 near the East Gate, West Smith offers stocked brook trout. It is unconfirmed if any warm water species or panfish are also found in the 4 hectare lake.

Westward Lake (Map 44/D5)
Accessed by trail, this brook trout rests close to Highway 60. In early spring or the fall, the action is usually decent.

Wet Lake (Map 57/F4)
Wet Lake can be easily accessed by trail from the Sec Lake Access Point. There is an infrequently used campsite along with bass fishing for smallmouth in the 0.5–1.5 kg (1–3.5 lb) range.

Whitebirch Lake (Map 64/C7)
Part of a popular canoe route from the Kiosk Access Point, visitors will find four rustic campsites on the lake. Lake trout are found in the lake and fishing can be fair for small lakers in spring.

Whitefish Lake (Map 45/D3)
Easily accessed form the Highway 60 Corridor, there are drive-in sites as well as interior campsites to help explore the lake. Anglers will find fair fishing for lake trout, while smallmouth bass can be active at times.

White Partridge Lake (Map 56/C4)
There are six interior campsites scattered along the shore of this rather big lake. Fishing in the lake is good at times for lake and brook trout. Brook trout can be found to 45 cm (18 in), while lake trout can reach 65 cm (26 in) in size.

White Trout Lake (Map 54/F7)
South of Big Trout Lake, it is a long journey to reach White Trout. Both lakes are connected and offer similar fisheries for lake and brook trout.

Wright Lake (Map 55/F6)
Lake trout and smallmouth bass inhabit Wright Lake, which is often overlooked by trippers who are more concerned about getting to Dickson Lake. Lake trout are usually small and smallmouth bass average 0.5–1 kg (1–2 lbs). The bass fishing is usually better, especially during summer.

STREAM FISHING

Below, we have provided information on most of the major systems in Cottage Country. Be sure to ask permission before entering any private lands and note the various seasonal closures.

Amable Du Fond River (Map 53/D3–64/B2)
The Amable Du Fond River is an often-overlooked gem, flowing from Kioshkokwi Lake in Algonquin Park to Smith Lake near the Mattawa River. Brook and rainbow trout are found throughout the system in good numbers.

Aylen River (Map 46/G2–56/E7)
Brook trout can be found within the portions of the Aylen River inside of Algonquin Park. Outside of the park, anglers frequent the small stretch of river between Aylen Lake and the Opeongo River where smallmouth bass can be found.

Barron River (Map 56/F3–57/G3)
Flowing from the east side of Algonquin Park to the Ottawa River, the northern side of the river outside of the park is Canadian Forces Base Petawawa Property and trespassing is strictly prohibited. Fishing in the river is good in sections and generally gets better farther away from Petawawa. Smallmouth bass are caught to 1 kg (2 lbs).

Baxter and Cavan Creeks (Map 10/C5–F3)
These creeks flow into the Otonabee River southwest of Peterborough. The headwaters provide small brook trout and the odd brown trout. As the creeks begin to approach the Otonabee River you will find panfish such as perch.

Beaver Creek (Map 20/E3–29/D7)
Beaver Creek offers some of the best paddling and fishing in the Tweed/Marmora area. Access is easiest near Crowe Lake near the mouth or off Highway 62 to the north. The stream holds most of the popular warm water species: muskellunge, bass, pike and a whole lot of small panfish. Try fishing in the back eddies and pools at the base of the rapids; this is where you will find the best muskie and bass fishing.

Big East River (Map 34/B1–44/D3)
The Big East River flows from the west side of Algonquin Park, past Arrowhead Provincial Park, into Lake Vernon. Native brook trout can be found in the sections of the river between Algonquin and Arrowhead Provincial Park, while they have been stocked on occasion in areas closer to Lake Vernon.

Bissett Creek (Map 66/A6–C3)
Bissett Creek is a meandering waterway that flows from the Ottawa River to Reed Lake, inside Algonquin Park. Fishing is best south of Highway 17, but can be productive throughout the creek as small brook trout are found in good numbers.

Bon Echo Creek (Map 30/G2)
This small creek flows through Bon Echo Provincial Park and into Mazinaw Lake. Brook trout are stocked annually and provide for fair fishing.

Bonnechere River (Map 47/E1–56/E5)
The Bonnechere River is best fished by boat or canoe. Walleye and small northern pike are found in fair numbers in the river near Round and Golden Lakes. There is also a good population of smallmouth bass throughout this section. Above High Falls, the river offers a few small brook trout. Walleye spawn in the river in spring and no fishing is permitted at that time.

Burnt River (Map 17/E3–36/E7)
The Burnt River is stocked occasionally with brown trout around Lochlin, Ritchie Falls, Francis Bridge and Scott's Dam. These elusive trout provide fair fishing in the upper reaches of the river. South of Howland, the river has resident smallmouth bass and panfish throughout the year. Walleye and muskellunge due migrate up the river during the spring for spawning, but note the spring fishing sanctuary for these fish.

Commanda Creek (Map 51/G1–52/C5)
Flowing from Deer Lake north to Commanda Lake, this stream offers anglers fair to good fishing in sections for small brook trout. The most productive stretches of creek are often the hardest to reach.

Crow River (Map 55/D4–56/A2)
Most of the fishing on the river is done on the section between Big Crow Lake and Lake Lavieille deep within the Algonquin Park interior. There are a number of fast water sections and big pools that hold good-sized brook trout.

Crowe River (Map 20/D6–28/F1)
Best known for its fine walleye fishing, the Crowe River flows from Paudash Lake towards the Trent River in the south. Walleye have been known to reach 3.4 kg (7.5 lbs) on occasion, while smallmouth bass, largemouth bass and northern pike can also be found in the system.

Deer Creek (Map 28/E1–37/E7)
Deer Creek is a small creek that offers fair fishing in some sections for generally small brook trout. Portions of the creek are accessible by rough 2wd roads, although the most productive areas of the creek are accessible by only walking.

Duchesnay Creek (Map 62/D1)
Found outside of North Bay, this creek does see heavy fishing pressure. However, fishing for brook trout remains fairly active. Please avoid trespassing on private property.

Duffins Creek (Map 2/G5–8/F7)
From Lake Ontario to Whitevale, the creek is a great place to catch steelhead, while north of Whitevale, the creek is populated with plenty of brown trout and brook trout. The mouth and marsh area are great places to catch northern pike, while walleye yellow perch, bass and carp are also caught at various times of the year. There are two private fishing clubs in the headwaters of the creek and there are plenty of places for anglers to access the creek.

East Cross Creek (Map 9/E4–F2)
East Cross Creek flows into the Scugog River and small brook trout can be found in the lower section of the creek. As the creek gets closer to the Scugog River, panfish, such as bluegill and perch, are predominant.

Egan Creek (Map 29/E1–38/D6)
Egan Creek is a rust coloured, Bancroft area waterway that is inhabited by a small population of brook trout. The creek is generally accessible, although it does travel through large portions of private land.

Elephant Creek (Map 37/C6)
Generally small brook trout are found in this creek and fishing can be good at times. A vehicle can be parked on the side of Highway 648 where the creek passes under the road. Be conscious of private property.

Esson Creek (Map 28/A1)
The creek crosses under Highway 118 and provides a chance to catch small brook trout. The creek was stocked in the past.

Fleetwood Creek (Map 10/B2–5)
In the lower stretches of the creek near Bethany there is a small population of small brook trout available.

French River (Map 48/E2–61/D4)
The French River flows from Lake Nipissing to Georgian Bay. Along the way, it travels through some remote stretches before passing by some of the most accessible areas of the river near Wolseley Bay. The best way to explore the history and natural splendour of the French River is to travel the river by canoe. Fishing is good for smallmouth bass, which have been found to 2 kg (4.5 lbs). Good sized northern pike and walleye are also found throughout the system. One of the best fishing areas on the river is where the river breaks up into several different arms near the Georgian Bay.

Ganaraska River (Map 5/A2–10/B7)
This river is beginning to regain its reputation as a fantastic migratory fishery. Most of the action is for salmon near Port Hope, although further afield, anglers will find resident rainbow and brown trout throughout the year

Gibson/Musquash River (Map 23/E2)
The portion of this river from Highway 69/400 to the Georgian Bay is fairly rustic and provides fair to good fishing for average sized smallmouth bass and fair fishing for smaller northern pike. In spring, walleye spawn in the river and many are still found in the river when walleye season opens in late spring. The mouth of the river can be quite good for walleye in both fall and spring.

Go Home River (Map 23/D1)
The Go Home River is a fairly wide river that stretches from Go Home Lake to the Georgian Bay. The river holds a good population of smallmouth and largemouth bass along with nice sized northern pike. Walleye spawn in the river in early spring and fishing near the mouth of the river can be good.

Gull River (Map 17/D2–37/A3)
The Elliot Falls and Minden section of the Gull River has been stocked periodically with rainbow trout. The system is also home to smallmouth and largemouth bass as well as panfish.

Head River (Map 25/C7–26/C6)
The section northwest of Head Lake and Highway 503 holds a fair population of resident smallmouth bass and panfish. Bass average 0.5 kg (1 lb) in size and can be caught on spinner baits and minnow imitation lures and flies.

Hoc Roc River (Map 24/G2)
The Hoc Roc River flows from Gull Lake to Lake Muskoka and has decent fishing for stocked rainbow trout.

Holland River (Map 1/A1–7/E4)
The Holland River is found to the south of Lake Simcoe and offers fair fishing for a number of species including smallmouth and largemouth bass, panfish and northern pike. The mouth of the river is an area where big bass and northern pike can be found. Try fishing along the many weed lines for better action.

Humber River (Map 1/A3–E7)
The best places to fish this river are between Etienne Brule Park north to Eglinton Avenue. In the spring, the river produces well for spawning steelhead. In the fall, you will find Chinook and brown trout.

Irondale River (Map 27/A5–28/B1 ; 36/G5–37/B7)
The Irondale River seems to warm up. As result the past stockings of brook trout simply have not done well. More recently, brown trout have been stocked in the river around Furnace Falls, Goderham and Devil's Gap. Brown trout generally have a better tolerance for warmer water conditions and provide anglers with decent fishing on occasion.

Key River (Map 49/B4–50/A4)
Found south of the French River, this is a popular access river to the Georgian Bay and the river can get busy with boating traffic during summer months. Fishing during the early morning and evening periods can be good at times for smallmouth and largemouth bass, which are found up to 2 kg (4.5 lbs). Northern pike and walleye are less prevalent in the system. The stretches of the river east of Highway 69 can also be fairly productive angling waters.

La Vasse River (Map 62/E3–63/B4)
The La Vase Portage connects Trout Lake, at the head of the Mattawa River, to the La Vase. The portage was the main fur trade route to the west and the La Vase is best known for linking these two watersheds. The river does not have the fishing fame of either the Mattawa or the French, but it still offers reasonable fishing for bass, pike and walleye. The best place to fish is in Champlain Park, where the La Vase flows into Lake Nipissing.

Little Madawaska River (Map 55/A4–F2)
This remote Algonquin river offers fishing opportunities for brook trout. Large brookies have been found to 30 cm (12 in) in the river, but average about 20 cm (8 in). Try behind any one of the small dams that are found along the river.

Madawaska River (Map 45/A3–47/E3)
Due to the abundance of prime fishing lakes in Algonquin Park, the Madawaska is not fished that heavily except around the town of Madawaska. The river holds wild brook trout in the 20–35 cm (8–14 in) range but there is a chance you will find bigger fish. Worms are always productive; however fly-fishing with nymph patterns can be a fun alternative.

Magnetawan River (Maps 41, 42, 43, 49, 50, 51, 53)
The headwaters of the Magnetawan River are in the highlands of Algonquin Park, although the main body of the river is from Ahmic Lake to the Georgian Bay. The main sport fish are smallmouth and largemouth bass, walleye and northern pike. Bass occur through most of the river, while pike and walleye can be found in select areas, most notably in the region west of Highway 69.

Mattawa River (Map 63/A2–64/E1)
A large portion of the river is part of the Mattawa River Provincial Park, one of Ontario's first waterway parks. There are many access points to the river. Some sections are difficult to navigate, although most of the river is quite slow and meandering. Fishing is quite good. Smallmouth bass to 2 kg (4.5 lbs) are found in good numbers throughout the river, while largemouth bass are also present in a number of areas. Walleye is the most sought after species on the river and one of the best locations for bass and walleye is near the confluence of the Ottawa and Mattawa Rivers. Some 4 kg (9 lb) walleye have been caught. Muskellunge are much harder to find than their cousin, the northern pike. However, some big pike caught in the river.

McGillvray Creek (Map 53/A1–62/G7)
This small creek is found south of the town of Powassan and home to small brook trout that average 18–20 cm (7–8 in) in size.

Memesagamesing River (Map 51/A1–60/E7)
The Memesagamesing River is also referred to as the Sag River by locals. It is quite remote and is best accessed by canoe from Restoule Provincial Park. Fishing in the river is fair to good at times for generally small smallmouth bass. Northern pike and walleye also inhabit most sections of the river. To find good-sized fish, you have to find bigger holding areas.

Mississagua River (Map 18/F3–27/G7)
Resident smallmouth and largemouth bass can be found in this river from Mississagua Lake to Buckhorn Lake. Fishing is fair for bass in the 0.5 kg (1 lb) range. Walleye and muskellunge spawn in the river in spring and the odd late spawning

walleye can be found in the river at the walleye spring opener. The mouth of the river is fair for both walleye and muskellunge in fall and late spring.

Moira River (Map 13/E4–20/G3)
The Moira River is a long, large river that flows through several urban areas, such as Tweed and Belleville. Smallmouth and largemouth bass are found throughout the river, while northern pike and even muskellunge can be found in some sections. Walleye are also found in various sections as they use the river for spawning during the spring.

Moon River (Map 24/A1–32/B6)
The Moon River is renowned for its walleye fishery. Walleye run up the river to spawn and in late spring the fish begin to return to Georgian Bay. At this time, the mouth of the river becomes quite good for nice sized walleye. Resident bass and the odd northern pike can also be found throughout the river.

Murdock River (Map 59/B2–D7)
The Murdock River is a fairly large river that flows south from Nepewasi Lake down into the French River. The Murdock essentially follows Highway 69 allowing easy access and the chance to catch smallmouth bass and northern pike.

Muskoka River – North Branch (Map 34/A7–C2)
This portion of the Muskoka River follows closely to the east side of Highway 11. The river has been stocked with brown trout in the past and there are reports of some fair fishing at times along the river. Look for browns along tight shore banks.

Muskoka River – South Branch (Map 24/G1–34/E5)
The main sport fish species that are found in the Muskoka River are smallmouth and largemouth bass. Fishing for smallmouth and largemouth bass can be fair at times for decent sized bass. Walleye can be found in the section closer to Lake Muskoka, mainly in the spring.

Nipissing River (Map 53/F6–55/B1)
The Nipissing River flows from the west side of the Algonquin all the way to Cedar Lake on the park's northern side. Fishing for brook trout can be good.

Nogies Creek (Map 18/C1–27/C7)
Walleye run up Nogies Creek to spawn and a few late spawners can still be found during the walleye spring opener. Smallmouth and largemouth bass are also resident in the creek, while panfish add a bit of excitement for the younger anglers.

Nottawasaga River (Map 6/C7–14/A5)
The Nottawasaga River has a good spring run of steelhead. They average 3–5 kg (7–11 lbs). Similarly, a few big salmon can be found in the river in the fall. Walleye also spawn in the river in spring mainly in the Minesing Swamp section, although they are rarely found in the river by the spring walleye opener. Brown trout are found in a few sections of the river and are caught occasionally near the mouth of the river. Resident smallmouth bass and perch are found mainly in the section from Jack Lake to Nottawasaga Bay.

Opeongo River (Map 46/ G4–55/G7)
The Openogo River is a great brook trout river, although some of the lakes along the route also hold northern pike, which can sometimes be found in the river near these lakes. These pike can get up to 12.5 kg (28 lb), while the brookies are usually found in the 0.5–1 kg (1–2 lb) range. You may also find smallmouth bass in the river, although again, these are more common in the lakes.

Oshawa Creek (Map 3/D4–9/C6)
The best stretch of Oshawa Creek is from the Thomas Street Bridge down to Simcoe Street Bridge. Early in the season, it is a great place to fly-fish for rainbow when the ice is off but before spring run-off. Fishing the mouth of the river can be productive, too. Try casting a Kwikfish from here to the Simcoe Bridge.

Otonabee River (Map 11/B4–19/A6)
The Otonabee offers fair fishing for panfish, such as perch, as well as resident smallmouth and largemouth bass. The Otonabee also offers muskellunge and walleye fishing opportunities. These fish are often found in the river in the spring and regularly near the mouth of the river at Rice Lake.

Ottawa River (Map 64/E1–67/G5)
The Ottawa River has played an integral role in the development of Canada and the Ottawa Valley. Today, smallmouth bass are abundant in the river and have been caught in the 2 kg (4.5 lb) range. Northern pike can reach 6 kg (13 lbs) or more. Look in the slower back bays for cruising northerns. Walleye fishing can also be good for walleye that average 0.5–1.5 kg (1–3.5 lbs). Walleye travel in loose schools and still jigging is effective. Lake trout are found near Mattawa. The trout are stocked periodically, although fishing is usually slow. Muskellunge inhabit the river in several areas and fishing is usually slow, although there have been some big fish caught here. Several other sportfish inhabit the river, including sturgeon and whitefish.

Oxtongue River (Map 34/G1–44/E4)

The Oxtongue flows from the west side of Algonquin Provincial Park to Lake Of Bays. Both brook and rainbow trout have been stocked in the Oxtongue River section closer to Lake Of Bays. The portion of the river in and around Algonquin Park offers natural brook trout. Fishing for small rainbows and brook trout is fair in the area closer to Lake of Bays.

Parks Creek (Map 13/F1–21/G7)

Found in Tyendinaga Township, this small creek has been stocked with brown trout yearling, producing small to average size catches. These elusive trout are most often found early in the season, but can be tough to land.

Pautois Creek (Map 64/D5)

This small creek is easily accessible by 2wd roads not far from Highway 17. Small brook trout inhabit the creek in fair numbers. Fishing is generally fair, although can be good during overcast periods.

Petawawa River (Maps 44, 54–57, 66, 67)

The lower section of the Petawawa River flows from Cedar Lake to McManus Lake. Smallmouth bass are prevalent throughout this portion of the river and provide for good fishing at times. Northern pike and muskellunge are also found in sections of the river. Fishing for pike is fair for generally small pike, while muskellunge fishing is slow. Northerns have been found in excess of 4 kg (9 lbs) in some of the larger holes of the river. The lower section has some dangerous rapids and is off limits in Canadian Forces Base Petawawa. The upper section of the river, in contrast, is slow, meandering and home to a good population of small brook trout.

Pickerel River (Map 49/A3–51/F5)

The Pickerel River flows into Georgian Bay. Portions of the river pass through some remote territory, although the sections around Highway 69 are often busy during summer months. Fishing can be good for smallmouth and largemouth bass, which are found throughput the system and are the most predominant species in the river. You will also find average sized walleye and northern pike in some parts of the river. The most popular angling area is the river section from Highway 69 to the Georgian Bay.

Pigeon River (Map 9/G4–18/C7)

The Pigeon River from Omemee to Pigeon Lake offers fair fishing for smallmouth and largemouth bass. Panfish, which includes perch and bluegill, are prevalent throughout the river. Walleye and muskellunge can also be found in the river and more often found near the mouth of the river to Pigeon Lake.

Restoule River (Map 51/G1–61/A6)

The Restoule is a short river, flowing 40 km (25 miles) from the town of Restoule on Commanda Lake, through a number of lakes (including Restoule and Stormy) before flowing into the French River. The river holds good numbers of smallmouth bass and northern pike.

Rouge River (Map 2/C4–E5)

The Rouge River is a popular fishing destination that forms a natural barrier to the urban sprawl as it separates Scarborough from Pickering. In the summer, the river is fished for carp or perch using a dew worm. The best place to fish is near Rouge Beach, where the river flows into Lake Ontario. In the spring and summer, the river becomes a great place to catch spawning steelhead. Also try fishing the Rouge Marsh.

Scugog River (Map 9/F2–17/F7)

The river flows from Lindsay to Lake Scugog and offers fair fishing for average sized smallmouth and largemouth bass. The river is also a spawning ground for Lake Scugog walleye and muskellunge, but note the spring fishing sanctuary.

Seguin River (Map 32/A1–42/B6)

The section of the Seguin River from Isabella Lake to the Mountain Basin is rarely fished and offers good fishing for panfish and bass. Smallmouth and largemouth bass are found in the larger, deeper holes of the river. Walleye spawn in the western portion of the river in spring and there is a spring fishing sanctuary imposed during this time. The cooler upper reaches of the river have been stocked with brook trout and rainbow trout.

Severn River (Map 23/G5–25/A6)

The Severn River has fair to good fishing for smallmouth and largemouth bass, as well as walleye, northern pike and panfish. The more remote section of the river between Sparrow Lake and the Gloucester Pool offers the best fishing on the river.

Sharpe Creek (Map 34/B7)

Small brook trout and rainbow trout inhabit the creek in good numbers. Although much of the creek is accessible by 2wd dirt roads, the further you get from Highway 17, the better the fishing.

Silver Creek (Map 15/F2)

The Silver Creek is a small flowing stream that is inhabited by brook trout. Fishing can be quite productive at times for generally small trout. There is rough road access to some sections of the creek.

Skootamatta River (Map 21/F3–30/G3)

Smallmouth and largemouth bass are the most popular sportfish to be found, reaching memorable sizes in some of the more difficult spots to access. Northern pike typically remain small, while the occasional walleye surfaces from time to time in deeper sections.

Soper Creek (Map 4/A3–9/G7)

Soper Creek flows to Lake Ontario and offers slow fishing for brook trout, brown trout and rainbow trout. Brook trout can be found in the northern portion.

South River (Map 53/D4–62/C6)

The South River offers anglers a variety of different habitats and sport fish species. In sections closer to Powassan and north of the town of South River, smallmouth bass, northern pike and walleye can be found. Fishing is fair for smallmouth bass and small northern pike. Walleye are the most popular species on the river, while the sections east of the town of South River offer brook trout.

Squirrel Creek (Map 10/G4)

In the southern most section of the Squirrel Creek there are tributary streams that support a small natural brook trout fishery. The closer the creek approaches the Otonabee River the less the possibility of finding trout and the greater the possibility of finding panfish.

Sturgeon River (Map 61/B2)

The Sturgeon River flows into Lake Nipissing at the town of Sturgeon Falls. Some sections of the river offer angling opportunities for smallmouth bass and northern pike. At certain times of year, sections of the river closer to Lake Nipissing are inhabited by populations of walleye.

Tim River (Map 53/F7–54/E6)

It is a slow, meandering river that flows from the west side of Algonquin Park to Big Trout Lake. The section of the river between Rosebary Lake and Big Trout Lake is less travelled and offers the best angling opportunities. Brook trout inhabit the Tim River and are generally small.

Trent River (Map 11/F1–13/A5; 20/A7–D6)

The Trent River flows east to Campbellford and then south to Lake Ontario at Trenton. The river is part of the Trent Severn Waterway and heavily frequented by boaters during the summer season. Fishing is fair for decent sized smallmouth and largemouth bass. Walleye and northern pike can be caught through most of the river's entirety, although fishing is much slower than for bass. Muskellunge are also present in even smaller numbers.

Trout Creek (Map 52/G2)

Trout Creek flows near Highway 11 and is easily accessed throughout. Fishing is fair for small brook trout that are best caught on small nymph fly patterns or with a spinner and worms.

Veuve River (Map 60/F1–61/A2)

The Veuve River flows into Cache Bay of Lake Nipissing, which is a favourite hot spot for both walleye and northern pike. Close to Lake Nipissing there are also resident populations of small northern pike, while muskellunge and walleye can be found in the river system in the spring as they spawn for the season. Watch for special restrictions on the river and area.

Wasi River (Map 62/F4–63/D7)

Smallmouth bass and walleye are found in most areas of the river, especially in the section from Callander Bay to Wasi Lake. Some big walleye are caught each year and fishing can be good at times. Brook trout and rainbow trout are also found in the river in the sections closer to Algonquin Park.

White Partridge Creek (Map 56/C3)

White Partridge Creek flows from the north end of White Partridge Lake to the Crow River. The creek is navigable by canoe and offers good fishing at times. Brook trout inhabit the creek and average 20 cm (8 in).

Wilmot Creek (Map 4/A1–B3)

Wilmot Creek is a small stream between Bowmanville and Newcastle that flows into Lake Ontario. The creek produces well for steelhead in the spring. The best time is just after ice off, but before the water gets too dirty from spring run-off.

York River (Map 36/E2–38/F2)

The York starts west of Algonquin Park and flows through the Panhandle, Elephant and Baptiste Lakes, Bancroft and Conroys Marsh, eventually joining the Madawaska River near Combermere. The upper sections of the York rarely see a lure or fly and only local residents fish the lower section of the river. Fishing is fair to good throughout the year for brook trout.

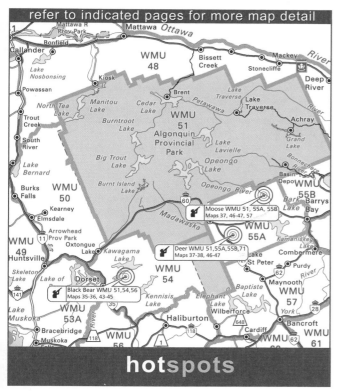

*H*unting has long been a popular activity for thousands of Ontario residents and visitors to the province. While there are many trophy hunters who come to this area to hunt, there are also plenty of sustenance hunters, too. Every year, these people head out in pursuit of the main big game species including moose, deer and bear. Small game hunters chase after fox, rabbit or hare and squirrel, while birders hunt geese, duck, wild turkey, partridge, woodcock and grouse. Cottage Country in Ontario is home to these and a number of other species to hunt for.

Traditionally, hunting seasons are in fall of each year, but there are sometimes hunting seasons in spring and winter as well. Season dates and bag limits vary from year to year and sometimes change without warning. Again, it is the responsibility of the hunter to keep up to date on changes to regulations, dates and bag limits. In addition to the regular seasons, there are a number of special hunting seasons. Every year, round the second week of October is the youth season for hunting deer, when youth age 16 and 17 can hunt deer with a firearm, providing that they are certified, have a license and are under the immediate supervision of a person over the age of 18 who is certified to hold a deer hunting license. The Ministry of Natural Resources is currently reviewing the moose hunt and how the moose draw system works. This is partly due to the varying moose populations in certain areas. As it stands now, resident hunters can apply for a moose tag as an individual or as a member of a group (the latter offers a better chance to obtain a tag).

Hunting is a highly regulated activity. It is your responsibility to know the rules and regulations before heading out. Hunters must pass both the Canadian Firearms Safety Course exam and the Ontario Hunter Education Course exam. Find out more at www.ohep.net. There are also two styles of hunting in Ontario: gun hunting and non-gun hunting. The latter includes archery and falconry. Each group needs an outdoor card. Gun hunters need a Class H1 card, while non-gun hunters need a Class H2 card. There is also an apprenticeship card for each of these hunting classes. Other things to note include the use of "hunter orange" during the open season and most areas also require non Ontario residents to use a licensed guide when hunting some big game species. For more on hunting, visit the hunting section of the Ministry of Natural Resources website at www.mnr.gov.on.ca.

GAME SPECIES

The main big game species in Cottage Country Ontario are moose, deer and bear. Others prefer the challenge to pursue small game such as fox, rabbit or hare and squirrel. Birders also have a good variety of species to look for from geese and duck to upland species such as wild turkey, partridge, woodcock and grouse. The seasons for each species vary as does the bag limit. Listed below is a summary of some of the main species to look for in the north.

Black Bear

There are about 100,000 black bear estimated to reside in Ontario, over 10% of the world's population. A large male black bear can get up to 175 kg (400 lb), although the average bear is usually about half that size.

The black bear population is distributed fairly equally across the entire area, even in areas that are quite heavily populated. This leads to an almost annual occurrence of problem bear having to be destroyed, as young males go looking for a place to call their own, and wind up in people's back yards.

Most hunting guides maintain baiting sites and generally have good success rates through the hunting season, typically from mid-August to end of October. Bear baiting involves using food (often human foods such as doughnuts, cookies and popcorn) to attract bear.

Coyote

Coyote are usually considered more of a pest than a popular species for hunting or trapping. Although coyote are technically classified as a fur-bearing animal, you are authorized to hunt them under your small-game license. In most WMUs, you also need a coyote game seal.

Coyotes are not pack animals, and usually hunt alone or in pairs, although several may gather at carcasses or other communal feeding sites. In the wild, they feed on hare and mice as well as blueberries and other fruit. They are opportunists, feeding on carrion of livestock, especially in winter. They will also feed on chickens, cats and other small farm animals, reinforcing their reputations as nuisance creatures. Note that if you happen to kill a coyote in order to protect your property in any WMU that requires a game seal, you must report that to your local MNR office.

Despite the often-aggressive attempts to destroy as many coyote as possible by landowners, coyote still survive and thrive. They are fairly common from the mixed forests of the Canadian Shield and the Clay Belt, southward, and can even be found in urban centers.

On Crown land, the coyote season is from mid-September until the end of March. As always, check the Hunting Regulations for changes to these rules before heading out. If you're lucky enough to bag one of these crafty creatures, you must fill out and submit a mandatory questionnaire for the MNR.

Ducks

There are, broadly speaking, two types of ducks, Dabbling and diving. Dabbling ducks are typically found in fresh, shallow marshes and rivers. They are good divers, but usually feed by dabbling or tipping, rather than diving underwater, thus the name. The speculum, or colored wing patch, is generally iridescent and bright and often a telltale field mark. Dabbling Ducks include blacks, mallards and green winged teals. They are most commonly found in this area in the many fens, bogs, marshes and lakes. Diving ducks also get their name from their feeding habits. They dive deep below the surface of the water to find food, such as fish and aquatic plants.

Diving ducks include canvasbacks, redheads, ring-necked ducks and greater and lesser scaup. Since their wings are smaller in proportion to the size and weight of their bodies, they have a more rapid wing beat than dabbling ducks. Diving ducks are sometimes found in small marshes (especially ring-necks), but are more frequently found in larger lakes and bays. They favour deeper open water areas where there is a good growth of underwater vegetation.

The classic set-up for hunting divers includes a boat, a dog and lots of decoys. The boat is needed to transport gear, set out decoys, retrieve birds and just get onto the water and away from the launch. A boat blind can be invaluable. Any ducks feeding on land will likely be a dabbling duck, for these sure-footed birds can walk and run well on land. Their diet is mostly vegetables and they are just as likely to be found in a farmer's field as they are in a marsh. These ducks will more readily land if the area is already "safe", so having decoys out will certainly help. Good camouflage is also essential, as ducks are very skittish. Some duck hunters even go so far as to paint their gun.

Migrating waterfowl are not regulated by the Ontario Government but by the Canadian Government, who has broken the province into four zones. Note that the season for each of these areas is different, but generally runs through fall and early winter; check the regulations for exact dates.

Geese

There are three types of geese hunted in Ontario: the brant goose, the snow goose and, by far the most common, the Canada goose. Canadian Geese are one of the most popular waterfowl, period. In the early season, they can be found in agricultural areas, but when the weather gets colder they move to saltwater flats. Hunting geese in a field is like similar to hunting dabbling ducks. Find an area, put out decoys and get under cover, either with camouflage gear or with netting. Geese like to land near where other geese are feeding, so set your decoys up so that you lead the birds to where you want them. The more decoys you use, the more likely geese are to land, as they find security in numbers. Feeding geese tend to make lots of noise, especially when they see competition approaching, so a goose call usually helps.

Duck hunters who are not used to hunting goose often use too light a load and fire from too far away. While geese are big birds, they have a relatively small vital zone and it can be hard to get a clean shot in. And their huge wingspan makes them look deceptively slow. The birds should be within 50 metres (50 yards) of you before firing.

Grouse

Not known for being the most cunning bird on the block, grouse are a popular bird to hunt in Ontario. But what they lack in brains they make up for in colouring. You can nearly step on one of these birds before they take off in a chaotic explosion of feathers. On a still autumn morning, this burst of activity can get the heart racing and the hands shaking. Once in the air, grouse are quick and often fly a random pattern through the forest, making them hard to hit. In fact, that's grouse hunting in a nutshell: go walk through the woods until you flush a grouse and then try and shoot it down in the two second window you have. More often than not, grouse hunters will walk for hours without success. Grouse like to hang out in dense young forest or along transition zones near the edge or streams. Because they are often found in the thick brush, they are even harder to flush and the thick woods will often block your shot.

Currently, the season for ruffled and spruce grouse is mid-September to the middle or end of December. There is a bag limit of five a day and a total possession limit of 15.

Moose

Moose are one of the most prized animals to hunt in Ontario. They are the largest member of the deer family and the largest ungulate in North America. Because of their size, they have few predators. Wolves will sometimes attack young or infirmed moose, but a healthy, grown moose is rarely targeted. Moose are quite distinctive looking (some would say downright ugly). They have long legs, a large, drooping snout and a flap of skin in the shape of a bell under their throats. The have broad hooves and are usually dark brown to black. Male Moose have large, broad antlers that are extremely prized among hunters. A full sized bull moose can stand 2.75 metres (9.25 ft) tall. Moose are usually found in wooded areas next to swamps, lakeshores and streams. They feed on leaves, grass and water plants in the summer.

In spite of their large size, moose can move through the underbrush quickly and quietly. Moose cannot see very well, but they have an acute sense of smell and hearing. When frightened, they will trot away with long smooth strides, threading their way through bush and trees that you wouldn't think they'd be able to navigate.

Rabbit or Hare

There are a variety of rabbit and hare species found in Ontario. The most common are snowshoe hare, which can be found across this entire area. Snowshoe hare are noted for their boom and bust population cycles. Once a decade or so, the population crashes, going from a high of up to 200 hare in a single hectare down to a low of one hare per 50 hectare. At last report, the population was climbing and the hunting should still be good across nearly the entire region.

There are other populations of hare and rabbit to be found in Ontario. European hare were in introduced as a game species in 1912 and are found mainly in southern Ontario. Cottontails can also be hunted. Their range is similar to the European hare.

Rabbit hunting season is currently from September 1 to June 15 of the following year. There is a daily bag limit of six cottontail rabbits and six European hares. In addition to the provincial small game license, a township or municipality license is required in regulated townships. As always, though, check the regulations before heading out.

White-tail Deer

White-tail deer are one of the most common large mammals in Ontario, with a population of over half a million deer across the province. They get their name from the notable white rump and tail. When the deer run, their tails are held erect, exposing the white underside. They are usually a grayish brown in winter and a reddish brown in summer. White-tailed bucks averaging 90 kg (200 lb.), while does average about 60 kg (130 lb.). Their antlers have un-branched tines extending up from single beams.

White-tail possess excellent senses of sight, smell and hearing and bound away gracefully when frightened. They are found in along the transition areas of forests or in open brush. They feed on buds, twigs, saplings and evergreen needles in the winter and on grass, fruit and leaves in the summer. They are frequently found in wooded river flats or in aspen groves. Their range is expanding westward into the foothills and they are becoming more common in the boreal forests of the north, too. They browse on forbs, chokecherry, Saskatoon and other shrubs. In addition to food, brushy patches also provide good cover.

White-tailed deer are found scattered throughout the region, with many rural areas like around Barry's Bay virtually shutting down during the first two weeks of November and the limited deer hunting season. The best hunting times are usually in the early morning and late evening, but deer can be bagged at any time of the day.

Wild Turkey

Wild turkeys are the largest game bird in North America with an adult male turkey weighing up to 11 kg (24 lbs) and females averaging about 4 kg (9 lbs). They do not look like domesticated turkey as they are darker and have a smaller breast and longer legs and necks. With their wattle, snood and caruncle, wild turkeys are not the prettiest bird. In fact, they're up there in the running for ugliest bird in the province. With a population of nearly 100,000 birds across the province, the opportunities to hunt wild turkey are increasing dramatically. This number should not be taken lightly. In 1984, there were an estimated 274 wild turkey in the entire province, having been hunted to near extinction.

Turkeys are generally hunted with shotguns, although there is an avid bow hunting community as well. They are generally hunted in spring, although there is a fall opening as well. In 2008, there were 10,492 wild turkeys harvested in the spring, but only 427 in the fall. Live decoys and electronic calls are not allowed. It is also illegal to hunt wild turkey using bait, although standing crops are not considered bait. Wild turkeys are often found on the edges of farmer's fields throughout the entire region.

People hunting wild turkey must have taken the Wild Turkey Hunter Education Course and be in possession of a wild turkey license. There is also a mandatory turkey harvest reporting worksheet.

Wolf

Wolves are the largest wild dogs found in the province, indeed, anywhere in the world. A full-sized male wolf can get up to 60 kg (130 lbs). Ontario has two types of wolf: the gray wolf and the eastern wolf. Gray wolves roam the boreal forests and semi-tundra in the far north, while eastern wolves rule the Canadian Shield and Great Lakes-St. Lawrence forests.

Wolves are a pack animal, travelling in groups that can be as small as two to over twenty. Pack sizes tend to be larger in winter. They mate in early spring and females give birth in May to a litter of five to seven pups. By fall, the pups are usually mature enough to participate in hunts. The primary food of wolves is moose, deer, elk and caribou, but can include beaver, hare, fish and even some plant material. In areas where wolves and ranchers occupy the same territory, there is often some predation. Ranchers and landowners often view wolves with suspicion and sometimes with downright contempt.

The majority of the wolf population in this area is around Algonquin Park and the northern areas where the deer population is growing. As with coyotes, wolves are classified as fur-bearing animals, but you are authorized to hunt them under your small-game license. In most WMUs you also need a wolf game seal.

Woodcock

The woodcock is a solitary game bird, often crouching amongst dead leaves and well camouflaged by its brown mottled plumage. Similar to grouse, a woodcock will remain motionless until almost stepped upon before taking off in a flurry of explosive movement. Most active at dusk, they live mostly on earthworms that they attract to the surface by drumming the forest floor with their feet. A single bird may eat twice its weight, or about 450 grams (1 pound), in worms per day.

The woodcock is about 28 cm (11 inches) long, including the long bill. With its eyes set farther back on the head than those of any other bird, they have a 360° field of vision. Their ear openings are located below, rather than behind the eye socket and their wings are very rounded. The outermost wing feathers are attenuated to produce vibratory sounds during flight, apparently at will. The woodcock pin feathers are also much esteemed as brush tips by artists, who use them for fine painting work. The pin feather is the covert of the leading primary feather of the wing.

WILDLIFE MANAGEMENT UNITS

Where to hunt seems to be the never ending question. So if you are new to an area or even a long-time resident looking for somewhere different, we have created this quick summary of each Wildlife Management Units (the large green numbers and boundaries on our maps).

WMU 42

Linking the south with the north, this unit stretches from the Georgian Bay north towards the Lake Temagami eco-region. Characterized by hilly terrain and mixed forests of red pine, white pine, yellow birch and maple, this area is one of the more heavily hunted parts of Ontario. The deer and waterfowl hunting is outstanding, while the bear hunting is no slouch either.

WMU 46

This massive unit is bordered on the west by Lake Huron from Severyn Sound northwards towards Georgian Bay and Big Parry Sound. Stretching approximately 180 kilometres through hundreds of bays, lakes, rivers and channels, this unit is home to a wide variety of wildlife including white-tailed deer, moose and black bear. Waterfowl by the thousands migrate to the area and small game can be found amongst the tall coniferous trees inland, providing a hunter's paradise. There are several provincial parks, reserves, estuaries and conservatories so consult the most recent information and regulations from the Ministry of Natural Resources.

WMU 47

This unit starts along the south end of the expansive Nipissing Lake and extends south through Restoule Provincial Park to the west and South Bay Provincial Park to the east. This management unit contains three big lakes within; Eagle Lake, Deer Lake and Bray Lake, all within a short distance from the towns of Sundridge and South River on the eastern side of the unit. Look for larger mammals to hunt like the moose and white-tailed deer as they stop for a drink along these pristine waters.

WMU 48

Spanning across the northern most tip of this region along the border of Quebec, this unit is especially rugged and features many spectacular views from Mattawa in the west through to Deep River and Petawawa to the east. In the surrounding areas, the moose hunting is sporadic, but improving. Bear hunting is reported as fair, while some of the smaller game hunting for rabbit and grouse is pretty consistent.

WMU 49

Running from Parry Sound along the southwest side of this unit and carrying along Highway 124 northbound through McKeller, this area is a spectacular drive with many hunting opportunities along the way. There are numerous lakes, streams and creeks which support many types of waterfowl. The southern areas are better for deer, while the further north you go, the better the moose hunting. Bear, rabbit and duck hunting are very good as well.

WMU 50

This unit is smaller than its eastern neighbour, taking you from South River to Huntsville along its western border then through hundreds of tiny lakes and rugged terrain as you travel eastward. Look for upland birds such as grouse and woodcock along the way as well as geese and ducks.

WMU 51

Algonquin Provincial Park covers over half of the western side of this WMU with literally hundreds of trails leading to lakes, streams and rivers with thousands of primitive campsites throughout. Fifty-three species of non-domestic mammals have been recorded within the boundaries of Algonquin Provincial Park, but hunters usually pursue the bigger game including white-tailed deer, black bear or wolf in the area around the park. Topping the list, however, is the mighty moose. Hunting is permitted in the Recreation/Utilization Zone in Clyde, Bruton and Eyre (McRae Addition) Townships. Hunting is also permitted in the east half of the park by the Algonquins of Ontario.

WMU 53A, 53B

Within these two units there are probably more lakes, rivers and bays than several other units combined. Travelling south along Highway 11 starting at Huntsville, you will pass Lake Vernon, Port Sydney, Mary Lake and into the northwestern side of Queen Elizabeth II Wildlands Provincial Park. This route takes you directly down the middle of these WMU's, 53A to the west and 53B to the east. Look for moose, white-tailed deer and black bear using the watering holes and grouse, duck and wild turkey lurking in the underbrush.

WMU 54

This unit is almost entirely engulfed by the Haliburton Forest Reserve to the west and the southern part of the Algonquin Provincial Park. The moose numbers tend to be better in the eastern portion of this area and there is excellent black bear hunting. There are also decent numbers of ruffed and spruce grouse, woodcock and wild turkey. In order to improve your chances of spotting game birds and animals, wear natural colours and unscented clothing. Be sure to stay downwind and keep your movements to a minimum.

WMU 55A, 55B

A long, skinny area skirting the southern borders of Algonquin Provincial Park, these two units travel along Highway 60 from Whitney through Madawaska to Barry's Bay. This area is excellent for white-tailed deer hunting, as well as the majestic moose. Given the popularity of deer hunting in this year, it is best to use deer stands near known food zones. Be sure to stay out longer in the day as deer can be bagged at any time of the day. Birders can also take a "gander" at Bark and Aylen Lakes for decent goose hunting and the surrounding underbrush for grouse.

WMU 56

Literally thousands of lakes are strewn amongst this medium sized unit from Fort Irwin in the north down through Haliburton, Minden and the shores of Gull Lake to the south. Queen Elizabeth II Wildlands Provincial Park sits in its southern area. Black bear are fairly common and there are some opportunities for deer and moose as well. For upland birds, grouse, woodcock and wild turkey hunting is a big draw to this area.

WMU 57

Migratory birds along the western side of this unit are what hunter's come for. Elephant and Baptiste Lakes host the majority of waterfowl, but don't rule out Bay and L'amable Lakes south of Bancroft. Travel east and you will find moose, elk, white-tailed deer and black bear populations.

WMU 58

This small unit includes the towns of Kaszuby, Combermere and Hopefield. Smaller lakes in the area provide hunters with the opportunity to bag a variety of big and small game including moose, deer, black bear and varying hares. For those interested in upland birds or waterfowl, this is a great place to find grouse, woodcock, a variety of geese and the large and wiley wild turkey.

WMU 60

This large unit starts in the north at the town of Bancroft and carries on to the southern border at Marmora and Havelock before heading west to Bobcaygeon. The bulk of this unit lies within the Kawartha Highlands Provincial Park, which encompasses 37, 587 hectares (92, 879 acres) and is the largest park in Ontario south of Algonquin Provincial Park. Situated along the southern edge of the Canadian Shield, this relatively undeveloped area features a rugged rolling landscape of small lakes, wetlands, forests and rocky barrens. You will find all types of big and small game, plus numerous upland birds and waterfowl. Hunting regulations have recently changed in the park so check for important information regarding hunting limits plus changes in specific hunting dates.

WMU 61

The main feature of this unit is the Bon Echo Provincial Park, renowned for Mazinaw Rock rising 100 metres above the deep Mazinaw Lake that also features largest visible collection of native pictographs in Canada. Due to its location, Bon Echo offers a unique chance to see species typical of both northern and southern Ontario, such as deer, moose, black bear, red fox and beaver. There are several reserves as you travel south so make sure to obey all hunting regulations along the way.

WMU 62

This unit rests in the eastern edge of Cottage Country, stretching from Actinolite in the extreme north down to Tweed along the eastern border. Stoco Lake is your best bet for hunting in this region as waterfowl by the thousands call this lake home.

WMU 68A, 68B, 69A, 70

These units all fall along the eastern border of Cottage Country down south through Belleville and Trenton before finally ending at Lake Ontario. The moose population is thin in these parts due to the proximity to the larger cities, but you should be able to find white-tailed deer, black bear, various species of hare and upland game birds such as grouse, woodcock and wild turkey. For the intrepid waterfowl hunter, the lakes in the southern section are a good bet for duck and goose hunting.

WMU 71

This small strip is bordered to the north by the Murray Marsh Conservation Area and leads south past the Brighton Provincial Wildlife Area all the way down to Presqu'ile Provincial Park and Lake Ontario. Murray Marsh at 667 hectares (1,648 acres) is a hotspot as the marshlands host a variety of wetland animal species and waterfowl. Presqu'ile Provincial Park is known for its excellent white-tailed deer hunting, as there is a large population within a relatively small area. Early morning and around dusk are generally the best times for hunting white-tailed deer. As always, check the regulations before heading out.

WMU 72A, 72B

These two units are sandwiched between Rice Lake to the northwest and Lake Ontario to the south. Port Hope, Newcastle, Bowmanville and the outskirts of Oshawa greet you as you travel west along the shores of the Great Lake. You will find all shapes and sizes of waterfowl the closer to the lakes you go, with white-tailed deer and black bear being the predominant big game animals. The deer population thins out as you move into WMU 72B and get closer to Oshawa, but there's plenty of upland bird hunting along the way.

WMU 73

Located southwest of Peterborough this unit has two main attractions. In the west, Port Perry and Lake Scugog provide all the waterfowl hunting you need as the marshlands are a haven for a wide variety of species of duck and goose. Heading further east, hunters look for grouse rustling amongst the underbrush and wild turkey roaming close to farmlands.

WMU 74A, 74B

There are several lakes, rivers and ponds within these two units. The towns of Bridgenorth, Lakeside and Donwood populate the area north of Peterborough providing hunters with easy access to supplies. Chemong Lake, in WMU 74A, is a good place to try your luck for duck and goose. The big game animals reside further north around Drummer Lake and Quackenbush Provincial Park.

WMU 75

This mid-sized unit is comprised of three massive lakes; Balsam Lake, Cameron Lake and Sturgeon Lake. All three have great waterfowl hunting with various species of goose and duck. If you're looking to bag that trophy moose or white-tailed deer, you may want to look elsewhere as the populations here are in decline.

WMU 76A, 76B, 76C

These units rest on the northern shore of Lake Simcoe and stretch from Bayview Beach in the east, west up to Lake Couchiching, then through Copeland Forest Management Area all the way to the southern part of Georgian Bay. The most common animal here is the white-tailed deer, but you can also find the odd moose lurking about. The surrounding forests make for great upland bird hunting, while the marshes tend to have better waterfowl hunting. Be sure to remember your binoculars so you can observe from a distance or see better in thick brush. The trick to most successful hunts is to see the prey before they see or smell you.

WMU 76D, 76E

Two very small management units occupy this space, with the Minesing Wetlands Conservation Area covering over half the area. There is no hunting allowed in this conservation area, so make sure you are within the proper boundaries before bagging any game. There are however, other marshes in the area that provide good hunting for varying species of geese and ducks.

WMU 77A, 77B, 77C

Straddling Highway 89, these units have a little bit of everything from Barrie to the north down to Tottenham to the south. There is no hunting in WMU 77A as this is Canadian Forces Base Borden; the folks there may shoot back! Better to try your luck in the other two units as they are well stocked with white-tailed deer, varying hares, grouse, woodcock, duck and the ever flamboyant wild turkey.

WMU 78A, 78B, 78C

Nestled between Lake Simcoe to the north and the major Metropolis of Toronto to the south, there are many lakes, rivers, streams and ponds for the hunter not wanting to tread too far into the great beyond. Look for white-tailed deer for bigger game and various species of hare for smaller game. Amongst the forests of deciduous trees you will also find grouse and woodcock, plus goose and duck populations along the waters edge.

WMU 78D, 78E

These two units reside within the Greater Toronto area and offer no hunting for the general public.

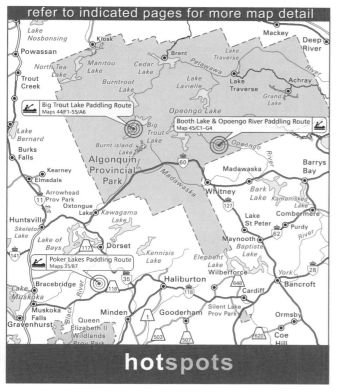

refer to indicated pages for more map detail

Big Trout Lake Paddling Route
Maps 44/F1-55/A6

Booth Lake & Opoengo River Paddling Route
Map 45/C1-G4

Poker Lakes Paddling Route
Maps 35/87

hotspots

Visitors from around the world come to Ontario for its endless array of lakes and rivers. It is one of the most popular paddling destinations in the world and Cottage Country is home to a lifetime of paddling opportunities including fantastic river routes and scenic lake circuits.

Algonquin Provincial Park is ground zero for paddling in Ontario. Canoe routes that begin near the Highway 60 corridor are normally busy throughout the year, but there are other places to start from, with roads touching the park on all four sides. In general, the easier it is to get to an access from Toronto, the busier it will be. Summer is the most popular time of year, although during the trout fishing season in spring can also be busy. When looking to find some seclusion, it is recommended to try a trip from one of the lesser-used access points or plan trips during the week or in the fall.

Trip equipment is very important to help reduce fatigue and increase enjoyment. For long tripping with numerous portages, a dependable, lightweight Kevlar canoe is recommended. Good planning is essential to minimize weight and maximize comfort. If planning is not done properly, an enjoyable trip can easily become hard work.

In general, the average paddler should be able to cover 10 km (6.2 mi) to 20 km (12.4 mi) in a six hour day. Of course, a number of factors must be accounted for when estimating the rate of progress, such as the number and difficulty of portages, wind on large water bodies and individual physical condition. Good paddlers on easy routes (short, easy portages on smaller lakes) can likely cover the larger distances, while difficult routes that involve longer or overgrown portages certainly slow progress.

For whitewater enthusiasts, the Algonquin Region offers some of the best whitewater rivers in the province. The rivers flow from the top of the watersheds down to the lowland valley areas, producing amazing whitewater runs. Many rivers are renowned for their rolling runs and attract adventure seekers from around the world. For those who are a little timid of rapids, several good novice rivers can be found in the region.

We use a modified version of the international scale to grade rivers. The Grade of a run tells you how difficult overall a stretch of river is. Class rates individual rapids, chutes and other features. A run might be rated Grade II overall, but one section might feature a Class IV drop. Please remember that river conditions are always subject to change and advanced scouting is essential.

LAKE & RIVER PADDING

Amable Du Fond River Route (Map 64/B6–B2)

Put-in/Take-out: The route begins at Kiosk within Algonquin Provincial Park. Parking is available at the access point. A second vehicle can be left at Samuel De Champlain Provincial Park or the Eau Claire Gorge Conservation Area.

There are 11 established portages along most of the needed sections, although there are no portage markers along the riverbank. Canoeists must be alert when approaching whitewater in order to spot the portages. The river is rated a Grad II-III whitewater river based on water level conditions. It is about 40 km (25 mi) from Kiosk to Samuel De Champlain Provincial Park. The river begins in the highlands of the park and slowly travels downward to the lowlands of the Mattawa River. Allow two full days to complete this entire stretch. Fishing can be good along the river for small trout. There are no organized campsites on the route, although no-trace camping is permitted. Be sure to respect private property.

Anstruther Lake/Long Lake Route (Map 28/B6)

Put-in/Take-out: Take Anstruther Lake Road to the public boat launch road that veers off of the main road. Parking is available at the boat launch. A second vehicle can be parked off of Long Lake Road at Long Lake Lodge for a small fee.

This moderate route travels across some large water bodies that can be challenging during high wind periods. From Anstruther Lake, the route begins by paddling to the most southerly portion of the lake and across the two short portages into Gold Lake. From Gold Lake the route continues south onto the secluded Cold Lake. From Cold Lake the route takes you to Cox Lake and then you follow a small stream to reach Loucks Lake. From Loucks Lake it is a short paddle to Long Lake where your second vehicle will be waiting at the lodge. Cottages dot the shoreline of Anstruther and Gold Lakes, although solitude can be found once you reach Cold or Cox Lakes. There are campsites scattered across the route, with some scenic sites being found on Cold Lake.

Bay of Quinte Paddling (Map 13)

Put-in/Take-out: There are many access points to the Bay of Quinte, although the most popular starting points are from local Belleville marinas or boat launches. Paying for parking is often required, although most marinas and boat launch areas do not charge for canoe/kayak launching.

The Bay of Quinte is world renowned for its quality walleye fishery, which attracts a large boating crowd. More recently, outdoor enthusiasts have begun to explore the bay by canoe and open water kayak. Although boating traffic can be heavy at times, larger canoes and ocean kayaks have proven to be an intimate way to travel the bay. From the preferred launching point, the paddling possibilities are limitless. This paddle is not for the inexperienced since you need appropriate skills and experience to deal with the turbulent waters and heavy boat traffic.

Beausoleil Island Routes (Map 23/D4)

Put-in/Take-out: From Highway 400 take Muskoka Road 5 west to Honey Harbour where parking and a boat launch are available at the marina north of the town.

Beginning in Honey Harbour, you have a few options to access Beausoleil Island of the Georgian Bay Islands National Park. The south access leads around Little Beausoleil Island to Tonch Point. The northwest route leads around Little Beausoleil Island to Beausoleil and Chimney Bay or to the northern point of the island near Honeymoon Bay. All routes travel through large water areas that can be difficult to manage during high wind periods. Also, be alert at all times for motorboat activity throughout the channels. The area is very scenic and camping is available at one of the many National Park campsites. Beausoleil Island also offers several trails that can be explored for added adventure and is home to the rare (and shy) Massassagua Rattlesnake. National Park passes must be purchased for overnight stays.

Big East River Canoe Route (Map 43/E6)

Put-in/Take-out: From Highway 60, follow Limberlost Road (County Road 8) past Brooks Mill to Billie Bear Road, which leads to Distress Dam Road. Follow this road to the dam and parking area. A second vehicle can be parked at Arrowhead Provincial Park.

This moderate to difficult (Grade II-III) route is exciting to run but is not well used and portages can be difficult to locate. You may have to line or bushwhack to portage around some areas of the route depending on your experience. The route travels about 17 km (11 mi) from the dam to Arrowhead Provincial Park and can be done in a full day. Rustic camping is available along the route, although an actual site may be difficult to find. The run does travel through some rapids, including the McArthur Chute, a waterfall that must be portaged around.

Big Sound Kayaking (Map 31, 40)

Put-in/Take-out: The main access area for this paddling excursion is the town of Parry Sound, although Killbear Provincial Park is an ideal home base location for exploring the sound.

A Popular destination for sea kayakers is Big Sound. Many that travel this loop usually begin from the town of Parry Sound and travel north or south along the shoreline. The trip takes two days to complete with the midpoint being Killbear Provincial Park. Stick close to shore as boating traffic in the middle of the sound can be heavy, especially in the summer months. Paddlers will experience some great scenery as they explore the rugged rocky terrain of the Big Sound. While cottages and camps dot a good portion of the shoreline, there are vast stretches of uninhabited shoreline, especially around the Killbear Park shore area.

Bissett Creek Canoe Route (Map 66/C3–C6)

Put-in/Take-out: The put-in is located off Highway 17 where parking is available. Alternatively, travellers can drive down Bissett Creek Road to a point where the road comes close to the creek and put-in at the creek. A second vehicle can be parked at the Algonquin Park interior access point near Bissett Lake to allow travel in one continuous direction.

While it can be done in a day, this moderately difficulty route is best done in two. Some of the portage points are overgrown, adding to the difficulty of the route. Although there are no designated campsites along the creek, camping is permitted. There are four portages along this stretch with two of them spanning over 600 m (1,970 ft). Once at Big Bissett it is an easy paddle to the access point on the eastern shore of the lake.

Black Lake Loop (Map 35/B4)

Put-in/Take-out: West of Highway 35, just south of Dorset, the Shoe Lake Access Road takes you directly to Shoe Lake where parking for about five vehicles is available.

This semi-wilderness route travels across nine beautiful lakes and over 11 portages. Visitors will paddle past a few cottages on Shoe Lake, but civilization begins to become as you travel through Blue and Red Chalk Lakes to Carcass and Pairo Lakes. The total distance of the loop is about 21 km (13 mi) with the longest portage being the 1,463 m (4,800 ft) trip from Pairo Lakes to Black Lake. The loop can be completed in two days and there are campsites scattered along the route. Birders will revel in bird watching opportunities, especially through the wetland area closer to Wren Lake and most of the lakes offer fishing for bass. Overall, most of the portages are generally short, although there are three that are over 1,000 m (3,281 ft) in length including the first one to Blue Chalk Lake and last one from Five Mile Bay on Raven Lake back to the parking area.

Black River, Lower (Map 21/D2)

Put-in/Take-out: The put-in for the Lower Black River is also the take-out for the upper section. Follow County Road 12, north of Madoc, to County Road 20 and Queensborough. The put-in is located below the dam. The take-out is on the Black River Road near its junction with Highway 7.

The lower section of the Black River is easier than the turbulent waters of the upper section, though easy is a relative description. This 10 km (6.2 mi) stretch is generally rated Grade III, although there are a few significant Class IV rapids. One of the highlights of the trip is a small canyon-like stretch, which should be scouted or portaged around. Another impressive natural obstacle is a set of waterfalls, which are a Class IV-V drop and should only be attempted by expert paddlers. The lower section of the Black River can be run in a day, although travellers may be able to find a few rustic campsites along the shore for an overnight stay. Although this section of the Black River may be easier than its Upper Black River counterpart, it is still recommended only for closed kayaks and tandem canoes.

Black River, Upper (Map 30/C7–21/D2)

Put-in/Take-out: Access to the Upper Black River portion can be found by following the Lingham Lake Road east from the town of Cooper. The put-in is located below the first bridge over the river. The take-out for the route is found just before the dam near Queensborough.

The Upper Black River is a rustic, Eastern Ontario whitewater river that snakes its way through 12 km (7.5 mi) of the forests and granite shorelines of the southern Canadian Shield. The upper section of the river can be run in one day, although those who enjoy play boating may want to divide the trip into two days. There are a few opportunities to camp along the river. This section of the Black River offers a number of Class IV rapids as well as its fair share of Grade II and III whitewater sections. This trip is mainly for whitewater kayaks and tandem canoes.

Black River Route (Map 25/B7–F5)

Put-in/Take-out: At the settlement of Cooper's Falls head east along Cooper's Falls Road (County Road 6) to the unpaved Black River Road. Continue east to the parking area at Victoria Falls. A second vehicle can be left at County Road 169 near the crossing of the Black River.

This moderate, Grade I-II semi-wilderness route takes you along the secluded Black River for about 21 km (13 mi). There are about six portages along the route that are all relatively short in length. The longest is the 650 m (2,133 ft) portage found near the beginning of the route. It will take most people two days to complete the trip and there are a few scenic campsites found about half way through the run. One of the more popular campsites is the island site located before Cooper's Falls. This river route offers an added pleasure during the fall when the forest leaves burst out into arrays of orange, yellow and red.

Buzzard Lake Route (Map 28/C7–19/C2)

Put-in/Take-out: Take Long Lake Road off of Highway 28 to Long Lake Lodge where parking is offered for a small fee. To drop off your second vehicle, take Coon Lake Road off of Highway 28 near Burleigh Falls and follow this road to the lake. Your second vehicle can also be parked at the end of Julian Lake Road on Big Cedar Lake.

On busy summer weekends, the Buzzard Lake Route is a good alternative to the Turtle Lake Loop. There are seven portages, none over 1,000 m (3,281 ft) in length. From Long Lake the route passes through Buzzard, Vixen and Shark Lakes before moving on to Coon Lake. For a longer route, a 180 m (591 ft) portage can be made into Big Cedar Lake. In the fall, some fantastic leaf colours can be witnessed and campsites are available on every lake on this moderate route.

Clear Lake Loop (Map 32/A4)

Put-in/Take-out: From Highway 69/400 take the Rankin Lake Road to Blue Lake Road, which leads to Three Legged Lake Road. Follow this road to the access point at Three Legged Lake.

The Clear Lake Loop is set amid the splendour of The Massasauga Provincial Park wilderness. You can pick up a park pass at either Oastler Lake Provincial Park on Highway 69/400 or at one of The Massasauga Provincial Park gate-houses. This moderate route takes you through a part of the Georgian Bay wilderness. The route travels from Three Legged Lake to Spider Lake and then on to Clear Lake, with a possible side-trip to Georgian Bay. The total distance of the loop is approximately 31 km (50 mi) with five portages. There are many campsites along the route that are clearly marked for your convenience. If the route is not very busy, it should be easy to find a preferred island site on either Spider or Clear Lake. Good fishing is also available on all the lakes, including the Georgian Bay.

Conroys Marsh Canoe Route (Map 47/G7–38/F2)

Put-in/Take-out: The access to this route is found at Negeek Lake on McPhees Bay. Off Highway 515, the McPhee Bay Road is found about 4.7 km from the junction with Highway 62 at Combermere.

Conroys Marsh is a vast wetland that is truly a unique place. The marsh has played a number of roles in history from a great provider to natives to a transportation line for the early log drives. Today, the marsh is wetland habitat for waterfowl and other birds, including the great blue heron. Walleye used to thrive in the marsh, although increased human pressure has reduced the species to a rarity. From the access area on Negeek Lake, paddle into the York River past the mouth of the Madawaska River. From Negeek Lake, the York River is a meandering waterbody that slowly opens into the wetland. Outdoor enthusiasts can paddle for hours in the marsh, exploring the many bays and inlets. The route is an easy, relaxing day trip.

Dividing Lake Provincial Park [Rockaway Lake] Route (Map 44/F7–45/A6)

Put-in/Take-out: One of the main access points follows County Road 12, east of Highway 35, to Livingstone Lake. Parking is available off the road shortly after the Livingstone Lake lodge. This route leads into Algonquin Park where park passes are required.

The Dividing Lake Provincial Park route is a difficult trip mainly due to the exhausting 2,750 m (9,022 ft) portage from Kimball to Rockaway Lake. Kawagama Lake can also hinder travel if winds are strong. One of the rewards of this challenging trip is the stand of beautiful, ancient white pines found between Minkey and Dividing Lake. For the more adventurous, paddlers can continue onto Minkey Lake and then to Dividing Lake in the Algonquin interior. All the lakes along the route offer fishing for brook trout, while camping is found at Rockaway and Dividing Lakes to name a few.

Dokis Canoe Route (Map 61/F7–50/E1)

Put-in/Take-out: The access to this route is Restoule Provincial Park, located at the end of Highway 534. The put-in is found on Stormy Lake in the north end of the park.

The Dokis Canoe Route begins from Stormy Lake in Restoule Provincial Park and travels west to Lennon Lake, before branching south on Woodcock Creek and the series of portages into Portage and Memesagamesing Lakes. Continue west along the Memesagamesing River, which turns north to link with the French River. From the French River, the route travels back along the Restoule River to the start. The terrain is typical southern Canadian Shield country, with smooth rocky shorelines and rugged pine landscapes along much of the route. The trip travels over 90 km (56 mi) and is not heavily travelled, therefore, portages may be difficult to find and traverse. No camping is permitted on the Dokis Native Reserve.

Drag River/Burnt River Route (Map 26/G2–17/F3)

Put-in/Take-out: Most start this route from the Canning Lake Dam to the east of Minden. Across the dam off County Road 17 there is a short portage down to the put-in. A second vehicle can be parked at Balsam Lake Provincial Park, where County Road 121 passes near Cameron Lake in Fenelon Falls or at the town of Rosedale near Highway 35.

The faster waters of the Drag River begin below the Canning Lake Dam and lead quickly to the Burnt River. Overall, this is a moderate (Grade II-III) semi-wilderness river that travels south towards Cameron Lake at Fenelon Falls. The route can be up to 80 km (50 mi) if you include the bigger lakes like Kashagawigamog and Canning in the north and Balsam in the south. A few campsites are scattered along the Burnt River, as are a number of short portages to avoid low water or heavy rapids. Shortly after the Irondale River connects with the Burnt River, a well-worn portage takes you around the magnificent Three Brothers Falls.

Eels Creek Route (Map 19/D2)

Put-in/Take-out: One put-in is located off of Highway 28 at Haultain, where the highway crosses the creek. For a longer route, take Julian Lake Road to the Big Cedar Lake access point. Your second vehicle can be parked off of Northey's Bay Road (County Road 56), where the creek passes under the road before entering Stoney Lake.

The Eels Creek Route is an easy (Grade I-II) 8-11 km (5-7 mi) trip that can be done in a day. One of the natural features of the trip is High Falls. The falls can be heard from a good distance away and do not pose a real danger unless they are foolishly run. There are campsites scattered along the route with some very scenic sites near High Falls. Fishing for bass is offered along various stretches of the creek and there are 8 portages along the route that are all quite short with the longest being only 540 m (1,772 ft).

Eighteen Mile Island Loop (Map 49/D1–60/E7)

Put-in/Take-out: The main access to this French River route is from the Loon's Landing Resort on Dry Pine Bay, just off Highway 69 north.

From the put-in on Dry Pine Bay, the route travels to the North Channel of the French River and then joins the main French River Route that follows the park corridor back to the start. In the northern portion of the trip, the terrain is typically farmland and mixed forests. As you venture down the main channel of the French River, the Canadian Shield landscape becomes much more evident. There are a few rapid areas that require attention before portaging/running. All of the more challenging rapids can be portaged around, making the trip much easier. Rustic campsites are numerous and are well distributed throughout the route.

French River Canoe Route (Map 61/A6–48/D3)

Put-in/Take-out: Parking and boat launch facilities are available at Dokis Bay at the end of Dokis Reserve Road, which branches east off of Highway 64 near Monetville. To avoid the first portage, the trip can begin at the Chaudiere Dam to the southwest. The route ends on the shores of Georgian Bay.

The French River Route is steeped in the history of native travellers, early explorers and the fur trade. The difficult 77 km (48 mi) journey contains plenty of rapids and takes users on a five to seven day journey back to the days of birch-bark canoes and unexplored land. At Recollet Falls, numerous crosses were erected to mark several locations where the river is documented as taking the lives of ill-fated voyagers. A plaque has been placed at the Highway 69 junction to mark this historic river's famed travellers. From here the route continues onward to the shores of Georgian Bay.

Frost Centre: Haliburton Highlands Water Trails [HHWT] (Map 35)

Over a dozen maintained canoe routes are found in the Frost Centre area. The portages are well-marked and the campsites offer pit toilets and fire pits. The routes range in difficulty from easy to moderately difficult and are ideal for planning a backcountry trip anywhere from one to seven days. Permits are required to stay at the canoe-in sites in order to manage the volume of visitor traffic the area receives.

Big Hawk/Sherborne Lake Loop (Map 35/E5)

Put-in/Take-out: The put-in for this route is the Big Hawk Lake Access Point, which is found at the end of County Road 13. Watch for the Big Hawk Lake Road heading north (left). The take-out is the same.

This route starts on Big Hawk Lake and passes through No Name Pond, Summit Pond, Sherborne Lake and returns to Big Hawk. You will probably want a couple days to complete the route.

Black River Route – Frost Centre (Map 35/C4–E3)

Put-in/Take-out: This is an out and back trip that starts from the put-in on Little Wren Lake north of the Frost Centre. There is a picnic site on the east side of Highway 35 where parking is found.

This is one of the longest and most remote routes in the Frost Centre and Haliburton Highlands systems. It will take most people four or five days to complete and features a couple of long portages en route to the north-east boundary of the Frost Centre. The trek takes you from Little Wren Lake and along the Black River to Hosiery Lake passing Raven, Gun, Knife, Jean and Mooney Lakes to name a few. The best time to go is early summer, as water levels can get low during dry months.

Gun Lake Loop (Map 35/D3)

Put-in/Take-out: At the north end of the Frost Centre, this route starts or ends at the Deer Narrows on Raven Lake. From Highway 35, north of Dorset, turn east onto Kawagama Lake Road (County Road 8) and follow this road for about 7.4 km to Deer Narrows Drive, which leads to an access point. The Herb Lake access point is found off Herb Lake Drive about 1 km past the Deer Narrows turnoff.

This short, easy route can be done in a long day, but is best split across two or even more. There are a number of route options that can be followed once you're on the route. The main route heads south to Gun Lake. A short portage links Raven with Gun and a short stretch of the Black River links Gun and Herb Lake.

Kawagama Lake (Map 35/E2)

Put-in/Take-out: There are a number of places to access the lake, including Fletcher Bay, Old Mill and Mountain Trout House.

Kawagama Lake is a big lake with plenty of nooks and crannies to explore. You can spend an afternoon or a couple days exploring. However, the lake can get quite windy.

Kennisis, Red Pine & Little Hawk Lake Loop (Map 35/F4)

Put-in/Take-out: Put-in and take-out at the Kennisis Dam. To get there follow County Road 7 from West Guildford. Follow the road through the main gate of the Haliburton Forest Reserve and then along the north shore of the lake to the dam.

This two to three day loop starts at Kennisis Lake Dam, passes through Red Pine Lake, heads south through Clear Lake and into Little Hawk Lake. The route heads back via Cat Lake and into Kennisis Lake.

Little Hawk, Blackcat & Clear Lake Loop (Map 35/F4)

Put-in/Take-out: The put-in and take-out for this route is the Little Hawk Lake Access Point. To get there head east on Country Road 13 from Highway 35 just past Halls Lake. Follow the road to the access point.

This nice short loop starts at the Little Hawk Lake Access Point and continues north through Blackcat Lake. It then curves back south through Clear Lake, Big Hawk Lake and finishes back at Little Hawk Lake Access Point. It is a short 1-2 day route, but has experienced heavy impact due to large groups trampling through.

Margaret/South Jean Lake Route (Map 35/B5)

Put-in/Take-out: The access point is found at the end of the Margaret Lake Road, which is found south of the main Frost Centre buildings off the west side of Highway 35.

This nice short route is accessed at Margaret Lake and follows a chain of lakes down to South Jean Lake and returns to the Margaret Lake Access Point.

McKewan Lake Loop (Map 35/C4)

Put-in/Take-out: The access is found on Wren Lake, while parking is found at the picnic site off of the east side of Highway 35 across from Wren Lake.

This moderate semi-wilderness loop takes you over 15 km (9 mi) and across six beautiful lakes. There are eight portages along the route that leads from Wren to Horse and McEwan Lake. You can camp on McEwan or loop over to Three Island where the longest portage of 667 m (2,188 ft) leads to Margaret Lake. Continue onto Dan and then back to McEwan for the return trip. The loop is best completed in three days.

Red Pine Lake Loop (Map 35/E5)

Put-in/Take-out: The put-in and take-out for this route is also the Big Hawk Lake Access Point. From County Road 13, off of Highway 35, watch for the Big Hawk Lake Road heading north (left).

Give yourself up to four days to complete this trip through Big Hawk, Red Pine, Clear and Nunikani Lake. You will spend most of your time paddling and enjoying the scenery as the portages are fairly short and easy. The route passes through the Clear Lake Conservation Reserve, which is a particularly environmentally sensitive area.

St. Nora, Sherborne & Raven Lake Loop (Map 35/D4)

Put-in/Take-out: This route starts on St. Nora Lake, which is found off Highway 35 south of Dorset and returns the same way. The take-out is at Wren Lake, also along Highway 35.

The main stem of this route travels from St. Nora through Sherborne Lake, Raven Lake and finishes up at Wren Lake. But, like all the routes in the area, there are a couple or three side routes that can lengthen the trip. Options include side-trips into Orley, Silver Doe and Silver Buck Lakes, Ernest Lake, or a loop through Sundew, Little Avery, Bruin Lakes, Long and Roach Pond and Plastic Lake. There is good fishing in Orley, Silver Doe and Silver Buck Lakes.

St. Nora, Kabakwa, Big Hawk & Sherborne Lake Loop (Map 35/D5)

Put-in/Take-out: This route starts and ends on St. Nora Lake, which is found off Highway 35 south of Dorset.

Give yourself at least two and possibly three days to do this route, which heads south into Kushog and Kabakwa Lakes before heading into Big Hawk, Sherborne and back to St. Nora. You can explore No Name Pond or Orley Lake from this route as well.

Georgian Bay Paddling (Maps 14, 22, 23, 31, 32, 39, 40, 48, 49)

Put-in/Take-out: There are several access points for paddlers on the Georgian Bay. A popular paddling access is Pete's Place Access Point in Blackstone Harbour (Map 32/B5) of The Massasauga Provincial Park. Some of the other access areas can be found at Moon River (Map 32/B6), Go Home Lake (Map 23/E1) or Honey Harbour (Map 23/E4).

Sea kayaking is a popular outdoor recreation activity in Georgian Bay. With the hundreds of quite inlets and thousands of small islands, the bay provides a unique and rugged setting for kayakers. Whether you head out for the day or camp overnight at a scenic Massasauga Provincial Park campsite, the exploration possibilities are endless. Paddling in the bay is not recommended for novice paddlers, as strong winds can make this trip difficult. Also, boating traffic is heavy in the bay.

Gibson-McDonald Route (Map 23/E2)

Put-in/Take-out: Off Highway 400 there is access available at Six Mile Lake Provincial Park or further north off Georgian Bay Road at McDonald Lake.

This moderate 56 km (35 mi) semi-wilderness loop can be completed in 3-4 days from Six Mile Lake. There are nine short portages, most along the Gibson River, including the Three Rock Chute, a small but potentially treacherous waterfall. Experienced paddlers can run the last set of rapids into Georgian Bay. The stretch along the river and across Georgian Bay is quite scenic, but paddlers should be wary of boat traffic in the bay. During summer weekends, traffic on the route, especially near McCrae Lake, can also be overwhelming. Fishing is available on all the water bodies of this route.

Gold Lake Loop (Map 27/G6–28/A7)

Put-in/Take-out: Off of Highway 507 take Beaver Lake Road to the Catchacoma Lake Access Point.

The Gold Lake Loop travels through the heart of Haliburton Cottage Country. With no portages, this is an easy day trip for the family or for beginners. However, boat traffic can be heavy during the summer. From Catchacoma Lake, the loop takes you across Beaver Lake, Gold Lake and on to Mississagua Lake. Most of the shoreline on the lakes in the loop is private property.

Grant's Creek/Mackey Creek Canoe Route (Map 66/F3–G4)

Put-in/Take-out: The access point to this route is found off Highway 17, on Grant's Creek, about 2 km west of Stonecliffe. Parking is available off the highway on one of the nearby bush roads. Be sure to be aware of private property and obey any land use signs. A second vehicle can be left at Driftwood Provincial Park or off one of the bush roads that crosses close to Mackey Creek.

This two-day route travels in a loop from the put-in on Highway 17 to Driftwood Provincial Park on Holden Lake of the Ottawa River system. Starting on Grant's Creek, the route leads south before branching east over many small lakes, including Eeyore, before linking with the Mackey Creek system at Sweezy Lake. From here the route continues east and then north towards the Holden Lake/Ottawa River. The rustic route is moderately difficult due to overgrowth on the creek and on many of the portages, which may be hard to find.

Grundy Lake Provincial Park Route (Map 49/E3)

Put-in/Take-out: Grundy Lake Provincial Park is located between Highway 69 and Highway 522 north of Parry Sound. Access to the canoe route is available from Gurd or Gut Lake in the campground area of the park.

The Grundy Lake Provincial Park Canoe Route is a short route that can be extended into a multi-day river route. The first three lakes in the route, Grundy, Gut and Gurd Lake, have vehicle campsites along their shorelines, while the last two lakes, Beaver and Pakeshkag Lake, are much more secluded. Backcountry campsites are available on all the lakes in the system other than Gut Lake. For the more adventurous, you can begin your trip at the park and travel north to the Pickerel River from Pakeshkag Lake where there is an endless array of paddling possibilities available on the Pickerel and the French River systems.

Gull River Route (Map 26/F2–17/E3)

Put-in/Take-out: Parking and access is available at the public park in Minden off of Highway 35. A second vehicle can be left at Norland, Coboconk or Fenelon Falls off of Highway 35, near the river crossing points in each of the towns.

The Gull River is an easy Grade I-II day trip from Minden to one of the three potential destination points. From Minden to Norland there are three short portages, each around various dams (be aware of currents around the intake) along the easy route. Motorboat traffic on the lakes can be heavy. Past Norland the route snakes through Shadow Lake and Silver Lake before passing under Highway 35. Shortly after the underpass, the route leads into the popular Balsam Lake. You can take-out at Rosedale near Highway 35 or continue on into Cameron Lake and take-out at Fenelon Falls. It takes a fit and determined canoeist to make it all the way from Minden to Fenelon Falls. For a shorter trip, try putting in at Norland.

For whitewater paddlers, there is the Minden Wild Water Preserve found between Horseshoe and Minden Lakes. The play section is small but is home to Grade III to IV water and is a good challenge to whitewater enthusiasts.

Healey Lake/Moon River Route (Map 32/D5)

Put-in/Take-out: West of MacTier, take Healey Lake Road to Kapikog Lake/Healey Lodge Road, Earls Marina Road or Back Road. These roads offer a place to launch and park.

The trek begins at Healy Lake or Kapikog Lake and heads south towards Eagle Lake. The route is considered difficult due to challenging sections on the Moon River (Grade II-III) and the rough condition of some of the portages. The portage from Kapikog Lake to Eagle Lake will be your main concern as the terrain can sometimes be soggy. Once on the Moon River, the trip does not get easier. There are many obstacles such as rapids, sweepers, the Curtain Chute, as well as some tricky areas to navigate. However, the route gets easier beyond Moon River Bay and the portage that leads you to Healey Lake. Fishing is offered on all of the lakes on the route and the mouth of the Moon River is renowned for its spring walleye fishing. There are campsites scattered along the route, which can take anywhere from 2-4 days depending on paddlers experience. It is recommended to have a topographical map and compass to travel this route.

Hollow River Route (Map 35/E1–C3)

Put-in/Take-out: Follow Kawagama Road to Russell Landing Road where parking and access are available. A second vehicle can be placed at Rabbit Bay, off Highway 35, near Dorset or at any of the public boat launch areas on Lake Of Bays.

The Hollow River Route is a moderately difficult (Grade II-III) white water route that spans 20 km (12 mi) and can be completed in a day. Beginning at Russell Landing, travel northeast to the mouth of the Hollow River. Continue down the river past Dorset before heading north to Rabbit Bay and to the take-out point. There are four distinct sets of rapids along the river with the last two sets, the Hollow River Rapids, being the most difficult. Be sure to scout any rapids or tricky areas to avoid potential problems. The route is user-maintained only with unmarked portage points that may be difficult to locate.

Indian River Route (Map 19/D5–11/C2)

Put-in/Take-out: The main access points to this route are located at the Warsaw Caves and Hope Mill Conservation Areas or Lang Mill Pioneer Village. Please inform conservation area staff that you are travelling the route. A second vehicle can be parked east of the village of Keene where the river crosses under County Road 2.

From the Warsaw Caves Conservation Area the river meanders through semi-forested areas past Hope Mill Conservation Area and Lang Mill Pioneer Village. This easy (Grade I-II) route can be done in a day depending on your access point, although it is recommended to take 2 days to complete the route from

Warsaw Caves. Camping is available at the Hope Mill and Warsaw Caves Conservation Areas and fishing is offered along most stretches of the river. Portage points are generally short but are not maintained. In late summer, the river is quite low and it may be necessary to portage or line your canoe more often than in spring and early summer.

Irondale/Burnt River Route (Map 27/E2–26/G5–17/E3)

Put-in/Take-out: The put-in is at the south side of the village of Gooderham on the south side of Highway 503 near the bridge over the Irondale River. A second vehicle can be parked near the County Road 121/Highway 503 junction in Kinmount or much further south at Fenelon Falls.

There are many short (100-200 m/300-600 ft) portages along this moderate Grade II-III route to avoid low water, rapids and waterfalls that make the trip more challenging. The total distance of the trip is about 41 km (25 mi) from Goderham to Kinmount. One highlight of the trip is the beautiful Three Brothers Falls found shortly after the Irondale meets up with the Burnt River. The only designated campsite along the Irondale River is a site at the Devil's Gap, about a quarter of the way down the route. There are also a few campsites found on the Burnt River if you continue past Kinmount.

Key River/Pickerel River Route (Map 49/D4–D1)

Put-in/Take-out: The put-in to this route is the Key Marina, off Highway 69. The take-out is the Pickerel Marina on the Pickerel River, near Highway 69.

This easy canoe route begins on the Key River beside Highway 69. The 46 km (29 mi) route follows the Key River to Georgian Bay and then along the Pickerel River back to Highway 69. The Key River is a popular boating channel to the Georgian Bay and is quite busy in summer. Once you approach the Pickerel River, you will find more solitude. There are only two easy portages. Rustic campsites can be found along much of the route, but are easier to find along the Pickerel River section of the route.

La Vase River Route (Map 62/E3)

Put-in/Take-out: The put-in for this route is in the southern end of North Bay at Champlain Park, off Champlain Park Road. The take-out is behind the Pine Hill Motel, off Park Drive. Permission must be obtained to park at the motel.

The La Vase River Route is an ideal beginner or tune-up paddle near North Bay. The route is just over 4 km (2.5 mi) in length and can be easily done in a few hours. To extend your trip, you can follow the river out onto Lake Nipissing and paddle along the shore of the large inland lake. Callander Bay to the south of the La Vase River is a good area to explore.

Madawaska River, Middle (Map 47/C6)

Put-in/Take-out: The middle part of the Madawaska River can be accessed from the bridge where Siberia Road (County Road 69) crosses over the river or further up river at the Bark Lake Dam. The main take-out for this part of the river is located near River Road, before the river enters Kamaniskeg Lake or at the public access point on the lake's western shore.

This stretch of the mighty Madawaska River runs about 5 km (3.1 mi) between Bark and Kamaniskeg Lake The route is rated a Grade II-III difficulty, although during high water there is a stretch of Class IV whitewater at the Staircase Rapids. All of the larger rapids can be portaged around. Scout all whitewater before attempting to run it. For river conditions, call the Madawaska Kanu Centre at (613) 756-3620.

Madawaska River, Upper (Map 46/A4–B4)

Put-in/Take-out: There are two access points to the Upper Madawaska River. The first is found in Whitney, off Highway 60. A parking area and put-in is found at the west side of the river. The second access point is located east of Whitney, off a short road from Highway 60, just after the power lines cross the highway. The take-out is located down river, off Major Lake Road, north of the town of Madawaska. Algonquin Bound Outfitters offers shuttles and supplies for those looking to run the river.

The Upper Madawaska River is an exhilarating whitewater river. The river has a number of Class IV and V rapids, although all rapids can be portaged around via the old rail bed that follows the river. The river can really only be travelled in spring until about the end of May. After May, the water level drops to a point where many areas are impassable. The first portion of the river is lined with several difficult rapids that require whitewater experience. In the last 5 km (3.1 mi), the river begins to slow considerably leading to the take-out.

Magnetawan River Route (Map 51/A7–40/A1)

Put-in/Take-out: There are three access points to the Magnetawan River Route. The most popular put-in is from the public boat launch on Wah-washkesh Lake. To find this launch, follow Wahwashkesh Road from Highway 520 all the way to the lake. The other two access areas are at Harris Lake and Naiscoot Lake. Both of these are found near Highway 69 and may require a fee for launching or parking.

The Magnetawan River Route is one of the more popular canoe routes around. The route loops through the heart of the southern portion of the Canadian Shield. In many areas, the river passes through magnificent gorges. There are a number of different route options available. The main route is from Wah-washkesh Lake to the Magnetawan River and then along the south branch of the river to Timber Wolf Lake. From Timber Wolf Lake, the last half of the trip involves crossing several lakes, including Naiscoot, Miskokway, Bolger and Maple Lake, and portages before looping back to Wahwashkesh Lake. On the main route there are about 13 portages, with the longest being 2,370 m (7,775 ft) in length. The route is rated moderate in difficulty with some Grade II river travel. Established campsites along the route are numerous and easy to find.

Mattawa River Route (Map 63/A2–64/B2)

Put-in/Take-out: There are a number of different areas from which to access the Mattawa River. Since this route requires a two-vehicle system, it is recommended to leave one vehicle at a public campground up river and the other vehicle at Samuel de Champlain Provincial Park.

The Grade I-II Mattawa River flows from Trout Lake, near North Bay, to the Ottawa River near the town of Mattawa. From Trout Lake to Samuel de Champlain Provincial Park, the river is protected by Mattawa River Provincial Park. No facilities other than user-maintained campsites exist. Although portages are usually marked, in spring, some may be difficult to see. There are also a few Class I and II whitewater sections along the river that can be run. Between Trout Lake and Pimsi Bay, the river meanders past numerous cottages and homes, while the stretch from Pimsi Bay to Samuel de Champlain Provincial Park is more secluded.

Mercer Lake/Little French River Route (Map 60/C5–61/D3)

Put-in/Take-out: The access point to this long canoe route is located at Mercer Lake, just off Highway 64, east of Monetville. There is a public boat launch available with ample parking for visitors.

Beginning at Mercer Lake and the Hall River, this canoe route covers over 135 km (84 mi). From the Hall, the route travels to the Little French and French Rivers before branching northwest along the Wolseley River. River travel along the route is generally easy, depending on the time of year you travel and whether you portage around rapid areas. After crossing a few small lakes, the trip extends to the West Bay of Lake Nipissing. The return portion of the trip is along the French River from Lake Nipissing back to the Hall River. You will pass through the typical rugged, rocky terrain of the Canadian Shield and through the lowland areas of Lake Nipissing. There are very few portages along this route, with the longest being 525 m (1,722 ft), although campsites are relatively easy to find along the French River Provincial Park and Lake Nipissing's southern shore.

Minesing Wetlands Route (Map 14/E6)

Put-in/Take-out: The access point to the route can be found off of George Johnston Road just south of the village of Minesing. You can park anywhere off of the road and portage your canoe down to Willow Creek. Alternate access points are found along the Nottawasaga River including the launch near the end of McKinnon Road. The main take-out points are found near the bridge of Highway 26 over the Nottawasaga River or at the Edenvale Conservation Area north of the bridge.

The 6,000 hectare Minesing is a bio diverse wetland with many unique qualities, including one of the largest Great Blue Heron colonies in Ontario. During the spring, water levels in the swamp rise to create a large water body easy to paddle. The Willow Creek meanders through the heart of the swamp passing amid the magnificent flooded forest that is comparable to the Florida Everglades. The most difficult part of exploring the swamp is its immense size and lush forest cover make getting lost quite easy. To help navigate the route it is highly recommended to bring along a topographical map and compass.

Mississagua River Route (Map 27/F7–18/F3)

Put-in/Take-out: The put-in is located off of Highway 507 on Mississagua Dam Road at the dam. Your second vehicle can be parked near County Road 36 north of the town of Buckhorn, where the river flows under the highway.

The Mississagua River is a moderate to difficult Grade III whitewater route that offers a challenge to intermediate and expert canoeists and kayaking enthusiasts alike. The route has numerous sets of rapids and swirling water as well as short portages or areas where you must line your canoe through hazardous waters. The section of the river from the Mississagua Dam to Buckhorn is about 20 km (12 mi) long. There are a few campsites scattered along the route, with a particularly scenic site located at the gorge shortly after the Triple Falls.

Moira River Route (Map 21/F5–F7)

Put-in/Take-out: Access to this river route is from below the bridge over the river off Carss Road, south of Tweed. The take-out is below the settlement of Chisholm's Mills, off Scuttle Hole Road.

The Moira River Route is a Grade II-III river route that offers a few more challenging whitewater sections in high water. Beginning at the put-in, the river offers an immediate taste of the action with a mix of Class I-III rapids before reaching the first bridge and an old dam. The dam can be run in high water and is rated Class III in appropriate water conditions. Luckily, users can take a short portage around the dam or use it to scout the run. From the dam, the route is a mix of Grade I-II water (with more flat water than whitewater) until you reach the dam near the Chisholm lumberyard. After the short portage around the dam, the river begins to offer more challenging whitewater again with a mix of Grade I-III water until the take-out. Depending on personal preference, paddlers can simply play in the very top section between the put-in and dam or the bottom section between the Chisholm Dam and the take-out.

Muskoka River Route [South Branch] (Map 34/D5–25/B1)

Put-in/Take-out: Public access and parking can be found in the town of Baysville off of County Road 117 below the dam. Additional access points are found along the river at the many road crossings en route to Muskoka Falls near Bracebridge.

The Muskoka River is a moderate Grade II-III semi-wilderness river that can be travelled from Baysville to the community of Muskoka Falls. The route takes about 2 days to complete. The river is quite slow at times, but speeds up in a number of areas, especially near the waterfalls. Be prepared for the portage points, as the waterfalls must be avoided. Most of the river travels through private property, although there are a few campsites located at about the half waypoint. Two of the sites are located on islands on the river and offer a unique setting for an overnight stay. The scenic river is even more stunning during the fall when the leaves turn colour.

Nottawasaga River – Angus to Wasaga Beach (Map 6/D1–14/A5)

Put-in/Take-out: This portion of the Nottawasaga River can be accessed from three different points. The Angus access is the most popular put-in for the route and is located at the Nottawasaga Conservation Authority office off County Road 90. North of the Angus, an alternate put-in is located near the end of McKinnon Road, while the Edenvale Conservation Area access doubles as a take-out. The end of the route is found at the Schooner Parkette at Wasaga Beach.

Beginning in Angus, this easy Grade I-II route travels through the magnificent Minesing Swamp. From the swamp the route travels past the Edenvale Conservation Area where the river has formed a deep gorge and is the only designated overnight camping area on the route past the Nottawasaga Conservation Authority office. The final stretch of the river passes through Doran and Jacks Lakes and on to the Schooner Parkette take-out. Camping is also possible in the Minesing Swamp as there is a well-used site available upstream about 2.5 km (1.6mi) south of the Edenvale Conservation Area.

Nottawasaga River – Nicolston to Angus (Map 6/F5–D1)

Put-in/Take-out: The most southerly access of the route is off of 5th Line, just north of the town of Nicolston. Along this stretch of the river, the route can also be accessed from Essa Centennial Park or from the Nottawasaga Conservation Authority Office on County Road 90 near Angus.

From Nicolston, this moderate Grade II-III portion of the Nottawasaga River meanders through the countryside and through some reforested pine stands. Much of the river's shoreline used to be forested with these great pines, before they were logged to make room for crop production. Just before the river reaches Essa Centennial Park, it flows through a stunning gorge that has slowly evolved over hundreds of years. There are rapids throughout this area and it may be necessary to portage around them depending on your skill level. The river continues past the Nottawasaga Conservation Authority Office, where overnight camping is offered. The trek to Angus covers over 32 km (20 mi).

Opeongo River Canoe Route (Map 46/C1–G4)

Put-in/Take-out: The route starts at the Shall Lake Algonquin Park Access Point, found at the end of Major Lake Road. The first take-out is located at the Aylen River/Opeongo River confluence. The other take-out is found where the river flows under Highway 60. Algonquin Park permits are required for camping inside the park or parking and can be purchased at the Access Point Office. Alternatively, Algonquin Bound Outfitters offers shuttles and supplies for those looking to run the river.

The Opeongo River is an exciting whitewater river that travels from Shall Lake within Algonquin Provincial Park, south to Bark Lake. The river flows over 30 km (19 mi) from the put-in point in Algonquin Park to the Highway 60 take-out. The section of the river from Victoria Lake to the Aylen River confluence is almost a continuous whitewater ride! The river drops over 80 metres (260 feet) in this stretch creating Class II to IV rapids. Portages can be spotted from the river. Be sure to scout all whitewater before attempting to run it.

Oxtongue River Canoe Routes (Map 44/F4–34/G1)

Put-in/Take-out: Off of Highway 60, within Algonquin Provincial Park, a short road takes you to the north end of Smoke Lake and the access point and parking area. For the river-only route to Lake Of Bays, access is provided at Oxtongue River/Ragged Falls Provincial Park. Algonquin Park passes are required within the park.

From Smoke Lake, travel west to Tea Lake to access the mouth of the Oxtongue River. The river meanders slowly at times, although there are a few areas with rapids that heighten the excitement of the trip. The river parallels Highway 60 until the portage to Park Lake where it is possible to loop back to Smoke Lake for a nice two or three day loop. The last portage is the longest covering 2400 m (7,874 ft) from Norman Lake to the south end of Smoke Lake. The actual river route continues past Oxtongue Lake and on to Lake Of Bays. The river section does have a few short, but well-marked portages, including Ragged Falls, before the Highway 60 crossing into Oxtongue Lake. From here there is another stretch of rapids (next to aptly named Rapids Road), before the final leg into Lake of Bays. A portion of the Oxtongue River is classified as Grade III-IV whitewater and is only recommended for experienced whitewater paddlers.

Poker Lake Canoe Route (Map 35/B7)

Put-in/Take-out: There are parking areas on both sides of Highway 118, west of Carnarvon. The parking area on the north side of the highway is quite small and many prefer to use the southern lot.

Part of the Haliburton Highlands Water Trails, the Poker Lake system is surrounded by crown land and offers several user-maintained campsites that help make it a peaceful experience for paddlers. In addition to good bass fishing, there are opportunities for bird watching and berry picking. The cluster of lakes is linked by nine portages, with the largest portage being a mere 375 m (1,230 ft). Canoe trips could entail an easy loop through Bentshoe, Cinder, Poker and Crane Lakes or an easy trip paddling along the larger Big East Lake to the south.

Port Rawson Bay Route (Map 32/A4)

Put-in/Take-out: Access and parking is located at Pete's Place Access Point of The Massasauga Provincial Park on Blackstone Harbour.

The Port Rawson Bay Route takes you through the bays and inlets of The Massasauga wilderness from Blackstone Harbour to Port Rawson Bay. Weather and boat traffic are the main hazards. The route makes a nice two-day venture and offers a variety of places to camp and endless coves and inlets to explore. Park passes can be purchased at the gatehouse.

Red Pine Lake Loop (Map 35/E4)

Put-in/Take-out: Access and parking are available for a small fee at the marina on Big Hawk Lake, off Big Hawk Lake Road.

This easy loop covers over 19 km (12 mi) and four different lakes, including Big Hawk, Nunikani, Red Pine and Clear Lakes. There are four portages along the route with the longest covering 440 m (1,444 ft) from Nunikani Lake to Red Pine Lake. During high water this portage can sometimes be reduced to about 30 m (98 ft). Many of the lakes do have cottages on them, although secluded Nunikani Lake offers a getaway from civilization.

Restoule River/French River Route (Map 61/F7–A5)

Put-in/Take-out: The access point to this route is Restoule Provincial Park, which is located at the end of Highway 534. The put-in is found in the north end of the park on Stormy Lake.

This isolated route begins on Stormy Lake of Restoule Provincial Park. The route travels west along the Restoule River towards the French River and then heads north to Lake Nipissing. The return route is from Lake Nipissing along Bass Creek and across a couple of small lakes back to Stormy Lake. Nearby,

where the Restoule meets the French River system, there is a 730 m (2,395 ft) portage around a scenic gorge and waterfall. On the French River, from the Chaudierre Dam to Lake Nipissing, the area is less secluded and you will certainly encounter boaters along the way. The trip along Shoal Creek is the most remote portion of the route, but low water levels in the summer on the creek can seriously hinder your progress. To avoid low water, it is best to travel the route before or after the summer season. There are 11 portages along the route with the longest portage being 1,200 m (3,937 ft). Allow about 4-5 days to complete the trip.

Seguin River Route (Map 41/E7–32/A1)

Put-in/Take-out: The access point for this route is located on the north side of Highway 518 between Maple and Little Seguin (Duck) Lakes. Your vehicle can be left off the highway and a second vehicle can be left off of Highway 518 at Haines Lake to the west.

This is a rustic route that is rarely travelled; therefore, be sure to stay alert at all times for whitewater, sweepers and other hazards. Portages are not marked and you may have to bushwhack your way around some of the rapids. The route can be difficult with Class III rapids but it is truly a hidden gem that leads north from Little Seguin Lake, through Isabella before venturing along the river. The route then leads past Mountain Chute, Greer and Mill Lakes before the last stretch along Haines Lake. Fishing can be enjoyed along the Seguin River and on all of the lakes along the route, however campsites are difficult to locate.

Serpentine Lake Loop (Map 28/B5)

Put-in/Take-out: From off Highway 28, take Anstruther Lake Road to the public boat launch. Parking is available at the boat launch.

The Serpentine Lake Loop is a great way to explore the heart of the Kawarthas. It traverses through a variety of vegetation including a wetland area, stands of mixed hardwood and beautiful tamarack. The route is generally easy, except for the gruelling 1,584 m (5,197 ft) portage from North Rathbun Lake to Serpentine Lake. Campsites are available on all the lakes except Anstruther Lake, with some particularly beautiful island sites available on Copper and Serpentine Lakes. The route can be busy during summer weekends, although the further you venture, the easier it becomes to find solitude. There are also bird watching opportunities along the route, especially along wetland areas.

Skootamatta River Route (Map 21/G1)

Put-in/Take-out: Paddlers can find the put-in to the Skootamatta River Route by following Flinton Road (Regional Road 25) south from Flinton. The put-in is below the bridge where the road crosses the river. The take-out is found before the bridge, off Upper Flinton Road.

The Skootamatta River Route is a Grade III-IV whitewater route, depending on water levels. The river is quite isolated and sports forested shores and breathtaking scenery. The entire run is about 10.5 km (6.5 mi) and can be easily run in a couple hours. The course offers a variety of water difficulties, ranging from easy Class I flatwater to very challenging Class IV rapids. There are also two significant natural obstacles that should be scouted and avoided at all costs. The obstacles are a 200 m (655 ft) long gorge and a set of waterfalls. After the gorge, the falls are not much further down the river with established portages detouring around both. Water levels are best during spring and early summer.

South Channel/Spider Bay Route (Map 32/A3–31/F4)

Put-in/Take-out: From Highway 400, look for the James Bay Junction. Take this road to Blue Lake Road, which leads to Three Legged Lake Road. Parking and a boat launch are available at Three Legged Lake. Since most of this route is set in the wilds of Massasauga Provincial Park, be sure to pick up a park pass at Oastler Lake Provincial Park on route to the access point.

The beauty and the awe of Georgian Bay draws people from across the province and this route travels through the heart of it all. Spider Bay is riddled with small islands and sleepy bays and is truly one of the more unique areas of the country. However, the large water bodies that are crossed on this route combined with the unpredictable winds of Georgian Bay can make this trip a challenge for even the most experienced canoeists.

This route travels north from Three Legged Lake and across McCoy, Jack and Canoe Lakes and onto the South Channel. From the South Channel, you travel southwest along the mainland past the many islands and inlets that line the area and on to Spider Bay. Travel in the South Channel and Spider Bay can be difficult due to high winds and boat traffic. From Spider Bay the portage to the secluded Spider Lake is located at the end of the northern arm. The route ends with a portage back to Three Legged Lake. This difficult route takes 3-5 days depending on weather and experience and rustic camping is available at various spots along the South Channel, Spider Bay or on Spider Lake. It is recommended to bring a good marine chart for navigation on the trip.

South River Canoe Route (Map 53/C4)

Put-in/Take-out: There are a few access points along this route with the main access point located near the Algonquin Park boundary. A bush road passes over the river near the confluence with Craig Creek and canoes can be put-in on the west side of the bridge. A second vehicle can be left down river at one of four other access areas off River Road, including on Forest Lake.

For centuries before the first settlers arrived, the river and the surrounding hillsides were the hunting grounds of Algonquin, Ojibway and Huron natives. The river was also one of Tom Thomson's favourite access points into Algonquin Park. The river travels through the picturesque Almaguin Highlands, offering travellers beautiful scenery and the chance to experience the solitude of nature. In spring, the higher water level of the river allows travel from the Craig Creek put-in all the way to Forest Lake. In summer, low water levels pose travel problems in a number of areas where extra portaging or lining canoes is often required.

Sucker Lake Route (Map 27/G6–28/A5)

Put-in/Take-out: To reach the access area, take Highway 507 towards Catchacoma. At Catchacoma take Beaver Lake Road east to the Catchacoma Lake Access Point.

This route is set amid the newly expanded Kawartha Highlands Provincial Park and takes you across three scenic lakes, through beautiful stands of mixed forest and along the secluded Bottle Creek. The total distance for this easy route is about 20 km (12 mi) and can be completed in two days. There are two short portages to access Sucker Lake from Catchacoma and Bottle Lakes and campsites are available at both Sucker and Bottle Lakes. Catchacoma Lake is quite busy sometimes with boat traffic and the route can be busy with canoeists during weekends in the summer.

Turtle Lake Loop (Map 19/A1–28/A7)

Put-in/Take-out: North from Lakefield, follow Highway 28 to the Long Lake Road. Parking is available at Long Lake Lodge for a small fee.

The Turtle Lake Loop is a popular route amid the splendour of the Kawarthas. During the summer the route can get quite crowded. The total distance of the loop trip is about 25 km (16 mi) and takes you across six beautiful lakes. The loop is moderate in difficulty due to two longer portages between Cox and Triangle Lakes and Turtle and Stoplog Lakes. The complete loop takes a minimum of two days and campsites can be found on most of the lakes including the scenic sites found on Stoplog Lake. Fishing is available on all of the lakes, with the best fishing being for bass.

Wolf Lake Route (Map 28/B6)

Put-in/Take-out: Follow Highway 28 to Anstruther Lake Road. Off the south side of Anstruther Lake Road, there is a short unmarked road leading to Wolf Lake and a boat launch.

This route is an easy day or overnight trip from Wolf Lake to Crab Lake. While there are quite a few cottages on Wolf Lake, Crab is secluded and offers the more picturesque campsites. The lakes are linked by a short portage found on the southeast side of Wolf Lake just past a couple of cottages. This is a fantastic trip to bring along younger kids or for beginning paddlers.

Wolf River/Pickerel River Route (Map 51/A2–50/C4)

Put-in/Take-out: Access to this river route is from the Wolf River, off North Road, north of Loring. The take-out is found at the public boat launch at Port Loring on Lake Wauquimakog. Unless you can arrange a shuttle, this route requires two vehicles or an ambitious biker willing to peddle the 10 km (6 mi) back to the put-in to retrieve their vehicle.

This easy to moderate canoe route is ideal for paddlers that are looking for a virtually portage-free river route. The main challenge along this route is the potentially strong winds that can develop on Dollars, Kawigamog and Wauquimakog Lakes. During the spring runoff, high water may create fast water with Grade II whitewater in some sections. The trip begins on the Wolf River and travels west to Dollars Lake. The route then heads south to the Pickerel River and finally to Lake Wauquimakog and the take-out. There is only one required portage of 130 m (426 ft). There is an optional portage that is located near the inflow of the Wolf River to Dollars Lake. At the southern tip of Dollars Lake, there is an alternative take-out off Highway 522 if you wish to shorten your trip. Since this canoe route travels through popular cottage country, you will certainly encounter plenty of other boat traffic, especially in the summer.

ALGONQUIN PARK PADDLING ROUTES

Algonquin Provincial Park is one of the premier canoeing destinations in the world. Many of the routes are well maintained and most provide campsites complete with fire pits and pit toilets as well as maintained portages. Orange or yellow signs mark these campsites and portages and usually indicate the distance of the portage to be travelled. Although many routes along the Highway 60 corridor and west side of the park can be busy, those looking for a bit more solitude will find the north and east sides of the park receive considerably less traffic.

Those new to the area or sport are well advised to use one of the many outfitters scattered around the park, such as Algonquin Bound. They offer canoe and camping rentals, delivery services, last minutes supplies and knowledgeable advice on where to camp or fish. Park permits along with a detailed trip itinerary are required to use the canoe routes.

Barron Canyon Route (Map 57/C3–E3)

Put-in/Take-out: The put-in and parking area for this route can be found at Algonquin Park's Grand Lake-Achray Access Point. Park permits can be purchased at the Sand Lake Gate.

The Barron Canyon is one of the most spectacular natural wonders of Algonquin Park. This easy route travels along the Barron River, where it travels through the immense gorge. In some areas, the canyon walls rise over 100 m (330 ft) above the river. From the put-in on Grand Lake, travel south to the Grand Lake Dam where there is a short portage into Stratton Lake, which is home to 19 rustic canoe access campsites. From St. Andrews Lake, trippers can travel across High Falls and Opalescent Lakes before entering Bringham Lake. Two portages from Bringham Lake, including one past the scenic Brigham Chute, bring adventurers to the marvellous Barron Canyon. The river is quite slow through the canyon, allowing time to relax and enjoy the scenery. It is about 13 km (2 or 3 days) from Achray to the Sand Lake Gate access point. Alternatively you can return to the start by backtracking or creating a loop south through Opalescent Lake and the various options from that lake back to the start.

Big Porcupine Lake Loop (Map 44/F4–45/A6)

Put-in/Take-out: The access point to this Algonquin Park interior route is the popular Smoke Lake. Parking and permits area available at the Access Point office at Canoe Lake.

Beginning at the north end of Smoke Lake, paddle south to the dam and portage to Ragged Lake. During summer, Smoke Lake can be busy with canoeists and motorboats. At the south shore of Ragged Lake, there is a very steep, 590 m (1,936 ft) portage into Big Porcupine Lake that brings visitors to a great first-day camping area. The 16 backcountry campsites are well spaced and secluded. The loop continues from Big Porcupine over Little Coon Lake, Whatnot Lakes and McGarvey Lake before reaching Bonnechere Lake. There are some lovely wilderness camping sites available at McGarvey or Little Coon Lakes. To keep the trip to three days, travellers can return from Bonnechere Lake through to Big Porcupine Lake and retrace back to Smoke Lake, although the trip could be extended for many days. Trout fishing is a popular attraction, especially in spring.

Big Trout Lake Canoe Route (Map 44/F3–55/A6)

Put-in/Take-out: There are two main access points for the Big Trout Lake Route. The most popular access is the Canoe Lake put-in. The other is the Source Lake Access Point, which is much less busy. The portages from the Source Lake put-in are a little longer, but well worth the effort. Permits can be found at the Canoe Lake Access Point office.

From the Source Lake Access Point, this moderately difficult route takes five nights to complete. The first day of the trip crosses a number of small lakes leading past Bruce, Raven and Owl Lakes. Linda Lake is a 1,315 m (4,315 ft) portage from Owl Lake. Both lakes make an ideal first night camp. Continue past Iris and the long 2,105 m (6,906 ft) portage into Alder Lake where a much shorter portage leads to Birdie and then the larger Burnt Island Lake. At the northeast side of the lake, there is a portage into Little Otterslide Lake. Paddling the north side of Little Otterslide brings onlookers to a small creek leading to the larger Otterslide Lake, which a great camping spot. The stretch down Otterslide Creek to Big Trout Lake travels through wetland habitat that is ideal for spotting moose, otter and beaver and includes a few generally easy portages. There are 36 campsites at Big Trout Lake that are all well-spaced, providing seclusion from other campers.

The return trip takes trippers to White Trout Lake, which empties into a seemingly endless 3 km (1.9 mi) marsh area reaching the portage to Hawkins Lake. Pay attention to route markers in the marsh area. From Hawkins

Lake, travel south over Canada Jay Lake into Sunbeam Lake. There are eight interior sites on Sunbeam Lake including three pleasant island sites. Burnt Island Lake offers 52 campsites, a testament to its popularity. From Burnt Island Lake, retrace the original route back to Source Lake or continue Canoe Lake if you have a second vehicle.

Bissett Lake Canoe Route (Map 66/C6–65/G6)

Put-in/Take-out: The put-in for this Algonquin Park route is at the park entrance at the Bissett Creek Road Access Point. Park permits can be picked up at Yate's Store, off Highway 17, near Stonecliffe.

The moderate Bissett Lake route is a quieter out and back route that is mostly used in spring by fishing enthusiasts. The journey begins with a long, 7 km (4.3 mi) portage along a cart trail that is actually a continuation of the access road. At the end of this relatively smooth hike is a more rugged and hilly 2,210 m (7,250 ft) portage to Gerald Lake, where a campsite awaits tired travellers. From Gerald Lake, paddlers have the option of continuing onward to Fitz and Reed Lakes, which are also each equipped with a campsite. The final leg of the journey continues down Bissett Creek before carrying on with another challenging portage of 1,510 m (4,954 ft). Bissett Lake and two shorter portages bring trippers to the terminus at Weasel Lake, where the route ends. Trippers should note that portages may no longer being maintained along the creek and may be difficult to cross.

Bonnechere River Canoe Route (Map 56/F5–57/E7)

Put-in/Take-out: The access point for this Algonquin interior trip is the hydro line at the end of Basin Depot Road. Once at the hydro line, the road turns south towards the river where parking is available. Permits can be picked up at Bonnechere Provincial Park, while a second vehicle can be left at any of the roadside campsites next to the river.

The route is difficult due to the long physically demanding portages and river travel involved. There are also few backcountry campsites between the access point and Algonquin Park boundary some 30 km or so downstream. From the put-in at the hydro line, river travel is quite smooth for the first 5 to 6 km. However, this soon changes with a series of daunting portages, including one spanning approximately 6,400 m (21,000 ft) leading past High Falls. Eventually, the river courses close to Basin Depot Road and Basin Lake. It is possible to camp on nearby Basin Lake by portaging down the road and back to the river. The route opens up from here and there are only a few short portages required before the river flows outside of the park and into Couchain Lake. The route from Couchain Lake to Turner's Camp is a much easier journey, as it crosses over Curriers and Beaverdam Lakes. Roadside campsites are found in this stretch of river, while it is possible to continue down river to Round Lake as well.

Booth Lake Canoe Route (Map 46/C1–A1)

Put-in/Take-out: The route begins and ends at Algonquin Park's Shall Lake Access Point at the end of Major Lake Road. Permits can be picked up at the access point, while rentals, shuttles or supplies can be found at Algonquin Bound Outfitters at the junction of Major Lake Road access road and Highway 60 in Madawaska.

The Booth Lake Route is an easy two to three day out and back trip that involves a bit of river travel. From the access point at Algonquin Park's Shall Lake it is short paddle to Farm Lake where four interior sites are available. The trip continues west towards Kitty Lake, past the popular Kitty Lake Cabin, which is one of the oldest standing cabins in the park. (The cabin can be rented.) Across from the cabin, a short portage moves into Kitty Lake proper. At the west end of Kitty Lake, there is a portage around a small dam before entering Booth Lake. The river flow entering into the portage can be a bit tricky to navigate. However, a trip into Booth Lake is well worth the effort as it is truly a beautiful lake with 18 well-spaced campsites, excellent fishing and a lot of nearby places to explore. McCarthy Creek, in particular, is a great place for moose sightings. The return trip is much easier as it is all downstream.

Cache Lake Canoe Loop (Map 45/A4–B5)

Put-in/Take-out: This Algonquin Park route starts from the Cache Lake Access Point found off the south side of Highway 60. Permits are available at the Canoe Lake Access Point office.

A popular three or four day route begins on Cache Lake. The first day travels from Cache Lake to Bonnechere Lake and is the most physically demanding stretch. There are nine portages and eight lakes to cross before reaching Bonnechere. Alternately, take the extra day and spend the first night at Hilliard or Delano Lake. Beyond Delano, you hop past South Canisbay, Kingfisher, Mohawk and Plough Lakes before entering Bonnechere. At the northeast corner of Bonnechere Lake, paddle through the narrows

into a small pond before reaching the short portage into a creek that leads to Phipps Lake. At the east side of this lake, there is a small waterfall that must be carried around before reaching Kirkwood, then Lawrence and Pardee Lakes. From Pardee Lake, there is a short portage into Harness Lake, which has 11 campsites, including five hiker only campsites. Two 1,000 m (3,280 ft) portages and the crossing of Head Lake is all that remains before concluding at Cache Lake.

Canoe Lake Canoe Route (Map 44/E3)

Put-in/Take-out: The Canoe Lake Route begins at the Canoe Lake Access Point and office off Highway 60.

The canoe traffic on the stretch from Canoe Lake to Joe and Tepee Lakes is so popular that it has been nicknamed 'Yonge Street', after the busy street in downtown Toronto. The Cairn to Tom Thomson, a famous group of seven painter, on the northwest point of the Canoe Lake is worth investigating before leaving the lake.

This easy route can be completed in three days, although four days allows a more leisurely pace. Beginning at Canoe Lake, it is about a 4 km (2.5 mi) paddle north to the first short portage around the Joe Lake Dam. Continue north under the old railway bridge into Joe Lake and stay to the left of Joe Island to proceed to Tepee, Littledoe and Tom Thomson Lakes. Camping is offered here or at the smaller Bartlett Lake to the northeast. From Bartlett, travel to Burnt Island Lake via Sunbeam Lake. The trip from Sunbeam to Burnt Island Lake involves four portages over some hilly terrain, with the last portage being the longest at 680 m (2,230 ft). Burnt Island Lake is a large lake where winds can sometimes play havoc. The big lake makes a popular last night stop with 56 well-spaced, backcountry campsites. The portage out of Burnt Island Lake is found on the most southerly tip of the lake. There is a short portage around a dam and into Baby Joe Lake. From Baby Joe Lake, there are two easy portages to the east arm of Joe Lake before the return back to Canoe Lake.

Catfish Lake Canoe Loop (Map 65/B7–55/A2)

Put-in/Take-out: The access point for this loop is the Cedar Lake-Brent Access Point. Backcountry camping permits can be obtained at the Access Point office at the turnoff to Wendigo Lake, before entering the park.

From the north shore of Cedar Lake, continue south to the first portage, which is directly across from the access point where the Petawawa River flows into the big lake. There are a few portages and campsites as well as some scenic waterfalls to negotiate along the river leading to Narrowbag Lake. The longest is a challenging 2,345 m (7,690 ft) trail past a stretch of whitewater. At the west end of Narrowbag Lake, there is a short portage that moves into Catfish Lake, which is a perfect place to spend a few days. There are 13 campsites at the lake with three sites lying on picturesque islands. The remains of an old steam tug found on one of the northern islands can also be explored. If so desired, guests can stay a night at Lynx or Luckless Lakes, which are accessible from the western side of Catfish Lake. The loop continues beyond these lakes to the gruelling 2,875 m (9,430 ft) linking Luckless Lake with the Nipissing River. From here, the Nipissing River flows over 8 km (5 mi) into Cedar Lake.

Dickson/Lavieille Lakes Canoe Route (Map 45/E1–56/A5)

Put-in/Take-out: This route begins at the Opeongo Lake Access Point and office north of Highway 60.

The Dickson Lake/Lake Lavieille Route is a moderate route due to a challenging portage and the large size of the lakes that are travelled. From the access point at the south end of Opeongo Lake, it is a full day's paddle to the first portage that most avoid with an Opeongo lake water taxi. For water taxi reservations, call Algonquin Outfitters (888) 280-8886 or Opeongo Outfitters at (613) 637-5470. A short portage takes visitors into Wright Lake where there is one pretty campsite found on the lake that makes for a good overnight spot. A short portage from Wright Lake's east side spreads to Bonfield Lake. The next portage is a backbreaking 5,305 m (17,400 ft); however, the reward is beautiful Dickson Lake and Lake Lavieille. It is only a 90 m (290 ft) portage at the north end of Dickson into Hardy Bay of Lake Lavieille where days could be spent exploring the many bays and inlets along the lakeshore. To return to the access point, follow the same route back to Opeongo Lake.

Erables/Maple Lake Canoe Route (Map 64/B6–54/E1)

Put-in/Take-out: The Algonquin Park Kioshkokwi Lake-Kiosk Access Point is the put-in for this canoe route. Permits for backcountry camping can be acquired at the Kiosk park office. The lakes are referred to as cousins because the French for maple is "erables".

This moderate, three day route begins with a paddle to the southeast corner of Kioshkokwi Lake, which takes its name from a native word meaning "lake of many gulls." The big lake can be windy. The route continues past Little Mink and Mink Lakes to the 985 m (3,230 ft) portage linking to the weedy narrows on Club Lake. The first night can be spent on Club Lake or on Mouse Lake to the south. Beyond Mouse is a challenging 1,705 m (5,595 ft) portage over hilly terrain, which leads to Mink Creek and Big Thunder Lake, a small lake with only one isolated campsite. The 1,495 m (4,905 ft) portage out of Big Thunder Lake is also difficult, due to the hilly terrain. At the end of the trek, canoeists will be at the southern arm of Erables Lake where the second night of the trip can be spent. The last leg of the trip heads back to Kioshkokwi Lake via Maple Creek. From Maple Lake, the creek travels about 5.5 km to Kioshkokwi Lake. There are six portages along the route with the longest being 805 m (2,641 ft).

Greenleaf Lake Canoe Route (Map 57/C3–56/F3)
Put-in/Take-out: Park permits can be purchased at the Sand Lake Gate. The put-in and parking area is found at Algonquin Park's Grand Lake-Achray Access Point.

This moderate four day out and back route travels across a number of small lakes en route to Greenleaf Lake. Beginning at Grand Lake, paddle south towards scenic Carcajou Bay where moose can be seen on occasion. From Carcajou Bay, you will travel over Lower and Upper Spectacle and Little Carcajou Lakes before reaching Wenda Lake. Backcountry campsites are available on all four lakes and the Wenda Lake Cabin makes a great place to spend the night if reserved in advance. The remainder of the trip involves numerous short portages and one larger portage into Greenleaf Lake. Due to changing water levels between Wenda and Carcajou Lakes, the portage distances change throughout the year. Carcajou Lake takes its name from the native word for "wolverine", while Greenleaf Lake offers impressive cliffs that bank the lake and support the rare Algonquin wood fern. There are three scenic campsites available on Greenleaf Lake. The route returns the same way to Carcajou Bay.

Hogan Lake/Lake La Muir Canoe Route (Map 45/E1–55/B4)
Put-in/Take-out: This route begins at the Opeongo Lake Access Point and office north of Highway 60. For water taxi reservations call Algonquin Outfitters (888) 280-8886 or Opeongo Outfitters (613) 637-5470.

This moderate route can take anywhere from three to five days to complete depending if you use the Opeongo Water Taxi to the portages leading to Proulx Lake. There are two portages into Proulx, with the second being 965 m (3,166 ft), where a series of backcountry campsites are found. At the north end of Proulx Lake, the Crow River leads through a marshy area to Little Crow Lake. Moose can be seen on occasion here. Big Crow Lake is found via a passage off Little Crows Lake's east side. Both lakes offer prime interior campsites that are all well-spaced and maintained. There is also an old ranger cabin on Big Crow Lake's southeast shore that is available for rent as well as a trail to an old fire tower.

The Crow River flows out of the big lake from its eastern shore where another trail can be explored. The trail is about 2.5 km return and passes through a stand of mature virgin white pine. On the opposite shoreline lays a daunting 3,750 m (12,300 ft) portage to Hogan Lake, which offers ten wilderness campsites. Lake La Muir can be found via the Little Madawaska River that flows into Hogan Lake's southwest side. Moose often frequent the banks of the river. Lake La Muir offers eight backcountry campsites with two of them situated on a large island. To return to Opeongo Lake, retrace your route back to the Proulx Lake or continue southeast to Merchant and Happy Isle Lakes. This alternate return creates a very challenging return loop.

Hurdman Lake Canoe Route (Map 64/E6)
Put-in/Take-out: Brain Lake, at the northern part of Algonquin Park, is the access point for this route. Park permits for backcountry camping can be picked up at the Mattawa Travel and Info Center in Mattawa.

This fairly remote route has a number of low use portages and can be done in two or three days. It is an out and back route that is mostly visited in spring after the trout season opens. The route follows Hurdman Creek crossing four portages from Brain Lake to Stretch Lake. Trippers can spend a night at Stretch or West Corbeau Lake. Hurdman Lake can be found about 1.6 km (1 mi) from West Corbeau Lake after hopping three short portages along the creek. On Hurdman Lake's northeastern shore, there are two scenic interior campsites. Hurdman is a long and slim lake that measures nearly 3 km (1.9 mi) in length and about 250 m (820 ft) at its widest point.

Madawaska Lake Canoe Route (Map 46/B7–36/E1)
Put-in/Take-out: South of Whitney, follow the McRae-Hay Lake Road to the public boat launch area where access and parking are available. Algonquin Park permits can be obtained from the East Gate of the park.

This moderate route is a good trip for seclusion seekers. From the Hay Lake Access Point travel west to Cauliflower Lake and down Cauliflower Creek, which links to the South Madawaska River. During spring, Cauliflower Creek is easier to travel than in late summer when water levels in some areas become quite low. There are a few portages along the creek, with the longest being the 1,440 m (4,724 ft) trip across the hydro line area to the South Madawaska River. This waterway meanders through wetland areas all the way to Madawaska Lake, providing an excellent opportunity for bird watching and a chance to see moose. At Madawaska Lake, there are four beautiful campsites to enjoy. It is possible to shorten the route by travelling the powerline road to the Cauliflower Creek portage.

Manitou Lake Canoe Loop (Map 53/C3–G1)
Put-in/Take-out: The access point to this interior canoe loop is the Kawawaymog Lake Access Point, east from the town of South River.

The Manitou Lake Loop is a moderately difficult, four to five day trip that begins on the west shore of Kawawaymog Lake. The Amable du Fond River can be picked up at the east side of the lake and travels into North Tea Lake, which was once named "Waskigomog Lake". The first portage of the trip is located on the northeast shore of the big lake, just east of Lorne Creek. Once on Lorne Lake, you can stay at one of six backcountry campsites or continue to Kakasamic Lake. Two shorter portages and a short paddle separate Kakasamic and Mattowacka Lakes. Both lakes make good second night camping spots, with three pleasant campsites on each lake. There are five secluded campsites available on Fassett and Shada Lakes.

Fassett Creek can be found from Shada Lake's eastern side, which travels down towards Manitou Lake. This is another large Algonquin Park lake where winds can play havoc with the rate of progress. There are about 50 backcountry campsites on this big lake, including a number of great island sites. The north end of the lake also contains the remains of the old Dufond Farm from the early 1880's. The last leg of the trip is the paddle down Manitou Lake and North Tea Lake. It is best to spend the last night at the south end of Manitou Lake or on North Tea Lake in order to limit the final day's battle with potentially high winds.

Misty Lake Canoe Route (Map 44/A2–54/C7)
Put-in/Take-out: The access point for this route is located at the Rain Lake Access Point, east of the village of Kearney. Park permits can be picked up at the park office in the Kearney Community Centre.

The Rain Lake Access Point is a popular area due to the easy access to numerous canoeing and camping options in the area. From Rain Lake, the easy three day route travels to Misty Lake via several small interior lakes. The first portage is found at Rain Lake's northeastern side, travelling to Sawyer Lake where six backcountry campsites are found. From Sawyer Lake, you portage into Jubilee, Juan and Moccasin Lakes. Next up is Bandit Lake (a 'bandit' was the nickname of rangers who cleared park portages), followed by Wenona and Muslim Lakes. The portage between Muslim Lake and Misty Lake is the longest of the trip at only 1,030 m (3,380 ft). Misty Lake is a long, picturesque lake with numerous inlets and bays to explore. There are a number of lakes that can be accessed by one or two portages from Misty Lake in addition to the 19 wilderness campsites, including three sites located on one of the lake's large islands. Follow the same access route back in order to return to Rain Lake or plan a longer looped trip.

Nipissing River Canoe Route (Map 53/C3–55/B1; 63/G7–65/C7)
Put-in/Take-out: There are few different access points that can be used to find this route. The main access is the Kawawaymog Lake Access Point, although it is also possible to access the river from the Tim River Access Point to the south.

The Nipissing River travels from Big Bob Lake on the park's western side all the way to Cedar Lake on the park's north side. The river was once used as a transportation vein for the early log drives inside the park and remnants of this era can still be found along the shoreline to this day. The moderate route is quite long and involves several portages to cross lakes and around the more challenging sections of the river.

From North Tea Lake, paddlers will continue onward to Mangotasi, Hornbeam and Biggar Lakes, incorporating 21 wilderness campsites into the stretch. From Biggar Lake, canoeists can travel up Loughrin Creek, moving over some long portages, to Lawren Harris Lake, which is named after another member of the 'Group of Seven' artists. From Barred Owl Lake, continue onward to Nod Lake and the Nipissing River. Travellers can also take a different route from Nod Lake through Gibson Lake and then down to the Nipissing. The advantage is spending the next night at the Highview Cabin, which is found off the portage to the Nipissing.

Once at the river, you will travel all the way to High Falls, a natural gem of the park's interior. This stretch consists of many long portages and several sets of rapids. Beyond High Falls, the river travels over 25 km (16 mi) with six portages that journey around four different dams and one whitewater section, en route to Cedar Lake. Much of this stretch is through a lowland area with marshland riverbanks allowing for prime moose spotting territory. The Brent Store is situated on the north shore of Cedar Lake to stock up on supplies before heading back.

From the west side of Cedar Lake, Little Cedar and Aura Lee Lakes can be found. Two short portages are found between Cedar and Little Cauchon Lake and another 440 m (1,444 ft) portage links Cauchon and Mink Lake, which has 11 campsites lining its north shore near an old railway bed. The next leg of the journey includes travel from Mink to Manitou Lake via Kioshkokwi Lake. A number of beach areas along Manitou Lake's shore make an ideal spot for an evening dip. The last day involves a short portage to North Tea Lake and the long paddle to the access point. Wind can be a major hindrance to travel on these last three lakes.

North Depot Lake Canoe Route (Map 65/F6)

Put-in/Take-out: The access point and parking area can be found at Wendigo Lake on the northern side of the park. Backcountry camping permits can be acquired from the Access Point Office shortly after you turn onto the Brent Road.

This lake route is a short, easy two to three day out and back trip that can be done in one day, if necessary. The route is popular in spring after trout season opens. From the access point on Wendigo Lake, paddle to the southernmost tip of the lake to the first, short portage to Allan Lake where there are nine backcountry campsites. At the southern tip of Allen Lake lies the 255 m (840 ft) portage into North Depot Lake, which travels around a set of rapids found on a small stretch of the North River. There are nine well-spaced campsites on the lake, with three of the sites resting on an island.

Park Lake Loop (Map 44/E4–C7)

Put-in/Take-out: This access is found off Highway 60 at the north end of Smoke Lake.

This route begins along the Oxtongue River taking you west past Tea Lake to Park Lake near the western boundary of the park. The river meanders slowly at times next to Highway 60, although there are a few areas with rapids that heighten the excitement of the trip. Look for the portage to Park Lake where the route then loops back to Smoke Lake via a series of small lakes and portages. The longest portage is the last in the loop and is a gruelling 2,400 m (7,874 ft) trek from Norman Lake to the south end of Smoke Lake. Campsites are scattered along the river and on a few of the park lakes.

Petawawa River Whitewater Route (Maps 55–57, 66–67)

Put-in/Take-out: There are several access points, including Cedar Lake to the north, Lake Traverse in the middle and McManus Lake in the park's southeastern side.

The Petawawa River is perhaps the best-known river of Algonquin Provincial Park. The river travels from one side of the park to the other, taking on a different character with every kilometre. From the marshy meandering flow in the west to the rushing rapids of the east, the Petawawa is a dynamic and exciting river to travel. From Cedar Lake to Rapid Lake, the river offers Grade II-IV whitewater as it flows through a steep valley. From Radiant Lake to Lake Traverse, the river is very rigorous, as the majority of rapids are rated as Class III-V. In one location just before Lake Travers, a falls called "the Fury," is not runnable during most of the year. Between Lake Traverse and Lake McManus the rapids vary from Class I to Class IV whitewater, depending on the water level encountered. Although, there are portages around the rapids, it is essential to scout any whitewater before attempting to run it.

The most popular stretch for whitewater trippers is the section between Lake Traverse and McManus Lake due to the proximity of the put-in and take-outs from each other. It is recommended to allow at least three days to run this section. From Lake Traverse to the large rapid known as the Natch, the scenery is set amidst a forested valley. Down river from the Natch, the scenery begins to change to a more southern feel with maples and other deciduous trees lining the shoreline.

Note: Travel beyond McManus Lake is strictly prohibited as the Petawawa River travels through a live artillery training range at Canadian Forces Base Petawawa.

Pinetree Lake Canoe Route (Map 45/E3–46/A5)

Put-in/Take-out: The Pinetree Lake Route can begin at the Sunday Creek or the Pinetree Lake Access Points. Our description begins at Sunday Creek. Travellers can park a vehicle at the Spruce Bog Board-walk Trail entrance and a second vehicle can be left at the Galeairy Lake public boat launch in the town of Whitney. Backcountry camping permits can be picked up at the East Gate of the park.

From Sunday Creek, just before it crosses under the highway, the creek meanders through a wetland habitat and into Norway Lake. A short paddle south of Norway Lake brings paddlers to Fork Lake, another common area to see wandering moose. A long portage links to the smaller Rose Pond Lake followed by another long portage to Pinetree Lake where there are three secluded campsites. The last leg of the trip begins with a 1,825 m (6,000 ft) portage into Fraser Lake. A single campsite lies on Fraser Lake, which makes a great second night camping spot for those ambitious enough to travel the gruelling portage. From Fraser Lake, there are two portages and a short paddle to access David Thomson Lake, which is named after David Thomson, a renowned Canadian mapmaker who once explored this part of the park for a possible canal route from Ottawa to Georgian Bay. A 1,580 m (5,180 ft) portage from the lake takes you to Mud Bay on Galeairy Lake. The take-out is about a 5 km paddle on the big lake.

Ragged Lake Loop (Map 44/F5)

Put-in/Take-out: The route starts at the Smoke Lake Access south of the Highway 60 Corridor in Algonquin Park. Permits can be picked up at the park permit office at Canoe Lake just across the highway from the Smoke Lake Access.

Beginning from the dock at the Smoke Lake Access, the Ragged Lake Loop is a great weekend getaway. The route heads southeast to towards the 240 m (787 ft) Ragged Lake portage. Smoke Lake is a northwest facing lake so going towards Ragged Lake you will often have a tailwind that can help you along your way. The only downfall is that that same wind can make the trip back a little more challenging at the end of your trip. There is also boat traffic on the bigger lake from time to time. Once on Ragged Lake, there are plenty of great campsites to choose from and moose can be seen on occasion around Crown Bay. You can return the same way or loop back to Smoke Lake through Claude Lake. The three portages are generally easy to travel with the longest, and last, being 770 m (2,526 ft) long.

Rosebary/Longbow Lake Canoe Route (Map 53/F7–54/B6)

Put-in/Take-out: The put-in is found at the Tim River Access Point. To find the access point, take the Forestry Tower Road from the village of Kearney and follow the signs to the access area. Park permits can be acquired at the Kearney Community Centre.

The Rosebary/Longbow Lake Canoe Route is an easy, two to three day out and back trip that follows the Tim River Canoe Route below. The easy paddling and lack of portages make this a popular trip throughout the year, especially with anglers in spring. From the put-in on the Tim River, the route meanders down into Tim Lake. There are six rustic campsites on the lake with three of the sites located on the lake's only island. The paddle to Rosebary Lake is slow, but scenic with only one easy, portage around a set of falls on the river. Longbow Lake can be found through a narrows on Rosebary's southeast shore. Rosebary Lake offers six wilderness campsites and Longbow has three to choose from. Paddlers can also take a day trip into Floating Heart Lake to the north or continue along the Tim River to the east.

Sec Lake Loop (Map 57/G4)

Put-in/Take-out: The Sec Lake Loop is found on the east side of Algonquin Provincial Park not far from the Ottawa Valley towns of Pembroke and Petawawa. Look for the park signs directing you to the Barron Canyon Road off Highway 17 west of Pembroke. Once on the Barron Canyon Road it is about a 20 minute drive to the Mallard (Sec) Lake Access Point. Permits are actually found beyond the access road to Sec Lake at the Sand Lake Gate, which is about 5 minutes down the road.

This loop is a popular local destination for long weekends and a great area for a quick two to three day trip anytime of the year. There are plenty of campsites on Sec Lake for your first night including a few highly prized island sites. From the bigger lake it is an easy, but wet at times, 890 m portage into Wet Lake where there is a single campsite. The last leg of the trip heads in a loop back through Norm's Lake across a 750 m and 1,005 m series of portages. Alternatively you can head back to Sec Lake through a linear pattern or if you want to vary things up there is also the secluded Log Canoe Lake found off the south side of the bigger lake for night number two. The trip ends back at the access point and parking area.

Shirley Lake Loop (Map 46/C1–56/C7)

Put-in/Take-out: The Shirley Lake loop begins from the Shall Lake Access, which is found at the end of Major Lake Road from Highway 60 and the village of Madawaska. The road can be found next to Algonquin Bound Outfitters, who specialize in delivery service to the access point and also provide last minute supplies or camping or fishing advice. Permits are available at the access point.

The Shirley Lake Loop is an easy three day loop that begins at Crotch Lake, which is part of the Shall Lake Access. Follow Crotch Lake north to the fairly flat 1,050 m (3,445 ft) portage into Shirley Lake. Remnants of an old logging chute can be found near the portage, while campsites are scattered amid the mature white and red pine trees. For the more adventurous, you can hike into nearby Fog or Ryan Lake for a chance at some trout fishing. The route continues by traversing 1,600 m into the secluded Bridle Lake, which hosts only one campsite and decent smallmouth bass fishing. From Bridle the route continues south along a 730 m portage into Farm Lake. The Opeongo River flows into the lake and its current will help you on your way east. As you proceed down Farm Lake you will pass the historic Kitty Lake Cabin. Kitty Lake itself is a short portage to the west. Your trip continues east through the weeds, lilies and reeds of Farm Lake until it opens up into the larger water and the final paddle back to the access point.

Tim River Canoe Route (Map 53/F7–54/E6)

Put-in/Take-out: The access point is the Tim River Access Point. Backcountry camping permits can be picked up at the park office in the Kearney Community Centre. Be wary of low water levels during summer that may add extra portaging.

Most begin this route from the put-in on the Tim River outside of the park, which leads to Tim Lake. Continue down the river to Rosebary Lake, which offers six campsites and small dam. A short portage takes you around the dam and back to the river, which is ideal for spotting moose. A series of small portages are found along the river as you trek deeper into the interior towards Big Trout Lake. To loop back to the beginning you will need to keep your eyes peeled for the daunting 2,860 m (9,380 ft) portage to Stag Lake. This is followed by another difficult 2,000 m (6,560 ft) portage to Devine Lake. Alternatively, canoeists can camp at Ranger or Stingman Lake, found west of Devine Lake. Ranger has one nice wilderness site while Stingman offers two sites to choose from. To reach Rosebary from Devine Lake, visitors will pass through Ranger, Stingman and Longbow Lakes, with five generally easy portages en route. From Rosebary Lake, it is an easy paddle back to the Tim River Access.

Welcome Lake Canoe Route (Map 45/D4–D6)

Put-in/Take-out: The access area is the Rock Lake Access Point, south of Highway 60. Look for the put-in on the Madawaska River between Rock and Whitefish Lakes. Permits for backcountry camping can be picked up at the Rock Lake Campground office.

This moderate two to three day route begins at the put-in on the Madawaska River. Paddle south on Rock Lake to the portage around the Pen Lake Dam and chute. It is a long paddle to the Galipo River on Pen Lake's southwestern shore where a fair bit of portaging to Welcome Lake. The first portage travels around a pretty waterfall, but the second portage is much more challenging, as it traverses 2,170 m (7,120 ft). Welcome Lake is a picturesque interior lake with a sandy beach and rock outcroppings. Paddlers can then continue along the Galipo River to Harry and Rence Lakes, where scenic campsites can be found. The last leg of the trip involves completing the loop back to Rock Lake via Lake Louisa.

From Rence Lake, follow a small stream north to Frank Lake, Florence Lake and Lake Louisa. From Florence Lake, there are two different portages to Lake Louisa, a 1,725 m (5,660 ft) portage or a 3,455 m (11,336 f) portage. The longer route will shorten your paddle considerably on Lake Louisa, which could be a great advantage when winds are heavy. Louisa is very scenic, although it is also very popular during the summer. The last portage is a gruelling 2,895 m (9,500 ft) back to Rock Lake and the access area.

Wilkins Lake Canoe Route (Map 47/A2–57/A7)

Put-in/Take-out: The access and permits for this route can be found on Aylen Lake at the marina, off Aylen Lake Road. An alternate access can be found at the end of North Road.

Depending on where you start and how far you travel, the Wilkins Lake Route can be an easy weekend trip or a challenging four to five day route. The longer trip begins with a long paddle on Aylen Lake beginning at the marina access point leading to the O'Neill and Robitaille Lake portages. The weekend trip starts and ends at the 4 km cart track from the park boundary directly to Wilkins Lake. The Aylen Lake option includes travel on the big lake that can be windy and busy with boat traffic. Many trippers take a water taxi up to the O'Neill Lake portage, a 1,425 m (4,670 ft) jaunt. There is another 1,235 m (4,050 ft) portage into Robitaille Lake where there are six wilderness campsites. From Robitaille Lake, continue onward to Breezy Lake and Wilkins Lake, a large lake with six well-spaced campsites itself.

Canoeists may continue to Alsever Lake via the Aylen River. The river is generally slow and meandering and requires a 970 m (3,180 ft) portage from Wilkins Lake. Continue over the beaver dams for about 3 km to the more challenging portages (780 m and 670 m) that take you into the secluded Alsever Lake. Visitors will find seven rustic campsites and decent trout fishing. Roundbush Lake to the north of Alsever Lake also makes a good day trip.

York River Canoe Route (Map 37/A3)

Put-in/Take-out: At the south end of the park, this route starts from the Kingscote Lake Access Point. Park permits can be purchased at the Pine Grove Point Lodge, located just after Benoir Lake. A second vehicle can be left here or you can taxi back to the start with through the lodge.

This moderately difficult route receives limited use. From Kingscote Lake, two portages will take paddlers to Byers Lake and to the mouth of the York River, which is a Grade II-III river. There are five short portages along the river, which avoid dams and circumnavigate the magnificent High Falls. Allow a few days to enjoy the peace and solitude of this beautiful area. Camping is available at Byers Lake and along the York River, while brook trout fishing along the river can yield surprising results.

CANOE ROUTE TIPS

Information provided by Algonquin Bound Outfitters
www.algonquinbound.com

Packing and Planning

Good planning is essential to minimize your weight and maximize your comfort on portages. If planning is not done properly, an enjoyable trip can easily become hard work. Be sure to consider the weight of items you are taking along on your trip. Items such as a water purifier, lightweight camp stoves and even small things like plastic cutlery, all contribute to making a pack lighter and easier to carry on portages.

Packing your packs may seem like a simple thing to most, but with a little extra consideration you can turn a grueling portage into a manageable one. A good rule of thumb is to pack in groups of two. One pack should be for the lighter items such as clothing and the second pack should be a much heavier load with food and equipment. This way, whoever is carrying the canoe, will wear the lighter pack and the other person will carry the heavier pack.

For long tripping with numerous portages, a good lightweight Kevlar canoe is highly recommended. This helps increase your endurance and reduce the physical stress of portages.

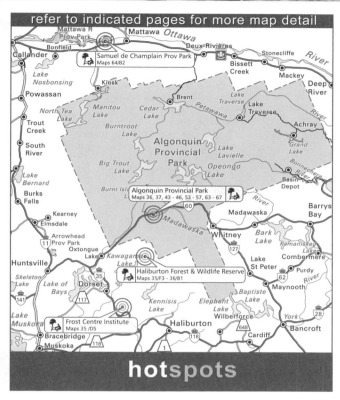

refer to indicated pages for more map detail

hotspots

Protecting some of the most spectacular areas the province has to offer, the parks system in this region is quite extensive and includes not one but two of the provinces showcase parks: Georgian Bay National Park and Algonquin Provincial Park. These two are the crown jewels, but there are dozens of other protected areas to explore.

These parks protect significant and vulnerable areas in an area where recreational activity is becoming progressively more popular each year. Virtually every park offers its own unique feature and presents visitors a chance to experience the great outdoors. The Ministry of Natural Resources oversees the vast network of protected area that is comprised of a variety of provincial parks, including Recreation, Historical, Wilderness, Nature Reserve, Natural Environment and Waterway Parks. Ranging from non-operating parks that rely mainly on user maintenances to recreation parks that have developed for enjoyment of outdoor activities and provide camping along with many amenities, there really is a park for everyone. Even the natural environment or nature reserves are great places to get out and experience the wildness of nature.

In the last decade, as part of the Living Legacy initiative, there were hundreds of new non-operating parks and conservation reserves established. Conservation Reserves usually have very limited facilities, if any and have a primary goal of preserving the natural environment of the area. Unlike non-operating provincial parks, these sites discourage outdoor recreation due to the delicate nature of the areas. With this in mind we have not listed all of these reserves.

Conservation Areas are a different sort of park all together. They are managed by a series of Conservation Authorities, which have been established across the province to manage areas that are heavily affected by human activity. Conservation areas should not be overlooked. They provide some of the best outdoor recreation opportunities and are often less crowded than the popular provincial parks. The development of these also varies greatly, ranging from full fee camping areas to day-use only sites.

Because Cottage Country is found just north of one of the most populated areas in the entire country (the Greater Toronto Area), there is often heavy pressure on many of these areas. Campsite reservations are available for all operating parks in Cottage Country and can be made at www.OntarioParks.com or by phone by calling (888) ONT-PARKS.

Algonquin Provincial Park (Maps 36, 37, 43–46, 53–57, 63–67)

Algonquin Provincial Park is internationally renowned as one of the premier wilderness areas of Canada and is one of the province's greatest treasures. From beautiful clean lakes and rocky hills, to the howl of the wolf or the call of the loon, this park is an outdoor paradise. Thousands of primitive campsites dot a seemingly endless collection of lakes and rivers. You can literally spend a lifetime exploring the park, as many people have. The Algonquin interior offers seclusion from our busy urban lifestyles and helps us get a little more in touch with the magnificence of nature.

Wildlife viewing is a standard pastime of interior trippers. Moose, deer, beaver, wolves and bear are often seen throughout the park, while. Fishing opportunities also abound in the interior of the park with the elusive brook trout and lake trout luring anglers from around the globe. In spring, just after ice off, fishing enthusiasts are the first to brave the interior in search of trout. The black flies of late May and June and mosquitoes into early July keep some of the trippers and campers away. Seclusion seekers will find this period (June and early July) some of the best times to be in the park. As the heat of August comes on, camping on a lazy lake is a great way to enjoy summer. The heat can be easily forgotten after a refreshing swim in a cool Algonquin Lake. One of the best times to travel the park is in September and early October, during its annual autumn display.

There are over one million visitors to the park annually. While most of those visitors stick to the Highway 60 Corridor, many of them head into the park's

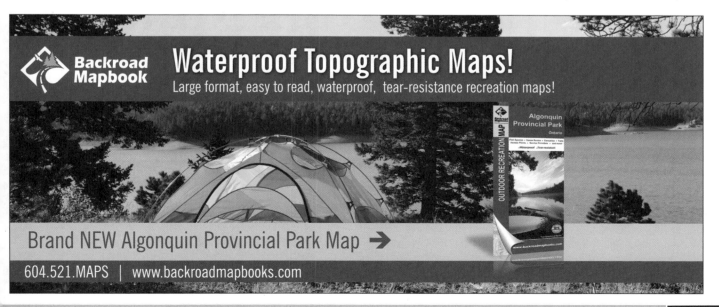

parkadventures

backcountry. In an effort to reduce the impact, there are certain limitations on the number of people who can access certain areas and interior camping permits are needed for all parties heading into the backcountry. To help maintain the park experience for yourself and others, be sure to leave campsites clean or cleaner than when you arrived.

Parking permits are also needed and available at most access points. For more information, see the Friends of Algonquin Park website www.algonquinpark.on.ca or call the park information line at (705) 633-5572. To reserve a cabin or campsite visit www.ontarioparks.com or contact the reservation line at 1-888-668-7275.

Accessing Algonquin
The main road into the park is Highway 60, which passes through the southern section of the park. Several vehicle accessible camping areas, a trio of lodges and yurts are available for overnight stays, while nine access points, trails, picnic areas, museums and a host of other attractions can also be easily found.

In addition to Highway 60, there are a number of gravel roads that enter the park. The gravel roads are used primarily by paddlers looking to access different routes within the park. There are twenty other access points abutting the east, north, west and southern parts of the park. Some, like the Brain Lake Access Point are seldom used. Others, like McManus Lake are used mostly as an exit point for paddling trips, while others, like the Kawawaymog or Shall Lake Access Points are popular locations for anglers.

Day-use Areas
In addition to the day-use areas found at many of the campgrounds (including Canisbay, Kearney Lake, Lake of Two Rivers, Mew Lake, Pog Lake and Rock Lake), there are a number of picnic areas off of Highway 60. These sites usually provide picnic tables, flush toilets, running water and some point of interest. From the west, there sites are found at: Oxtongue River, Tea Lake Dam, Lake of Two Rivers Beach, East Beach and Picnic Pavillion, Costello Creek and the Algonquin Visitor Centre.

Backcountry Campsites
There are about 1,900 campsites in the interior of Algonquin. Most of them accessed by canoe, but a select few are also accessible by trail. Smaller lakes have only one or two sites, while larger lakes might have ten or more. It is recommended to reserve your interior campsite ahead of time by providing an itinerary with dates, number of people, access and exit points, along with the lakes you will be camping at each night. Nightly permits are required. You are also well advised to bring along a compact stove, especially during summer when fire bans may be in effect and a water filter system.

Ranger Cabins
In the early 1900s, park rangers travelled on foot and by canoe through the park in search of poachers. Cabins were built throughout the park to house equipment and provide a more comfortable place to stay while the rangers were on duty. These days, the cabins have become a popular alternative to tenting for interior trippers, while a select few are accessible by vehicle and offer running water (Brent, Brent Deputy, Kiosk & Rain Lake). The backcountry cabins are more rustic and and often only a simple one room log cabin with a small wood stove, table and bunk beds. No mattresses, dishes, dishes or pans are provided. Some of the more popular destinations include Kitty Lake, Lost Coin, McKaskill, Tattler Lake and Wenda Lake). Visit www.algonquinpark.on.ca/visit/camping/ranger-cabin for more information. Call 1-888-668-7275 to make reservations.

Vehicle Campgrounds
There are a number of vehicle access campgrounds in Algonquin Park, ranging from large sites with full comfort stations that are equipped with flush toilets, showers and laundry facilities to small sites with pit toilets. The bulk of the campgrounds are found along the Highway 60 Corridor of the park, while the Achray Campground at the east end and the Brent and Kiosk Campgrounds on the north end can be accessed along gravel roads from outside the park. Those looking for electrical sites can visit Canisbay, Lake of Two Rivers, Mew, Pog and Rock Lake for an additional fee. Mew Lake also offers winter camping. Overnight fees vary depending on the amenities available and time of year. Reservations are recommended by calling 1-888-668-7275.

Algonquin Park Vehicle Campgrounds
Listed below are the drive-in campgrounds found around the park.

Achray Campground (Map 57/C3)
Located on the eastern side of the park via 50 km of gravel road, there are 45 well-spaced sites next to Grand Lake at this campground. A picnic area, beach, boat launch for motorized boats, interpretive centre and yurt are a few of the amenities here. The Eastern Pines Backpacking Trail and canoes routes to Barron Canyon or Greenleaf Lake are also found here.

Brent Campground (Map 65/B7)
Brent Campground is found at the Cedar Lake-Brent Access Point via 40 km of gravel road. The site offers 30 campsites, a beach, a boat launch for motorized boats, the Brent Cabin and a store nearby. Canoe trips including venturing down the mighty Petawawa River, while fishing on Cedar Lake or exploring the Brent Crater Trail is also popular.

Canisbay Lake Campground (Map 45/A3)
Canisbay Lake is one of the larger campgrounds in the park with 242 sites, including 66 with electrical hookups, and showers. The campground also offers a sandy beach, hiking and biking trails and paddle in campsites for those looking for a bit more seclusion. It is found off the north side of Highway 60 at km 23.

Coon Lake Campground (Map 45/D4)
This is a popular staging area for a number of different hiking and biking trails as well as fishing and paddling on the lake. The campground is found 6 km from km 40.3 of Highway 60 on the gravel road to Rock Lake. There are 48 rustic campsites and a small beach area.

Kearney Lake Campground (Map 45/D3)
Kearney Lake has 104 sites and showers set amidst splendid stands of pine trees. A beach area and fishing are available on Kearney Lake, while a number of trails are within a short walk from the campground.

Kiosk Campground (Map 64/B6)
Accessed by 30 km of gravel road along County Road 630, there are 24 campsites and the Kiosk Cabin at this site. Found at the north end of the park at the Kioshkokwi Lake-Kiosk Access Point, there are a number of different canoe routes in the area. Fishing and lazing around the beach are also popular pastimes.

Lake of Two Rivers Campground (Map 45/B3)
Located off the south side of Highway 60 near km 32, this big campground hosts 241 sites, including 160 with electrical hook-up. Comfort stations with showers and laundry, a store, a beautiful sandy beach and access to the Madawaska River and nearby trails are some of the attractions here.

Mew Lake Campground (Map 45/B3)
This is a year round campground found off the south side of Highway 60 at km 30.8. Offering 131 campsites, 66 of which have electrical hook-ups, the comfort stations with showers and laundry are closed in winter. The beach area on Mew Lake is a popular spot during the summer as are the yurts, which are also available to rent throughout the year.

Pog Lake and Whitefish Group Campgrounds (Map 45/C3)
Found 2 km south of Highway 60 and km 37, there are 286 campsites, including 83 with electrical service at the popular Pog Lake Campground. Comfort stations include showers and laundry. A number of trails can be explored in the area, including the Old Railway Bike Trail, while canoeing and swimming at the sandy beach areas are also popular pastimes on Pog Lake. Also in the area is the Whitefish Group site. Offering 18 rustic campsites with space for up to 40 people this site is for youth or special groups by reservation only.

Rock Lake Campground (Map 45/D4)
Home to a couple beach areas, 121 campsites (72 with electrical hook-ups) and comfort stations with showers, this is a popular campground 8 km south of Highway 60. Look for the access road near the 40 km mark of the corridor. In addition to swimming or lazing on the beach, fishing and paddling opportunities are available on Rock Lake and beyond. The Booth Rock Trail is also found here.

Tea Lake Campground (Map 44/E4)
Found off the north side of Highway 60 at km 11.4, this campground offers 42 campsites, vault toilets and a small beach. The lake is popular for fishing and a number of trails are within close proximity of the campground.

Algonquin Park Ranger Cabins

Listed below are many of the old park ranger cabins that have become a popular alternative to tenting for interior trippers. Visit www.algonquinpark. on.ca/visit/camping/ranger-cabin for more information.

Big Crow Cabin (Map 55/D5)

Built in 1956, the Big Crow Cabin is found accessible by canoe only. Without the water taxi on Opeongo Lake, the trip takes about two days. The cabin is equipped with a kitchen, living area, wood burning stove and two bedrooms.

Bissett Road [Twelve Mile] Cabin (Map 66/C6)

Accessed via the Bissett Creek Road, an active logging road, this one-room log cabin set amidst a beautiful mature stand of white pine. Despite the road access, it is a rustic cabin like the other backcountry cabins. Built in 1922, the cabin is known locally as the Twelve Mile Cabin because of its distance from Bissett Creek.

Brent Cabin & Brent Deputy Ranger Cabin (Map 65/B7)

Located on a peninsula on Cedar Lake, not far from the campground, the Brent Cabin is equipped with four bedrooms, a kitchen, living room, wood stove, propane, fridge and fire pits. It is close to the beach, store and boat launch and the Brent Crater Trail is only a short drive away. Nearby Brent Deputy Ranger Cabin is a smaller one room cabin.

Crooked Chute Cabin (Map 66/G7)

This larger, 8 person cabin lies on the impressive Petawawa River, south of the treacherous Crooked Chute. It is long day or two travel from the Lake Travel Access Point. The cabin was completed in 1929 at a cost of $33.97 to house the rangers patrolling log drives on the river.

Highview Cabin-Nipissing River (Map 54/A4)

Allow two days to access this cabin on the serene Nipissing River from the Tim River Access Point. The single room cabin was re-built in 1928 for $37.50 after the original cabin was set ablaze by a lightning strike.

Kiosk Cabin (Map 64/B6)

Found at the Kiosk Access Point, adjacent to the Kiosk Campground, this is one of the few cabins in the park that has vehicle access and electricity. The two bedroom cabin was built in 1936 on Kioshkokwi Lake and offers a refrigerator, stove, electric heat, couch, a table with chairs and running water. Fishing is presented in Kioshkokwi Lake for the elusive lake trout and there is a nearby boat launch and lovely beach area.

Kitty Lake Cabin (Map 46/B1)

This single room cabin is a short paddle from the Shall Lake Access Point. It was constructed in 1935 and is one of the largest cabins available in the park housing up to eight people. The cabin actually sits on Farm Lake and offers plenty of fishing opportunities in the many nearby lakes.

McKaskill Lake Cabin (Map 56/D7)

The single room log cabin was built in 1932 and rests in a prime fishing area. Access is easiest from the end of Basin Depot Road at the hydro line where a rough forest access road cum cart trail travels 8 km to the lake. The more exciting, but longer route requires crossing five lakes with challenging portages from the Shall Lake Access Point.

Rain Lake Cabin (Map 44/A2)

With drive-in access from the village of Kearney, this is one of the more modern cabins in the park. In the late 1970s, the cabin was moved from Cache Lake to its current location on Rain Lake. Equipped with a propane stove, fridge, lights and heat the 2 bedroom cabin sits adjacent to a beach and boat launch. A number of different canoe routes and the Western Uplands Backpacking Trail are also found in the area.

Tattler Lake Cabin (Map 46/A1)

Originally constructed as a shelter for the person who manned a nearby fire tower, it is estimated that the cabin was built in 1932. Today, it is a great location to enjoy Tattler Lake after the easy one day canoe trip from the Shall Lake Access Point.

Wenda Lake Cabin (Map 57/A4)

This one room cabin sits on picturesque Wenda Lake amidst a mature stand of red pine trees. The most direct option is to travel from the Grand Lake-Achray Access Point and cross the challenging 3.5 km portage off Grand Lake. Alternatively, you can travel from across to Carajou Bay and through the Spectacle Lakes to Wenda Lake.

Ahmic Forest & Rock Barrens Conservation Reserve (Map 41/E3)

This large area contains over 55 different habitats and was set aside because so many diverse features were present in one area. The rugged landscape features sugar maple forests growing on hills of fine glacial deposits called tills, rock barrens with balsam fir and white cedar forests as well as white pine, ash, red oak and maple forests growing on bare bedrock uplands. Wetlands also occur on a variety of landforms. The area is frequented by snowmobilers and hunters and there are a number of recreation camps in the area.

Alliston [Beattie] Pinery Nature Reserve (Map 6/E5)

Found just south of the town of Alliston, this new nature reserve was established to help protect one of the last mature sand plain forest stands in southern Ontario. Visitors will find some magnificent white pine tracts along with sugar maple and white cedar. There are no facilities at this reserve, and if you do plan to visit, please tread lightly.

Amable du Fond River Provincial Park (Map 64/A5)

Falling along a popular canoe route north of the Kiosk Access Point of Algonquin Park, a section of the Amable du Fond River is protected as a waterway park. In addition to the canoeing possibilities available, the waterway also affords visitors some decent angling and wildlife viewing opportunities.

Ancor Park (Map 7/E4)

Formerly known as the Holland Landing Conservation Area, the park is located off County Road 51, north of the town of Holland Landing. In addition to a picnic area, there is also a 2 km (1.2 mi) trail that can be used year round.

Arrowhead Provincial Park (Map 43/C7)

Named after the bright crimson arrowhead aquatic plant, which is uncommon in this region, this 1,237 hectare park encompasses Arrowhead and Mayflower Lakes, including three sandy beaches. A peaceful stretch of the Big East River meanders through the south side of the park and is a great spot for an easy canoe paddle or swim. There are also over 13 km (8 mi) of easy hiking and biking trails as well as 22 km (14 mi) of groomed cross-country ski trails that give visitors a chance to explore the area further. The park offers 378 campsites (185 with electrical hook-ups), toilets and showers. In winter, tobogganing, tubing and skating are also popular activities. Call (705) 789-5105 for more information.

Atlee Conservation Reserve (Map 58/C5)

Located north of Broker Lake, this 263 hectare conservation reserve protects bedrock of ground moraine situated on a slightly rolling landscape.

Axe Lake Wetland Conservation Reserve (Map 42/D7)

The 793 hectare reserve is regarded as one of the most important areas in Ontario for Atlantic coastal plain plant life. Visitors will find vast conifer wetlands as well as rare aquatic plants. The reserve is popular with nature lovers, hunters in the fall and snowmobilers in the winter.

Awenda Provincial Park (Map 23/B4)

Encompassing 2,917 hectares, including Methodist Bay and Giants Tomb Island of Georgian Bay, one of the unique natural features of the park is the Nipissing Bluff that rises sharply 60 metres (197 feet) above the bay. Campers will find 333 spacious sites (102 with electrical hook-ups) set amid red oak and sugar maple trees. Six beautiful beaches are spread across the mainland and Giants Tomb Island, while trail enthusiasts will find 27 km (17 mi) of summer trails and over 32 km (20 mi) of groomed cross-country ski trails. Canoe rentals are available. Call (705) 549-2231 for more information.

Ball's Mill Conservation Area (Map 11/D7)

Ball's Mill is located north of Cobourg in Hamilton Township. The 15.7 hectare area offers woodland trails and a pond for exploring and spotting wildlife. You can walk, fish or relax near the dam, pond or stream.

Balsam Lake Provincial Park (Map 17/C2)

Located off Highway 48, this three-season park sits on beautiful Balsam Lake of the Trent Waterway System. There is a resource centre and an Outdoor Adventure Theatre, while boating, swimming, windsurfing and fishing on the lake are the main attractions. Nature trails provide year round adventure.

parkadventures

Campers will find 505 campsites (213 with electrical hook-ups), as well as 3 group camping sites. Camping amenities include comfort stations featuring toilets, showers and laundry facilities as well as a small store for supplies and a playground. Rental equipment such as canoes, kayaks and boats are available and you can even borrow a PFD or fishing tackle to enhance the enjoyment of your stay. One cottage is also available for rent. For more information call (705) 454-3324.

Bass Lake Provincial Park (Map 15/E3)

Only a short drive from Orillia on Highway 12, Bass Lake is a popular weekend retreat. The park has 182 campsites (92 with electrical hook-ups) and an additional 3 group site that can accommodate anywhere from 45 to 75 people. Camping amenities include comfort stations with flush toilets and showers, playground and a boat launch. The 3 km (1.8 mi) nature trail gives a good view of the lake and surrounding habitat, while the beach area is often busy with sun lovers. During winter, the nature trail is used for cross-country skiing and there is snowshoeing and tobogganing opportunities. Rentals include canoes and pedal boats and PFDs can be borrowed with deposit. For more information call (705) 326-7054.

Bear Creek Conservation Reserve (Map 43/F4)

This 212 hectare conservation reserve protects winter habitat for deer and a yellow birch forest around Bear Creek.

Bear Lake Peatland Conservation Reserve (Map 42/B5)

This large conservation reserve was recently established to help preserve one of the largest bog and peatland sites in the region. The area is prime moose habitat and is also home to a variety of wetland bird species such as the sandhill crane. The Seguin Recreational Trail passes along the southern boundary of the reserve in several places.

Bell Bay Provincial Park (Map 46/G4–47/A4)

Found on Highway 60 east of Madawaska, this non-operating park protects a large section of Bark Lake's northern shoreline. Separate parcels to the west protect a stretch of Parissien and Pergeon Lakes. In total, the park covers 404 hectares of land and is home to the very rare encrusted saxifrage, which grows mainly on the park's large cliff that overlooks Bark Lake. The plant is a remnant of the glacial retreat over 10,000 thousand years ago. Although there are no facilities, hiking along the old roadway and informal trails through the park and canoeing or fishing on Bark Lake are possible.

Big East River Provincial Park (Map 43/E6–47/A4)

Long utilized as a canoe route, the majority of the Big East River has now been established as a provincial park. Linking Algonquin Park to Arrowhead Provincial Park, a rustic canoe route exists along the river, although portage points are not well established and can be hard to spot on occasion.

Bigwind Lake Provincial Park (Map 34/F7)

This 1,970 hectare, non-operating, provincial park is found in a remote area of Muskoka, south of the southern shore of Lake of Bays. Canoeing and fishing are available at three of the park's lakes; however, there is no camping available. The park is forested with a variety of trees including hemlock, birch and maple, while moose, deer and a few bear can sometimes be spotted. Geological features of interest include a ground moraine and Precambrian rocks that exist as part of a gneiss belt.

Bissett Creek Provincial Park (Map 65/G4–66/D4)

This waterway class provincial park protects 1,676 hectare around Bissett Creek. In addition to the canoeing possibilities available, the waterway also affords visitors some decent angling and wildlife viewing opportunities.

Bleasdell Boulder Conservation Area (Map 13/A4)

The Bleasdell Boulder is one of the largest glacier erratic in North America. This small conservation was set aside to protect the boulder and surrounding area.

Bon Echo Provincial Park (Map 30/F2)

One of the more popular provincial parks Ontario, the park encompasses several lakes including a large portion of Mazinaw Lake. Along the eastern shore of the lake is a 1.5 km long, 100 metre (328 foot) high cliff that is home to the largest single native pictograph collection in North America,

which includes over 260 markings. The park's main vehicle access campground and day-use facilities can be found on the western shore of Mazinaw Lake. There are 528 campsites, split between eight locations, including interior camping. There is also group camping and a historic log cabin available for rent. Amenities, such as laundry facilities, a park store, visitor centre, picnic area, boat launch and rental facilities are available, while five hiking trails offer spectacular views of the lake and forestlands. Fishing or lounging on the sandy beaches are also common pastimes. Call (613) 336-2228 for more information.

Bonfield Park Conservation Area [Kaibuskong Park] (Map 63/C3)

The 8 hectare area offers a parking and picnic area, a small beach on the river for swimming and sunbathing, as well as a kid's playground. Other popular features of this day-use park include a lit ball field, a tennis court, basketball hoops, volleyball court and a skating rink in winter.

Bonnechere Provincial Park (Map 47/F1–57/G7)

On picturesque Round Lake, this park is home to 128 campsites (24 with electrical hook-ups), comfort stations with showers as well as a laundry area, park store and visitor centre. Four rustic cabins can also be rented through the reservation system. There are fishing opportunities on both the Bonnechere River and Round Lake, which is an ideal place for a beach picnic or a refreshing swim. Canoes and kayaks are available for rent at the park for a nominal fee. For more information call (613) 757-2103.

Bonnechere River Provincial Park (Map 47/F1–57/C7)

Encompassing 1,198 hectares of shoreline, this non-operating park allows for camping and canoeing along on the historic waterway. The river was once a vital component of the log drives in the area. Between Round Lake and Algonquin Park, there are six rustic camping areas, several trails, while deer, moose, bear and waterfowl are often seen among the maple and pine dominated forest. The river, also known as the "Little Bonnechere", is quite meandering and there are few areas of difficulty for canoeists.

Bowmanville/Westside Marshes (Map 4/A3)

This conservation area protects not just one, but two provincially significant coastal wetland areas within its 80 hectares. The area provides habitat for nesting birds, waterfowl and shorebirds migrating along Lake Ontario. There is a 1.5 km wheelchair friendly trail through the area. For a longer hike or bike, the Waterfront Trail can be accessed from the parking lot.

Boyd Conservation Area (Map 1/C5)

Boyd is set next to the Humber River in the steep sided river valley. The park is a popular picnic destination and has 7 km (4.5 miles) of hiking trails.

Bruce's Mill Conservation Area (Map 2/A2)

Known locally as the home of the Sugarbush Maple Syrup Festival, which attracts upwards of 20,000 people annually, this area has 11 picnic areas, 10 km (6 miles) of hiking trails, a driving range, playing fields for soccer or baseball and a pool which can be rented.

Callaghan's Rapids Conservation Area (Map 20/E5)

This area protects a number of karst features, including caves and sinkholes. There are some trails in the area.

Cardwell Township Old Growth Conservation Reserve (Map 33/B2)

As part of the Living Legacy initiative, this fabulous area has been created to protect some of the oldest white pine stands in Southern Ontario. Some of these amazing trees are over 100 years old. Please tread lightly.

Carruthers Memorial Conservation Area (Map 6/A2)

This 20 hectare reserve encompasses a portion of the Mad River Bottomlands near Airport Road (County Road 42). The area offers 25 sites for camping along with a short trail that can be used for hiking, snowshoeing or cross-country skiing. For day-trippers, there are picnic facilities at the area and the Mad River provides opportunities for canoeing and fishing. For more information call (705) 424-1479.

Carson Lake Provincial Park (Map 47/C4)

Carson Lake Provincial Park is a small non-operating park found off Highway 60, about 6 km (3.7 mi) west of Barry's Bay. Currently, the park is gated, but is accessible by foot or boat. Swimming is a major attraction, while it is possible to canoe south past Trout Lake into Kulas Lake via a series of culvert or channels. Fishing is also popular in the area.

Chain Lakes Conservation Reserve (Map 43/B2)

Most commonly visited by hunters (there is a recreation camp in the area), this conservation reserve has a mixture of forests and other habitats including open muskeg. The rolling hills and rugged terrain are mixed with flat sandy deposits from ancient waterbodies.

Cherriman Township Conservation Reserve (Map 59/E4)

This reserve protects an area of Precambrian Shield, as well as areas of wetlands and forest.

Cobourg Conservation Area (Map 5/C1)

A popular place for picnics, playing sports and games in the open space or taking a stroll near the river, this park covers 13 hectares.

Cognashene Lake & Point Conservation Reserves (Map 23/D2)

The Cognashene Lake Conservation Reserve helps protect wetland habitat next to the Georgian Bay, Cognashene Lake, Go Home Lake and Go Home River. The 2,945 hectare reserve can only be accessed by canoe or boat off Georgian Bay or Go Home Lake. Also in the area is the Cognashene Point Conservation Reserve, which encompasses wetland and rock barrens that are home to the endangered Massasauga Rattlesnake.

Commanda Creek Conservation Reserve (Map 52/C4)

This 1657 hectare reserve is located a few kilometres north and west of Mikasew Provincial Park. The area has a few rough hunting trails and hunting is the most popular recreational activity here.

Conroys Marsh Conservation Reserve (Map 38/F2–47/G7)

Part of the York River system, the 2,400 hectare marsh was once an abundant wildlife and fishing area that provided furs and fish to the first settlers and to natives. Today, it acts as a refuge to many fur bearing animals, including fox, beaver and marten. Mayhews Landing, up river, can provide a means of access for a 4 km (2.5 mi) paddle down to the peaceful marsh.

Copeland Forest Resources Management Area (Map 14/G3–15/A3)

Off Ingram Road north of Barrie lies this 1,650 hectare park was developed by the MNR for educational and practical resource management activities. The forest offers a variety of recreational opportunities for the public, including a 35 km (22 mi) multi-use trail system. Facilities include picnic tables at three separate wooded areas and washrooms along with group campsites. Fishing for trout is also available in the various streams in the forest.

Corbeil Conservation Area (Map 63/A3)

This 36.5 hectare area protects the headwaters of the La Vasse River, an important floodplain that helps to maintain proper water levels during spring thaws. There is a small parking area off Highway 94 where a short interpretive trail loops through the conservation area. For more information call (705) 474-9793.

Crane Lake Forest Provincial Conservation Reserve (Map 32/B3)

Located along the northwest part of Crane Lake, this 392 hectare reserve helps protect an older stand of maple and hemlock. There are no facilities available at the reserve, but naturalists, canoeists and anglers use the area.

Crowe Bridge Conservation Area (Map 20/D6)

Found north of Campbellford, this 10 hectare site is a popular outdoor recreation area. The weir dam located on the Crowe River creates a swimming area with picnic sites and hiking trails. There is even a mini putt on site.

Crowe River Swamp Conservation Reserve (Map 28/G5–29/A5)

This 189 hectare site is found in Peterborough County. It is a provincially significant wetland complex and is the largest and least disturbed wetland in the area. There are also landforms known as kame moraines, which are found only in a few other spots in the area. Please tread lightly if visiting.

Darlington Provincial Park (Map 3/E3) 6B8OAVC(9.

Found on the shores of Lake Ontario, there are 315 campsites here including 135 with electrical hook-ups and an additional two group sites that can accommodate up to 150 people. Camping amenities include flush toilets, showers, laundry facilities, a playground, park store, visitor centre and boat launch. The waters of McLaughlin Bay are protected from the open waters of Lake Ontario by a barrier beach, creating a warm, sheltered area for swimming and canoeing, while larger boats can head out onto the open waters. There are four easy trails in the park, the longest one, at 2.6 km (1.5 miles) is the Waterfront Trail, which is follows the shores of Lake Ontario. It is a short excerpt of a much longer trail that runs from Niagara on the Lake to Trenton. For the explorer, remnants of past American settler inhabitants remain with a small log cabin and cemetery on site. Tobogganing and skating opportunities exist in winter.

Deerock Lake Conservation Area (Map 30/F6)

This small conservation area features a boat launch onto Deerock Lake, which is a popular destination for anglers. The lake is supported by a dam, but remains fairly shallow in most spots with many small islands and rocky outcrops.

Dividing Lake Provincial Nature Reserve Park (Map 44/G6–45/A6)

Dividing Lake Park can only be accessed by canoe from Rockaway Lake, which in turn is accessed by a gruelling 2,745 m (9,006 ft) portage from Kimball Lake. The reward is well worth the effort since the park protects one of the last stands of old growth white pine in southern Ontario. There are a few rustic campsites available at Rockaway and Dividing Lakes but an Algonquin Park permit must be acquired in order to stay at these sites.

Draper Township Wetland Conservation Reserve (Map 25/D2)

This small reserve is located just east of Gravenhurst and helps protect a unique natural environment. The area highlights include wetland, stands of white pine and sugar maple.

Driftwood Provincial Park (Map 66/G4–67/A4)

This park sits on a quiet bay of the Ottawa River that was formed in 1950 with the completion of the Des Joachims hydroelectric dam. The bay was a collection point for large amounts of driftwood from the flooding, thus the name. The park offers a number of different recreational activities, including fishing, hiking, water sports and boating. There is a large sandy beach, perfect for swimming, with 80 campsites (20 with electrical hook-ups) as well as two group camping areas. Easy hikes to nearby lookouts provide panoramic views of the river.

Duclos Point Nature Reserve (Map 8/C1)

Located east of the popular Sibbald Point Provincial Park, Duclos Point is a 111 hectare reserve, which is home to a variety of interesting plants, such as tamarack swamp and wild rice. There are no facilities available; however the area is visited by birdwatchers.

Dutcher Lake Conservation Reserve (Map 41/F6)

This large 1,952 hectare tract of Crown land preserves a vital portion of the Seguin River watershed. The reserve encompasses Dutcher Lake as well as a few other lakes. Hunting and paddling are popular activities here.

Earl Rowe Provincial Park (Map 6/D5)

Amid the rolling hills and valleys of southern Ontario, the main attractions are a large swimming pool and a man-made lake. Campers will find 365 sites available, with almost half providing electricity, as well as toilets, showers and laundry facilities. There are 11 km (6.7 miles) of trails and nice picnic areas throughout the park. The Boyne River also flows through the park and offers fishing, canoeing and bird watching opportunities. For more information call (705) 435-2498, for reservations call 888-ONT-PARK.

Eau Claire Gorge Conservation Area (Map 64/A3)
This 120 hectare conservation area protects the magnificent Eau Claire Gorge and its 18 metre (60 foot) high rock walls. The gorge was a natural barrier to the historical transportation route on the Amable Du Fond River requiring a log chute to be built to bypass the gorge. Remnants of the chute and the logging camp can still be seen today. An interpretive trail, a reconstructed squatter's cabin and 80-year-old pines are also featured.

Edenvale Conservation Area (Map 14/D6)
On the shore of the Nottawasaga River, this small reserve provides picnic tables for day-use and campsites for organized groups or users of the Nottawasaga River Canoe Route. Fishing and canoeing is offered on the river. Call (705) 728 4784 for more information.

Egan Chutes Provincial Park (Map 38/D5)
This is a small, 322 hectare nature reserve that was established to help protect a portion of delicate wetland of the York River system. A variety of waterfowl and small mammals, such as muskrat, rely on the wetland as habitat. There are no visitor facilities, although hikers can walk an unmaintained road to a series of three pictorial waterfalls.

Elks Lodge 25 Family Park (Map 62/E3)
This small park is ideal for spending a day at the beach with family and friends. Set along the shores of Trout Lake, the park provides an alternative to La Vase Portage Conservation Area, which lies adjacent to the park.

Emily Provincial Park (Map 10/C1)
Located in the Kawartha Lakes Region on the Pigeon River, this 83 hectare park has 299 campsites (170 providing electricity) as well as comfort stations with flush toilets, showers and laundry facilities. A playground and park store are also on site. Three, more rustic, group camping sites are available that can accommodate up to 80 people. There are two beaches for swimming and a boardwalk trail along the Pigeon River to a lookout tower where a nesting pair of Osprey can sometimes be spotted. The river offers fair fishing for a wide variety of species and there are boat launches adjoining the river. In winter, the park can be utilized for cross-country skiing or snowshoeing. Rentals, such as canoes, boats and even tents are available to visitors. Call (705) 799-5170 for more information.

Enniskillen Conservation Area (Map 3/E1)
Found along the south slopes of the Oak Ridges Moraine, this 65 hectare conservation area has a 3 km (1.8 mile) network of trails, a picnic area and an earthen dam that held water for the Moorey Grist Mill (built in 1874). Bowermanville Creek is a good fishing creek.

Ferguson Township White Pine Forest Conservation Reserve (Map 41/A5)
The Ferguson Township White Pine Forest Conservation Reserve is found about 18 km (11 miles) north of the town of Parry Sound. The 364 hectare site provides habitat for the threatened Eastern Massasauga rattlesnake. The area is dominated by white pine forests on low sandy hills with bare bedrock patches and flat sandy deposits.

Ferrie Township Forest Conservation Reserve (Map 51/E7)
This 474 hectare site is about 15 km (9 miles) northwest of the village of Magnetawan. The remote forest is most commonly visited by hunters.

Ferris Provincial Park (Map 12/D1)
Located along the Trent River, this park is situated on hilly drumlins south of Campbellford. One of the most popular features in the park is Ranney Falls although visitors will also find stone fences and cleared meadows, dating back from the farms that were once in the area. The park has 163 campsites, split between two areas, as well as 3 km (1.8 miles) of hiking trails.

Fleetwood Creek Nature Area (Map 10/B5)
This 380 hectare reserve offers a few picnic tables, privies and hiking trails. The trails are a great way to explore the area and offer a scenic route through forested and undisturbed areas to a lookout. If you are lucky, you may be able to get a glimpse of a wild turkey. The wily bird has been reintroduced to the area.

Fort Willow Conservation Area (Map 14/E7)
During the War of 1812, the Americans cut off access to the lower Great Lakes route. In order to maintain British outposts on Lake Huron and Lake Superior, a new supply route had to be found. The Nottawasaga River and

Willow Creek became an integral part of this new route. Fort Willow was built to house supplies and munitions that were essential for the survival of the upper Great Lakes posts. Fort Willow is now gone, although the clearing where the buildings stood still remains. A picnic area and a short hiking trail are available for visitors. For more information call (705) 424-1479.

Foy Property Provincial Park (Map 47/G1–57/G7)
Foy Provincial Park is a non-operating provincial park that was established to help protect a portion of Round Lake's shoreline, its impressive forests of old pines and hardwoods and the fine sand beach left over from glacial activity. The park is 48 hectares in size and can be explored on foot if desired. Camping is not permitted, although canoeing, swimming and picnicking are acceptable activities. Visitors are strongly encouraged to contact the park at (613) 757-2103 if they wish to visit.

Freeman Township Sugar Maple Forest Conservation Reserve (Map 32/F6)
A magnificent stand of older sugar maple trees is one of the reasons why this site was established. The site is 123 hectare in size and lies near the east side of Highway 69/400 just south of Mactier. Due to bordering private lands, there is limited public access.

French River Provincial Park (Maps 48, 49, 58, 59, 60, 61)
Linking Georgian Bay with Nipissing, the French River was once a vital transportation route for French fur traders. This 105 km designated waterway park, made up of linked lakes, rapids and gorges, makes for one of the most popular outdoor recreation areas in Ontario. The park protects 51,740 hectares and is home to a wide range of animal species including one of the largest white-tailed deer populations in Ontario and the Massasauga rattlesnake. Although there are 230 boat-accessible campsites available in the park for rustic camping; users should be sure not to trespass on the pockets of private property (campsites, lodges and camps) that dot the park. Access to the park can be from one of many public or private boat launch locations. For river information and more detailed maps, visit the new Visitor Centre located at the junction of the river and Highway 69, about 65 km south of Sudbury.

Frost Centre Institute (Map 35/C5)
The Frost Centre Institute is a 24,000 hectare playground for outdoor enthusiasts. The former MNR training area still offers outdoor education and environmental research. Visitors can explore a variety of canoe opportunities exist within the reserve, including the Black Lake and Sherborne Lake Canoe Routes. Permits are required to stay at the canoe-in sites. Alternatively, there are many trails throughout the property that are used for hiking, biking, cross-country skiing, snowmobiling and snowshoeing. The two main access points for the trails are behind the main buildings or from the parking area across Highway 35 from the centre. For reservations, call 1-866-364-4498 and for information call (705) 766-9033.

Ganaraska Forest (Map 10/C6)
The Ganaraska Forest is a 4,200 hectare reserve on the Oak Ridges Moraine. The rehabilitated area provides a great recreational playground for outdoor enthusiasts. There are many multi-use trails as well as backroads that travel through the forest and there is a forest centre that offers educational programs to local schools. The area is divided into three sections-west, central and east-that each have their own access. Permits must be purchased for use of each area. Call (905) 885-8173 for more information.

Ganaraska Millennium Conservation Area (Map 5/A1)
North of Port Hope the protected area provides trails around the old Molson Pond and along the Ganaraska River as well as a covered picnic area to enjoy the natural environment. Demonstration sites are also on sight to show local landowners how to protect and enhance their properties through the use of native plants and conservation techniques for home landscaping projects.

Gannon's Narrows Conservation Area (Map 18/D5)
Located along the northern shore of the narrows, west of Black Pool Road, this is a busy boating area in the summer months. Fishing can also be productive in this area. For more information call (705) 745-5791.

Garden Hill Conservation Area (Map 10/E6)
This 53 hectare conservation area preserves a portion of the headwaters of the Ganaraska River west of Rice Lake. There is a picnic area for visitors and swimming opportunities at the large pond. Fishing for trout is also quite popular at the pond and in the river. Call (905) 885-8173 for more information.

Georgian Bay Islands National Park (Map 23)
This national park is comprised of 59 separate islands scattered throughout the majestic Georgian Bay. Access to the park is by boat only, with the more popular access route being from Honey Harbour to Beausoleil Island, the largest island of the park. Honey Harbour can be found at the end of County Road 5, off Highway 400. There are many mooring areas, 13 different campgrounds with over 179 sites as well as a visitor centre on the southeastern shore on the big island. Bikers can explore the forest roads on the island, while 11 separate trails covering over 27 km (17 mi) offer endless hiking. The park also has a few campsites located on Centennial Island and Island 95B. Another unique feature of the park is the endangered, and rarely seen, Eastern Massassauga Rattlesnake. It is recommended to make advance reservations for camping during the busy summer periods. Call (705) 756-5909 for more information.

Gibson River Nature Reserve (Map 23/G2–24/A2)
The 168 hectare non-serviced park is situated along a southern portion of the Gibson River shoreline and was established to help protect a number of types of vegetation rare to Ontario. The river is one of the few in the region that remains undammed and it is a popular canoe and camping destination. A short trail travels through forested areas and near the wetlands. Access to the river is available from Gibson Lake or from near the Highway 69/400 crossing.

Glen Miller Conservation Area (Map 13/A4)
North of Trenton, off County Road 4, there is a boat launch providing access to the Trent River System and its many fishing opportunities. Visitors can also enjoy a large picnic area and shelter complete with outhouse toilets.

Glencairn Conservation Area (Map 6/B2)
This small conservation area encompasses a portion of the Mad River amid beautiful stands of large cedar trees. In addition to picnic facilities, the Mad River offers fishing and canoeing opportunities. Call (705) 424-1479 for more information.

Goodrich-Loomis Conservation Area (Map 12/C5)
The Goodrich-Loomis Conservation Centre is a highlight of the area, offering educational programming and facilities to the public. The 179 hectare site also offers several outdoor recreation options, including fishing, 12 km (7.5 mi) of hiking and mountain biking trails that convert into groomed cross-country skiing trails in the winter months, picnic shelters and privies. Significant here are remnants of prairie species within many of the protected land's open areas.

Grant's Creek Provincial Park (Map 66/D6–F4)
This waterway provincial park protects 1,444 hectares around Grant's Creek. In addition to the canoeing possibilities available, the waterway also affords visitors some decent angling and wildlife viewing opportunities.

Grundy Lake Provincial Park (Map 49/E3)
Encompassing 2,554 hectares of the beautiful Canadian Shield, the park offers three easy trails along with maintained portages between a number of lakes. You can also choose one of nine camping areas encompassing 475 vehicle accessible sites (138 electrical hook-ups) all of which are close to a lake or collectives of 15 to 60 people can book one of three large group sites. Some camping areas are designated noise and/or pet-free zones for your preference. There are showers, flush toilets, laundry facilities and a park store for campers, while horseshoe pits, beach volleyball, a sports field and boat rentals also help to make your stay fun and relaxing. Also scattered along Gurd, Grundy, Beaver and Pakeshkag Lakes are 10 canoe-access interior campsites that offer a more secluded camping experience. For more information call (705) 383-2286.

Gut Conservation Area (Map 29/A5)
The Gut is a gorge on the Crowe River, a fissure 30 metres (100 feet) high and ranging from 5 to 15 metres (16-50 feet) in width. It is the central feature of this 162 hectare site. Archaeological evidence suggests that first nations used this area as a battleground. More recently, the river was used to transport logs.

H.R. Frink Centre (Map 13/F1)
Formerly known as the Plainfield Conservation Area, the H.R. Frink Centre is located north of Belleville, not far off Highway 37. The 138 hectare expanse helps to protect natural habitat, including wetland habitat of the Moira River. For a better view of the area, visitors can enjoy 13 km (8.1 mi) of trails that meander through the site. At the Outdoor Education Centre, students and visitors can take part in organized educational events or enjoy a sugar bush demonstration. For more information call (613) 477-2828.

Haldimand Conservation Area (Map 5/G1)
One of the most recreation focused conservation areas on these maps, this is one of the few that has a campground. There are 235 campsites (178 with full hook-ups) and picnic area on the shores of Lake Erie.

Haliburton Forest and Wildlife Reserve (Map 35/F3–45/C7)
The privately owned Haliburton Forest Reserve encompasses over 20,243 hectares and 50 lakes. Guided and non-guided recreation opportunities, educational programs, a restaurant and store as well as both lodge and cottage rentals are some of the services provided. Visitors will find over 300 km (186 mi) of trails, including the ever popular Forest Canopy Trail that are utilized throughout the year. Rentals for everything from bikes to snowmobiles are available. Canoeing and fishing is offered on most of the lakes in the reserve and 17 of the 50 lakes have semi-wilderness campsites available. For more information call (705) 754-2198 or visit www.haliburtonfoest.com.

Hardy Lake Provincial Park (Map 24/D1)
When ancient Lake Algonquin receded thousands of years ago it left behind plants that were once submerged beneath the great water body. These plants were stranded and survived among the inland vegetation that is prevalent in Ontario today. The plants are typical for Atlantic coastal areas and this park was created to protect this unique array of vegetation that was established in the region over 12,000 years ago. There are no facilities at the park other than a small series of trails. Canoeing can also be enjoyed on Hardy Lake.

Harry Smith Conservation Area (Map 13/D6)
This 17 hectare conservation area is the site of the 1842 Roblin's Mill, which can be explored here. Picnicking is a favourite attraction as is hiking along the few short trails. One of the trails leads up to a 25 metre (80 foot) natural escarpment to a nice vantage point.

Heber Down Conservation Area (Map 3/A2)
One of the more recreation-based conservation areas in the Central Lake Ontario Region, Heber Down even offers group camping for up to 500 people. There is good fishing in Lynde Creek and Devil's Den Pond, 5 km (3 miles) of hiking trails and several picnic locations.

Himsworth Crown Game Preserve (Map 62/G5)
The purpose of the preserve is to provide a wildlife refuge for deer, waterfowl and moose. If you do visit the area, be sure to abide by private property and all Crown Game Preserve restrictions.

Holland Prairie Landing Nature Reserve (Map 7/E5)
The former Algonquin Lake Plain left behind sand and silt deposits providing the perfect environment for one of the few remaining remnant patches of tallgrass prairie in Ontario. Currently, Red Pine is planted in the reserve, but plans are afoot to restore the native prairie ecosystem. This non-operating provincial park has no visitor facilities; however visitors are welcome to pursue day-use activities such as nature appreciation, hiking and cross-country skiing. Limited parking is available at the access point at Cedar Street. Due to the very sensitive nature of the tallgrass prairie ecosystem, off-road and motorized vehicles are prohibited in this nature reserve.

Hope Mill and Lang Mill Conservation Areas (Map 11/C2)
Located off County Road 34 (Heritage Line) east of Peterborough, the Old Hope and Lang Mills have been restored. The Lang Mill Pioneer Village is a collection of restored and reconstructed pioneer homes that are staffed often by volunteers in period clothing. Alternatively, the Hope Mill Conservation Area offers 65 campsites (20 with electrical hook-ups) as well as group camping. The main recreational feature in the area is the Indian River. There are also sheltered picnic facilities available at both conservation areas. For more information call (705) 745-5791 or (705) 295-6250.

park adventures

Indian Line Conservation Area (Map 1/B6)
Indian Line is the closest campground to downtown Toronto. Needless to say, the 247 campsites (some with full hook-ups) are extremely popular. There's public transit just outside the park leading downtown, as well as a swimming pool and high speed internet, along with the usual campground amenities. To book a campsite, call toll free at 1-800-304-9728 or email iline@trca.on.ca.

Indian Point Provincial Park (Map 17/D1)
Indian Point Provincial Park is a 947 hectare reserve that contains the longest stretch of undeveloped shoreline in the Kawartha Lakes region. This is a non-operating park with no visitor facilities, although you can enter the park by vehicle at the north end of Balsam Lake. There are a few short walking trails set amid forest and wetland areas.

Island Lake Forest and Barrens Conservation Reserve (Map 50/F5–51/C7)
This 15,452 hectare site is located in one of the most diverse natural areas in its district. It is located about 45 km (28 miles) north of Parry Sound. The area includes several rare plant species and is habitat for the threatened Eastern Massasauga rattlesnake.

J. Albert Bauer Provincial Park (Map 43/G6)
J. Albert Bauer Provincial Park borders on Solitaire and Estell Lakes, protecting mature hardwood forests, a small sand plain and a steep escarpment. The 163 hectare non-operating park offers canoeing, hiking and fishing opportunities.

Jevins and Silver Lakes Conservation Reserve (Map 25/B3)
This 2,144 hectare parcel was put aside to help protect three rare species found just north of Kahshe Lake. The reserve is home to pine forests, wetlands and rock barrens as well as the rare Massasauga Rattlesnake and the five-lined skunk. Various outdoor recreation opportunities exist at this reserve including fishing and snowmobiling around the wetland.

John P. Webster Nature Preserve (Map 52/E1)
A highlight of the J.P Webster Nature Preserve is a number of bright green boulders scattered throughout the property. The green colour is a result of the lichens that live on the rock's surface. The conservation area is found south of Alsace Road, but is not marked.

Kahshe Lake Barrens Conservation Reserve (Map 25/B4)
The diverse 3,200 hectare ecological area is home to a mix of pine and oak forest along with some beautiful wetland and rocky areas. Due to the rustic nature of the terrain, backcountry travel is limited; however, snowmobiling is popular during the winter months.

Kawartha Highlands Provincial Park (Map 18/F1–28/C4)
Kawartha Highlands is a fantastic outdoor recreation resource. Stretching beyond the borders of Bottle and Sucker Lake, the park encompasses dozens of remote lakes that can only be accessed by canoe via Bottle Creek from Catchacoma Lake and from Coon Lake to the southeast as well as Anstruther Lake to the east. The park is currently being developed to offer more services.

Keating-Hoards Conservation Area (Map 12/G2)
Intended as being a low use area without visitor facilities, the 261 hectare reserve protects part of the Trent River, near the community of Stirling.

Ken Reid Conservation Area (Map 17/E6)
The 110 hectare area offers a beautiful beach on the south shore of Sturgeon Lake as well as an easy series of year round trails. During spring, the wildflower bloom is a popular attraction and in fall the vast array of colours is always welcoming. There is also a wooden boardwalk that travels through the McLaren Creek Marsh, which is an ideal place for bird watching and classified as a class 1 wetland area. Picnic facilities are available at the area as well as camping for organized groups. For more information call (705) 328-2271.

Killbear Provincial Park (Map 31/E1)
Killbear is an extremely popular site on the Georgian Bay peninsula. There are 881 campsites (181 with electrical hook-ups), spread out between seven separate camping areas that range from sites on sandy protective beaches,

to rocky headlands. A lodge is also available for summer and winter bookings. Camping amenities include showers, flush toilets, laundry facilities and a park store. In addition to the boating, fishing, swimming and sailing, there are 6 km (3.6 miles) of hiking and biking trails. Note that when water levels in Georgian Bay are quite low, launching a boat might be problematic. Call the park at 705-342-5492 for information.

King's Mill Conservation Area (Map 20/G7)
Encompassing 25 hectares, King's Mill Conservation Area is highlighted by its historical buildings. The mill site allows for picnicking opportunities with privy facilities and the possibility of participating in a day of fishing as well.

Kortright Conservation Area (Map 1/C4)
Home to the Kortright Centre for Conservation, there are 16 km of trails through the 324 hectare area.

Lake St. Peter Provincial Park (Map 37/E1–46/E7)
Found on the southern boundary of the Canadian Shield north of the town of Maynooth, the park's landscape is characteristic of the Algonquin highlands. The 478 hectare park offers 65 campsites and stretches from the shore of Lake St. Peter all the way north to McKenzie Lake.

La Vase Portage Conservation Area (Map 62/E3)
Natives and voyagers of the early 19th century frequently used this portage, which was one of the more challenging portages along the Mattawa River. Currently, there are no established facilities at the area other than a rustic year round trail. Call (705) 474-5420 for further information.

Lakefield Marsh Conservation Area (Map 19/A6)
The Lakefield Marsh is a rehabilitated wetland area that offers visitors a boardwalk along the marsh. The two level tower is an excellent place for viewing the entire wetland and its wildlife.

Limestone Islands Provincial Nature Reserve (Map 39/E7)
There are two limestone islands, unique in that most others in the region are made of granite bedrock and wind-swept pine trees, within this 450 hectare nature reserve in Georgian Bay. Herbaceous and shrubby vegetation dominate the low-lying shelves providing valuable habitat for many species of colonial water birds. Day-use for nature-watching and hiking is permitted outside of the May 1 to August 1 nesting period with the permission of the Park Superintendent. However, due to the sensitivity of this site, visitation to the islands is generally discouraged.

Lingham Lake Conservation Reserve (Map 30/C5)
Fashioned to preserve the bass fishery and extensive beaver pond activity, which creates ideal waterfowl habitat, this 20,291 hectare site is most often used by anglers, hunters and fur trappers. Paddlers also use the lake as a recreation area for primitive camping. The numerous trails that meander around the lake are serviced by only one main access road.

Little Spring Lake Conservation Reserve (Map 51/G7)
Located about 8 km (5 miles) northwest of Magnetawan, this 106 hectare site features gently rolling landscape with tamarack forests and wetlands.

Long Lake-Lancelot Creek Conservation Reserve (Map 33/E2)
North of the popular Skeleton Lake, this 627 hectare reserve is made up of a few different land parcels found around Long (Cardwell) Lake. The area is quite beautiful as it combines open wetlands with mature stands of sugar maple and balsam fir. Snowmobiling and some rustic all season trail systems can be found.

Long Sault Conservation Area (Map 9/F7)
This 214 hectare conservation area helps preserve a portion of the Oak Ridges Moraine and can be accessed off Regional Road 20 (Boundary Road) south of Blackstock. There are picnic facilities available along with over 15 km (9 mi) of trails that are used year round. There is also a chalet that is used as a warm up area in winter and can be rented for summer group activities. For more information call (905) 579-0411 or for reservations call 888-ONT-PARK.

Loon Lake Wetland Conservation Reserve (Map 24/E3)

West of Gravenhurst, the reserve lies between Loon Lake to the north and North Muldrew Lake to the south. The wetland is an extremely diverse ecological area with over three hundred identified species of plants, including some provincially rare specimens. There are no visitor facilities; however, there is road access along the border of the wetland from where nature viewing can be enjoyed.

Lower Moon River & Moon River Conservation Reserves (Map 32/C6)

Combined, these newly established reserves encompass over 3,170 hectares of area surrounding the Moon River. The reserve stretches from near Highway 400 northwest all the way to Woods Bay and is prime habitat for the endangered Massasauga Rattlesnake as well as the Eastern Hognose Snake. Interesting natural features include impressive rocky cliff formations, as well as chutes and the Moon Falls along the river. Canoeing, fishing and boating are all popular recreation uses of this area. Access can be found via the boat launch at the end of Arnold's Bay Road west of Highway 400.

Lynde Shores Conservation Area (Map 3/B4)

This area is known for its wildlife viewing. There are hiking trails and a canoe launch, but both these are to help people see the wildlife better. The canoe launch is only open from July 15 to September 15, to minimize disturbances to the wildlife during breeding and migration. There is good fishing in the marsh.

Mabel Davis Conservation Area (Map 7/F7)

This small conservation area is located in the city of Newmarket between the Bayview Parkway and Davis Drive. The area is situated along the Holland River and offers a small series of hiking and biking trails. There are also picnic facilities at the conservation area. Call (905) 895-1281 for more information.

Magnetawan River Provincial Park (Map 40/C1–50/F7)

Steep, rocky shorelines and deep main channels will appease canoeists and anglers looking for a day of fine fishing, while hunters can also utilize the park. Remnants of early logging activity can still be seen along the 3,424 hectare waterway park, although there are also mature red and white pine and hardwoods stands. There are no amenities available at this park.

Manitou Islands Provincial Nature Reserve (Map 62/C2)

This 1,925 hectare water access provincial park encompasses a series of islands in the eastern section of Lake Nipissing. The islands host colonies of birds as well as a population of small mammals such as muskrats. Visitors will find a few nice beach areas as well as a few walleye fishing hot spots nearby.

Mara Provincial Park (Map 15/G3)

This 40 hectare park is located east of Orillia off Highway 12 near the narrows between Lake Simcoe and Lake Couchiching where indigenous peoples have fished for over 4000 years and anglers still come for bass, muskie and trout. The narrows is part of the Trent Severn Waterway, a popular route for vacationing boaters travelling to the Georgian Bay. A beautiful sandy beach is the main attraction, although the 105 campsites (36 with electrical hook-ups) and picnic areas are equally busy. Amenities include flush toilets, showers and a playground. The park also provides a boat launch. For more information call (705) 326-4451.

Mark S. Burnham Provincial Park (Map 11/A1)

Located off Highway 7 just east of the city of Peterborough, this 43 hectare park was a Burnham family estate woodlot that was bequeathed to the province with the wish that "people would continue to make their way to this quiet spot." It is home to some of the oldest hardwood stands in the province. The park also protects a portion of the Peterborough Drumlin field that was left behind after glaciers retreated from the area thousands of years ago. The park has picnic tables and open shelters making it a perfect place to stop for lunch. Alternatively, a small series of trails allow you to explore the area throughout the year. Call (705) 799-5170 for more information.

Mashkinonje Provincial Park (Map 60/B3)

Named after the mighty muskellunge, Mashkinonje Provincial Park is a 2,000 hectare reserve that is located between the West Arm and the West Bay of Lake Nipissing. Extraordinary bird watching and wildlife viewing op-

portunities complement the park's many plant species that inhabit the wetlands, bogs and rocky shores. A trail system is currently being developed, while several user-maintained campsites have been created by visitors along the shoreline of the park. Fishing in Deer Bay is one of the more popular pastimes of park visitors. For the more adventurous visitors, it is possible to explore inland along the Amateewakea River.

Massassauga Point Conservation Area (Map 13/F4)

The former site of a bustling, late 1800's hotel, this 24 hectare reserve offers 3 km (1.9 mi) of hiking trails, a sheltered picnic area, a boat launch and washrooms. In addition to the ruins of the hotel, visitors also enjoy access to the Bay of Quinte.

Massasauga Provincial Park, The (Maps 31, 32)

Established to preserve almost 12,000 hectares of Georgian Bay wilderness, access is from Pete's Place Access Point off Healy Lake Road or the Three Legged Lake Access Point found further north. Paddlers can access the Spider Bay, South Channel and Clear Lake Canoe Routes, while hikers can explore the interior of the park along three trails. The largest trail is the challenging Nipissing North Arm Orienteering Trail, a 30 km (19 mi) one-way trek across the Massasagua wilderness. There are 135 water-accessed tenting sites, including 48 inland sites that require a short portage to reach, along with overnight boat mooring at Echo, Three Finger, Clear, Port Rawson, Ritchie, Gilman Bays and on the east side of Vanderdasson Island. The visitor information centre is an early 19th-century Georgian Bay cottage site known as the historic Calhoun Lodge. The park also protects the endangered and very shy Eastern Massasauga Rattlesnake habitat. For more information call (705) 378-0685.

Mattawa Island Conservation Area (Map 64/D2)

West of the town of Mattawa, there are privies and a picnic area in this 3 hectare park. The beach area and swimming in the Mattawa River are popular activities, especially in the heat of summer.

Mattawa River Provincial Park (Map 63/B2–64/A2)

Established in 1970 as Ontario's first waterway park, the river was designated as a Canadian Heritage River in 1988. The river was an essential native transportation and trading route for over 5,000 years. With the arrival of Europeans, the river not only moved people, but endless amounts of lumber to the mills of the St. Lawrence until the early 20th century. The 3,257 hectare park protects the river from Samuel de Champlain Provincial Park to Trout Lake, incorporating cliff faces, canyon walls and a fault line that is believed to be 600 million years old. Rustic campsites, portages and access points can be found along the shoreline for experienced whitewater paddlers to enjoy. Grasswells Point is a popular area in the park.

McCrae Lake Conservation Reserve (Map 23/E3)

Through the Living Legacy initiative this reserve has been expanded significantly to include a much larger area including much of McCrae Lake. Canoeists often enjoy one of the scenic user maintained campsites around the lake as it is part of the Gibson-McDonald Canoe Route.

McGeachie Conservation Area (Map 29/E4)

This 500 hectare conservation area protects a fairly typical patch of hardwood forest. There are no special features here, but it is a nice place to get away to, especially when the leaves are starting to change. There is a cottage available for rent here. Call (613) 472-3137 or email info@crowevalley.com.

McRae Point Provincial Park (Map 16/A3)

On Lake Simcoe east of Orillia, this 138 hectare park offers a variety of recreation opportunities including ball fields and volleyball nets on the beach. There is a boat launch on Lake Simcoe, where fishing and water sports such as windsurfing, water-skiing and of course, swimming are popular. Campers will find 203 campsites available, 166 of which have electricity and 125 are pull-through sites, well-suited for large recreational vehicles. The comfort stations are equipped with showers and flush toilets, while children will enjoy the play area. For the nature lover, explore the Water's Edge Nature Trail in the park, which is home to 79 different species of birds. Reservations are recommended. For more information call (705) 325-7290.

Medd's Mountain and Millpond Parks (Map 10/E4)

Medd's Mountain is a natural area that provides access to the Millbrook Valley Trails. Adjacent to this park is the Millpond, which is a scenic picnic area and home to the annual spring fishing derby.

Mikisew Provincial Park (Map 52/D5)

'Mikisew' pronounced 'mic-su' is Ojibwa for 'eagle'. Most of the activity in this 138 hectare park involves swimming, paddling, or fishing in or hiking and camping around Eagle Lake. On top of 265 campsites (62 with electrical hook-ups) the park offers showers, laundry facilities, flush toilets, a playground, a boat launch and three beach areas. The park can also accommodate group camping for parties of 15 to 50 people. For hiking enthusiasts, there is a series of hiking trails found in the southern portion of the park. Remember not to bring you own firewood as it will be seized when entering any of the Ontario Provincial Parks to prevent the spread of pests like the Asian long-horn beetle and the Emerald ash borer. For more information call (705) 386-7762.

Miller Creek Wildlife Area (Map 18/G6)

This beautiful 202 hectare wetland is found west of the town of Lakefield. The wetland area is teeming with bird life and is a popular location with bird watchers and other naturalists. There is a short trail along the wetland area and a two level tower that provides a great way to view of the area. In winter, the trails can be used for cross-country skiing or snowshoeing. For more information call (705) 745-5791.

Minesing Wetlands Conservation Area (Map 6/D1–14/D6)

The Minesing Wetlands is renowned as a diverse area with unique features that are rarely found in any other parts of the world. The Minesing is not entirely a swampland, it is actually made up of a variety of wetland geographies such as marsh, bog and fen and covers over 6,000 hectares. The swamp is an excellent area for bird watching. In addition to the fifth largest blue heron colony in the province, there are over 200 species present at various times of year. The best way to explore the Minesing is by canoe. There are also a small series of trails that travel along the Nottawasaga River and into the Hackberry Levee Forest. These trails can be used in summer for hiking or in winter for cross-country skiing or snowshoeing.

Mono Cliffs Provincial Park (Map 6/A7)

This 732 hectare park protects a significant section of the Niagara Escarpment. There are parking lots available along with toilets and scenic walking trails for visitors interested in exploring the unique rock formations, including talus slopes and crevice caves. The Bruce Trail also passes through the middle of the park. Please stay on the trails as the natural features in the area can be easily damaged.

Monteith Forest Conservation Reserve (Map 42/C6)

Formerly called Cashen Lake, this site was renamed to better reflect its location. Protecting significant hemlock stands, the 185 hectare reserve can be found northeast of Parry Sound, about 5 km south of Bear Lake and Highway 518. Hunting is the main activity here, but be wary of private property in the area.

Moreaus Bay Conservation Reserve (Map 23/C1)

Moreaus Bay is located near the outlet of the Go Home River along the Georgian Bay. This 141 hectare conservation reserve encompasses Tate Lake as well as a large portion of Big Island. The reserve was established through the Living Legacy initiative and contains several rare plant species and is also ideal habitat for the endangered Massasagua Rattlesnake.

Morrison Lake Wetland Conservation Reserve (Map 24/E4)

This fabulous wetland lies along the southwestern shore of Morrison Lake and is home to many rare plants and animals. The wetland is quite rich with aquatic vegetation and visitors are asked to please tread lightly to preserve this important natural area.

Mount Moriah Conservation Reserve (Map 30/C6)

Rising above the surrounding landscape by hundreds of feet, the 'mountain' gives way to unique topography. The rocky area houses a variety of trees such as red oak, pine, maple and spruce as well as numerous small, shallow bogs and ponds. Supporting a plethora of wetland life, wildlife viewing is the most popular activity at this 2,319 hectare site. Fishing and hunting are also permitted.

Muldrew Barrens Conservation Reserve (Map 24/G4)

The Muldrew Barrens is an 803 hectare reserve found between Highway 11 and the Muldrew Lakes. The landscape of the reserve is typical southern Canadian Shield terrain with interesting rock barrens combined with the odd wetland and forest cover.

Murray Marsh Conservation Area (Map 12/D3)

Designated as a natural habitat area, this 667 hectare site is intended for low use and offers no visitor facilities. The marshlands host a variety of wetland animal species, waterfowl and heronries. Hunting is permissible by permit only.

New Lowell Conservation Area (Map 6/B1)

Developed mainly for a campground offering close to 100 campsites (most with electrical hook-ups) as well as comfort station with showers, the conservation area also encompasses a large reservoir, created from the damming of Coates Creek. There are two beach areas and a covered picnic site that can be reserved for group use. A small trail through the area provides opportunity for a short hike and cross-country skiing or snowshoeing in winter. Call (705) 424-1479 for more information.

Noganosh Lake Provincial Park (Map 50/D5)

This remote waterway park is found south of Highway 622. While there are bush roads in the area, the best way to access this park is by canoe, as the main feature of the park is a series of interconnected waterways. There are no facilities, but canoeing is popular, as is fishing and wildlife viewing.

Nonquon Provincial Wildlife Reserve (Map 9/B5)

The Nonquon Provincial Wildlife Reserve is located near the town of Port Perry. The reserve helps protect a large portion of the Nonquon River and its many wetland areas. Numerous roads intersect the reserve providing viewing opportunities for naturalists and bird lovers.

Oastler Lake Provincial Park (Map 32/B2)

Set next to a beautiful lake not far from Parry Sound and Georgian Bay, this park provides a home-base to venture from or stay and enjoy the leisurely pace of the cottage life. Water activities such as canoeing, water-skiing and swimming are popular attractions and canoe rentals are available. There are 148 regular campsites (22 with electrical hook-ups), showers, a park store and boat launch. Tenters can find more seclusion at the walk-in sites on the northern peninsula of the park, while there is a day use area as well as trails enjoyed year round. For more park information, call (705) 378-2401.

O'Donnell Point Nature Reserve Park (Map 31/G6–32/A7)

This 875 hectare nature reserve can only be accessed by boat on the Georgian Bay. A total of 34 amphibians and reptiles live in this reserve, including two rare species of spotted turtle and the endangered Massasauga Rattlesnake. O'Donnell Point is also home to the largest growth concentration of White-fringed Orchids in the province. This is a natural area, so please take care when exploring in order to help maintain the reserve in a wild and undamaged state.

Opeongo River Provincial Park (Map 46/F1–G4)

This waterway provincial park protects 955 hectares of shoreline stretching from Algonquin Provincial Park to Highway 60 that covers 34 distinct forest communities. Travelling the entire stretch of the river makes a great two or three-day trip in spring. Whitewater paddlers will find no developed campsites and more challenging rapids where the Opeongo River meets the Aylen River. Portages are also not marked.

Ottonabe Gravel Pit Conservation Area (Map 11/B3)

Once home to a gravel pit, volunteers are working hard to restore the area to a more natural state. Trail enthusiasts will find a series of short trails to explore. Call (705) 745-5791 for more information.

Oxbow Lake Forest Conservation Reserve (Map 40/D2)

This 200 hectare site is found west of Oxbow Lake. It features a white birch forest on a low sandy till plain and bare bedrock plain.

Oxtongue River-Ragged Falls Provincial Park (Map 44/B6)

This day-use waterway park can be accessed off Highway 60 on the west side of Algonquin Provincial Park. A marked gravel road on the east side leads to a parking area and the lookout over Ragged Falls and the rolling hills of Algonquin Park.

Papineau Lake Conservation Area (Map 64/D4)

A 2wd dirt road from the road to Brain Lake leads to a boat launch area on Papineau Lake. The park also hosts a parking area, picnic tables and basic privies. Swimming and fishing are the major attractions of this conservation area.

Peterborough Crown Game Preserve (Map 19/E2–28/F6)

Protecting approximately 15,268 hectares of forest land northwest of Burleigh Falls, the preserve provides a wildlife refuge for white-tailed deer, waterfowl and moose. There are ATV & snowmobile running through the area along with the Kawartha Nordic Trail system. If you do visit the area, be sure to abide by private property and all Crown Game Preserve restrictions.

Petroglyphs Provincial Park (Map 19/E2)

Protecting the largest known concentration of indigenous people's rock carvings in Canada, this day-use park is home to The Learning Place Interpretive Centre, which is surrounded by meandering hiking trails. There are 900 carvings depicting turtles, snakes, humans, birds and other images carved in the white marble of the area. Please note, for spiritual reasons, capturing images of the carvings by either photograph or video is prohibited. As well the park is closed on Mondays and Tuesdays in the spring and fall.

Petticoat Creek Conservation Area (Map 2/F5)

Best known as the home of Ontario's largest outdoor pool, this site on the shores of Lake Ontario is quite popular. There are also picnic sites and hiking trails in the area.

Pigeon River Headwaters Conservation Area (Map 9/G5)

This 125 hectare conservation area is located off Gray Road and preserves a stretch of the Pigeon River and its surrounding inflow streams. There is a small series of easy hiking trails that take you through beautiful stands of 100-year-old hardwood trees and a marsh boardwalk where bird watching opportunities are available. There is also a picnic shelter at the conservation area where you can have lunch amid the splendour of the forest. For more information call (705) 328-2271.

Plastic Lake and Dawson Pond Conservation Reserve (Map 35/D4)

Tucked in the Frost Centre, this 200 hectare reserve is one of the top sites in Ontario to find Atlantic Coastal plant species. The reserve protects the Dawson Ponds/Plastic Lake watershed. This is a popular paddling area.

Pointe au Baril Forests & Wetlands Cons Area (Map 39/F3)

Mainly visited by hunters, this area is home to a number of different wetland areas. These swamps, marshes and peatlands provide habitat for a number of rare plant and animal species.

Port Hope Conservation Reserve (Map 5/A1)

This 90 hectare area is tucked alongside the Ganaraska River and is a popular spot for fishing. The woodland trails along the river are also great for a picturesque stroll or nature photography. The Ganaraska Fishway (fish sanctuary) is on the south side of Highway 401.

Powassan Mountain Conservation Area (Map 62/G7)

Offering users a stunning view atop Powassan Mountain, the trail system extends well beyond the 2 hectare site and is used year round.

Presqu'ile Provincial Park (Map 12/E7)

Taking its name from a French translation meaning "almost an island", Presqu'ile attracts visitors from afar who converge on the park each spring and fall to get a glimpse at the this major flyway for migrating birds and monarch butterflies. The second oldest operating lighthouse in Ontario stands at the tip of the park overlooking Lake Ontario. Also present here are an elaborate selection of trails, which are groomed during the winter for cross-country skiing. The long, sandy beach is popular in summer, while campers will find a large 394 site (71 with electrical hook-ups) at the High Bluff Campground. There are also ten group sites. Other attractions include a nature centre, lighthouse interpretive centre, park store, boat launch and rental facilities. For more information, call (613) 475-4324.

Price Conservation Area (Map 21/F3)

The Price Conservation Area lies near the junction of Highways 7 and 37. The 9 hectare site helps to preserve a portion of the Skootamatta River and the surrounding natural habitat of wetland and mixed forest. Picnic areas are situated along the scenic river. The remnants of an old dam and footbridge are also interesting features.

Proctor Park Conservation Area (Map 12/E6)

Conveniently situated along County Road 30, this 36 hectare park allows for families and friends to enjoy a day of picnicking, while taking in the site's historical features. The Proctor House Museum displays a restored 1800's household. Approximately 2.5 km (1.6 mi) of trails are available for hiking and cross-country skiing, meandering through cedar lowlands and hardwood forests.

Purple Woods Conservation Area (Map 9/C7)

South of Port Perry, the reserve is a fun place to take the kids to explore nature and is home to the annual maple festival in the early spring. Visitors to the festival can enjoy seeing hoe maple syrup is made and, of course, try the many sweets that are made from the natural sugar.

Quackenbush Provincial Park (Map 19/F3)

There are no recreational facilities in this provincial park and use is discouraged, as it is the fragile historical site of the indigenous peoples of this region; thought to be connected to the Iroquoian culture.

Queen Elizabeth II Wildlands Provincial Park (Map 25/C5–26/D3)

Formerly known as Dalton Digby Provincial Park, the 33,500 hectare park name was changed in honour of Queen Elizabeth II. The non-operating park is one of the largest parks in southern Ontario. One of the primary access routes to the interior is via the Ganaraska Trail that travels east to west through the northern reaches. There are also many other established trails through the park that can be explored via foot in the summer months. Crown land campsites are available on several of the lakes in the park. Please practice low impact camping and pack out all garbage you find as these sites are user maintained.

Quinte Conservation Area (Map 13/D4)

Guests can find the Quinte Conservation Area off County Road 2, just to the west of Belleville. The park includes a 6 km (3.7 mi) trail series, which is ideal for hiking and visits former farm complexes. During the winter, the trail system is also used for cross-country skiing and snowshoeing.

Restoule Provincial Park (Map 61/A6–F7)

Much of the Restoule area's settlement is due to logging in the area. Today a 2,800 hectare park protects the land between Restoule Lake and Patterson (Stormy) Lake that is connected by the Restoule River. The full facility park, including flush toilets, showers, laundry facilities and park store, offers 278 drive-in campsites, walk-in or paddle-in campsites, as well as three group camping areas. For boaters and anglers, there are boat launches available on both Restoule Lake and Patterson Lake. Canoeists can paddle the nearby lakes or embark on a five-day, 72 km (45 mi) journey that follows the path of Samuel de Champlain to the French River and Lake Nipissing. Trail enthusiasts will find three short trail systems as well as cycling trails. Bike rentals are available. Call (705) 729-2010 for more information.

Rice Lake Conservation Area (Map 11/A6)

The 182 hectare Rice Lake Conservation Area is located on the southwest shore of Rice Lake and can be accessed via the Cavan Road near Bewdley. There are a few picnic tables available. The conservation area contains an important wetland habitat that is popular for bird watching. Watch out for poison ivy here.

Richardson's Lookout Conservation Area (Map 10/E6)

Richardson's Lookout is located on Northumberland Road 9 (Ganaraska Road), west of Highway 28. The small conservation area has a few picnic tables but the main attraction of the area is the lookout tower. The tower provides a great view of Rice Lake and perhaps one of the best panoramic views of the eastern Oak Ridges Moraine.

Rogers Reservoir Conservation Area (Map 7/F6)

Found north of the city of Newmarket, between Green Lane and 2nd Concession Road, access and picnic areas for this urban outdoor hideaway are found off both roads. The reservoir and surrounding marshland are a part of the Holland River system and provides good opportunities for bird watching and some fishing. The 39 hectare site also protects the historical locks, a swing bridge and canal that were once an integral part of transportation in the area. There are two short, easy trails as well as the Nokiida Trail, which travel through forested areas. Group camping is by reservation only. Call (905) 895-1281 for more information.

Round Lake Nature Reserve Park (Map 40/E4)

This quiet 2,585 hectare nature reserve is located about 40 km (25 mi) north of Parry Sound. The reserve was established in order to help preserve rare Atlantic coastal plain flora and provincially significant reptile species, including a small population of Massasauga rattlesnakes. Access into the park is via a rustic trail from Highway 69, canoe from Partridge Lake or snowmobile in winter. Wiwassasegen and Round Lakes make for an enjoyable canoeing destination and offer some fishing opportunities. There are no amenities available at this park.

Sager Conservation Area (Map 13/A2)

Situated north of Trenton on the east side of the Trent River and Highway 33, this 19 hectare park offers visitors a hiking trail that boasts a lookout tower that oversees the surrounding area. Picnic facilities include a shelter and privy washrooms.

Samuel de Champlain Provincial Park (Map 64/B2)

Found off Highway 17, west of Mattawa, this 2,550 hectare park helps protect a stretch of the Mattawa River and Amable du Fond River. The Mattawa River is a Canadian Heritage River where you can learn more about the history of the area at the Voyageur Heritage Centre. The scenic park offers over 30 km (19 mi) of trails throughout the hilly terrain, while canoeing during the summer and whitewater paddling and rafting in the spring are popular attractions of the park. Campers will find 215 campsites (106 with electrical hook-ups), six group sites, a park store, visitor centre, play area, rental facilities, showers, flush toilets, laundry facilities and French language services. In winter, the outdoor fun continues with a series of cross-country skiing and snowshoeing trails that are groomed for use for a nominal fee. For more information, call (705) 744-2276.

Scanlon Creek Conservation Area (Map 7/D5)

This 283 hectare area lies north of the town of Bradford and helps protect a provincially significant wetland area. Picnic sites are scattered throughout the park and are connected by a series of year round trails. Also in the area is the Scanlon Reservoir, which is home to a small beach area that is a great place to relax or to have a cool swim on a hot summer day. For organized groups, canoe rentals and overnight camping is available for a marginal fee. There is also a nature and educational centre at the area where public and local school programs on the outdoors are offered. For more information call (905) 895-1281.

Seguin River Conservation Reserve (Map 41/B7)

Formerly called Seguin Chutes, this conservation reserve is a 275 hectare tract that includes a portion of the Seguin River. This section of the river is best known for the Mountain Chute, which is a tight and fast flowing rocky section of the river. The river is used primarily by whitewater canoeists in the spring. The reserve also contains a portion of the Trout Lake deer yard, where large collections of deer spend much of the year. The closest access to the reserve is the McDougall Road bridge to the east.

Selwyn Conservation Area (Map 18/G5)

This 29 hectare conservation area was established to preserve a portion of the shoreline of Chemong Lake in the beautiful Kawartha Lakes region. Accessed off Birch Island Road north of Peterborough, the main attraction is the beach area complete with a covered picnic area and washrooms. There is also a public boat launch to access the lake and a short year round trail

north of the beach. Group camping is offered at the area and must be arranged in advance. Call (705) 745-5791 for more information.

Serpents Mound Park (Map 11/D3)

This family campground was used as a provincial park until 1995, but is now owned and operated by Hiawatha First Nation. It is a location of great aboriginal significance. On a high point of land near Rice Lake, the burial mounds that mark the graves of the Point Peninsula People. The largest mound has a zigzag, serpentine appearance, thus the name of the park. In 2002, the area was designated as a National Historic Site. There are 157 unserviced and 4 serviced campsites, a boat launch and good fishing for walleye, bass, muskie and panfish. The site is often used by boaters on the Trent-Severn Waterway.

Seymour Conservation Area (Map 12/C2)

A great picnicking destination for residents of the Campbellford area, the 82 hectare space provides hiking and cross-country skiing opportunities.

Severn River Conservation Reserve (Map 24/B2–C4)

One of the largest reserves in southern Ontario, this reserve protects a large tract of the northern shore of the Severn River. Along with the shoreline, massive portions of rock barrens, wetlands, lakes and forests are included in the reserve. These areas can only be accessed by snowmobile in the winter. Access to the reserve is mainly by boat along the Trent Severn Waterway. Canoeists should note that the river is quite busy during the summer months with boating traffic from the waterway.

Shack Creek Wetland Conservation Reserve (Map 34/E6)

East of the town of Bracebridge, this remote 288 hectare tract of land contains a large conifer swamp and wetland teeming with plant and wildlife. Surrounding the wetland, visitors will find mixed forests, which include birch and sugar maple.

Sharpe Bay Fen Conservation Reserve (Map 19/D1–28/D7)

This 636 hectare site protects an area of undisturbed fen and peatland that supports large black spruce and cedar stands, fen forests, as well as open black ash and cedar swamps.

Shawanaga Lake Conservation Reserve (Map 41/B3)

The large protected area is visited throughout the year by anglers, hunters and snowmobilers. There are several recreation camps and a trapper's cabin, while Pike's Peak is quite scenic. This conservation reserve also provides inland habitat for the nationally threatened Eastern Massasauga rattlesnake.

Sheppard's Bush Conservation Area (Map 1/F1)

Found in the heart of Aurora, this beautiful woodlot is a natural oasis. There are groomed trails, a small stream and a covered pavilion. The area is popular with walkers and picnickers.

Shields-McLaren Conservation Area (Map 63/E1)

The McLaren Family donated the Shields-McLaren Conservation Area in 1993. Informal trails and information about the logging history of the area are provided. The area can be found to the east of North Bay, off Highway 17 and Pine Lake Road.

Shirley Skinner Memorial Nature Preserve (Map 63/C6)

This nature preserve was donated in 1994 to help provide another a place to enjoy the outdoors. The 20 hectare property will entail a self-guided, interpretive hiking trail as well as a demonstration area for the production of maple syrup and the logging industry. To reach the conservation area, travel Highway 11 south from North Bay and take Chiswich Line east.

Sibbald Point Provincial Park (Map 8/A1)

One of the busiest parks in Ontario can be found on the southern shore of Lake Simcoe near Highway 48. The 225 hectare park is named after the Sibbald family, who owned the lands from 1836 to 1951. Visitors can get a glimpse of the family and park history at the Eildon Hall Museum which was the family manor and St. George's Church near the shore which was the family chapel. Additionally, Lake Simcoe provides a great place for water activities such as swimming, wind surfing, sailing and fishing. There are powerboat and canoe rentals available at the park along with a small series of interconnecting trails for a leisurely stroll or ski in winter. Campers will find 604 campsites (289 with electrical hook-ups) within walking distance to the beach and an additional 6 group sites which can accommodate between 15 and 50 people. Other amenities at the park include flush toilets, showers, a playground and a park store. For more information call (905) 722-8061.

Sidney Conservation Area (Map 13/B2)
Located just west of the village of Foxboro at 379 Airport Road, the Sidney Conservation Area was once an experimental farm for the Federal Department of Agriculture. Trail enthusiasts can enjoy the 2 km (1.2 mi) of hiking and cross-country ski trails, which traverse the red pine plantation and mixed forest habitat.

Silent Lake Provincial Park (Map 28/D2)
Before this area was a park, it was a popular hunting and fishing destination for American sportsmen. These days, fishing and hunting are still popular, but camping, mountain biking and canoeing are also popular. There are three mountain bike trails in the park, with a total of 38 km (23.6 miles) of trails that are groomed for cross-country skiing in the winter. There is also a rough hiking trail around the lake. While the marshes around the lake are popular destinations for wildlife watchers, these areas are best accessed by canoe (there are rentals on site). Campers will find 167 sites, 10 of which have electrical hook-ups.

Six Mile Lake Provincial Park (Map 23/F4)
Home to several rare species including: yellow-throated vireos, five-lined skinks and yellow-eyed grass, this provincial park located conveniently off of Highway 400, offers three sandy beaches and calm water ideal for swimming, paddling and fishing. There are 217 campsites, including 53 electric service sites. Camping amenities include flush toilets, showers, laundry services, park store, visitor centre, playground, boat launch and even canoe rentals. For more information please call (705) 756-2746.

South Bay Provincial Park (Map 62/B6)
Along the southeastern shore of Lake Nipissing, the only public access to this 1,525 hectare park is by boat. The area is home to several unique rock formations such as neohelikiam muscovite, which is a thinly layered, mica rock formation. Rustic trails lead from the shore into the interior of the park. The closest water access point to the park is found at the small settlement of Wade's Landing off Lake Nipissing Road.

Springwater Provincial Park (Map 14/F6)
This 145 hectare day-use park is dedicated to the enjoyment and education of the natural environment. At one of the many wildlife displays in the park, visitors can view animals such as deer, wood ducks and beavers. There are walking trails throughout the park, including the self-guided Woodland Nature Trails, as well as 13 km (8 mi) of groomed cross-country ski and snowshoeing trails for winter use. For more information call (705) 728-7393.

Squirrel Creek Conservation Area (Map 10/G4)
Located off Wallace Point Road (County Road 21) south of Peterborough, visitors will find a variety of recreational opportunities available at the 111 hectare park. There is a rustic boat launch and docking facilities on the Otonabee River, which is part of the Trent Severn Waterway. In addition, there is a picnic shelter with washrooms as well as an easy, year round trail leading to a wetland area that provides a great place for bird watching. Organized group camping is available on a reservation basis only. For more information call (705) 939-6079 or (705) 939-6405.

Stephen's Gulch Conservation Area (Map 3/G1)
Found north of Bowmanville, this conservation area protects a large area of deciduous forest and coniferous forest/swamp that help maintain both water quantity (through seeps and springs) and water temperature along a section of Soper Creek. The reserve also includes a portion of the provincially significant Soper Valley Area of Natural and Scientific Interest (ANSI). Recently re-opened, please tread lightly when visiting.

Stewarts Woods Conservation Area (Map 10/G3)
Found not far off Wallace Point Road (County Road 21) south of Peterborough, there are currently limited visitor facilities available. Please call (705) 745-5791 for more information.

Stoco Fen Provincial Park (Map 21/G4)
Stoco Fen is a 101 hectare nature reserve that was established to help protect a treed fen and cedar swamp community, which lies east of Tweed. The fen is a natural habitat to a variety of rare plants and animals.

Sturgeon Bay Provincial Park (Map 39/G2–40/A2)
Situated among the 30,000 islands that dot Sturgeon and Georgian Bay, the park offers amenities such as a park store, flush toilets, boat rentals and a boat launch onto the lake. There are 81 campsites at the park (31 with electrical hook-ups) and three cottages available for rent. The large beach area is a popular spot on hot summer days, while fishing, canoeing and sailing are also popular. Both canoes and motorboats are available for rent through the park office. Call (705) 366-2521 for more information.

Sylvan Glen Conservation Area (Map 4/G1)
This small property is located alongside a good fishing creek. There is a picnic area, but little else.

Thornton Bales [99 Steps] Conservation Area (Map 7/E7)
Known for its steep slopes and rugged beauty, the area also features some trails that offer some stiff climbs and a challenging workout. Along with hiking, wildlife watching is a popular activity.

Thurne Parks Valley Conservation Area (Map 4/A2)
Located off 4th Concession road to the west of Highway 115/35, this is a great spot for fishing, bird watching and nature photography.

Tiffin Conservation Area (Map 6/F1)
This 203 hectare area has recently been developed into a unique and informative outdoors area. There are full modern facilities at the centre with an environmental learning centre, maple sugar shack and a picnic pavilion suitable for large groups. The series of interconnecting trails that travel through the property are a great way to get some exercise and can be used for hiking or biking in summer and for snowshoeing or cross-country skiing in winter. There are 3 small ponds at the centre that are stocked regularly with rainbow trout and are great for fishing. The centre can be found not far off County Road 90 between Barrie and Angus. Organized group camping is available with a reservation. Call (705) 424-1479 for more information.

Tilton Forest Conservation Reserve (Map 58/B2)
This 727 hectare forest reserve protects a beautiful area of hardwood forest.

Torrence Barrens Conservation Reserve (Map 24/D3)
Found off Highway 169 on Clear Lake Road, the area was set aside to help protect a unique geographical area of Ontario. The character of the park somewhat resembles what you might find on the moon. The land is quite barren with little soil to sustain life with. There are no facilities other than a series of trails that travels through the area.

Trenton Escarpment Conservation Area (Map 13/A5)
Found near the south end of Trenton, the 8 hectare conservation area was established to help protect the fragile escarpment environment. The natural habitat area offers no visitor facilities.

Trenton Greenbelt Conservation Area (Map 13/A5)
The Trenton Greenbelt Conservation Area lies in the north end of Trenton and is about 13 hectares in size. The area encompasses a stretch along the Trent River and is a great spot for a summertime picnic. A boat launch onto the Trent River allows for paddling, boating and fishing. The area also hosts a nature trail that travels along the scenic riverside.

Trent-Severn Waterway Canadian Heritage Park (Maps 10–13, 15–20, 23, 24)
The Trent Severn Waterway is a 386 km (240 mi) water route from the Bay of Quinte, near the city of Belleville, to Georgian Bay, near the town of Port Severn. The route is comprised of many different waterbodies and a system of historic locks in order to transport watercraft across southern Ontario. The locks are operational from mid-May to mid-October and can become quite busy during July and August. The entire trip takes about a week and overnight mooring is available at all lock stations, with camping areas available at some stations.

The route has been designated as a National Heritage Park due to its historical significance in helping develop the areas it passes through. A few of the highlights of the route are the century old hydraulic lift lock in Peterborough and the unique marine railway. Fishing is offered along the majority of lakes and rivers that are a part of the waterway. Call (800) 663-2628 for more information.

Upper Madawaska River Provincial Park (Map 46/B4–E4)

This 1,085 hectare park was established to protect the upper stretch of the mighty Madawaska River. This stretch of the river is best known for its whitewater, especially in spring. The main put-in is near Whitney with the take out being near Madawaska. Rustic, no trace camping and fishing are also possible along the river.

Upper Shebeshekong Wetland Cons Reserve (Map 40/B5)
This site is habitat for the Eastern Massasauga rattlesnake and protects portions of the Georgian Bay shoreline. Recreational uses here include hunting.

Utopia Conservation Area (Map 6/E1)
This 44 hectare conservation area is located east of the town of Angus. The reserve encompasses a pond where an old mill still stands as a reminder of the past. The fish ladder that carries trout and salmon to spawning grounds upstream is one of the more interesting features of the area. There is a small trail through the conservation area that is used for hiking, cross-country skiing and snowshoeing. For more information call (705) 424-1479.

Vanderwater [Colonel Roscoe] Conservation Area (Map 21/F6)

This 257 hectare conservation area is stretched along the shores of the Moira River, just east of Thomasburg. It was named after the founder of the Moira Conservation Authority, Roscoe Vanderwater. The conservation area has a number of picnic sites, hosting 15 km (9.3 mi) of hiking and cross-country skiing trails. Other amenities include picnic shelters and public washrooms.

Warkworth Conservation Area (Map 12/B3)
The Warkworth Flood Control Dam is located in this conservation area, as is Mill Creek, which the dam dams. The creek offers good fishing.

Warsaw Caves Conservation Area (Map 19/D5)

This interesting conservation area offers a unique look at the power of the glacial retreat that occurred over 10,000 years ago. Encompassing 225 hectares the main feature is the series of magnificent caves and potholes. The Indian River also flows through the area, where swimming, fishing and canoeing are offered. If needed, canoe rentals are available. There are over 13 km (8 mi) of trails through the conservation area that can be used throughout the year, while washrooms, a picnic shelter and 60 sites for family camping are also found here. Call (705) 745-5791 for more information.

Wasaga Beach Provincial Park (Map 14/A4)

The main attraction of this day-use park is the 14 km (9 mile) long stretch of beautiful white sand beach. Visitors partake in swimming, wind surfing, beach volleyball, picnicking or cycling along the beach bike path. Further inland, the sand dunes of the park can be explored on the Blueberry Plains Trail system, which offers over 30 km (18.6 miles) of year round trails. For more information call (705) 429-2516.

Waubaushene Beaches Provincial Nature Reserve (Map 23/G6)
This 34 hectare nature park was created to preserve geographically significant landforms that were created over 12,000 years ago. The area contains distinct markings of the retreating shoreline of ancient Lake Algonquin. The most pronounced and oldest markings can be seen outside the park near the town of Coldwater. There are no facilities at the park.

Whitechurch Conservation Area (Map 2/A1–8/A7)
Located 10 km east of Aurora, this conservation area is a popular place to hike and view wildlife.

Whytock Conservation Area (Map 21/B3)
Near Madoc, at the intersection of Highway 7 and Highway 62, is this 40 hectare municipal park. It incorporates a soccer field, swimming pool and lawn bowling park and is a busy summertime place for local residents.

Willow Beach Conservation Area (Map 7/F1)
Located on Lake Shore Drive on the southern shore of Lake Simcoe, this small conservation area offers a popular beach area for public use. There is a large parking area with change rooms available with picnic tables scattered along the beach. For more information call (905) 895-1281.

Windy Ridge Conservation Area (Map 10/B2)
Windy Ridge offers a panoramic view from the lookout perched atop the area's tallest ridge. Directly below lays Fleetwood Creek wetlands, where the Pigeon River and Fleetwood Creek join. There is a short trail here, which is used by hikers, bikers and in the winter, snowshoers.

Wolf Island Provincial Park (Map 19/A3)
Preserving a unique crescent shaped formations in the bedrock created by retreating glaciers thousands of years ago, this non-operating 222 hectare park offers a short series of undeveloped hiking trails that provide access throughout the park. Note that swimming off the island is not permitted due to the inherent danger of the Trent Severn Waterway.

Wye Marsh Wildlife Area (Map 23/D7)
The Wye Marsh Wildlife Area is a large reserve established to help protect a diverse and unique wetland. Set along the southern shore of Wye Lake, a wildlife centre is available for visitors to learn more about plants and animals in the region. In the winter, visitors can enjoy a series of cross-country ski trails.

CAMPING TIPS

Below are a few tips to help you enjoy your camping experience:

- Each year dozens of forest fires are started by human negligence. Be sure your fire is completely out and cool to the touch before moving on.

- Canada is home to hundreds of kilometres of cool clear streams and lakes. However, it is ideal to carry a water filter, iodine tablets, or boil water for a minimum of 10 minutes before consuming, as many water bodies carry the bacteria commonly referred to as Beaver Fever.

- One of the first faux pas of backcountry sanitation is to use soaps in lakes or streams. For any soap or shampoo to biodegrade, they must be disposed of on land a good distance from water sources.

- Be bear aware. Be sure to never bring in any food into your tent or even items such as toothpaste. All food items should be properly stored in a pack that is hung from a tree at least 5 metres from the ground. Keeping a clean campsite will ensure a fun and bear free camping adventure.

- Keep black flies away with a safe homemade formula. Combine four parts vegetable oil with two parts aloe vera gel and one part citronella, cedar oil or sassafras oil (available at pharmacies). Apply liberally and remember to wear light-coloured clothing.

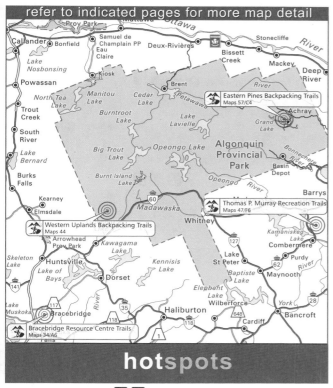

refer to indicated pages for more map detail

hotspots

*T*his is not a landscape to be seen out the window of a car. Not if you truly want to experience it. No, to truly experience this region, you have to get out onto the land to explore. To see the miles pass by at a much more leisurely pace than what is seen from the 400 or 401.

Fortunately, the people who live and play here have realized that and this region has one of the most extensive trail systems anywhere in the country. Some are well marked and maintained for the enjoyment of visitors and some that are faint footpaths that take you to some of the most remote wilderness areas the province has to offer. These trails pass through all manner of landscape, along rocky shorelines into low-lying valleys and through thick forest. There are trails that wind their way through the green spaces of cities and trails that are miles from crowds. There are trails that are well used and trails that see only a few visitors each year. There are trails that are popular with hikers, with mountain bikers, with horseback riders and with ATVers and motorcyclists. Some routes will tax the abilities of experts, while others can be navigated with ease. No matter what you are looking for in a trail, you will find something that satisfies.

Hikers, in particular, will find plenty of trails to keep them happy. Indeed, most of the trails listed in this section are designed primarily for hiking. From the Western Uplands Hiking Trail of Algonquin Park to the Seguin Trail, the opportunities abound. Of course, there are also hundreds of kilometres of old rail beds that have been converted into fantastic multi-use long distance trails.

The trails listed below are open to a variety of different trail users. We have marked the main methods of use on both the maps and beside each trail name below. If possible, we have also included return distance and time, elevation gain and a short description of the route. The trails have been rated according to difficulty with an easy trail generally requiring little uphill or downhill travel. These trails are ideal for inexperienced users and families. On the opposite side of the spectrum are difficult trails or routes. In addition to challenging climbs, orienteering skills may be required to track the trail that can often be overgrown. Even moderate trails should not be under estimated.

Note: Day use or overnight use passes must be purchased and displayed on your dashboard for use of all facilities and trails within National Parks, Provincial Parks and many Conservation Areas.

Ajax Trails (Map 2/G4)
The town of Ajax is located just east of Toronto, near Pickering. There are 74 km (46 mi) of trails in and around the town, the longest of which is the 6 km (3.6 mi) paved Waterfront Trail, which runs east and west along the shores of Lake Ontario from Pickering to Whitby. There is a trail along Dufferin Creek and in the Greenwood Conservation Area, both of which are part of the Trans Canada Trail system.

Algonquin Highlands [Stanhope] Trails (Map 35/F5)
A short drive off Highway 35 leads to four trails that are available for hiking, biking, cross-country skiing or snowshoeing. The longest route here is the Algonquin Highlands Ridge Trail. It travels north along a scenic ridge to Little Hawk Lake. The difficult trail treks through some rough terrain covering approximately 16 km (10 mi) return. The other three trails are all between 1.3 and 1.5 km long, the most difficult of which is the James Cooper Lookout Trail, a moderate 1.5 km (0.9 mi) route leads to a scenic lookout tower. It is not recommended for biking due to some steep cliff areas on the route.

Algonquin Motel Mountain Biking Trails (Map 52/G5)
Situated on Highway 11, just south of South River, the Algonquin Motel hosts a series of mountain biking trails. Ranging from easy to difficult, several kilometres of trails travel in and around sand dunes, big rocks, beaver dams, up and down a mountain and within the town of South River itself. There are also many trails that

spread many kilometres from the Algonquin Motel to other trail systems in the area. Some trails also double as snowmobile routes in the winter months. For more information, please call 1-800-263-7537.

Algonquin Provincial Park Trails (Maps 36, 37, 43–46, 53–57, 63–67)

From the extended backpacking trails that travel deep into the park's interior to the more gentle day-trails that offer spectacular scenery and an abundance of wildlife, Algonquin is rich in the history, geology and natural characteristics that keep people coming back to the outdoors. Be sure to obtain a park permit to use the trail system within the park.

Algonquin South Trails (Map 37/B3)

The quieter southern arm of Algonquin Park was one of the last major additions to the park. The main access points are the Kingscote Lake and the High Falls parking area, near the end of Elephant Lake Road. There are four main trails in the area: The Bruton Farm Trail, a 5 km (3.1 mi) moderate hike to an old farm site; the High Falls Trail, a 4 km (2.4 mi) moderate hike to the not-as-high-as-you-might-expect-from-the-name falls; the 2 km (1.2 mi) moderate Scorch Lake Lookout Trail and the Byers Lake Bike Trail, a 5 km (3.1 mi) one way ride. You can hike a short ways off this trail to Gut Rapids. Also in the area are about 40 km of cross-country ski trails maintained by Algonquin Eco-Lodge.

Basin Depot Trails (Map 56/E5–57/C7)

From the Basin Depot Road, a series of trails help you explore the Bonnechere River area. Most of the trails are short, but strung together this is an excellent place to get back in touch with nature. The High Falls on the Little Bonnechere River Trail is a 4 km return trail leading to the scenic High Falls where a timber slide once helped loggers bypass the falls. Further east, the easier, three hour long McGuey Farm Trail is named after the homestead that was a popular stopover for lumbermen travelling the Old Bonnechere Road. At the end of the road, the McIntyre's Clearing Trail leads to another former homestead of the logging days gone by. Other trails in the area include the Basin Depot Trail and Payne's Pine Trail, which are both found closer to the park boundary.

Barron Canyon Trail (Map 57/E3)

Once an important pipeline for the log drives, The Barron Canyon is one of Algonquin Provincial Park's natural treasures. This 1.5 km trail takes you to the edge of the canyon where breath-taking panoramic views are offered. From the canyon edge, you can view the sheer, 100m (328 ft) high canyon walls and the Barron River that flows between them. An interpretative guide is available at the trailhead, which explains a little history, ecology and geology of the canyon.

Bat Lake Trail (Map 45/B3)

This trail is an easy 5 km (3.1 mi) loop that travels through a bog area and past Bat Lake. The trail is located off Highway 60, across from Mew Lake or about 30 km (19 mi) from the West Gate. A parking area is available off the highway and interpretive trail guides can be found at the trailhead that are coordinated with various checkpoints along the route to inform users about the basic ecology of the area.

Beaver Pond Trail (Map 45/F2)

This easy 2 km (1.2 mi) trail traverses a mixed forest and past a couple of beaver dams. If you are lucky you may even see a beaver, but be sure to be quiet or they will quickly head for shelter. The trail also passes Amikeus Lake, which is the result of the beaver's work.

Berm Lake Trail (Map 57/C3)

Adjacent to the Achray Campground in the eastern portion of Algonquin Park, visitors will find a number of trails, including the Berm Lake Trail. This easy 4.5 km (2.8 mi) loop travels around Berm Lake and through some brilliant stands of oak and pine trees. At one point along the trail, you will pass through a stand of white pine that is over 150 years old. The trees in this area measure over 30 m (100 ft) tall and 80 cm (31 in) in diameter. Along with the trail guide, the trail will help you learn more about the ecology of the pine forests and the drier climate that is common to this side of the park. This part of the park is also prime territory for blueberries. If you happen to visit during blueberry season, keep your eyes open along the trail for a tasty snack.

Big Pines Trail (Map 45/E2)

Incorporating old growth white pines and the site of an old, 1880's logging camp, the Big Pines Trail loops 2.9 km (1.8 mi) through a forest

setting. An interpretive guide is available to allow visitors to learn about the early logging history and ecology of white pines that play such an integral role in the park's past. In all, there are approximately 75 of these 200 year old, big pines for onlookers to gaze up at along 12 interpretive stops. The largest such specimen reaches an impressive 37 m (122 ft), with a diameter of 1.14 m (45 in), weighing in at an estimated 20 tonnes.

Booth's Rock Trail (Map 45/E4)

Booth's Rock Trail is named after the famous lumber baron J.R. Booth. In addition to early logging in the park, he was instrumental in building the Ottawa, Arnprior & Parry Sound Railway (O.A. & P.S.) to help ship lumber. The railway stretched from Ottawa to the Georgian Bay and travelled right through present day Algonquin Park. In fact, the last leg of this moderate 5 km (3.1 mi) loop is a part of the old railbed. The trailhead and parking area are located just past the Rock Lake Campground.

Brent Crater Trail (Map 65/C7)

Located just within Algonquin Provincial Park's northern boundary is the Brent Crater Trail. The trailhead and parking area can be found en route to the Cedar Lake-Brent Access Point, where trail guides are available. The trail is an easy 2 km (1.2 mi) loop that travels from the ridge of the crater to its present day floor. There is also a lookout tower to help provide a better view of the crater. From the lookout, you can see the far rim and Tecumseh Lake on the crater floor.

Centennial Ridges Trail (Map 45/D3)

The Centennial Ridges Trail of Algonquin Provincial Park was established in 1993 to coincide with the 100th birthday of the park. The moderate 10 km (6.2 mi) loop can be found 2 km (1.2 mi) off Highway 60, 37 km from the West Gate of the park. A parking area is located at the trailhead, as is a trail guide. The route scurries along a number of cliff tops climbing 107 metres (351 feet). From the cliffs, magnificent views of the park's rolling highlands and a number of lakes can be seen.

Eastern Pines Backpacking Trail (Map 57/C4)

The Eastern Pines Backpacking Trail can be accessed from the Achray Campground. The trail is made up of two moderate, connecting loops totaling 15.9 km (9.9 mi). The shorter loop takes you around Johnston Lake where five backcountry campsites are offered. The larger loop travels to a lookout over the lake then down to Stratton Lake, where five more hike-in campsites are offered. From here, the trail travels over some fairly hilly terrain before coming down to the northern tip of Stratton Lake. Three more hike-in campsites are available at the tip of the lake as well as a 2 km side trail to High Falls. The main trail passes an old logging camp location and single campsite on Buckholtz Lake as it circles the lake and passes through some glacial boulder gardens. Eventually you meet up with the shorter loop that heads back towards the parking area.

The trail is monitored under Algonquin Park's quota system. Call (800) 668-7275 for reservations.

Hardwood Lookout Trail (Map 44/F4)

This easy 800 m (2,625 ft) trail loops through a hardwood forest typical of the western side of the park. Along the trail, you will pass a number of different hardwood tree species, including red maple, black cherry and yellow birch. With the interpretative guide, the trail will help to educate visitors on the ecology and significance of the hardwood forest. Walkers will pass a natural lookout area that offers a great view of Smoke Lake set among a backdrop of rolling hills that are typical of much of Algonquin. At the parking area, there is also a short side trail called the Red Spruce Side Trail. The Red Spruce is quite rare in Algonquin as it is only found occasionally in solitary pockets on the park's west side.

Hemlock Bluff Trail (Map 45/A3)

This trail can be found about 27 km (17 mi) from the west gate, on Highway 60. There is a parking area across the highway from the trailhead where trail guides are available. The trail is an easy 3.5 km (2.1 mi) route that passes through a predominantly hardwood forest, including an enchanting stand of Yellow Birch trees. Shortly after beginning the trail, hikers will ascend a cliff to a lookout that provides a gorgeous view of Jack Lake. Along the trail, the guide gives you valuable information on research in Algonquin Park. One such example is the extensive studies done on wolves in Algonquin Park. Much of what has been learned has played a big part in changing people's perception of wolves from a nuisance to an important part of nature.

Highland Backpacking Trail (Map 45/B4)

The Highland Backpacking Trail is one of three Algonquin Provincial Park interior hiking trails. This route is generally moderate in difficulty, although some sections can be more challenging due to steep ascents. The trailhead and parking area can be found near the Mew Lake Campground, off Highway 60. The trail is made up of two connecting loops totaling 40 km (25 mi), giving hikers some flexibility in the distance they wish to cover. Rustic camping is offered at a number of areas along the trail, although site reservations must be made in advance. The trail is monitored under Algonquin Park's quota system and can be quite busy. You should make reservations well in advance of your trip to avoid disappointment. For reservations and availability call (800) 668-7275.

Lookout Trail (Map 45/D2)

The Lookout Trail can be found off Highway 60, approximately 40 km (25 mi) from the park's west gate. The trail is an easy 1.9 km (1.2 mi) loop that will help users learn more about the geology of the area. There are numbered posts along the trail that co-ordinate with the trail guide, which is available at the trailhead. The main feature of the path is the natural lookout, which sits approximately 525 m (1,700 ft) above sea level, offering a humbling view of the park. From the lookout, you can see the rolling hills of Algonquin along with Kearney Lake, Little Rock Lake and Lake of Two Rivers. Parking is available at the trailhead.

Minnesing Mountain Bike and Ski Trail (Map 44/G3–45/A3)

The Minnesing Mountain Biking and Cross-Country Ski Trail is found about 23 km (14 mi) from the west entrance to Algonquin Park, off Highway 60. Alternatively, the trail can be accessed from the Canisbay Campground. The trail is named after the Minnesing Road, which ran from Cache Lake to Minnesing Lodge on Burnt Island Lake. The lodge was demolished in the early 1950s and the old road now makes up much of the western portion of the Minnesing Trail. There are four interconnected loops, with a combined distance of 55.3 km (34.3 mi). In spring and late fall, the route is extremely muddy, so the trail is only open from late June to Thanksgiving. Check with the Park Information Office for conditions at (705) 633-5572.

Mizzy Lake Trail (Map 44/F3)

The Mizzy Lake Trail is located across from Smoke Lake, off Highway 60. Parking and trail guides are available at the trailhead. The path is 11 km (6.8 mi) in length and is rated moderately difficult due to the distance of the trail and the sometimes-soggy terrain. The trail travels past nine different water bodies of various sizes and is one of the better routes for spotting wildlife, particularly in early morning or towards evening.

Old Railway Bike Trail (Map 45/B3)

The Railway Bike Trail travels along the old O.A. & P.S. (Ottawa, Arnprior and Parry Sound) railway. The trail is about 10 km (6.2 mi) in length and can be ridden from the Mew Lake Campground, off Highway 60, to the southern tip of Whitefish Lake. The trail traverses the Algonquin forest, Whitefish Lake, the Madawaska River and Lake of Two Rivers. The old railway bed makes travel quite easy and is ideal for all skill levels.

Peck Lake Trail (Map 44/G3)

The Peck Lake Trail is an easy 1.9 km (1.2 mi) loop that encircles Peck Lake. Along with the trail guide, visitors will learn more about the ecology of lake and how they support life. The parking area and trail guides can be found approximately 4 km (2.5 mi) past Smoke Lake on the north side of Highway 60 at the trailhead.

Spruce Bog Boardwalk Trail (Map 45/E2) (JK.

The 1.5 km (0.9 mi) looped trail begins by traveling through a spruce forest and then proceeds along a boardwalk across the Sunday Creek Bog to a smaller kettle bog. With the guide and trail markers, hikers will learn about the different stages of a bog and the ecology of the area. The forests of the bog are also a great place for bird lovers. Near the end of the trail, there is a lookout area where you can get a better view of the bog in its entirety. The parking area for the trail can be found off Highway 60, across from the road to the Algonquin Park Visitor Centre. Interpretative guides are available at the trailhead. Users should be sure to remain on the boardwalk at all times and refrain from picking any of the plants that may be encountered.

Track and Tower Trail (Map 45/A3)

This is an easy 7.7 km (4.8 mi) hike from the parking area and back, unless walkers choose to venture down one of the side trails. A short side trail is available at the 3 km (1.9 mi) leads to the site of the former Skymount Tower, a fire tower that was torn down in the early 1950's. Shortly after the tower site, onlookers can walk atop a cliff where a fine view of Cache Lake is offered. Once back on the main trail users are able to travel along an old railbed, built by the famous lumber baron, J. R. Booth. It stretched from Ottawa to the Georgian Bay and, during World War I, was the busiest railway in all of Canada. A second side trail travels for 4.4 km (2.7 mi) to the Mew Lake Campground area.

Two Rivers Trail (Map 45/B2)

The Two Rivers Trail can be found across from the Mew Lake Campground entrance, off Highway 60. There is a parking area and interpretative guides available at the trailhead. The trail is an easy 2 km (1.2 mi) loop that traverses a mixed forest to a lookout area atop a cliff. With the interpretative guide, guests can learn more about forest ecology in and outside of Algonquin Provincial Park. The hike informs users about the effects humans have had on the forest, in addition to natural events, such as fire and predatory insects. From the lookout, you will find a great view of a pine forest set amidst the rolling highlands of Algonquin.

Western Uplands Backpacking Trail (Map 44/D5)

The largest trail system in Algonquin Provincial Park is the Western Uplands Backpacking Trail. It is comprised of three large interconnected loops that span over 100 km (62 mi) through the interior of the park. Rustic campsites are available at numerous areas along the trail and are usually set on the shore of a lake. The trail can be accessed from either the Oxtongue River Picnic Area off Highway 60 or from the Rain Lake Access Point at the east side of the park. The moderately tough trail is well marked and can be busy during the months of August and September.

Trail use is regulated under the Algonquin Park quota system, with only so many users permitted at one time. Included in this quota system is a maximum camping party of nine people. It is recommended to make reservations well before your trip date to reserve your space on the trail at (800) 668-7275. Call (705) 633-5572 for more information.

Whiskey Rapids Trail (Map 44/E5)

This trail is located just inside the west park gate, off Highway 60. A parking area and interpretative guides are available at the trailhead. The footpath is an easy 2.1 km (1.3 mi) loop that traverses a mixed forest along the Oxtongue River to the Whiskey Rapids. The theme of the trail and its corresponding trail guide are the ecology of Algonquin rivers. The last leg of the trail follows a tote road built in the late 1800's, where horse drawn wagons once carried supplies to Canoe Lake where they could be disbursed to the logging camps.

Altona Forest Trails (Map 2/E4)

Located near the city of Pickering, there is a series of easy interpretive trails found in this 53 hectare forested area.

Arrowhead Provincial Park Trails (Map 43/C7)

Located off Highway 11 north of Huntsville, the park offers four easy interpretative trails to explore. In winter, the trails are groomed for cross-country skiing. The longest trail, the Beaver Meadow Trail, is only 3 km (1.9 mi).

Ardagh Bluffs Loop Trail (Map 6/G1)

The access for this series of trails is in Cumming Park on Cumming Drive in the city of Barrie. A total of 17 km (10.5 mi) of trail exist in this 524 acre park. This trail provides some outstanding vistas over Barrie and the surrounding landscape. Due to some steep ascents on the trail, it is rated as moderate but can be used year long for walking, snowshoeing, skiing and cycling. There is limited municipal parking on Cumming Drive which can be found by leaving Highway 400 at Essa Road, driving southwest to Ardagh Road. From there, one heads west to Ferndale Road South where a left turn is taken. Continue onto Cumming Drive.

Aspen Valley Wildlife Sanctuary (Map 33/C3)

A series of hiking and snowshoeing trails are found at the Aspen Valley Wildlife Sanctuary near Rosseau. They are well signed and range in distance from 800 metres to 8 km. The registered charity rescues, rehabilitates and releases Ontario wildlife. A map of the trails is found at http://www.avws.ca/webimages/trails/AVWS_trail_map.pdf.

trailadventures

Avery Park Trail (Map 34/C1) 🥾🚴
The Avery Park Trailhead is located off Yonge Street in Huntsville at Hunters Bay. The trail is presently 1 km in length and follows along the bay and through a hardwood forest area. Eventually, the trail will extend all the way to Highway 11.

Awenda Provincial Park Trails (Map 23/A4) 🥾🎿🚻
This scenic natural park has three trails that will challenge both cross-country skiers and hikers. In winter, activity on the trails is sparse. Park direction signs are easily visible along Highway 93 near Penetanguishene. The longest of the three trails is a 13 km (8 mi) loop called the Bluff Trail. The Beach Trail is 4 km (2.5 mi) long and leads to a lookout point, while the 5 km (3.1 mi) Wendat Trail loops around Second Lake. All three trails are easy hiking and moderate cross-country ski routes.

Barrie Waterfront Trails (Map 15/A7) 🥾🚴🎿🚶
A set of connected urban waterfront trails run along the beautiful shoreline on Kempenfelt Bay of Lake Simcoe in the city of Barrie. Covering more than 11 km (6.8 mi), the longest is the 5 km long Nine Mile Portage Heritage Trail. This trail actually extends beyond the city for an additional 10 km in the Township of Springwater. The trails are generally flat and easy.

Bear Mountain Hiking Trail (Map 46/G4–47/A4) 🥾🚻
This hidden gem has plenty to offer hikers. The route consists of two connecting loops totaling 8 km (5 mi) and traverses rustic terrain. Hikers can travel a short loop past the first lake or there is a longer loop that extends all the way to Spectacle Lake and back. Shortly after the start of the trail, there is a small side loop that takes users to Kluke's Lookout, where a humbling view of a chain of lakes and the distant rolling hills can be seen. The first loop is used more often than the longer loop and is moderate in difficulty. The longer loop, however, is difficult due to low usage and could be tricky to keep track of as trekkers venture further into the forest. The trailhead is found about 13 km west of Barry's Bay Cottage Resort, off the south side of Highway 60, marked only by an opening in the trees.

Beaver River Wetland Trail (Map 8/G1–2) 🥾🚴🐾🛹♿🚶
The Beaver River Wetland Trail follows an old abandoned rail bed from near the village of Sunderland north spanning approximately 12 km (7.5 mi) one-way to Cannington. The trail is easy to travel and treks through a variety of terrain while following near the Beaver River. The area is a great birding location and if desired, can be followed further north or south.

Beetle Lake Trail (Map 44/A7) 🥾🚻
Integrating a great lookout over Oxtongue Lake, the Beetle Lake Trail also entices trekkers with a rocky ridge, a quaint creek, an interesting bog and hardwood forests. The difficult, 5 km (3.1 mi) linear path originates on the north shore of Oxtongue Lake, near the bridge, along Highway 60.

Belleville Urban Trails (Map 13/E4) 🥾🚴🎿
There are a series of year round, multi-use trails that join to form a system that follows the Moira River to the Bay of Quinte. Starting close to Highway 401, the Riverside Trail is 5.2 km (3.2 mi) long and follows the west side of the river until it meets the Parrott Riverfront Trail that crosses the river at College Street and continues for 1.6 km (1 mi) to the Bay of Quinte. As it forms somewhat of a loop, one can return via an alternate route to College Street or continue along the bay on either the Kiwanis Bayshore Trail that goes 2.6 km (1.6 mi) to the east of the Moira River mouth or cross the bridge at Dundas Street to take the Zwicks Trail 3.2 km (2 mi) to the west of the river's mouth.

Birdland Trail (Map 62/B7) 🥾🚻
Birdland is a small privately owned area that is a popular birding site where up to 320 different species of birds could be spotted throughout the year. The site can be reached via Highway 534. A parking area is located off the highway where there are also washrooms available for visitors. The 6 km (3.7 mi), easy trail system is made up of three interconnecting loops that travel through a mixed forest setting.

Bon Echo Provincial Park Trails (Map 30/F2) ⛺🥾🚵🚻
Bon Echo Provincial Park is located north of Kaladar, off Highway 41. The park is home to the magnificent pictographs of Mazinaw Lake as well as a number of superb hiking trails.

Abes & Essens Trail is comprised of three interconnecting loops and begins off the north side of Joeperry Road after Echo Lake. The trail is 17 km (11 mi) in length and is quite difficult due to the distance and the rustic terrain involved. Visitors can expect to see beautiful views of the surrounding area, a kettle lake, huge boulders and remnants of past logging practices. It is possible to camp at one of the five interior campsites located along the route.

Bon Echo Creek Trail is an easy 2 km (1.2 mi) linear route that follows the creek down to where it empties into Mazinaw Lake. Exploring the creek habitat is a favourite among birdwatchers.

Cliff Top Trail lies on the east side of Mazinaw Lake and is only accessible by canoe, boat or the Mugwump Ferry. The trail is a moderate, 2 km (1.2 mi) hike that meanders to the top of the cliff of Bon Echo Rock via a staircase and rocky walkway. Once the summit of the cliff is reached, a 100 m (328 ft) picturesque view of Mazinaw Lake and the surrounding countryside can be enjoyed.

High Pines Trail is a moderate, 1.4 km (0.9 mi) interpretive loop that travels through a mix of tall pines, hemlock stands and a series of ponds. Along the route, hikers will pass a natural viewpoint, which offers a fine view of Bon Echo Rock on the east side of Mazinaw Lake.

Shield Trail is a moderate, 4.8 km (3 mi) loop that travels from the east end of Echo Lake to the border of the park and back. The track traverses some dense forest and follows a portion of the historic Addington Settlement Road. A series of interpretive stops allow visitors to discover the area's link to early settlers and their life in the Canadian Shield. The conversion of a drained beaver pond into a meadow can also be observed.

Bondi Village Resort Trails (Map 34/G2) 🥾🚶
Bondi Village Resort is located off Highway 35 on Muskoka District Road 21 and offers 16 km (10 mi) of cross-country ski trails and over 8 km (5 mi) of hiking trails. The routes traverse through mixed forests and provide great viewpoints of the beautiful Lake of Bays. The trails vary in difficulty from easy to moderate. Detailed maps of the trail system are available at the resort office. Although there is no fee for use of the trails, donations are always welcome.

Bonnechere Provincial Park (Map 47/F1–57/F7) 🥾🚵🚻
A series of short trails can be explored in the popular park next to Round Lake. These include the Beaver Marsh, Meandering River and Oxbow Loops. Further up the river are also a series of historical walks that would make a fine day of exploring.

Beaver Marsh Loop is an easy, 1 km (0.6 mi) trek past a beaver pond within a marsh ecosystem. The trail visits a historical site called the Depot.

Meandering River Nature Loop is an easy, 2 km (1.2 mi) looped hike that integrates a boardwalk into its walkway that allows visitors to investigate the many plants, animals and birds that this wetland habitat has to offer.

McNaughton's Walk (Map 47/G1–57/F7) is also found in Bonnechere Provincial Park, near the River Loop Campground. The easy, 2 km (1.2 mi) trail is on a sand delta that was formed as a result of glacial activity thousands of years ago.

Oxbow Loop (Map 47/G1-57/F7) is an easy 2 km (1.2 mi) trail that follows the shoreline of the Little Bonnechere River, circling an old river oxbow. The trail also can be accessed from the Beaver Marsh Trail.

Bonnechere River Trails (Map 47/F1–57/A6) 🥾🚴🎿🚻
Linking Round Lake with Algonquin Park, Bonnechere River is a hiker and paddlers dream. Most of the trails are short, but strung together this is an excellent place to get back in touch with nature. In addition to trails in Bonnechere River Provincial Park, there are a few more to explore off the Basin Depot Road in Algonquin Provincial Park itself.

High Falls on the Little Bonnechere River Trail (Map 57/A7)
This trail is situated within Algonquin Provincial Park, just west of the old cabin marking Basin Depot. The 4 km return hike requires little elevation gain as it follows an original section of the Old Bonnechere Road and terminates at the scenic High Falls. In 1847, a timber slide existed here that allowed outgoing timber to bypass the falls.

Lafleur Homestead Trail (Map 57/E7)
An easy, 30 minute hike features a preserved pioneer homestead and log house that was once the only dwelling in the entire municipality. It is found off Lafleur Lane, just south of Turner's Camp.

McGuey Farm Trail (Map 56/G6)
Named after a homestead built by Dennis and Margaret McGuey, this was a popular stopover for lumbermen traveling the Old Bonnechere Road who were able to obtain a meal and bed for 25 cents a night at a time when a dollar a day was the going wage. The linear route is easy to navigate, but takes about three hours to complete as it provides access to the Bonnechere River in Algonquin Provincial Park.

McIntyre's Clearing Trail (Map 56/E5)
Starting at the end of Basin Depot Road at the cart trail within Algonquin Provincial Park, this trail passes through an area that was a busy lumber spot in the 1870s. William McIntyre and family cleared ten acres of land and built a log house and several other outbuildings here.

Omanique's Mill Trail (Map 47/E1)
All that remains of the mill that once stood here is a large depression near the river's edge that is hidden by a pine plantation. The easy 30 minute trail is found off the White Mountain Chute Road, near the Omanique Mill Road sign.

Payne's Pine Trail (Map 57/C7)
This trail starts within Algonquin Provincial Park, but travels outside of the park to Stringers Lake. The easy loop contains a spruce bog habitat that hosts a multitude of plant life, including sphagnum moss, pitcher plants and cotton grass. The trail culminates at a silver maple swamp on the banks of the Little Bonnechere River.

Whispering Winds Lookout on Egg Rock Trail (Map 57/C7)
This difficult, but rewarding journey climbs to two parallel fault lines that form the sides of an impressive trench that once formed the spillway for volumes of glacial meltwater. Located near the Algonquin Provincial Park boundary, off Basin Depot Road, this 40 minute, linear jaunt crosses the valley bottom before climbing a steep ridge where hikers are compensated with a panoramic vista from the Whispering Winds Lookout.

Boyd Conservation Area Trails (Map 1/C5)
There is a series of easy hiking trails found in this small conservation area near Toronto.

Bracebridge Bay Trail (Map 34/A7)
This easy 1.5 km (0.9 mi) trail begins at the Bracebridge Visitor Centre at the southern end of Manitoba Street or at Kelvin Grove Park on the south side of the bay. The route travels around Bracebridge Bay and over the beautiful Muskoka River Falls. There are information plaques, which provide historical information, on the route.

Bracebridge Resource Management Centre Trails (Map 34/A6)
North of Bracebridge off Highway 11 at High Falls Road, the Bracebridge Resource Management Centre offers some of the best hiking and biking trails in southern Ontario. The 8 km (5 mi) series of trails are rated from easy to moderate. During winter, cross-country skiing is offered at the centre.

Brydon's Bay Trail (Map 24/G2)
Located just north of Gravenhurst, the Brydon's Bay Trailhead is accessible off the Old Portage Road. The trail is an easy 2.3 km (1.4 mi) loop that treks through a beautiful pine forest tract close to the shores of Lake Muskoka.

Buckwallow Cycling Centre/KOA Trails (Map 25/A2)
The KOA Campground just outside of Gravenhurst has long been a popular cross-country skiing destination, however the trail system has been adapted in the summer for mountain biking. Over the years, some fantastic trails have been established, from easy runs for beginners to routes that will challenge expert riders. In all, there is approximately 16 km (10 mi) of trails for bikers to explore. There is a small fee to use the system.

Burk's Falls Heritage River Walk (Map 42/F2)
This short trail is found in the village of Burk's Falls and is an easy 1.4 km (0.9 mi) walk along the graceful Magnetawan River. The route begins at the Burk's Falls Welcome Centre at the foot of Yonge Street and travels to the racetrack in the village. The trail offers a scenic viewing area of the Thompson Rapids, where picnicking is possible.

Callander Bay [Cranberry] Trails (Map 62/E4)
The Cranberry Trail is a beautiful 2.5 km (1.6 mi) trail leading from the end of Cranberry Road to the north end of Callander Bay. There is a viewing platform overlooking the Cranberry Marsh, interpretive signage, benches and a nice view of the bay. A less formal route follows the old logging road leading west. This more challenging 4 km (2.5 mi) route passes by a wild cranberry bog en route to the shore of Lake Nipissing. It can be muddy in spring and is utilized as a bike route in summer and by snowmobiles trail in winter.

Central Muskoka Trail (Map 24, 25, 32, 33)
Currently under construction, the Central Muskoka Trail will eventually stretch from Kahshe Lake in the south all the way to the Seguin Trail in the north. For updates on the location and progress of the trail please inquire with local visitor centres.

Central Ontario Loop Trail (Maps 9, 10, 17, 18, 26–28, 36–37)
The Central Ontario Loop Trail (COLT) is a collection of mainly established railway trails that combine to create this 450 km (280 mi) loop through Ontario's Cottage Country. The more notable trail systems that are a part of the loop network include the Hastings County Trail, Victoria Rail Trail and the Haliburton Rail Trail.

The trail begins near Lake Ontario at Port Hope and travels north all the way to Gelert, south of Haliburton. The route continues east to Bancroft before turning south to Trenton. From Trenton, the trail follows close to the shore of Lake Ontario west returning to Port Hope. The terrain along the trail is obviously quite varied. Travelers along the route will pass by urban areas, open fields and the more rustic terrain further north. For more information visit www.looptrail.com.

Chalk River/Deep River Bike Trail (Map 67/G6)
This route can begin in either Chalk River or Deep River. Essentially, it incorporates side roads and snowmobile trails that link the two towns in a 30.5 km (18.9 mi), moderately difficult loop. The trip is a great way to explore the northern region of the Ottawa Valley. The trail runs east off these maps.

Chamberlain Trail (Map 24/F2)
Off Muskoka Road North the easy 3 km (1.9 mi) trail traverses through softwood and hardwood forests. En route, a 1 km side trail leads to a lookout point over beautiful Lake Muskoka. This trail can be wet in the spring and fall months.

Cooper's Falls Trail (Map 25/C5)
The Cooper's Falls Trail is scheduled to become a part of the Trans Canada Trail. The trail is a moderate 8 km (5 mi) one-way hike that travels through some rustic terrain, including the new Kashe Barrens Conservation Reserve. From wetlands to rock barrens to dense forest cover, visitors will thoroughly enjoy this route. Parking is available at both ends of the route.

Copeland Forest Management Area Trails (Map 14–15)
North of Barrie, the 1,754 ha Copeland Forest Management Area is accessed off Ingram Road. This forested area offers over 35 km (22 mi) of easy to moderate trails that can be used for hiking, biking, snowshoeing and cross-country skiing. From May to October, horseback riding is also permitted on some of the backroads throughout the forest. The trail system traverses through mixed forest and along some marshy areas, which make ideal sites for bird watching. Washrooms and picnic areas are available.

Cordelia Levering Broadmeadows Trail (Map 42/A1)
Located just outside of the town of Magnetawan, at the Ahmic Lake Golf Course, is an easy 3 km (1.9 mi) loop down towards the Magnetawan River and back. The trail travels through a mixed forest that is known locally as the Broadmeadow Wildlife Area and passes close to the shore of Ahmic Lake.

Coulson's Hill Trails (Map 7/B5)
This 12 km (7.5 mi) set of trails is located off the 11th Line northwest of the town of Bradford. A small parking area is located off the south side of the road about 1 km east of Highway 400. The forested trails were developed locally by riders and are used on occasion for organized racing.

Covered Bridge Trail (Map 34/A7)
The Covered Bridge Trail is located in the west end of Bracebridge and can be found off Ball's Drive, behind the shopping centre. The easy trail begins at the covered bridge and follows Beaver Creek, eventually breaking out into a subdivision. The route is approximately 3 km (1.8 mi) in length. Also in the vicinity is the South Monk Trail.

Cranberry Trails (Map 33/B7)
The Cranberry Trails are a collection of six easy to moderate trails found at the Cranberry Marsh. The trails total over 13 km (8 mi) and traverse through a mix of terrain, including forest cover, past wetlands and rocky areas. There are several picnic tables along the trails, which vary from multi-use to hiking or winter use only. Parking can be found at the trailhead area off County Road 169 north of Bala.

trailadventures

Darlington Nuclear Trail (Map 3/F3) 🚶🚴⛷️
This 7.5 km (4.6 mi) section of the Waterfront Trail is a popular hike for day users. In the winter, it doubles as a cross-country ski trail.

Darlington Provincial Park Trails (Map 3/F3) 🚶🚴⛷️
There are 5 km (3 mi) of hiking (and biking and skiing) trails to be found in this park. Split between four trails, including a chunk of the Waterfront Trail. The trails are easy and popular with wildlife watchers.

Deep River Trail (Map 67/G5) 🛶🎣🚶🚻
Beginning at Lamure Beach, the Deep River Trail follows the edge of the Ottawa River to Centennial Rock, offering visitors a great opportunity to see the beauty of the river. The easy, 4 km (2.5 mi) walk is set within the heart of Deep River, the walk incorporates a cedar forest, waterfowl viewing and sandy beaches. The easternmost section of this trail is off these maps.

Devil's Gap Trail (Map 24/E2) 🚶🚴⛷️
North from Gravenhurst off Snider's Bay Road, this 6 km (3.8 mi) moderate trail traverses through dense forest and past many lakes and wetlands. About 3 km (1.9 mi) from the trailhead, the path squeezes through the Devil's Gap. The legend of Devil's Gap began many years ago when stories tell of a farmer who got his wagon and oxen stuck between the gap. After returning with help hours later, the farmer came up on the gap with the wagon and oxen completely gone. The route can be extended via the Southwood Road.

Dorset Scenic Lookout Tower Trail (Map 35/B3) 🚶🚻💲
The 25 metre (82 foot) lookout tower featured along this walk was used from 1922 until 1961 by the former Department of Lands and Forests as a forest fire lookout because of its 500 square km (310 sq mi) viewing radius. Today, for a small fee, visitors can hike to the tower and climb the steps to take in this awesome view. Many tree and plant species are marked along the trail to allow visitors to learn about local vegetation. The lower portion of the trail is also a popular deer spotting area. The moderately difficult trail and tower climb spans approximately 2 km (1.2 mi) and can be found along Highway 35, across from the Dorset School. Restrooms and drinking water are also available.

Driftwood Provincial Park Trails (Map 66/G4–67/A4) 🚶⛷️🚶🚻
Driftwood Provincial Park is located on Highway 17, north of Rolphton on the historic Ottawa River. The three trail systems are mainly for hiking and cross-country skiing. The access points can be found at the parking areas just past the park office. Both trails are also a good area for blueberry and raspberry picking while they are in season. There are a total of 14.5 km (9 mi) of trails.

Durham Demonstration Forest Trails (Map 8/F7) 🚶🚴⛷️
The Durham Demonstration Forest is a public land tract that lies just north of Glen Major Conservation Area. The forest is home to a collection of over 14 km (10 mi) of multi-use trails scattered throughout a few parcels of lands in the Claremont area, including North Walker Woods, Walker Woods, Glen Major Forest and the Brock Tract. There are over 60 trails in the area, meaning that most of the trails are short. But you can string the trails together into a nice long walk.

Eastern Pines Backpacking Trails (Map 57/C4) ⛺🚶🎣🚻
One of a series of backpacking trails in Algonquin Park, this 15.9 km (9.9 mi) trail is made up of two moderate loops near the Achray Campground. The trail is monitored under Algonquin Park's quota system and is described in more detail under the Algonquin Park Trails above.

Eau Claire Gorge Interpretive Trail (Map 64/A3) 🚶🏕️🚻
Within Eau Claire Gorge Conservation Area is a relatively easy, network of hiking trail loops that span approximately 3 km (1.9 mi) in total distance. There is a wonderful viewpoint overlooking Smith Lake and picnic tables for visitors to enjoy. Guests can also explore the gorge itself with its many waterfalls and steep rock walls. The trailhead is located on the Amable du Fond River, west of Highway 630 and south of Samuel de Champlain Provincial Park.

Egan Chutes Provincial Park Trails (Map 38/D6) 🚶🚻
There are a few rustic trails within Egan Chutes Provincial Park for visitors to venture into the outdoors. The relatively easy trails wander 5 km (3.1 mi) along both sides of the York River and are a favourite among those looking for minerals in the Bancroft area. The reserve is located east of Bancroft, off Highway 28. Please note that collecting minerals within the park boundaries is strictly prohibited.

Emily Forest Tract Trails (Map 10/C1) 🚶🚴⛷️🚻
The Emily Forest Tract is located just west of Emily Provincial Park off County Road 14. The forest tract is home to a short collection of trails that help visitors better explore the natural features of this area.

Emily Provincial Park [Marsh Boardwalk] Trail (Map 10/C1) 🚶🚶🚻
The Marsh Boardwalk Trail is an easy route that travels along a boardwalk through a cattail marsh to a sphagnum moss island. The trail also leads to a lookout tower where osprey can sometimes be spotted diving into the water for prey.

Fairy Vista Trail (Map 34/D1) 🚶🚴⛷️
This easy 5 km (3.1 mi) trail is fully paved and can be accessed from the north side of Highway 60 at Fairyview Drive. The trail passes through a variety of farmland and forest tracts and ends at Canal Road. Near the east end of the trail the route passes some ruins of an old farmhouse, a reminder of past attempts to settle the area. The trail is for non-motorized use only.

Frost Centre (Map 35/C5) ⛺🏕️🛶🚶🚴⛷️🚶🚣🚶🎣🚻🏠
The Frost Centre is located on Highway 35, south of Dorset. It offers over 12 km (7.5 mi) of trails through a beautiful portion of the Haliburton Highlands. All trails to the east of the centre are for hiking and snowshoeing use only, due to the difficult terrain. The other series of trails across the highway from the centre offer access to 21 km (13 mi) of cross-country ski trails. These trails can also be used for hiking or biking in the summer as well as limited snowmobiling. The two main access points for the trails are behind the main buildings or from the parking area across the highway from the centre. For campsite reservations, call 1-866-364-4498 and for information call (705) 766-9033.

Trails East of the Frost Centre:

- **Acclimatisation Trail** is a moderately difficult, 4 km (2.5 mi) loop that traverses some hilly sections through a mixed forest and past a marsh area.

- **Dawson Ponds Trail** can be accessed from the Steep Rock Trail. It is a moderately difficult, 1.4 km (0.9 mi) linear trail that travels over some steep sections to a gravel road that leads to the Dawson Ponds. The ponds provide an ideal location for bird viewing.

- **Fire Tower Trail** is an easy, 1.2 km (0.7 mi) loop that travels through a mixed forest to the fire tower where a great view of the surrounding Haliburton Highlands can be enjoyed. The trail can be accessed from both the beginning and end of the Acclimatisation Trail.

- **Forest Management Trail** is located across the highway from the Resources Centre and is an easy 1.5 km (0.9 mi) loop. The trail is used mainly for cross-country skiing, although snowshoeing and hiking are becoming increasingly popular.

- **Lakeshore Trail** is an easy, 0.8 km (0.5 mi) loop that travels along the shore of St. Nora Lake. The trail connects with the Acclimatisation Trail for the trip back to the Resources Centre.

- **Steep Rock Trail** is really a 1.8 km (1.1 mi) extension of the Acclimatisation Trail. The moderately difficult trail traverses some steep cliff sections and should always be approached with caution. There is also a rest/warm up shelter found along the route that usually has a small supply of wood available. Stoke a fire to warm you and your friends on those cold winter days.

- **The Geomorphology Hike** is a combination of the Steep Rock and Acclimatisation Trails. The hike is a 3.5 km route (2.2 mi) organized to inform users of the various landscapes in the area and the forces that have shaped it. An interpretive guide for the hike can be picked up at the Frost Centre.

- **Vista Trail** extends from the Acclimatization Trail and Steep Rock Trail, leading to a great lookout. The steep hills make this 1.4 km (0.9 mi) hike difficult.

Ganaraska Forest Centre (Map 10/C6) 🚶🚴🐎⛷️🚶🏇🏍️🚣🚶
The Ganaraska Forest Centre, which is located just over an hour from Metro Toronto, offers a variety of great recreational trails for public use. The forest centre can be accessed from a number of different areas, with the main access located shortly off County Road 9 about 3.5 km after the town of Kendal. The Forest is divided into three recreational use areas; west, central and east. Each area has a certain recreational focus and accordingly has restrictions on their use. There is also a great snowmobile trail that travels through most of the Ganaraska Forest area that begins at Bewdley off the west side of Highway 28 and ends at the Highway 115/35 junction north of Kirby.

Forest West offers over 50 km (31 mi) of forest roads for snowmobiling, dirt biking or mountain biking. You can also hike or horseback ride in the west section, although at times, motorbike activity is extensive. The trailhead access is located at the north section of the Forest off the main access road.

Forest Central is a great spot for hiking orienteering, snowshoeing, cross-country skiing or horseback riding. This section is designated as a 'passive use zone' and motorized vehicles are not permitted. There are a series of interconnecting trails in this area for your recreational pleasure. The trail centre, where conservation programs have been developed to enhance your visit, also doubles as a rest area in the summer or a welcomed warm up area in the winter.

Forest East is much smaller than the other two forest areas, although it still offers some great forest roads for dirt biking, snowmobiling and mountain biking. This eastern section is sparsely patched together with some areas being surrounded by private land. Please do not trespass on private property. Travel on some trails, such as the main snowmobile trail, is permitted through private property.

Ganaraska Hiking Trail (Map 5/A1–23/D6)

The Ganaraska Trail is a long distance route extending from Port Hope along the banks of the Ganaraska River, to Midland and eventually Glen Huron, where the trail connects with the Bruce Trail. The trail traverses through a great variety of different natural areas including rolling farmland, the Pre-Cambrian Shield, the shores of the Georgian Bay and the Niagara Escarpment. It also crosses through private property on occasion. Parts of the trail travel over easy terrain such as country roads, whereas other portions traverse steep hills along narrow foot trails. Camping is available along the trail at various provincial parks, conservation areas and private campgrounds. If you are planning an extended outing, it is advised that you pick up the detailed Ganaraska Trail Guide to aid in your trip preparations.

The Southern Section (Map 5/A1–26/D5) of the Ganaraska Trail extends over 165 km (102 mi) from the town of Port Hope to the settlement of Moore Falls. Much of this portion of the trail is easy and travels along roads or abandoned rail beds. From Port Hope, the first large stretch of rustic footpath can be found as the trail passes through the Ganaraska Forest Centre. Roads once again become the main pathway after the Forest Centre. As you begin to approach the wilderness section of the trail, the route becomes more rustic, but still easy. Past Highway 503 the trail becomes more challenging as it traverses past wetland areas, lakes and through sometimes heavily wooded areas.

The Wilderness Section (Map 26/D5–15/G2) is rustic and often difficult and should only be traveled by experienced users. If you decide to travel this portion of the trail it is recommended to carry a compass and a good topographical map of the route. This part of the trail spans over 65 km (40 mi) from Moore Falls to Sadowa Road outside of Orillia. The route passes numerous lakes and streams where fishing may be enjoyed. At about the 40 km (25 mi) point from Moore Falls, there is a side-trail called the Ragged Rapids Loop. The loop trail travels along Montgomery Creek and then along the shore of the Black River, where you can catch a glimpse of the powerful Ragged Rapids.

The Northern Section (Map 15/G2–14/A7) mostly follows quiet country roads and across rolling fields. This section is over 172 km (107 mi) long from Sadowa Road to the Mad River Side Trail near Devil's Glen Provincial Park outside of Collingwood.

The Midland Section (Map 15/A3–23/D6) is an addition that stretches over 40 km (25 mi) from just south of Midland to Horseshoe Valley, where it connects with the main trail. This section travels through the Copeland Forest Resources Management Area and across the Sturgeon River before meeting the main trail. Much of the geography of this route is rolling hills with a few wetland areas.

The Wasaga Section (Map 14/A5) route traverses through Wasaga Beach Provincial Park and over the Nottawasaga River before meeting the main trail.

For updates on trail changes and closures contact the Ganaraska Trail Association.

Georgian Bay Islands National Park Trails (Map 23/D4)

On Beausoleil Island of the Georgian Bay Islands National Park there are over 27 km (16.8 mi) of scenic recreation trails, spread between eleven trails around the island. The rare Eastern Massasauga Rattlesnake can sometimes be spotted along these trails, although does not pose any danger unless it is provoked. All trails are suitable for hiking only unless otherwise noted. The trails are easy or moderate and bikes are permitted on the Christian Trail and the Huron Trail. A popular trip is the 3 km (1.9 mi) trail to Treasure Bay.

Gibson Lake Trail (Map 23/G2)

This year round trail parallels the South Gibson Lake Road from Highway 400 to the small parking area found east of Hungry Bay Road. The trail is an easy 10 km (6.2 mi) trek that passes wetland habitat and through mixed forest cover. You can return to your vehicle via the same route or by the South Gibson Lake Road.

Gibson River Wilderness Trail (Map 23/G2)

The Gibson River Wilderness Trail lies within the nature reserve, although the parking area is found just west of the reserve. The moderate 3.5 km (2.2 mi) one-way trail follows the Gibson River through a wilderness setting ending at the scenic Long Falls. Sightings of deer, moose and even black bear are a possibility along this route.

Glebe Park Trails (Map 36/B7)

The Glebe Park Loop and the other trails in the area are used mainly for cross-country skiing in the winter. Over the past few years, however, the trails are beginning to be used more frequently for hiking. There is approximately 20 km (12.4 mi) of trails available for exploration. Most of the trails are an easy hike. Please drop a donation in the drop box to help maintain these trails.

Goodrich-Loomis Conservation Area Trails (Map 12/C5)

Found about 5 km east of County Road 30 near Orland, lies the Goodrich-Loomis Conservation Area. Six trails cover 12 km (7.5 mi) and cross an assortment of diverse ecosystems including oak savannah, wetland, extant prairie and a varied woodland. The more difficult Esker Trail offers a beautiful view after a strenuous climb.

Granview Inn Nature Trails (Map 34/D1)

Located off Highway 60, 5 km (3.1 mi) from Huntsville, the Grandview Inn resort offers 15 km (9.3 mi) of trails that can be used for hiking or biking. Nature tours along the trails are also available for a modest fee. The trails vary in difficulty from easy to moderate and a detailed map is available at the resort.

Grundy Lake Provincial Park Trails (Map 49/E3)

Grundy Lake Provincial Park is located north of Parry Sound at the junction of Highway 69 and Highway 522. Over 8 km (5 mi) of interpretive trails are found between three separate systems. The longest trail is the Beaver Dam Trail, at 4.5 km (2.8 mi).

Hahne Farm Trail (Map 24/G3)

Located in the southern end of Gravenhurst, this easy 5 km (3 mi) trail system traverses through a mixed forest, home of a variety of trees such as pine and birch. The highlight of the loop is the view over a small marsh area.

Haliburton County Rail Trail (Map 26/G5–36/B7)

The Haliburton County Rail Trail is a 36 km (20 mi) one-way route along an old rail bed between the towns of Kinmount and Haliburton. From Kinmount the route heads north over an impressive trestle over the Irondale River. Shortly after the river crossing you will be rewarded with a fantastic view at the Bunt River Lookout. Another highlight of the route is the Ritchie Falls found south of the village of Lochlin. The trail is part of the Central Ontario Loop Trail system.

Haliburton Forest and Wildlife Reserve Trails (Map 35, 36, 45)

This wonderful nature reserve is privately owned and encompasses over fifty lakes, 300 km (185 mi) of trails and access roads and over 50,000 acres of beautiful nature. The reserve is open year round and charges a nominal fee for outdoor activities. In summer, the Forest offers mountain biking, hiking, canoeing, camping and the spectacular forest canopy tour. The canopy tour takes you along an exciting suspension bridge that is mounted over 20 m (66 ft) high amid a beautiful old growth white pine canopy. In winter months, many of the trails are groomed and provide endless cross-country skiing and snowmobiling opportunities. The Forest offers snowmobile and mountain bike rentals if needed and there is a small supply store open daily. The main gate to the Haliburton Forest and Wildlife Reserve can be accessed from Kennisis Lake Road off Highway 118. Call (705) 754-2198 for more information.

Hardwood Hills Trails (Map 15/C4)
This facility is designed for cross-country skiing in winter and biking in summer. For a marginal fee, Hardwood Hills provides access to over 86 km (53 mi) of trails for visitors to enjoy. The trails are rated from easy to difficult and offer rest areas complete with picnic tables and toilets. The facility at the centre offers a variety of services such as equipment rentals and training programs to improve your skills. Hardwood Hills is located north of Barrie off Doran Road, just past the village of Edgar.

Hardy Lake Provincial Park Trail (Map 24/D1)
Hardy Lake Provincial Park can be found just outside the village of Torrance off County Road 169. This undeveloped park offers an easy 3 km (1.9 mi) trail that leads to the site of some turn of the century abandoned buildings on the shores of Hardy Lake.

Harrison Woods Trail (Map 35/F7)
Found just west of the town of Carnarvon, the Harrison Woods was donated to the province by the Harrison family, who enjoyed the beauty of Ontario's Cottage Country. The trail is an easy 1.2 km (0.7 mi) hike through a scenic pine forest that eventually gives way to a hardwood forest.

Hastings Heritage Trail (Maps 12, 13, 20, 21, 29, 30, 37, 38)
The Hastings Heritage Trail is a fabulous long distance trail that follows an old railbed from Lake St. Peter south to Bannockburn, Marmora and eventually Trenton. The trail travels through a variety of different terrain, such as wetland habitat, remote forest, the rolling hills of the Madawaska Highlands and many small towns and villages. In total, the trail stretches about 156 km (97 mi) and is well maintained throughout. During the summer months, hiking, biking, horseback riding and ATVing are popular uses of the trail. In the winter, the trail transforms into a great ski, snowshoe or snowmobile path.

Hazlewood Trail (Map 33/B6)
The trailhead for this historic trail is located west of Port Carling. The trail was named after one of the first pioneers that settled the area and was the original route between Port Carling and Port Sandfield. Today, the trail is a moderate 5 km (3.1 mi) route that leads through forest cover and past a beaver pond.

Highland Backpacking Trail (Map 45/B4)
Found along the Highway 60 Corridor near the Mew Lake Campground, this trail is made up of two connecting loops totaling 40 km (25 mi). Those wishing to explore the entire route or stay overnight should note that the trail is monitored under Algonquin Park's quota system and campsite reservations are necessary. It is described in more detail under the Algonquin Park Trails above.

Hog's Trough Trails (Map 52/F2)
The Hog's Trough is a local swimming hole on the scenic South River. To find the trailhead, follow Highway 11 south from Trout Creek to McFadden Line. Follow McFadden Line to a parking area near the end of the maintained road. From the parking area, you can continue by foot or bike along the older portion of the road. Shortly along the trail, you will come to a fork. The north fork follows a trail directly to the South River and the Hog's Trough, while the second fork is a loop trail that follows an old road. Both trails are generally easy and are about 2 km (1.2 mi) in length offering good views of the river.

Horseshoe Resort Nordic Trails (Map 15/B3)
There is a fine collection of cross-country ski trails available for visitors to explore in the summer. The trails vary in difficulty from easy to difficult and are often used by mountain bikers. Some decent views of the countryside can be found from several points along the trail system.

H. R. Frink Centre Trails (Map 13/F1)
Part of the Loyalist County Trails, this set of trails can be found just southeast of Madoc, at the H. R. Frink Centre, off Thrasher's Road. There are a number of hiking trails, which interconnect near a variety of wetland habitats near the Moira River and Parks Creek over boardwalks, as well as through mixed forest areas, a silver maple swamp and some open fields. During winter, the trail system doubles as a fantastic cross-country ski trail system.

Huckleberry Rock Trail (Map 33/E6)
Located southeast of Port Carling, the trailhead for this trail can be found off Milford Bay Road. The route is a moderate 2.5 km (1.6 mi) loop that traverses

over some hilly, rocky terrain to a scenic lookout. En route to the lookout, visitors will pass through a stand of pine and past a bog.

Huntsville Urban Trails (Map 34/C1)
There are two connected, moderate 4.1 km (2.5 mi) loops that take visitors through a variety of industrial, residential and parkland areas. Parking can be found near the intersection of Highway 11 and West Road. Other local trails make up sections of the Park to Trail system and the Trans Canada Trail.

Hybla to Graphite Trail (Map 38/A3–4)
Formerly an important rail link in the early commerce of the region, this railbed has since been converted to a wide and easy 6 km (3.6 mi) loop. It follows a picturesque portion of the Madawaska Valley and is suitable for year round travel by most trail users. The trail can be accessed from the old village of Graphite, which lies 4 km to the east of Highway 62 on Graphite Road.

Kahshe Barrens Trail (Map 25/B4)
The trailhead for this easy 4 km (2.5 mi) hike is found at the parking area of the Muskoka Tourism office. The office can be found south of Gravenhurst off the east side of Highway 11. The trail passes over a few small streams, past beaver ponds and over a rocky ridge where a fine view is offered.

Kerr Park Trails (Map 25/A1)
Located near Bracebridge on Beaumont Drive (County Road 16), these easy 2.3 km (1.3 mi) trails are utilized by hikers and bikers in the summer. In the winter they are a great place for cross-country skiing or snowshoeing. Kerr Park is also a regular area for bird watching and there is a bird-viewing platform along one of the trails.

Killbear Provincial Park Trails (Map 31/E1)
Killbear Provincial Park offers three hiking only trails through scenic portions of the provincial park, totaling 6.5 km. The Lookout Point Trail is the longest of the three at 3.5 km (2.2 mi), leading to Ouimet Point.

Kortright Conservation Centre (Map 1/C4)
Located in the Humber Valley, there are 16 km (10 mi) of easy hiking trails in this conservation area.

La Vase Portage Conservation Area Trails (Map 62/E3)
This 39 hectare conservation area was established in 1995 in order to protect a portion of the historic La Vase Portage. Natives and voyageurs of the early 19th century frequently used this portage. It was one of the more challenging portages along the Mattawa River and hence it received its name. Currently, there are no established facilities at the area other than a series of three portages that total 11 km (6.8 mi). The trailhead can be found on Highway 17, 5 km (3.1 mi) east of Highway 11, east of North Bay. Contact the North Bay-Mattawa Conservation Authority at (705) 474-5420 for further information on the conservation area.

Lafontaine en Action Trails (Map 23/A6)
This year round facility is located off County Road 26 near the old French settlement of Lafontaine. It offers great cross-country skiing trails in the winter and hiking and camping in the summer. There are a total of seven trails that vary in difficulty and cover over 20 km (12 mi). Minimal fees are charged for use of the facilities. For more information call (705) 533-2961.

Lake Bernard Circle Tour (Map 42/G1–52/F7)
Encircling Lake Bernard, this cycling route or footpath basically makes use of existing side roads that surround the lake to create an easy, 10 km (6 mi) loop. Lake Bernard claims the title of being the largest freshwater lake in the world without an island.

Lake St. Peter Provincial Park Trails (Map 37/E1)
Lake St. Peter Provincial Park can be found near Highway 127, south of Whitney. There are two connecting trails available for hiking at this park, totaling approximately 6.7 km (4.2 mi). Permits can be picked up at the gate and parking is available at the trailhead. In winter, the trails can be used for cross-country skiing or snowshoeing, although they are not groomed.

Lakefield Trail (Map 19/A6)
The Lakefield Trail was established as a commemorative for Lakefield's 125th year. The trail travels along roads in town, over the Bridge Street Bridge, along the Otonabee River and in a loop around Lakefield Beach. Trail parking is available in several locations, including at the Lakefield Marina and Lakefield Beach.

Laurentian Escarpment Conservation Area Trails (Map 62/E1–2)

Located in the vicinity of the Laurentian Ski Hill to the northeast of North Bay, this moderate trail system rewards visitors with some spectacular vistas over North Bay, Lake Nipissing and the general area. The two trails, the McNutt Family and the Richardson Ridge, join to provide a 6.6 km (4.1 mi) trek. The trailhead starts behind the ski tower at the Janey Avenue parking lot.

Little River Road Interpretive Trail (Map 51/F3)

The Little River Road Interpretive Area is a small, informal preserve that is the site of one of the largest deer wintering areas south of the French River. Over 10,000 deer migrate to this area in winter and spend the cold season foraging on twigs and other vegetation before the spring thaw. There is a small set of easy self-guided interpretive trails that meander through the area amid a peaceful forested setting. The interpretive area is located off Little River Road from Highway 522.

Long Sault Conservation Area Trails (Map 9/F6)

Long Sault Conservation area offers about 18 km (11 mi) of trails and is located off County Road 57 on Durham Road 20. There are four trails to explore, the longest of which is the Black Trail, a 6.5 km (4 mi) easy hike.

Lookout Tower Nature Trail (Map 35/B3)

Off Highway 35 just north of Dorset, is the access to a series of trails at the lookout tower and picnic area. The tower is over 30 metres (98 ft) high and offers a stunning panoramic view of Dorset and the surrounding hills. The connecting trails are easy and generally short in distance. Signs are also posted along the trails, which describe various points of interest.

Loxton Beaver Trail (Map 53/B2)

The Loxton Beaver Trail is found off Chemical Road, northeast of the town of South River. This easy 8.5 km (5.3 mi) loop travels through mixed forest, past the Loxton Lake Dam. The trail is maintained as a cross-country ski trail in the winter and doubles as a hiking and biking trail during the summer months. The route passes both Loxton and Beaver Lakes before returning to the trailhead.

Loyalist County Trails (Maps 11–13, 19–21)

The Loyalist County Trails are a large series of trails made up of old railway beds that travel throughout several regions. Part of the system follows the Trans Canada Trail, while other sections see no maintenance at all. Hikers, bikers and horseback riders frequent the trails during the summer months, while in the winter, the trails are very popular for snowmobiling, although cross-country skiing and snowshoeing are also possible. While the trail can be accessed from a number of spots, the three main sections are from Peterborough to Belleville, from Belleville to Madoc and from Bonarlaw to Glen Tay. The H. R. Frink Centre off Thrasher Road is a common access point.

Mabel Davis Conservation Area Trails (Map 7/F7)

Located in the north portion of the town of Newmarket, these trails can be accessed off Bayview Avenue or Davis Drive. This 6.4 hectare area is surrounded by urban development but is a great place to find the quite of nature so close to the city. There is an easy 1.4 km (0.9 mi) hiking trail through the conservation area that travels from the north portion of the park all the way to Davis Drive. There are also picnic facilities available throughout the area.

Magnetawan Trails (Map 42/A1)

In and around the quaint town of Magnetawan are a series of trails that allow visitors and locals to explore this beautiful area. The Ahmic Lake Golf Course features a number of easy trails, including a 3 km (3.1 mi) loop. The Old Greenhouse Trail is the same length, passing a number of wetlands along the way. There are also a number of shorter trails in the area.

Mansfield Outdoor Centre (Map 6/A4)

For a small fee, this outdoor centre offers over 30 km (18 mi) of trails for cross-country skiing, mountain biking or hiking. The centre was developed mainly for educational purposes and focuses on providing outdoor education to area schools, although all trails are open to the public. There is a main building that has a small cafeteria and offers equipment rentals if needed. If you wish to stay more than one day at the centre, there are small rustic cabins available for weekend rental. The centre is located on Airport Road just south of the town of Stayner.

Mark S. Burnham Provincial Park Trail (Map 11/A1)

This small non-operating park is located just outside the city of Peterborough. The park is a popular trail destination for city residents and visitors and offers an easy 2.5 km (1.6 mi) loop. The trail travels through a mature forest, which is a favourite spot for wildflower enthusiasts and bird watchers.

Mashkinonje Provincial Park Trails (Map 60/B3)

Situated on the West Arm of Lake Nipissing, Mashkinonje Provincial Park straddles Highway 64. Ten hiking trails traverse this geologically and topographically interesting park in a series of joined loops totalling more than 30 km (18.6 mi). The trails range from 1 km to more than 5 km long and travel ridges of bedrock, tread through marsh and bog, lead past beaver ponds and next to the lakefront. Atakas Trail, at 5.4 km (3.4 mi), is the longest and best approached in the dry season as it is quite wet in places. The 3.4 km (2.1 mi) Samoset Trail is the most southern trail and offers a better opportunity to see moose that dwell in this lowland marshy habitat. The most remote of the trails is the Coastal Trail covering 4.3 km (2.7 mi).

Massasauga Provincial Park Trails (Map 31/F3–32/B5)

One of Ontario's newest provincial parks, there are a few boat access hiking trails in the park. The Baker Trail is a moderate 5.5 km (3.4 mi) interpretive loop near Woods Bay. The Nipissing North Arm Orienteering Trail is an undeveloped 30 km (19 mi) route that is best left for experienced backcountry travellers. Another popular trail destination is Wreck Island where visitors will find a couple short trails to explore.

Mattawa Valley Trek/Mattawa River North Trails (Map 63/E1)

A moderately difficult hike extends from the northern edge of Rice Bay of Lake Talon to the snowmobile/ATV trail system that permeates the area northwest of Mattawa. The 3 km (1.9 mi) trail travels through a forest setting where the opportunity to discover the local vegetation and wildlife is ever present. Beyond the trail, ATVers and snowmobilers have plenty of bush roads to explore.

McCrae Lake Conservation Reserve Trails (Map 23/E3)

The McCrae Lake Conservation Reserve lies off the west side of Highway 400 north of Six Mile Lake Provincial Park. The trailhead is found on Georgian Bay Road at the canoe launch to McCrae Lake. The moderate 3 km (1.9 mi) trail is marked with yellow trail markers and leads to the Crow's Nest Lookout. The lookout offers a spectacular view of the lake from atop a 30 m (100 ft) granite cliff. Experienced bushwhackers can navigate an additional 25 km (15.5 mi) of rustic trails but a compass and topographical are required to explore past the lookout.

Medd's Mountain Conservation Trails (Map 10/E4)

Established in 1991, this small interconnecting series of trails can be accessed at the south end of Distillery Street or from the Old Millbrook School in the town of Millbrook. The trails are all easy and generally short. There are also a number of benches along the paths where you can sit and just enjoy nature.

Memorial Park Trails (Map 34/C1)

Memorial Park is located in the southeast end of Huntsville off Brunel Road. The trailhead can be found behind the Centennial Centre. The trails are comprised of two loops totaling approximately 2 km (1.2 mi) that follow along the Muskoka River and through a mixed hardwood forest.

Midland Rotary Waterfront Trail (Map 23/D6)

The Midland Rotary Waterfront Trail links to the Penetanguishene Rotary Trail and is an easy route that follows close to the Midland waterfront. The trail travels through a number of scenic parks and past a few lookout areas.

Mikisew Provincial Park Trails (Map 52/D5)

Mikisew Provincial Park is located west of the town of South River on the western shore of Eagle Lake. This full facility park offers four interconnected loops that can be enjoyed by outdoor enthusiasts. The trails are excellent for spring and early summer wildflower and bird viewing. Each trail varies from 1 km to 3.2 km (2 mi) and is moderately difficult, due to some steep grades. Visitors can see a beaver pond as they travel over diverse locales that include boardwalks, meadows and cedar and mixed forests.

Millbrook Valley Trails (Map 10/E4)

This set of trails travels through a variety of ecosystems including forest, meadows, marsh and shrub land. Totalling 8 km (5 mi), the trails include the 2.7 km (1.7 mi) Meadow Loop Trail and the Baxter Creek Trail at 2.2 km (1.4 mi). There are two trailheads, one by the millpond dam in Medd's Mountain Park and the other at the Ministry of Natural Resources parking lot by the 4th line theatre. These trails are for hiking only, but there is a set of separate trails set aside for snowmobiling in winter.

Miller Creek Wildlife Area Trail (Map 18/G6)

Protecting a small wetland, this wildlife area is home to a set of easy, short trails. The trail travels through a mix of wetland and forest cover.

Moose Mountain Trail (Map 53/B2)

This 2 km (1.2 mi) loop is moderate in difficulty due to the climb that is required to ascend Moose Mountain. Once atop the 'mountain' you will be rewarded with a picturesque view of Loxton Lake and the surrounding countryside.

Muskoka Trail (Map 52/E5)

The Muskoka Trail follows the Old Muskoka Road, which was one of the first roads in the region. The old road now makes a great multi-use trail for all to enjoy. The easy 5 km (3.1 mi) route is suited for hiking, mountain biking, cross-country skiing and snowshoeing. To find the trailhead, take Eagle Lake Road from South River and look for the access road where Eagle Lake Road takes a distinct turn south. The trailhead can be found off the north side of the dirt road about 1 km from Eagle Lake Road.

Nipissing Colonization Trail [Ghost Trail] (Map 42/A7–62/D6)

The Old Nipissing Road is one of the first colonization roads to access Northern Ontario and the first to lead to Lake Nipissing. The old road actually begins near Seguin Falls in the south and stretches north, past the town of Magnetawan to the settlement of Nipissing. The road is now part of the Trans Canada Trail and makes a great outing for hikers, bikers and other trail enthusiasts. The most popular sections are between Magnetawan to Nipissing where a few sections of the old road have been converted to trail creating short walks no more than 5 km (3.1 mi) in length. Camping on Crown land is possible in the area.

Nordic Inn Trails (Map 35/A2)

Found across the road from the Dorset Lookout Tower on Highway 35, the Nordic Inn Trails are a rustic series of interconnected trails. The system is made up of a combination of generally easy loops totaling over 23 km (14 mi) in length.

North Bay Trails (Map 62/D2)

The city of North Bay offers a series of fine recreational trails in and around the city. Most are open to cyclists and double as fine ski destinations in the winter.

Canadore College Trails (Map 62/E1)

This group of trails is a fabulous, multi-use outdoor recreation area. The trails can be accessed from the west side of Canadore College's Education Centre off Larocque Road in the city of North Bay. The main trail is the Duchesnay Trail, a moderate 2 km (1.2 mi) loop that travels from the college to Duchesnay Creek. The trail follows the creek for about 450 m (1,476 ft) before heading back towards the education centre. Several secondary trails branch off the Duchesnay Trail, including one leading to Duchesnay Falls. Others offer great views of the city of North Bay, while the others offer a scenic view of Lake Nipissing. Picnic tables are located in several locations along the trails. An interpretive guide brochure for the Duchesnay Trail can be picked up at the Canadore College Library.

Kate Pace Way (Map 62/E2)

Named after Olympic skier Kate Pace, the 5 km (3.1 mi) one way paved trail is a popular trail in North Bay. While bikers and inline skaters can use part of the route, the southern portion is restricted to pedestrians only.

Kinsmen Ecology Trail [Chippewa Way Bike Path] (Map 62/E2)

This 5 km (3.1 mi) one way trail is a paved trail that links together a number of green spaces in North Bay. It is an easy paved trail that makes its way from Airport Road to Kate Pace Way on North Bay's waterfront.

North Bay Nordic Trails (Map 62/G1–63/A1)

These trails are popular with hikers in the summer, too. The trails are found east of North Bay on the north side of Trout Lake, off Northshore Road. There are over 40 km (25 mi) of well-marked trails in the area, ranging from easy to moderate. There are fees for skiing, but none for hiking.

Jack Pine Ski Hill Trails (Map 62/E1)

The 5 or so km of trails at Jack Pine covers popular, challenging terrain for mountain bikes. The trails are just east of the ski hill, near Janey Ave (between Wallace Heights and Graniteville) at the northeast portion of North Bay. It is easy to spend a whole day on the trails here.

Laurier Woods Trail (Map 62/E2)

Part of these trails are on private lands, the rest are owned by the city. There are three short, easy trails here, open to bikers and hikers. The small network of trails extends between Laurier Avenue and Winters Street.

North Simcoe Rail Trail (Map 14/D7–D2)

The North Simcoe Rail Trail begins from Pinegrove Road southwest of Barrie and follows and old rail line north past Elmvale to Flos Road 10 and County Road 27. The trail passes the east end of the Minesing Swamp and through a mix of fields and semi forested areas. Since the trail follows an old rail line, the grade is gentle but the distance (up to 32 km/20 mi one-way) can be taxing. Shorter sections are possible, while continuing north to Penetanguishene the trail is called the Tiny Trail.

Northumberland County Forest Trails (Map 11/E5–6)

This large, 2,195 hectare park is situated on County Road 45, about 15 km north of Colbourg and Highway 401. There are more than 45 km (28 mi) of multi-use, year round trails in the area. Included here are hiking trails that make up part of the Oak Ridges Trail system as well as roughly 20 km (12.4 mi) of mountain biking trails that can be accessed from the Beagle Club parking lot. Cross-country skiers can explore four shorter loops, all less than 4 km, or venture on the three longer trails that range from 5.2 km to 15 km and get progressively more difficult with distance. Hikers will also enjoy the three loops on the Purple Trail that progress from the easy 3 km loop to the moderate 6 km loop and finally the more difficult 9 km loop. The access for these loops is on the east side of County Road 45 at Woodland Road.

Oak Ridges Trail (Map 8/A7–11/B5)

This semi-urban trail travels from east to west along the rolling hills of the moraine. The route is a combination of roads and trails and is highlighted by fantastic hilltop views and sections of beautiful mature stands of forest. The complete route is over 200 km (120 miles) long and rated as moderate. The western trailhead is found at the Durham Demonstration Forest, while the eastern trailhead is found south of Rice Lake near Gores Landing. For more information please contact The Oak Ridges Trail Association by calling 1-877-319-0285 or visit www.orta.on.ca.

Old Stone Road Trail (Map 24/F3)

Located west of Gravenhurst, the trailhead can be found off North Muldrew Lake Road from County Road 169. The easy trail can be traveled in a 4.7 km (2.9 mi) loop by linking back along the North Muldrew Lake Road. For a longer trip, the trail can be continued west to Southwood Road. The route mainly follows the old colonization road that was once the only link between Gravenhurst and Bala.

Orillia Trails (Map 15/G2)

Set along an abandoned rail line, the main trail traverses from one end of the city to the other. The paved route is 10 km (6.2 mi) one-way and is intersected by a few other trail offshoots, including gravel trail sections. The trail is easy to travel and provides some great views of Lake Couchiching.

Oro-Medonte Trail (Map 15/A7–F2)

The Oro-Medonte Trail follows an old rail bed. The rail bed stretches from Barrie to Orillia and is an easy one-way journey of approximately 28 km (17.4 mi) in length. The route passes by a number of shoreline communities where some fine views of Lake Simcoe can be caught along the way.

Oshawa Urban Trails (Map 3/C3)

Three paved walking and cycling paths give access to downtown as well as some areas of natural beauty. The Michael Starr Trail, a former railbed, is a flat and easy 5 km (3.1 mi) route. The older 7 km (4.3 mi) long Joseph Kolodzie Oshawa Creek Bike Path and 4 km (2.5 mi) long Harmony Creek Trail follow a riverine route and have sharper turns as well as steep inclines that can challenge bikers. Please be wary of walkers on the routes.

Oxtongue River-Ragged Falls Provincial Park Trail (Map 44/B7)

This non-operating provincial park was established to protect a stretch of the Oxtongue River. The park joins Algonquin Provincial Park at its western boundary and envelops the river up to Highway 60. There is a short turnoff from Highway 60 where parking and public toilets are available. From the parking area, there is an easy 2 km (1.2 mi) trail that leads to a lookout over the brilliant Ragged Falls.

trailadventures

Park to Park Trail (Map 31–33, 42–45)
The Park to Park Trail links Algonquin Provincial Park in the east to Killbear Provincial Park on Georgian Bay, a 230 km (143 mi) span. The multi-use route piggybacks on several established trails, such as the Seguin and Trans Canada Trail. At the time of printing, parts of the trail were still under construction, but the trail was officially open. Please check www.parktoparktrail.com for details and updates on the trail progress or call 1-800-746-4455.

Parry Sound Fitness Trail (Map 32/A1)
This easy 5 km (3.1 mi) one-way trail passes along the shore of the Georgian Bay and through the streets of Parry Sound. The trail can be accessed from Waubuno Park, off Bay Street or at Great North Road. It is popular for walking and biking.

Partridge Lake Trail (Map 35/D5)
This trail is located off Highway 35 just past Partridge Lake, about 700 metres down the old highway roadbed. It is an easy 6.5 km (4 mi) trail that treks through the forest all the way to Sherborne Lake. There are also few unmarked side trails available for further exploration. The area is a popular wildlife area and larger animals such as deer, moose and bears are spotted occasionally.

Petawawa Crown Game Reserve (Map 57/G1–67/G7)
Although sections of this reserve are found in this book, most of the actual trails are actually found to the east off Highway 17, north of Pembroke. The reserve is great for cross-country skiing and a number of local athletes have used the area for training in the past. There is a small parking area available and a detailed route map at the trailheads. The trails are also suitable for hiking and biking during summer months.

Peterborough Trails (Map 10/G1, 11, 19)
Within the city of Peterborough there are a series of trails that help locals and visitors explore the beautiful city on foot or bike. Described below are some of the bigger trail systems.

Rotary Greenway Trail (Map 10/G1–19/A7)
One-way, this easy paved trail traverses over 20 km (12.5 mi) and travels along a portion of the old railway line that travels from Beavermead Park in Peterborough past Trent University towards Lakefield. The scenic route follows the Otonabee River and is scheduled to be part of the Trans Canada Trail.

Otonabee River Trail (Map 10/F1)
This easy trail begins behind the Holiday Inn off George Street in Peterborough. The trail follows an old rail line north past the Ministry of Natural Resources Head Office building to Simcoe Street. From Simcoe Street, it is possible to continue west to link up with the Jackson Creek Trail.

Jackson Creek Kiwanis Trail (Map 10/G1)
The Jackson Creek Trail travels from beautiful Jackson Park in Peterborough to Ackison Road just outside of the city. The trail is an easy 4 km (2.5 mi) one-way route and can be accessed at the corner of Parkhill Road and Monaghan Road in Peterborough. The trail is a part of the Trans Canada Trail system and traverses through mixed forest areas, open fields and a portion of the Cavan Swamp. It is used for hiking, biking, skiing and snowshoeing.

Pine Grove Resort Trails (Map 51/F3)
Pine Grove Resort is located just east of the settlement of Port Loring, off the south side of Highway 522. The resort lies on the shore of the rugged Pickerel River and offers a series of easy interconnecting routes that span approximately 7.5 km (4.7 mi). During the summer, hikers and mountain bikers are welcome on the well-maintained trail system. The trails meander through a mainly hardwood forest and lead to the shore of the Pickerel River. Be sure to check in with the resort operators before heading out on the trails.

Petroglyph Provincial Park Trails (Map 19/E2)
This park is fond 11 km east of Highway 28 on County Road 56 and is home to one of Canada's largest collections of Native rock carvings. There are a number of trails in this park ranging from easy to moderate. The West Day Use Trail is an easy 5 km (3.1 mi) multi-use trail. The High Falls Trail crosses a variety of terrains on its 16 km (10 mi) course to the learning centre and waterfalls. The Marsh Trail, at 7 km (4.3 mi), is considered the most difficult due to its up and down terrain while the 5.5 km (3.4 mi) Nanabush Trail is focused on a number of Native legends.

Pine Grove Resort Trails (Map 50/F4)
Pine Grove Resort is located just west of the settlement of Port Loring, off the south side of Highway 522. The resort lies on the shore of the rugged Pickerel River and offers a series of easy interconnecting routes that span approximately 7.5 km (4.7 mi). During the summer, hikers and mountain bikers are welcome on the well-maintained trail system. The trails meander through a mainly hardwood forest and lead to the shore of the Pickerel River. Be sure to check in with the resort operators before heading out on the trails.

Pine Interpretive Trails (Map 51/A3)
Formerly the Powassan Trails, this collection of connected loop trails can be found behind the retirement home at 62 Big Bend Avenue in the town of Powassan. Covering approximately 4.3 km (2.7 mi), the trails range from easy to moderate as they climb to some nice viewpoints over Powassan and the highland region. Interpretive brochures are available at the municipal office.

Pine Ridge Ski Club Trail (Map 15/A3)
The Pine Ridge Ski Club is a popular downhill ski area in the winter that offers an excellent mountain biking area in summer. The main trail forms about a 12 km (7.5 mi) loop and climbs the ski hill where some fantastic views can be found. The route is regarded as moderate in difficulty and will definitely get your heart rate up.

Pines Wetland Trail (Map 24/G2)
This small hiking trail is located off Muskoka Beach Road, before the main entrance to the Muskoka Sands Resort. The trail is found just after the drainage pools and travels through dense forest, past active beaver ponds and offers a good view of Lake Muskoka.

Presqu'ile Provincial Park Trails (Map 5 Inset)
Best known for its birdwatching opportunities, Presqu'ile also tenders some great trail systems for visitors to enjoy. Present here are ideal marsh habitats for waterfowl, a staging point for Mexico-bound monarch butterflies and the second oldest operating lighthouse in Ontario. It is located south of Brighton and Highways 2 and 401. There are 11 km (6.8 mi) worth of trails in the park.

Quinte Conservation Area Trails (Map 13/D4)
Located west of Belleville, visitors will find a fine series of easy hiking or cross-country ski trails. The 6 km (3.7 mi) trails traverse the mixed forest of the conservation area and offer views of the Bay of Quinte. Abandoned farmlands with former apple orchards and derelict equipment are reminders of days gone by and can also been seen from the trail network.

Ramara Trail (Map 15/G2/16/A2)
A 5 km (3.1 mi) multi-use, year round trail is built on the railbed of an abandoned CN line outside of Orillia. The trail begins at the Mnjikaning Fish Weirs National Historic Site. The end of the trail is a little to the east of the junction of Rama and Monck Roads, but there are plans to expand this trail further north.

Ravenshoe Trails (Map 7/G4–8/A4)
Located just east of the settlement of Ravenshoe, the trailhead can be accessed from a parking area off the west side of McCowan Road. There are about 20 km (12.5 mi) of interconnected trails that wind through this mixed forest setting. The trails are mainly used for mountain biking; however, hikers do enjoy exploring the forested area.

Raymond Trail (Map 33/F4)
The trailhead for this moderate 7 km (4.3 mi) trail can be found off the side of Skeleton Lake Road 1 north of the general store. The trail follows the road for some distance before following the old right of way through forest cover, which turns vibrant with colour in the fall. This route tracks part of the former colonization road from Parry Sound to Skeleton Lake.

Recollet Falls Trail [French River] (Map 49/D1)
Situated beside one of Ontario's most historic waterways, the Recollet Falls Trail is a moderately difficult hike that spans a return trip distance of 3 km (1.9 mi). As the name suggests, the falls and river are main feature of the trail, which is located at the Highway 69/French River junction.

Restoule Provincial Park Trails (Map 61/F7)

Restoule Provincial Park is located south of Lake Nipissing at the end of Highway 534. There are three trails, the longest of which is the 8 km (5 mi) trek to an old fire tower with great views of Patterson Lake. The most popular trail is a 3 km (1.9 mi) walk along the Restoule River. Angels Point Trail is a series of connected loops totaling 3.5 km (2.2 mi). Designed originally as the roads for a new section of campground, they now serve as fine biking or walking paths.

Ridge Road Trail (Map 53/C4)

The Ridge Trail is an exhilarating ride along an easy 19 km (12 mi) path, incorporating old logging roads throughout the Almaguin Highlands. The route begins at the Algonquin Provincial Park access point on Kawawaymog Lake. Visitors can park vehicles there and use the area as a base for trips. From the access point, the route takes cyclists and more recently ATVers past a number of small, semi-wilderness lakes and through some quiet forests. The route also passes the trailhead to the Tower Trail, which can be a fun side trip.

Rogers Reservoir Conservation Area Trails (Map 7/F6)

Rogers Reservoir is located on the banks of the Holland River off Green Lane and Concession Road 2. The area is 39 hectares in size and offers a series of small, easy hiking trails throughout the natural setting of the conservation area and along the old Newmarket Canal. The trails also pass through wetland areas and past the reservoir leading to a fun swing bridge over the lock.

Rossmore Trail (Map 13/E4)

Volunteers from Rossmore have created a nice 1 km trail leading from the Rossmore Park on County Road 28 through to the Bay Breeze Estates.

Russ' Creek Trail (Map 11/G4–5) (NT

This walk has some uncommon flora and fauna along its forested and grass prairie portions. The 5 km (3.1 mi) route travels through an area that was farmed in the distant past. Keep to the left when the track forks, 0.5 km after crossing Dunbar Road. The trailhead is found on Russ' Creek Road, 1 km south of County Road 29 on Covert Hill Road.

Samuel de Champlain Provincial Park (Map 64/B2)

This park rests on the Mattawa River north of Highway 17. It offers three separate trail systems providing different native and natural history experiences. The short, interpretive Forestry Research Trail offers a look at the work that researchers do in the field while the Kag Trail, at just less than 2 km, covers a range of elevations that make it a moderately difficult hike. The 17 km (10.5 mi) Etienne Brule Trail network is a series of loops that are coloured coded with a corresponding category of geology, nature, history and ecology. It is mostly a natural trail, but there are boardwalk sections and there are some difficult sections that require good footwear. The many climbs are rewarded with magnificent views.

Santa's Village Cycling Centre (Map 33/G7)

Santa's Village offers over 25 km (15.5 mi) of mountain biking trails from May 17 to the first weekend in September. There is a marginal fee for use of the trails as well as bike rentals if needed. The trails vary in difficulty and provide plenty of opportunities for all levels of experience.

Scanlon Creek Conservation Area Trails (Map 7/D5)

Scanlon Creek can be accessed on Concession Road 9, east off Highway 11. The conservation area protects 281 hectares of forest and meadows and has a large picnic area with washroom facilities. The area offers 13 km (8.1 mi) of easy to moderate trails that are used for hiking, biking, cross-country skiing and snowshoeing. The trails travel through open fields and mixed forests and traverse past the Scanlon Reservoir. Wildflowers in the spring and the fall colours attract many visitors.

Scout's Valley Trails (Map 15/F3)

The Scout's Valley Trails is a small collection of easy trails found just outside of Orillia. Parking is available off the 15th Line and the Old Barrie Road.

Seaton Hiking Trail (Map 2/E3)

Named after the planned community of Seaton, which was envisioned in the 1970's to accompany the new airport planned for the area, the Seaton Trail is located along West Duffins Creek. It runs for 12.9 km (8 mi) from 3rd Concession near Brock Road northwest to Highway 7 at Green River. In pioneer times, the creek and valley became the site of several water powered mills and a former grist mill stills exists at Whitevale.

Seguin Trail (Map 32/D2–43/C6)

The Seguin Trail is part of an old railway line that stretched from Ottawa to the Georgian Bay. The trail runs 61 km (38 mi) from the Highway 69/400 access point at the Parry Sound Visitor Centre to the Fern Glen Road, west of Highway 11. The route can also be accessed from the many access points along Highway 518. This rustic trail is a popular snowmobile and ATV route and is becoming increasingly used for hiking, biking and horseback riding, especially in the stretch closer to Highway 69/400. It is also well groomed for cross-country skiing and snowshoeing. The geography of this great trail is based in the beautiful Canadian Shield, where visitors will travel over rocky areas, through dense forest and past many lakes and wetland areas. Please avoid trespassing on private property and practice low impact camping at all times to ensure that future users can enjoy the beauty of the trail as well.

Selwyn Conservation Area Trail (Map 18/G5)

The undeveloped northern portion of the conservation area offers a nice hiking/cross-country ski trail. This easy route passes through wetland areas, open fields and mixed forest next to Upper Chemong Lake.

Seymour Conservation Area Trail (Map 12/C2)

As well as an educational interpretive centre, visitors can explore the moderate 6.5 km (4 mi) Quarry Trail. This loop trail starts at the parking lot and circumnavigates a body of water. It is found 3 km south on County Road 30 from Campbellford.

Shawanaga Trail (Map 40/C4–G2)

The Shawanaga Trail is a semi-wilderness route that begins near the Shawanaga River at Highway 69 and stretches all the way to the settlement of Ardbeg at the end of Highway 520. Future plans for the trail will have a section of the route beginning near the Point au Baril Community Centre. The total distance of the route is about 52 km (32 mi) return. The eastern and western sections follow old roads, although the middle section is still difficult and quite rough. The trail winds through many picturesque kilometres of the southern Canadian Shield landscape and passes numerous lakes and wetland areas. The route also passes through an important deeryard where a large herd of deer gathers during winter months. Rustic camping is available along the trail, which is used by snowmobilers in winter.

Shields-McLaren Conservation Area (Map 63/E2)

The McLaren Family donated the conservation area to the North Bay-Mattawa Conservation Authority in 1993. The area is about 61 hectares in size and offers users some informal hiking trails and a chance to learn about the local logging history and trading activities. The easy trails meander through a mixed forest setting, highlighting historical and natural points of interest. Shields-McLaren Conservation Area is located on Lake Road, off Highway 17, east of North Bay.

Silent Lake Provincial Park Trails (Map 28/E2–3)

This park lies 24 km to the south of Bancroft on the south side of Highway 28. Its mixture of hardwood and softwood forests, as well as marshes, host three mountain bike loops, the longest of which is 12 km (7.5 mi). The trails get progressively more difficult as the distance increases. The same can be said for the three hiking trails that range from the easy 1.5 km Lakehead Loop to the moderate 3 km Bonnie's Pond Trail or the Lakeshore Trail that stretches 15 km (9.3 mi) around the lake while offering some beautiful views from lookouts. Bonnie's Pond Trail is accessed from the Pincer Bay parking lot.

Simcoe County Trails (Map 14/F6)

The Simcoe County Trails are found on the site of the old tree nursery just west of Midhurst. Parking is available at the administration buildings. There are over 6 km (3.7 mi) of trails that allow visitors to explore the old nursery.

Sir Sam's Inn/Eagle Lake Trails (Map 36/C5)

Sir Sam's Inn, located on beautiful Eagle Lake, is the starting point for a series of year round trails. During summer the rarely used bush roads are popular mountain biking routes that lead to the top of an open plateau where a great view of Eagle and Moose Lakes is offered. The inn can be found northwest of Haliburton off County Road 6 or County Road 14 on Sir Sam's Road. In all, there are about 31.5 km (19.5 mi) of trails to explore, most of that being the 19 km (11.8 mi) North Road Loop.

Snowdon Park Preserve Trails (Map 26/G3)
The Snowdon Park Preserve is a lush wetland area that is located north of the settlement of Galert off County Road 1. Visitors will find about 3 km (1.9 mi) of easy trails that dissect the wetland and lead to a viewing platform.

Somerville Forest Tract Trails (Map 26/F6)
The Somerville Forest Tract lies about 5 km (3.1 mi) west of the town of Kinmount off the south side of County Road 45. Visitors will find a collection of three loops, which total over 8 km (5 mi) in length. The trails are all generally easy and traverse through mainly mixed forest cover.

South Monck Trail (Map 34/A7)
This trail can be accessed off Ball's Drive by the Bracebridge Shopping Mall. The trail traverses through a mixed forest and along country lanes and can be used by both hikers and bikers. This moderate 7.5 km (4.7 mi) route has steep ascents and descents that can be tricky on a mountain bike.

Springwater Provincial Park Trails (Map 14/F6)
This year round day-use park offers three hiking/cross-country skiing trails totaling 12.4 km (7.7 mi). Facilities at the park include a covered picnic area, washrooms and two log warm up shelters that each furnish a wood stove and a good supply of wood in winter.

Strawberry Bay Point Trail (Map 24/G1)
Next to Lake Muskoka, this scenic 5 km (3.1 mi) hiking trail cuts through an evergreen forest to a lookout area that offers a great panoramic view of the lake. From the lookout area the trail continues to the lake where you can take a refreshing dip or have a picnic. The trail can be accessed at Strawberry Bay Road just off Stephen's Bay Road.

Tay Shore Trail (Map 23/E7–G7)
Totalling 18.5 km (11.5 mi) this railbed trail starts at the Wye River in Tay Township, continues on to Victoria Harbour and then on to Waubaushene before finishing at the Trestle Trail section. This easy, flat, paved trail is designated for multi-purpose, year round, non-motorized activities such as running, walking, cycling and rollerblading in summer as well as snowshoeing and cross-country skiing in the winter.

Theodore Fouriezos Wetlands Park Trails (Map 61/B2)
Located at the Sturgeon River House Museum near the town of Sturgeon Falls, these three interconnecting trails total approximately 3 km (1.9 mi) in length. To find the park, take Leblanc Road south, off Highway 17, to the trail kiosk at the end of Fort Road. Along the route to scenic Cache Bay, you will pass lush wetland environments with a number of viewing platforms to look for waterfowl and other small mammals.

Thomas P. Murray Recreational Trails (Map 47/F6)

Found south of Barry's Bay along Highway 62. There are six trails here, totaling about 16 km (10 mi). The longest trail is Drohan's Trail, at 4.5 km (2.8 mi). Many of the routes are quite challenging, climbing to lookouts and skirting rock outcroppings.

Thompson Forest Loop Trail (Map 23/C6)
This easy 5 km (3.1 mi) loop is situated in the town Penetanguishene just off the harbour on beautiful Georgian Bay. It makes a nice forest walk during most of the year.

Thornton-Cookstown Trail (Map 6/G2–7/A4)
The abandoned rail line that lies between the towns of Cookstown and Thornton offers trail enthusiasts approximately 9 km (5.6 mi) one-way of easy travel. The terrain along the route varies form forest stands to open fields and is ideal for biking or skiing.

Timber Trail (Map 63/G2–64/B2)
Spanning approximately 5 km (3.1 mi), the Timber Trail follows the Mattawa River from the Ecology Centre in Samuel de Champlain Provincial Park to Pimisi Lake in the west. The moderately difficult journey also serves as part of a portage system for paddlers navigating the Mattawa River Canoe Route. Visitors can enjoy the waterfront nature viewing opportunities that exist.

Tiny Trail (Map 14/D3–23/C6)
An extension of the North Simcoe Rail Trail, this 23 km (14 mi) follows County Road 6 from Elmvale before looping north to Penetanguishene. The section along Copeland Creek features over 14 bridges. There are several access points along this easy, multi-use trail.

Torrence Barrens Trail (Map 24/D3)
Torrence Barrens reserve is truly a unique geographical area of Ontario. The landscape of the area resembles something that you would imagine the moon to look like, a barren surface with almost no soil. An easy 2.5 km (1.3 mi) loop trail traverses through this unique area and along a boardwalk around a pond, where the rare Cooper's Hawk and Eastern Bluebird can sometimes be spotted. Visitors will also find a 2.5 km (1.3 mi) trail extension as well as another connecting 3.5 km (2.2 mi) loop. The trailhead is found off Highway 169 on Southwood Road, 2 km past the second railway crossing.

Tower Trail (Map 53/B3)
The Tower Trail can be found off the Forest Access Road northeast of South River. The trail was originally used to travel to a fire tower, which helped monitor forest fire activity in the area. The tower is now gone, but the cement blocks where it used to stand still remain. The 2 km (1.2 mi) trek is somewhat difficult due to the steep ascent.

Trans Canada Trail (Maps 2, 6–15, 17, 20-21, 23-25, 33, 34, 42-43, 52-53, 62)
Once completed, the Trans Canada Trail will extend from coast to coast across all provinces and territories of Canada. In this region, several disjointed sections of the trail are complete. Most of the pathway rests on former railway corridors in and around Highway 7. Because the trail is a multi-use pathway, a wide range of activities are possible, including hiking, biking, horseback riding, cross-country skiing, snowshoeing and, in some places, snowmobiling and ATVing. Much of the trail incorporates existing trail systems into its network, requiring users to be sure their chosen activity is acceptable on a specific portion of trail. Rustic camping and an abundance of side trail possibilities also exist. For more information or an update on the status of the trail in Ontario, call (705) 743-0826 or visit www.tctontario.ca. For national information, call 1-800-465-3636 or visit tctrail.ca.

Trent University Wildlife Sanctuary (Map 19/A7)
This sanctuary was established in 1964 as a migratory bird refuge. Over the years a series of recreation trails has been developed for public use. The main parking lot is located near the Trent University Campus off Nassau Mills Road on University Road. There are a number of short trails here, adding up to over 10 km (6 mi) of trails. The longest trail is only 2.9 km (1.8 mi) long.

Trenton Greenbelt Conservation Area Trail (Map 13/A5)
Located at the Trenton Greenbelt Conservation Area, hikers will find a short, easy hiking path along the Trent Canal. The path is an ideal for a stopping point in Trenton and offers a splendid view of the Trent Canal.

Twentyseven Lake Loop (Map 53/B4)
This loop is best suited for mountain biking or ATV enthusiasts. It spans approximately 15 km (9 mi) along two moderately difficult loops that circle Twentyseven Lake and skirt the shore of Kawawaymog Lake. The trailhead is situated off the Forest Access Road northeast of South River.

Uhthoff Rail Trail (Map 15/F2–24/B7)
The Uhthoff Trail is a 25 km (15.5 mi) one-way route that stretches from the town of Orillia northwest to Coldwater. The trail provides easy travels along an old rail line that passes through a mix of farmland and woodland areas.

Vanderwater Conservation Area Trails (Map 21/E6)
Approximately 15 km (9.3 mi) of easy trails can be found at the Vanderwater Conservation Area, found southeast of Madoc. A longer trail complements a short, 1 km nature interpretation trail called the Cedar Trail. The longer nature trail travels through mature forest areas, open grasslands and scenic views with the highlight of the trip traversing a peaceful mature cedar forest tract. The conservation area entrance is located off Vanderwater Road, not far from Highway 37 and is also a popular cross-country skiing venue.

Victoria Rail Trail Corridor (Map 17/F7–26/G5)

Part of the COLT system, the Victoria Rail Trail originates in the north end of Lindsay, at the top of Williams Street North. There are also many access points along the easy 55 km (34 mi) route that can be traveled all the way to Kinmount. The trail passes through the Ken Reid Conservation Area and over Sturgeon Lake on its route to Fenelon Falls. In summer, the swing bridge over the Trent Canal becomes an exciting addition. From here, the trail follows the shore of Cameron Lake and the Burnt River before leading into the County of Victoria Somerville Forest Tract. The tract is heavily forested and contains some side trails for additional hiking opportunities. The rail line continues north from Kinmount along the Haliburton County Rail Trail.

Warsaw Caves Trails (Map 19/D5)

The Warsaw Caves Conservation Area is located off County Road 4 on Caves Road. It offers over 13 km (8.1 mi) of trails for hiking, snowshoeing or cross-country skiing. The Cave/Scenic Lookout Trail begins at the parking area off Caves Road and is an easy 4 km (2.5 mi) route. The trail leads to the caves and then over the Indian River, although there is no boardwalk. The river passes directly underground at this point and in spring the vibrations of rushing water can sometimes be felt underfoot. Shortly after the trail passes over the river there is a side trail that leads to the kettles area. The Limestone Plain Trail is an easy 7 km (4.2 mi) route that travels along the Indian River for a large portion of the trail.

Wasaga Beach Park/Blueberry Plains Trails (Map 14/A4)

Hidden from the summer fury of beach crazy tourists lies the Blueberry Plains Trails of Wasaga Beach Provincial Park. The trails cover over 26 km (16 mi) and provide hiking in the summer and cross-country skiing in the winter months. There is a trail centre facility marking the beginning of the system that provides detailed information on the various routes. In winter, the facility doubles as a warm up area and offers equipment rentals if needed. The most challenging trail is the High Dunes Trail, which climbs and descends a series of dunes in the area.

Wasaga Beach Trails (Map 14/A4)

Beyond the beaches and the park area, trail enthusiasts have a fine collection of trails to explore. The 20 km (12 mi) Beaches Loop passes a number of beach parks in the area and is a favourite to stroll. The McIntyre Creek Trail follows the creek through a golf course. It is an easy 4 km (2.5 mi) trail. At the east end of Wasaga Beach is Ski Wasaga, a popular cross-country skiing destination in winter that is used in summer by hikers. There is a small trail fee to access the 19 km (12 mi) of interconnected loop trails.

Wasi Cross-Country Ski Club Trails (Map 62/G4–63/A5)

The Wasi Ski Club Trails are located just south of North Bay, not far from Highway 11. To find the club and trails, follow Lake Nosbonsing Road from Highway 11 to the parking lot on the left just before Groulx Road. There are over 45 km (28 mi) of established trails available that were developed for cross-country skiing, but are becoming more popular with hikers. The trails are generally moderate in difficulty, due to the rustic nature of the trail system during summer months. One challenge on the trail system is that some sections can become overgrown and difficult to follow for hikers. For more information, call (705) 476-5717.

Waterfront Trail (Maps 2–5; 12–13)

Launched in 1995, the Waterfront Trail stretches 900 km (560 miles) from Niagara on the Lake all the way to the Quebec boundary. Following the northern and western shorelines of Lake Ontario and the St. Lawrence River, only 30% of the route is official trail. The rest is sidewalk, shoulders of roads and residential streets, while about 120 km (75 miles) of the trail has yet to be completed. The trail is well signed and incorporates 31 communities, almost 200 parks and natural areas and 170 marinas and yacht clubs into its repertoire. Only a portion of the trail is found in this book.

Western Uplands Backpacking Trail (Map 44/D5)

The largest trail system in Algonquin Provincial Park, this popular backpacking route is comprised of three large interconnected loops that span over 100 km (62 mi). The moderate trail is regulated on a quota system and can be accessed from either the Oxtongue River Picnic Area off Highway 60 or from the Rain Lake Access Point at the east side of the park. Call (705) 633-5572 for more information.

Wilno Trail (Map 47/G4)

Beginning at the Wilno Heritage Park, this 8.5 km (5.3 mi) walk incorporates country roads, earth paths and an old railway bed. The moderately difficult journey travels through Wilno Pass, which overlooks the many hills and valleys that are typical of the area. Shrine Hill Lookout is another of the central features of this route, which contains an historical plaque commemorating Wilno as being the first Polish settlement in Canada in 1859. Hikers can also visit the Pioneer Cemetery near the midpoint of the trail. To find the trailhead, follow Highway 60 to the Shrine Hill Lookout and the impressive architecture of St. Mary's Church on Church Street. ATVers and snowmobilers can enjoy the easy route along the railbed that links with Barry's Bay and points further west or east towards Renfrew.

Wilson's Falls Trail (Map 34/A7)

There are three main access points that lead to the picturesque Wilson's Creek Falls. The highlight of the trail is the bridge over the spectacular 12.6 m (41 ft) falls. The first route is the most demanding section and can be accessed at the Macaulay Public School off Cedar Lane. This 2 km (1.2 mi) route is generally easy, although there are some portions that are a little more rugged. The trail can also be accessed off Roger's Road just past Pine Street. From here it is an easy 2 km (1.2 mi) return hike to the falls and the river. The last route follows Wilson Creek Falls Road directly to the falls. This route follows the bank of the Muskoka River and can be hiked or biked over an easy 5 km (3.1 mi).

Woodland Trail (Map 42/A1)

The Woodland Trails are located just south of the town of Magnetawan at the Woodland Echoes Resort. Permission must be obtained for use of the private trails from the resort. The main trail is an easy 2 km (1.2 mi) loop; however, there are a few spur trails that can be explored. The well-maintained trails make their way through a peaceful forest setting and pass near the shore of the Magnetawan River. You can reach the resort entrance by taking Spark Street south in Magnetawan to Victoria Street. For more information on the trail system, call (705) 387-3866.

Wye Marsh Wildlife Centre Trails (Map 23/D7)

The Wye Marsh Wildlife Centre offers a series of interpretative trails for year round use. In the summer a naturalist hosts seminars and for a nominal fee you can access all centre facilities including an enjoyable series of trails. During winter, cross-country skis and snowshoe rentals are available. The longest trail by far is the Fox Trail, a moderate 11.5 km (7.1 mi) loop. The other two easy loops total 4.7 km (3 mi) together.

Yonge Street Trail (Map 34/C1)

This moderate 3 km (1.9 mi) hiking or biking trail travels from Chubb Lake Road to Yonge Street South through a beautiful part of Huntsville. The main access point is approximately 1.2 km (0.7 mi) north on Yonge Street South from Main Street West. The trail passes through some dense forested areas and is frequented by bird watchers.

YMCA Camp Wanakita (Map 27/C1)

Located on the beautiful shores of Koshlong Lake in the Haliburton Highlands, this year round camp and outdoor centre boasts a wealth of facilities to encourage learning and growing in all seasons. Trail enthusiasts will find 25 km of trails for hiking, skiing and biking here.

refer to indicated pages for more map detail

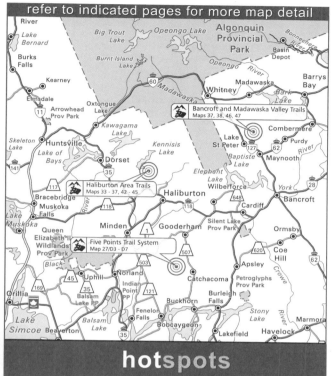

Algonquin Provincial Park

Bancroft and Madawaska Valley Trails
Maps 37, 38, 46, 47

Haliburton Area Trails
Maps 33 - 37, 42 - 45

Five Points Trail System
Map 27/D3 - D7

hot**spots**

▶ ATV/OHV & Snowmobile - Designated/Authorized Trails

OHV (off-highway vehicles) have a variety of designated/authorized trail riding opportunities within this region. Some trails permit the use of ATVs, OHVs and Snowmobile (Motorized Trails), while others are designated for ATV or Snowmobile use only. Other trail riding can be found in the multi-use part of the trail section so be sure to check that out for some other great adventures.

Line styles on the maps:

––––––––––   Snowmobile Trails (winter only)

– – – – – –   Motorized Trails (ATV/OHV/Snowmobile)

ATVs are quickly becoming a popular recreational pastime throughout Ontario. In response to this increased popularity, ATV clubs, organizations and trail systems continue to be developed. The results are impressive and the local HATVA system of over 3,000 km (1,800 miles) is the second biggest ATV system in the country.

In order to ride on ATV Ontario Trails or the Regional Trails of HATVA (including riding areas around the Haliburton, Kawartha, Madawaska, Muskoka and Peterborough) you need an ATV Ontario Power Pass (available from www.atvontario.com) or a Haliburton or Kawartha Club Membership riding pass. Confusingly, there is also an Ontario Federation of All Terrain Vehicles (OFATV) and Eastern Ontario TTN Gold Trail permits. These do not work in the HATVA area. Riders need to check ahead with the local club before heading out to avoid fines for riding the trails without proper passes.

The Ontario Federation of All Terrain Vehicles (OFATV) website has a comprehensive listing of clubs and trails and can be found at www.ofatv.org. Another useful website is www.gorideontario.com which has information for all motorized trail users. Most clubs also provide detailed maps of the trail systems which are updated annually. All of the clubs in Ontario work together with local landowners, the local community and all levels of government in an effort to address any problems as well as to promote the maintenance and expansion of existing trails. Many of their websites have current updates regarding open trails or trail conditions as well as notices or warnings.

The trails in this area include a mix of roads and rails-to-trails. Because these trails exist within the confines of the Canadian Shield, users can expect a rocky ride along some jagged and hilly terrain. Muddy areas abound the landscape, as trapped water is common, especially in spring and after heavy rainfalls. It is important for ATVers to stay on designated trails and roadways, as the damage these machines do to the environment and local ecosystems when left to run amuck is well documented, particularly in sensitive wetland habitats. Riders should also be wary of other trail users, especially on multi-use trail systems.

Since the implementation of Bill 11, ATV users can also now travel on the shoulders of most roads in the HATVA catchment area of Haliburton, Almaguin and Madawaska, allowing easier travel than ever before. For the most part, though, roads in Muskoka, Kawartha and Peterborough are not open.

Algonquin West (34–36, 42–45, 52, 53)

Part of the HATVA catchment, this area extends from Haliburton north to South River and offers over 250 km of trails to enjoy. In addition to extended riding west of Highway 11 in the Kearney area, the Park to Park and a nice loop north from Livingstone Lake around Luck Lake are popular riding areas. Visit the Algonquin West ATV Club www.algonquinwestatv.com for more information.

Ahmic Lake Trail (Map 41/F2–42/B2)

From the town of Ahmic Harbour, the 42 km (26 mile) moderate trail heads southeast along Ahmic Lake. Follow the signs until meeting the Old Nipissing "Ghost Road" at Spence where a turn to the left (east) will take you north past the cemetery and onwards to Magnetawan. Take County Road 520 northwest to the junc-

Image © Shutterstock

tion of Highway 124 where it is required to drive on the paved shoulder. Both the scenic Knoepfli Falls and the Fagan Falls on the Magnetawan River are visible before finishing back in Ahmic Harbour. Information can be found at www.discoveryroutes.ca.

Anten Mills Area Forest Trail (Map 14/E5)
Sandwiched between Wasaga Beach and Highway 400, the area around Anten Mills offers a few good riding areas. To the southeast of town, there is an easy 9 km (5.2 mile) trail that passes through a tall pine forest with sandy soil. Northwest of town, the Phelpston Forest Trail is a newly cut trail that offers about 10 km (6 miles) of riding. It is a little more challenging of a riding area.

Bancroft and Madawaska Valley Trails (Maps 37, 38, 46, 47)
From Bancroft north to Barry's Bay and west to Whitney, riders will find over 400 km of trails to explore. These include abandoned railways south of the Madawaska River and north of Barry's Bay, fire roads between Whitney and Lake St. Peter and the Thomas P. Murray Recreation Trails near Combermere. ATV users can also travel on the shoulders of most roads in the Madawaska Valley allowing easier travel than ever before. Part of the HATVA/ATV Ontario network, expect to find plenty of hills, wetlands and sharp turns to keep users of all experience levels satisfied. The Madawaska ATV club has a website at www.madatvclub.com, while the North Hastings ATV Association in Lake St. Peter also has information at www.northhastingsatv.com.

Baxter Riders ATV Trails (Map 23/F4)
Located in Port Severn, this club is part of the OFATV and is actively expanding its current system of approximately 40 km (25 mi) of permit required trails. Most of the trails are off road but there are some road connections between trails. Information on trails and membership is at www.baxteratvriders.comze.com.

Brentwood and Lawden Forest Trails (Map 6/A1-B2)
The Brentwood Forest offers a short, easy trail that is managed by the Central Ontario ATV Club. The 7 km (4.3 mile) trail runs through a pine forest with sandy soil to the west of Barrie. To the west riders will find the Lawden Forest Trail along Centre Line Road south of Wasaga Beach. This trail is only 5 km (3 miles) long and provides easy riding on a sandy trail through a pine forest. The ATV club can be found online at www.coatv.ca.

Deep River, Mattawa, Petawawa Area Trails (Maps 63–67)
Part of the ATV Ontario system, the Mattawa area has a fairly extensive series of ATV trails, totalling approximately 150 km (93 miles). The well-marked trails complement the network of logging roads that also present some distinct ATVing possibilities. They encompass the area around Kearney, Cahill and Purdy Lakes as well as Antoine Creek north of the Mattawa River. For more information on the ATV trail system, call the Voyageur Multi Use Trail System at 1-800-819-6888 or online at www.vmuts.com.

Five Points Trail System (Map 27/E5)
Called the granddaddy of all Crown land trail systems in Ontario, this popular system links the Haliburton and Kawartha Districts. The trails can be accessed west of Gooderham or several points to the south as it runs parallel to Highway 507. There are literally hundreds of square kilometres of every kind of trail imaginable within this system. In fact, the area has long been used by off-road motorcycle riders. Bring extra gas, a GPS and waterproof boots when exploring this vast area.

Haliburton Area Trails (Maps 33–37, 42–45)
Haliburton ATV Association has the largest mapped, signed and insured trail system in Ontario. In fact the HATVA Trails extend beyond Haliburton and into Muskoka, Kawartha, Peterborough and Madawaska regions offering over 3,000 km (1,800 miles) to explore. The trails include a mix of roads and rails-to-trails as well as more remote and challenging trails leading deep into the wilderness. The trails west of Highway 35 link Queen Elizabeth II Wildlands with the Frost Centre between Minden and Dorset. To the east of the highway are extended trails leading in all directions around Gooderham and Haliburton. The Haliburton Rail Trail and rail trail leading east to Gooderham access many of the trails in the east. As an added bonus, ATVers can also now travel on the shoulders of most roads in the Haliburton area. For a detailed list of Haliburton Highland area trails visit www.haliburtonatv.com.

IB & O Rail Trail (Map 35/B1–37/A7)
South of Wilberforce, this trail can be accessed from the intersection of Essonville Line (County Road 4) and Farr Road. Following the former railway line south to Gooderham, this 14 km (8.7 mile) multi-use trail is relatively flat and easy. It has some forested areas with rocky outcrops as well as some nice wetland areas to pass through. The wetlands become very muddy and challenging to ride after heavy rains or during spring thaw season and this trail is not recommended at these times.

Kawartha Area Trails (Maps 17–19, 25–28)
Between Peterborough and Haliburton, this area is home to many great riding areas including The Five Points Trail System, Somerville Forest and Victoria Rail Trail. A Kawartha ATV Association Membership pass gives access to all of the City of Kawartha Lakes riding areas as well as the HATVA system leading into the surrounding areas. A list of specific trails within these areas is found at www.kawarthaatv.com. Unfortunately, most roads in the Kawarthas are not open to ATV riders.

Kingston/Belleville Trails (Maps 13, 21)
While Kingston is east of our maps (see the Eastern Ontario Backroad Mapbook), the section of trail around Belleville offers some good riding. The terrain is mostly flat, although if you head north and east, to the areas north of Roslin, the landscape begins to become more rugged as the limestone base gives way to the less forgiving granite of the Canadian Shield. The Napanee and District ATV club can be found on the web at www.ndatvclub.org.

Madawaska Highlands Trails (Maps 37, 38, 46, 47, 57)
The area known as the Madawaska Highlands encompasses roughly from Bancroft in the west, Algonquin Provincial Park in the north, Carleton Place in the east and Sharbot Lake in the south, most of which is off these maps and can be found in the Eastern Ontario Backroad Mapbook. Still, the rocky, Canadian Shield north of Bancroft makes for great hills and forested logging roads and side trails to explore. Many of these bumpy corridors lead to scenic lakes and hidden fishing spots to complement ATV use. These trails are part of the Eastern Ontario Trail system, not HATVA.

Miserable Lake Trail (Map 27/B3)
Branching from the Haliburton Rail Trail along Milburn Road, this is a short but challenging trail to a lookout near the south end of Miserable Lake.

North Bay Area Trails (Maps 48–52, 58–62)
Spreading from the urban region of North Bay, this area is a rugged land of various forest settings that is commonly frequented by ATVers. In addition to the French River region, riders often explore the area north of Killarney Provincial Park to find more solitude. There are plenty of logging roads for users to discover without straying from established pathways. Most of the riding areas can be accessed via the major highways in the area, including Highways 69, 17, 11, 64 and 68. The West Nipissing ATV club has information at www.wnatvclub.com.

Northumberland County Forest (Map 11/E5–6)
A large forested area with 30 km (18.6 mile) of dedicated motorized trails. There are two separate staging areas for motorized trail users as well as parking lots for non-motorized users. Details of the forest as a whole can be found at www.northumberlandcounty.ca while the local ATV club information is located at www.northumberlandatvriders.com.

Outhouse Trail (Map 26/C3–35/C7)
From the Scotch Line Road northwest of Minden, this trail skirts the top of the Queen Elizabeth II Park along a hydro corridor. Beyond Beer Lake, the remote trail continues north to Highway 18 along the Regional Snowmobile Trail 6. It is possible to continue north on the Beaverdam Trail leading to the Frost Centre, but this requires crossing Anson Creek. There are several by-passes on the trail due to swampy areas.

Park to Park Trail (Map 32/B1–43/A6)
The Park to Park Trail links Algonquin Provincial Park in the east to Killbear Provincial Park on Georgian Bay, a distance of 75 km (46 miles). Most of the route follows the multi-use Seguin Trail and is the most popular ATV trail in the Parry Sound area. However, certain sections are closed to ATV use. Check www.parktoparktrail.com for more information.

Wildman Forest ATV Trail (Map 14/B2)
North of Wasaga Beach is another fine riding area to explore. This 15 km (9 mile) trail is northeast of Elmvale and passes through a scenic forest. The trail hooks up with the Tiny Trail, although only riders who purchase a Tiny Trail Pass can ride on the Tiny Trail.

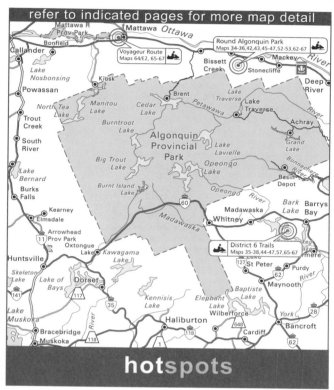

refer to indicated pages for more map detail

Round Algonquin Park
Maps 34-36,42,43,45-47,52-53,62-67

Voyageur Route
Maps 64/E2, 65-67

District 6 Trails
Maps 35-38,44-47,57,65-67

hotspots

Snowmobile trails span from one corner of the province to the other providing recreational riding and in some cases the main mode of transportation in winter. It is possible to travel thousands of kilometres on snowmobile trails in Cottage Country alone. In fact, is not uncommon to see snowmobiles used as the main method of transportation from town to town and even (on occasion) in town.

The Ontario Federation of Snowmobile Clubs (OFSC) has brought together snowmobile clubs from around Ontario in an effort to standardize and expand snowmobiling trail opportunities. To date the OFSC trail system spans over 34,000 km (21,000 mi) and include the OFSC Trans Ontario Provincial (TOP) Trails as well as local club trails. A great resource for finding the status of these official trails is through the interactive map, which is found at http://ofsc.mapbase.ca/viewer/

All users travelling on an OFSC trail must have a valid trail permit, which can be picked up at most local snowmobile retailers and outdoor stores. A permit grants you access to any OFSC trail in the province, but you should purchase it from the club in the district which you ride in most because that is the area's main source of funding for trail grooming and maintenance.

The trails in this book cover seven OFSC Districts: 2, 3, 6, 7, 8, 10 and 11. Each club and/or district has their own website where you can find more information on services and accommodations, poker rides and social events and, on occasion, the local hot spots and trail conditions.

In addition to the groomed and well signed trails, there are select Crown land riding areas along old roads and trails. Frozen lakes are also often used by all winter adventurers. While they are dangerous if not frozen solid (and some lakes don't ever freeze solid), frozen lakes can provide great opportunities for winter recreation. Snowmobilers, too, can access new terrain or even tour the lakes themselves. However before venturing over the ice, be sure to test the thickness to ensure it is safe. Snowmobilers should also note that ecological reserves, private property and most provincial parks are off limits.

Given the potential danger of extreme weather and motorized travel, it is important to familiarize yourself with local rules and conditions. A good resource for safety tips is this OFSC webpage: www.ofsc.on.ca/go-snowmobiling/preparing-for-your-first-ride/safety-tips. You should also review the standardize hand signals as described at www.ccso-ccom.ca/handsigs.

ATV/OHV & Snowmobile - Designated/Authorized Trails

OHV (off-highway vehicles) have a variety of designated/authorized trail riding opportunities within this region. Some trails permit the use of ATVs, OHVs and Snowmobile (Motorized Trails), while others are designated for ATV or Snowmobile use only. Other trail riding can be found in the multi-use part of the trail section so be sure to check that out for some other great adventures.

Line styles on the maps:

- - - - - - - - Snowmobile Trails (winter only)

- - - - - - - - Motorized Trails (ATV/OHV/Snowmobile)

District 2 Trails (Maps 9–11, 17–21, 26–30, 35–38)

District 2 comprises the area north of Highway 7 from Lindsay eastward, stretching north almost to Algonquin Provincial Park. There are 8 well established clubs operating in the district and most do a great job grooming the more than 2,000 km (1,250 miles) of trails. This area is not nearly as busy as neighbouring District 3, but the snow tends to be better and the landscape more scenic thanks to glacial activity.

Bancroft Area (Maps 29, 38)

The Old Hastings Snow Riders maintain more than 400 km (250 miles) of trails in this snowy and beautiful area. Visit www.bancroftoldhastings.com for trail conditions and more information.

Image © Shutterstock

One nice daytrip in this area is to take Trail 930 northeast from the clubhouse (near L'Amable) to the B106E Trail and then eastward on the E Trunk Trail. Turn south on Trail 910 and follow it until you reach Trail 951 and head west for a few kilometres until the trail ends at the 960. Take a short jog north and then turn onto the 950 and cross Mephisto and Limerick Lakes. The trail ends at the E106, which you should take northwest until you get to the E Trunk Trail. Head due west until just after Coe Hill, where you catch the start of the 930, which brings you back to the clubhouse.

Bobcaygeon Area (Maps 18, 27)

This is a compact area with a small, but great network of trails looping for a total of 130 km (80 miles) or so between Pigeon Lake and Crystal Lake. Visit www.twinmountainssc.ca for trail conditions and more information.

Bon Echo Area (Maps 21, 29, 30)

This is a beautiful and remote area, with few roads and even fewer human settlements. However, the Mazinaw Powerline Snowmobile Club does a decent job of maintaining some 350 km (220 miles) of trails. Be aware that once you leave Cloyne, it's a long way to the next fuel or service stop. Visit www.mazinawpowerline.ca for trail conditions and more information.

A popular route is the Cloyne to Bancroft Loop (Maps 29, 30, 38). This route will take you on a full day of sledding. Take the E101 north from Cloyne to the E Trunk Trail, which you head east on. You can either head south again on the 938 or head to Bancroft for gas or lunch, which is about 13 km (8 miles) up the B106E (and then backtrack west along the E Trunk Trail to the 938). Take the 938 to Trail 960 and turn west. Follow the 960 for a good while until you reach Trail 1009, which takes you through some amazing country before bringing you back to the E101 just south of Cloyne.

Buckhorn Area (Maps 17, 18)

The Buckhorn District snowmobile trail system is quite popular due to its close proximity to the metro Toronto area. Some fantastic trails can be found in the region, which include everything from open travel across large Kawartha lakes to woodland travel to secluded backcountry lakes. The system spans form the town of Buckhorn north all the way to Gooderham, with plenty of spots to get gas and food. There are around 200 km (125 miles) of very well-maintained trails, mostly branching off of the main routes going north from the clubhouse just outside of Buckhorn. You can do a nice 50+ km (30 mile) loop north of Buckhorn, but to really get out and experience the terrain, jump onto the Twin Mountains Trails to the west and do a much larger loop. Visit www.bdsc.ca for trail conditions and more information.

Haliburton Area (Maps 26–28, 35–37)

This area offers some of the more remote trail systems found in Cottage Country. Riders can explore hidden lakes or, if they prefer, spend the day out on some of the more popular routes. The region is characterized by the rugged terrain of the Canadian Shield, with plenty of opportunity to find lake travel or stopover for a great day of ice fishing. The main club in the area is the Haliburton County Snowmobile Association offering about 350 km (220 miles) of well-groomed trails. The trail system links numerous towns including Norland, Minden and Haliburton. Visit www.hcsa.on.ca for trail conditions and more information.

Haliburton County Rail Trail (Maps 26, 27, 36)

A popular alternative in the Haliburton area is the 36 km (20 mi) one-way route along an old rail bed between the towns of Haliburton and Kinmount. One of the highlights of the route is Ritchie Falls, which is found south of the village of Lochlin.

Haliburton Forest Snowmobiling Trails (Maps 35, 36, 44)

This private trail network offers seemingly endless riding around the forest and many secluded lakes. The region is quite isolated with little development on most of its backcountry lakes. In addition to a fee to ride here, there are also numerous facilities available for visitors including accommodations. For snow conditions call 1-800-267-4482.

Havelock Area (Maps 19, 20)

The Havelock & District is a small club that maintains around 150 km (90 miles) of trails, mostly north of Highway 7. A nice option is the Top Trail E108 (Maps 9–12, 20, 21), which trail takes you on an arcing route past some lakes with good ice fishing prospects and near Petroglyphs Provincial Park. You can drop down on a connector trail to Stonyridge for fuel or a bite to eat.

Kawartha Lakes Area (Maps 8–10, 16–18)

While the snow may fall a little later in the season for this area, there are still some fabulous snowmobiling opportunities in the Kawarthas. TOP Trails span from as far south as Rice Lake and trek north all the way to Bobcaygeon and Fenelon Falls. The systems are well marked and are an easy drive from metro Toronto. The local snowmobile club, 900 members strong, has been recognized as the top snowmobile club in both Ontario and Canada in recent years. They groom more than 200 km (125 miles) of trails. Visit www.klsc.ca for trail conditions and more information.

A favourite here is the Victoria Rail Trail Corridor (Maps 17/F7–26/G5). This rail trail originates in the north end of Lindsay, at the top of Williams Street North. The route can be travelled a total of 55 km (34 mi) all the way to Kinmount and makes for an ideal family snowmobile outing. Be aware that the speed limits are regularly enforced along this popular trail.

Kawartha Highlands (Maps 19, 27–28, 36–37)

This rugged area has some great trails that are groomed by the Paudash Trail Blazers, who look after 350 km (220 miles) of snowy fun as well as the Stoney Lake Sno Riders, who have 225 km (140 miles) of trails. The Paudash Trail system lies just to the west of Bancroft and stretches between the towns of Bancroft, Wilberforce and Apsley. Since these trails are a little further from metro Toronto, they receive less use compared to their Muskoka or Kawartha counterparts. This portion of Cottage Country is also one of the first areas to receive a good enough base of snow for riding and one of the last areas to lose it. Visit www.paudashtrailblazers.on.ca or www.stoneylakesnoriders.ca for trail conditions and more information.

District 3 Trails (Maps 2–5, 8–13, 16–17, 20–21)

District 3 comprises the area south and east of Lake Simcoe, running all the way to Tweed and Picton at the east edge of our maps (and a little beyond). There are 11 clubs in the area and over 2,000 km (1,250 miles) of often busy trails. The area features the rolling hills of Northumberland, forests and wide open countryside and farmland. The Ganaraska Forest and the Northumberland Forest get more snow than most areas in the district and are usually open sooner than the other areas too. One of the highlights of the region is the old railway bridge crossing the Trent River at Hastings. The refurbished bridge is 130 metres (400 feet) long and 18 metres (50 feet) high and now forms an important trail link through the district. In fact, many of the trails in the district are old rail grades and offer easy, family friendly riding.

Lake Scugog Area (Maps 8, 9)

These trails can be accessed quite easily from the large population centres to the south, so they can get quite busy. There are three clubs (Cartwright Dynos, Long Sault Snowmobile Club and Port Perry Snowmobile Club) in the immediate area who maintain a small number of easy trails. Visit www.cartwrightdynos.com, www.longsaultsnowmobileclub.com or www.portperrysnowmobileclub.com for trail conditions and more information.

Lake Simcoe Area (Maps 8, 9, 16, 17)

The area between Lake Scugog and Lake Simcoe is the domain of the Heart of Ontario Snowmobile Club. Their trails radiate out from the clubhouse in Cannington (where they recently built a snowmobile bridge over the Beaver River), stretching from Uxbridge to Fenelon Falls. Visit www.heartofontario.ca for trail conditions and more information.

Madoc Area (Maps 20, 21)

The Tweed Snow Scooters and the Centre Hastings Snowmobile Club look after the trails on either side of Highway 7 around Madoc and Tweed. There aren't a lot of club trails, but there are good access points for jumping onto on the E106, E108 and E212 TOP system. Visit www.centrehastingssnowmobileclub.ca for trail conditions and more information.

Rice Lake Area (Maps 10, 11)

There is a set of trails running between Highway 35 and Bewdley that are maintained by the Ganaraska Snowmobile Club. Although this is a fairly small area, there are numerous trails totalling more than 200 km (125 miles). The Ganaraska Forest remains one of the more popular areas, while other trails extend north and into the Rice Lake Snow Drifters area. This club has trails that extend to Peterborough and Highway 7, as well as a very popular trail along virtually the whole stretch of Rice Lake. On the east side of Rice Lake, the Great Pine Ridge Snowmobile Association has a further 200 km of trails branching off the E108. Visit www.ganaraskasnow.ca, www.ricelakesnowdrifters.com or gosledding.ca for trail conditions and more information.

Trent River Area (Maps 12, 13)
The Percy Boom River Rats do a great job of maintaining a few hundred kilometers of trails that straddle the Trent River from Trenton to Rice Lake. Visit www.percyboomriverrats.com for trail conditions and more information.

Top Trail E108 (Maps 9–12, 20, 21)
This trail is the main trail in the area that runs the length of the district connecting Tweed all the way to Port Perry and beyond. Nearly all of the trails in the district connect up to this one at one point or another.

District 4 Trails (Maps 1, 6, 7, 14, 15, 22–24)
District 4 sits at the northeast corner of Greater Toronto, linking Lake Simcoe to the Niagara Escarpment. This guide only covers the northern reaches of the 900 km (560 miles) of trails in the district. Although the trails, for the most part, don't get the impressive snowfalls that Districts 7 and 8 to the north do, there is some fine open riding on mainly farmland. Please stay on the trail or risk alienating the partnerships with the local farmers and ruining things for everyone else. You can get trail information and conditions for a number of the clubs from the Huronia Snowmobile Southern Zone Grooming Association (www.hssz.org).

Alliston Area (Maps 6, 7)
There are two clubs in this area: Alliston and District Snowmobile Club and Bonsecour Track and Trail. A popular option is the Thornton-Cookstown trail (Maps 6/G2–7/A4) that follows along an old abandoned rail line for about 9 km (5.6 mi) one-way between the towns of Cookstown and Thornton. If you want to plan a more extensive trip, consider including some of the Barrie Snowmobile Club Trails in your itinerary as well. Visit www.adsc.ca for trail conditions and more information.

Georgina Area (Maps 7, 8)
There are two clubs in this area: Georgina Trail Riders and Holland. Their trail network is quite modest, mainly serving as a way to access the Bonsecour or Heart of Ontario Club Trails (and beyond) from Newmarket or Keswick. Visit www.hlsc.on.ca for trail conditions and more information.

District 6 Trails (Maps 35–38, 44–47, 57, 65–67)
This dynamic district covers the area from Renfrew west to Deux-Rivieres and south to Bancroft and Haliburton/Minden, including the scenic Ottawa Valley and Madawaska Highlands. There are over 4,000 km (2,500 miles) of trails available to ride, including both TOP and club trails, with many loop and long distance tour rides available. From rolling farmlands to mixed forest areas with scenic vantage points to abandoned rail lines there is plenty to see and do here. Adding to the appeal of the area are lots of services and accommodations available along the trails. For information and trail conditions, visit www.snowcountrycsa.ca. Note that some District 6 clubs are not in the Snow Country Association.

Algonquin Snowtrail [B Trunk Trail] (Maps 35/G7–47/A5)
This trail stretches from Barry's Bay to the east all the way to Carnarvon in the west (it's actually a part of the massive B Trunk Trail that extends all the way to the Bruce Peninsula). One of the highlights of this trail system is the powerline trail through the southern panhandle of Algonquin Provincial Park. This is the only place in the park where public snowmobile use is acceptable. Take care making the crossing, as there are no services within the park.

Bancroft/Barry's Bay/Whitney Area (Maps 37, 38, 46, 47)
This beautiful piece of Ontario falls southeast of Algonquin Provincial Park. It is an area defined by rolling hills, marshy flatlands and the western extremity of the Ottawa Valley near Barry's Bay. Part of the Snow Country or District 6 trails, there is plenty of snow here to keep both snowmobilers and anglers looking for that secluded lake satisfied. The Maple Leaf Snow Skimmers, who groom and maintain more than 300 km (190 miles) of trails radiating out from Lake St. Peter, are one of the main clubs in the area. Visit www.snowskimmers.com for trail conditions and more information.

Route B106E (Maps 38/ B7–46/A5)
This trail is a main connector trail, linking the Bancroft area in the south to Whitney near the eastern edge of Algonquin Park. Beginning from L'Amable south of Bancroft, snowmobile enthusiasts will head northwest, travelling through Birds Creek, Maynooth and Lake St. Peter

before reaching Whitney. The route loosely follows Highway 62 and County Road 127, although the vast majority of the route offers seclusion and a wilderness feel.

Route D102B (Maps 34/D5, 43/E6)
This trail is a TOP Connector Trail that spans approximately 60 km (37 mi) in a north/south direction, linking Baysville with an area southeast of Kearney. Most of the route travels across a rustic environment, taking in the settlements of Newholm, Grassmere and Williamsport before connecting to Route D101B, just southeast of Hart Lake.

Route E109 (Maps 37/C4–47/E4)
This trail connects Elephant Lake and Lake St. Peter in the south to Barry's Bay at the junction of Highway 60 and 62. From Elephant Lake, just south of the southern tip of the southern panhandle of Algonquin Provincial Park, the route moves from the rugged landscape of the Canadian Shield to the rolling hills and flatter lands of the Ottawa Valley en route to Barry's Bay.

District 7 Trails (Maps 23–25, 32–35, 42–44)
District 7 comprises the justly famous land between Highway 11 and 400, better known as the Muskoka. With 1,600 km (1,000 miles) of trails, there are some fantastic sledding opportunities. It is also one of the largest snowmobile regions in Cottage Country and offers a variety routes that include a mix of remote backcountry runs to mainline runs between small towns. Some of the towns that can be visited in this region include Port Severn, Gravenhurst, Bracebridge, Baysville and Huntsville. The Muskoka Snowmobile Region is the large association in the district that is made up of nine clubs. In addition there are clubs based south of Huntsville in Port Sydney, the Hill & Gully Riders and the Snowcrest Riders in Gravenhurst. Visit the relevant site for more information and current trail conditions: www.msrsnowtrails.com, www.hgrsnowmobileclub.on.ca, or snowcrestriders.com.

Around Lake Muskoka (Maps 24–25, 33–34)
Using some of the local club trails and the TOP trails, you can do a memorable loop around Lake Muskoka. If you are more ambitious, a route to Lake Joseph can be added; as can a run along the well-known Seguin Trail.

District 8 Trails (Maps 6–7, 14–16, 22–25)
District 8 runs between Nottawasga Bay and Lake Simcoe, from Barrie up to the Muskoka or District 7 area. This is one of smaller districts that benefits from the "lake effect" with lots of snow and mostly easily accessible trails. The highlighted centres of this region include Collingwood, Barrie, Midland and Orillia. The region rivals the Kawarthas as the most popular snowmobiling destination in Cottage Country. There is one large association of five clubs, Mid Ontario Snowmobile Trails (MOST) and three independent clubs, two of which are in the coverage area for this guide: Georgian Bay Snowriders and Orillia Snowmobile Club (who have a very cool website that lets you view the groomers' progress on their trails). Trail systems are well groomed and well used, making for smooth riding from town to town. Visit www.most.on.ca, www.gbsr.on.ca and www.sledorillia.com.

North Simcoe Rail Trail (Maps 6/F2–23/C6)
Leading north from County Road 90 southwest of Barrie all the way to Penetanguishene, this old rail line stretches approximately 40 km (25 mi) each way. Between Anten Mills and Colwell the trail is 14 km (8.7 mi). This section of the trail begins at Anten Mills on Horseshoe Valley Road and runs south through the Minesing Swamp Conservation Area and a mixed forest area to the Essa Transformer Station near County Road 90.

Oro-Medonte Trail (Maps 15/A7–15/A2)
This trail lies along an old rail bed, which stretches 25 km (15.5 mi) one-way from Barrie to Orillia. Along the route, anglers can often be spotted trying their luck through the ice of frozen Lake Simcoe.

Penetanguishene Rotary Park Trail (Map 23/D6)
This trail is often used by snowmobilers travelling between Penetanguishene and Midland. The trail picks up at the end of the Tiny Trail, a rail trail that treks north from near Barrie and travels though Penetanguishene. Eventually the trail links up with the Midland Rotary Park Trail.

Tiny Trail (Maps 14/C2–23/C6)
Basically the northern portion of the Simcoe Rail Trail, this route leads north from near Barrie to Penetanguishene. It is a popular day trip that leads past the Tiny Marsh.

Uhthoff Trail (Maps 15/F2–24/B7)

This trail is a 25 km (15.5 mi) one-way route that stretches from the town of Orillia northwest to Coldwater. The old rail line trail passes through a mix of farmland and woodland areas.

District 10 Trails (Maps 31–33, 39–42, 49–52)

If you are looking for early season snow, this is the place to visit. This region sits near the shore of the Georgian Bay and regularly receives ample snowfall due the lake effect and regular snowfalls. The trails also offer some of the most scenic terrain in Cottage Country. From the local trails in and around the town of Parry Sound, you can quickly find a secluded system. Visit www.pssd.ca for local trail conditions.

Route C104D (Maps 40/G2–53/B5)

This trail connects the C Trunk Trail near the settlement of Ardbeg with the D Trunk Trail east of Lake Bernard and Sundridge. Snowmobilers will pass Dunchurch, Ahmic Harbour and Magnetawan along the way. There is some large lake travel involved and many stop to ice fish Ahmic Lake, Lake Cecebe or Bernard Lake.

Seguin Trail (Maps 32/D2–43/C6)

This trail stretches 61 km (38 mi) one-way from the Highway 69/400 access point at the Parry Sound Visitor Centre to the Fern Glen access point on Fern Glen Road west of Highway 11. This rustic, multi-use trail is a popular route that follows an old railway line that used to span from Ottawa to the Georgian Bay. Be wary of backcountry skiers and snowshoers.

District 11 Trails (Maps 48–53, 58–66)

This area spans the neck of land that connects southern Ontario with the north, roughly from Algonquin Provincial Park to the Georgian Bay and north to Lake Nipissing. Covering roughly 2,800 kilometres (1,750 miles) of trails, only the southern reaches of this district are covered in this mapbook. See the Northeastern Ontario Backroad Mapbook for additional options.

Deep River/Mattawa/Pembroke Area (Maps 63–67)

Encompassing the northwestern extreme of the Ottawa Valley, this area incorporates the narrow stretch of land that is sandwiched between the Ottawa River in the north and Algonquin Provincial Park to the south. The region is relatively flat compared with much of the remaining area surrounding the park, although some rolling hill and rocky outcrops make this place scenic and pleasant for those who are able to visit. The main corridor in this area is the A Trunk Trail that links Mattawa with Pembroke. This trunk trail travels past numerous town and villages, including Deux-Rivieres, Stonecliffe, Deep River, Chalk River and Petawawa. The trail loosely follows Highway 17, but strays far enough away from the roadway to offer a rustic feel through forested settings. In all, the trip from Mattawa to Petawawa spans approximately 150 km (90 mi).

North Bay/Mattawa Area (Maps 41, 42, 52, 53, 62, 63, 64)

Since a good portion of the area around North Bay is private land trails in the area travel more closely to road systems. As you approach Mattawa, however, it is easy to find yourself alone on the system. The many old and new logging roads provide for a seemingly endless array of great riding opportunities. The system also travels south from Mattawa to Pembroke or from North Bay to Parry Sound. Within this area, the D Trunk Trail (Maps 42/E5–62/D2) is the main corridor, linking Sprucedale in the south with North Bay in the north. Loosely following Highway 11, the route is a popular ride along the west side of Algonquin Provincial Park that links to Northeastern Ontario. Along the journey, users will pass by or come close to Burk's Falls, Sundridge, South River and Callander before reaching North Bay, travelling approximately 125 km (78 mi).

French River Area (Maps 49–52, 58–62)

The French River region is unique because you can travel from the flatter terrain of the Lake Nipissing area all the way to the rocky shores of the French River. A newer suspension bridge replaces the old shuttle service over the river. Most routes in this region follow old logging roads from the French River through hundreds of kilometres of forest and spans all the way to Lake Nipissing and North Bay. One alternative is Route C106 (Maps 60, 61) that crosses over the French River at the Dokis Indian Reserve. The trail begins north of Alban along the C Trunk Trail and travels east to the C105D Connector Trail, south of Golden

Valley. Along the path, snowmobilers will cross numerous roadways, rivers and marshy areas. In total, the route spans approximately 120 km (75 mi), although most users only travel on certain portions of the trail in order to link up with another of the many trails that connect to this route.

Ottawa River Area (Maps 65–67)

This remote and rugged area is sandwiched between Algonquin Provincial Park and the Ottawa River. The Missing Link and the North Renfrew Snowmobile Association are responsible for the trails, with most of the club trails being modest loops that offshoot from the A Trunk Trail. Visit www.nrsa.ca and www.morningmistresort.ca for trail conditions and more information.

Touring Routes

Central Ontario Loop Trail (Maps 9, 10, 17, 18, 26–28, 36–37)

The Central Ontario Loop Trail is a collection of railway trails that combine to complete 450 km (280 mi) loop through Ontario's Cottage Country. The more notable trail systems that are a part of the loop network include the Hastings County Trail, Victoria Rail Trail and the Haliburton Rail Trail. Since portions of the route are a part of the TOP trail system, trail pass are required. For more information visit www.looptrail.com.

D Trunk Trail (Maps 33, 34, 42, 43, 52, 53, 62, 63)

This trail is the main route travelled within the Muskoka region to move from Bracebridge to North Bay. From Bracebridge to Kearney, the route spans approximately 100 km (62 mi), stopping by Ziska, Utterson, Aspdin, Whitehall, Sprucedale and Scotia. Much of the route is quite rugged, although there are some flatter sections southwest of Kearney.

Ride Around Nipissing Tour [RAN Tour] (Maps 60, 61, 62)

This two-day route takes you in a 400 km (250 mile) or so circuit around Lake Nipissing. From North Bay, take the D Trunk trail to the D102C trail and then go south on C110D, which takes you through Nipissing. Go northwest on TSSR 706 to D102C through Restoule, where you can fuel up. Stay on D102C until you reach C Trunk trail and head north. Before you get to the French River (where you should probably spend the night), you will have the pleasure of crossing the snowmobile suspension bridge. The next day, continue on the C Trunk Trail until just after Alban, where you take the C106 Trail to the D104 trail, on which you head north all the way to NV502. That trail becomes the WN402, which takes you to the D103. Take that trail north until you reach the WN403, which takes you east to the D Trunk Trail. The D Trail merges with the A Trail for a while and then diverges before North Bay, returning you to your starting point.

Round Algonquin Park [RAP] Route (Maps 34– 36, 42, 43, 45– 47, 52, 53, 57, 62–67)

This 965 km (600 mi) tour around the perimeter of Algonquin Provincial Park is a fantastic winter trip for those looking to make an extended snowmobile vacation without travelling to the more remote sections of northern Ontario. Part of the North Bay/Mattawa Trails, this self-guided route utilizes many trunk trail networks (Trunk Trails A, B, C and D) that encompass the park. The route never strays too far from civilization, although it does offer a rustic feel with many isolated pockets. For more info, call 1-800-461-7677.

Voyageur Route (Maps 64/E2–67/G6)

This trail follows, for the most part, the A Trunk trail from Mattawa through District 6 (and continues onward). The whole route is around 350 km (220 miles) but you can do as much or as little as you like. There are some fabulous views of the Ottawa River and the Laurentians, as well as many side routes along club trails that also reward you with some fine vistas.

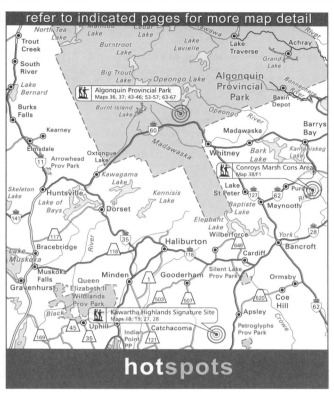

refer to indicated pages for more map detail

hotspots

As you move north from Toronto, man's influence on the landscape becomes less pronounced. Larger and larger swaths of land are still left in their natural state.

As the land becomes wilder, so to do the residents of that landscape: moose, white-tailed deer, wolves and black bear are regularly seen.

These are the biggest of the creatures to inhabit the rugged Canadian Shield landscape, but they are not the only ones. Smaller mammals like beaver and otter can be found and there are birds beyond number to appeal to the ornithologists.

This is not to say that wildlife cannot be spotted in the more populated areas of the province. Indeed Lake Ontario forms a natural barrier to migration, so birds fly around the shores of the lake and right through Toronto. In fact, the city has a lights out campaign, as the lights of the city lures birds that are often killed by flying into office buildings.

One of the most popular spots for wildlife watching is Algonquin Provincial Park. Because much of the area remains or at least has returned to a wilderness state, it is the ideal location for those hoping for the chance to spot some local wildlife. Because the area is so vast, spotting wildlife can sometimes be difficult. However, all that space has allowed larger mammals to flourish. And, with all the lakes, there are plenty of opportunities for birders, too.

In order to improve your chances of spotting birds and animals, wear natural colours and unscented lotions. Bring along binoculars or scopes so you can observe from a distance and move slowly but steadily. Keep pets on a leash, or better yet, leave them at home, as they will only decrease your chances to spot wildlife. Early mornings and late evenings are usually the best time to see most birds and animals.

Never approach an animal directly and for heaven's sake, do not try and bring animals to you by offering them food. Animals can become conditioned to handouts, which may put both of you, into harm's way. Rather, figure out what natural foods they prefer and situate yourself near where these animals will feed.

What follows isn't a complete list of where you can see animals and birds, but it is a fairly good start. Some of the sites below cater mostly to birders, while other sites feature large mammals. Still other sites focus on fish. All of them are worth checking out. There are also many organizations dedicated to wildlife watching and birding that would be more than happy to offer you suggestions of where to start looking.

Algonquin Provincial Park (Maps 36, 37, 43–46, 53–57, 63–67)

Algonquin Park has long been a favourite place for those looking for the chance to view some wildlife. There is no shortage of habitat within Algonquin to host close to 40 different mammals, over 130 bird species and over 30 species of reptiles and amphibians. Some of the more notable sightings include black bear, beaver, otter, white-tailed deer, moose, wolves and foxes. You don't have to go far. By far the most wildlife sightings are along the Highway 60 corridor. Other known wildlife viewing sites in the park include the Mizzy Lake and the Beaver Pond Trails where a variety of birds, reptiles and small animals are readily seen.

Amable du Fond River Provincial Park (Map 64/A5)

Moose frequent parts of the river that are sheltered by alders, while black bear and white-tailed deer are spotted less often.

Axe Lake Wetland Conservation Reserve (Map 33/E1–42/E7)

This 793 hectare reserve is regarded as one of the most important areas in Ontario for Atlantic coastal plain plant life. Visitors will find vast conifer wetlands as well as rare aquatic plants. Expect to see a wide array of waterfowl and aquatic life in this location. Migrating Canadian geese can often be heading flying above the reserve in the spring and fall.

Image © Shutterstock

Bear Lake Peatland Conservation Reserve (Map 42/B5)
This large conservation reserve is prime moose habitat and is also home to a variety of wetland bird species, such as the sandhill crane. The Seguin Recreational Trail passes along the southern boundary of the reserve in several places.

Bigwind Lake Provincial Park (Map 34/F7)
This 1,970 hectare park is home to moose, deer and a few bear. Geological features of interest include a ground moraine and Precambrian rocks that exist as part of a gneiss belt.

Blair Township Provincial Wilderness Area (Map 50/B4)
This area is an important habitat site for deer, bear and other animals. There are a few rustic trails that meander through the reserve.

Bonnechere River Provincial Park (Map 47/E1–57/C7)
This waterway park was created to protect the historic Bonnechere River and its shoreline. The river travels through a maple and pine dominated forest and there are opportunities to view wildlife, such as moose, bear and waterfowl.

Brighton Provincial Wildlife Area (Map 12/E5)
Accessible north of the 401 off Coltman Road, there are several trails passing forests, grasslands, streams and a 5 acre pond that provides excellent habitat for a variety of wildlife.

Conroys Marsh Conservation Reserve (Map 38/F1)
Conroys Marsh is located east of the town of Maynooth and is part of the York River system. The marsh, in its entirety, is approximately 2,400 hectares and the game preserve is about 2,100 hectares. The reserve is a refuge to many fur bearing animals, including fox, beaver and marten. Mayhews Landing, up river, can provide a means of access.

Cranberry Marsh (Map 3/B4)
Found just outside of Whitby, this is one of the best places in the region to see migrating bird. The marsh is part of the Lynde Shores Conservation Area and offers observation platforms for bird watchers.

Egan Chutes Provincial Park (Map 38/D6)
The wetland is part of the York River water system and is home to numerous provincially significant plant species. A variety of waterfowl and small mammals, such as muskrat, rely on the wetland as habitat. The reserve is located east of Bancroft, off Highway 28. Hikers can walk an unmaintained road to a series of three pictorial waterfalls.

Eighteen Mile Island Wilderness Area (Map 49/F1–59/F7)
Eighteen Mile Island is a large island that was formed by the separation of the north and main channels of the French River. The wilderness area is located on the western section of the island and encompasses a small lake and wetland area. The area is closed to the public, but a number of different bird species as well as other mammals such as deer, beaver and muskrat can be viewed from the water.

Eleanor Island National Wildlife Area (Map 24/G1)
This small, rocky island in Lake Muskoka is home to one of the few gull and heron nesting colonies in the region since it provides a refuge from predators. Other birds that nest here include double-crested cormorants. Visiting the island is discouraged, but it is possible to view these birds from offshore.

Holland Marsh Wildlife Area (Map 7/D4)
The marsh is home to thousands of bird species and is an important migration point for waterfowl. Although there are limited facilities, nature lovers and bird watchers will marvel at the complexity of this wetland.

Kawartha Lakes (Maps 17, 18, 19)
The Kawartha Lakes are a chain of popular lakes east of Lake Simco that include Balsam, Cameron, Sturgeon, Pigeon, Buckhorn, Chemong and seven other lakes. These lakes are known for their rich marshes, which provide great habitat for waterfowl, marsh birds and other aquatic wildlife. The best way to explore the area is by canoe.

Lingham Lake Conservation Reserve (Map 30/C5)
This 20,291 hectare site was created to preserve the bass fishery and extensive beaver pond activity in the area. The resulting wetlands have created ideal waterfowl habitat and birders can find a good number of species throughout the area.

Long Lake-Lancelot Creek Conservation Reserve (Map 33/E2)
North of the popular Skeleton Lake, this 627 hectare reserve is made up of a few different land parcels found around Long (Cardwell) Lake. The area

is quite beautiful as it combines open wetlands with mature stands of sugar maple and balsam fir. Expect to see a variety of waterfowl and smaller mammals within this quaint, wooded area.

Manitou Islands Provincial Nature Reserve (Map 62/C2)
This 1,925 hectare water access provincial park encompasses a series of islands in the middle of the eastern section of Lake Nipissing. The islands host colonies of birds as well as a population of small mammals such as muskrats.

Miller Creek Wildlife Area (Map 18/G6)
This beautiful 202 hectare wetland is found west of the town of Lakefield. The wetland area is teeming with bird life and is a popular location with bird watchers and other naturalists. There is a short trail along the wetland area and a two level tower that provides a great way to view of the area.

Opeongo River Provincial Park (Map 46/F2–F4)
This waterway provincial park protects 955 hectares of river shoreline stretching from Algonquin Provincial Park to Highway 60 that consist of 34 distinct forest communities. The park can be accessed from Highway 60 or from the Shall Lake Access Point. Wildlife viewing is a popular attraction within the river park with moose and white-tailed deer being the primary viewing species.

Oshawa Second Marsh/McLauglin Bay Wildlife Reserve (Map 3/E3)
The 123 hectare Second Marsh has been undergoing extensive restoration work. Together with McLaughlin Bay Wildlife Reserve and Darlington Provincial Park it is one of the largest waterfront spaces in the Greater Toronto Area. It is also the largest remaining wetland in the GTA. The area protects an ecosystem that provides food and cover for 305 bird species, as well as mammals, reptiles and amphibians.

Presqu'ile Provincial Park (Map 12/E7)
Presqu'ile attracts visitors from afar who converge on the park each spring and fall to get a glimpse at the major flyway for migrating birds and monarch butterflies. Trails access some of the better viewing sections of the park's fields and shoreline where the birds and butterflies tend to converge.

Thurlow Wildlife Management Area (Map 13/D1)
Designated as a provincially significant wetland, Thurlow Wildlife Management Area has limited access. It can be found off County Road 5 (Mudcat Lane), north of Belleville and east of Foxboro. There are no visitor facilities available in order to maintain the wetlands, red maple swamp and drumlins that are found in this location.

Tiny Marsh Provincial Wildlife Area (Map 14/C2)
Tiny Marsh Wildlife Area can be accessed from First Concession Road, off Highway 27. Over 250 different bird species have been observed at the marsh, including Osprey and Least Bitternsand Black Terns. There is a series of short trails along the marsh dikes that lead to observation towers where visitors can get a better view of the wildlife in the area.

Waubaushene Beaches Wildlife Area (Map 23/G6)
Set just outside of the town of Waubaushene, this small reserve is home to a thriving wetland area popular with nature and bird lovers. There are limited facilities.

Wellers Bay National Wildlife Area (Map 13/A7)
The wildlife area is comprised of four islands, totalling 40 hectares and is home to a large number of birds, from waterfowl and shorebirds to grassland birds and raptors. However visiting the area is not permitted, as the islands were used as a bombing range during World War II and the Korean War and unexploded bombs remain in the area.

West Sandy Island Nature Reserve (Map 61/C4)
Sandy Island lies within Lake Nipissing near the mouth of the fabled French River. The park itself is 266 hectares in size and encompasses the western half of the island, an important water bird breeding habitat home to relic shoreline flora, a red pine stand and a fen. Visitors are asked to try to avoid island contact if possible.

Wye Marsh National Wildlife Area (Map 23/D7)
Part of the Wye Valley near Georgian Bay, this area protects both marshlands and wooded uplands, providing habitat for a variety of animals. In particular, there are about 150 of Ontario's 400 trumpeter swans found here. The best times to visit are during spring and autumn migration and during June when the turtles are nesting.

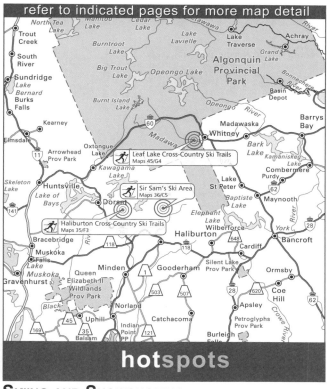

refer to indicated pages for more map detail

hotspots

There are two choices that outdoor types have when the weather turns to winter. Hide inside away from the cold or face it down and enjoy some of the best adventures that the province has to offer. Winter can arrive here as early as November and the last snowfall can happen as late as May. With snow on the ground for as long as half the year, many people choose the latter.

As a result, Cottage Country is literally littered with trails for winter travel. For cross-country skiers, there are few long distance trails, but there are literally hundreds of trails scattered throughout the region that are open to skiing (both Nordic and downhill). And if they're not groomed for skiing, chances are, you can snowshoe them.

Outdoor enthusiasts will find that Ontario is the battleground between cold arctic air from the northern and warm moist air pushing in from the Gulf of Mexico. This means that weather in the region can be varied to say the least. One day it can be sunny and cold, the next, warm and rainy. In a place like Algonquin Provincial Park, the average temperature in January is between -5 and -25 °C (23 to -13°F) with average annual snowfall of about two and a half metres (8 feet). While it is possible to ski as early as December, the season does not heat up until January and runs well into March and sometimes April.

In the section below, we have outlined a few places where you can go skiing and snowshoeing. But know that this is just the tip of a very large metaphorical iceberg. For the snowshoer and backcountry skier, many of the trails described in the Trails section of this book would make fine destinations. Then there are the endless bush road systems found on the maps. Only a few of these mainlines are ploughed. The rest make a wonderful playground for backcountry adventurers.

Frozen lakes are also often used by all winter adventurers. While they are dangerous if not frozen solid (and some lakes don't ever freeze solid), frozen lakes can provide great opportunities for winter recreation. Skiers can cross the lake to access areas that are mostly inaccessible in the summer. However before venturing over the ice, be sure to test the thickness to ensure it is safe.

Snowshoers should note that if you want to snowshoe in designated cross-country areas, please stay off the track set trails. Downhill skiers should also check the hours and snow conditions as some of the local hills are only open on weekends and conditions vary dramatically during the season.

SKIING AND SNOWSHOEING

Algonquin Ecolodge Trails (Map 37/C3)
Algonquin Ecolodge offers some of the best wilderness cross-country ski trails in southern Ontario along with snowshoe and dog sled trails. There are over 40 km of trails here, a mix of groomed or track set and ungroomed or wilderness, that lead inside the southern panhandle of Algonquin Park. Resting in the highlands area, visitors can expect a few hills and varying terrain that passes through a mixed forest and over beaver ponds. White-tailed deer winter in the area and there is the occasional sighting of wolf as well.

Algonquin Park Trails (Map 44, 45)
Algonquin Park is much quieter during the winter. While there are still places that see plenty of people except on the coldest and stormiest January days, the thick blanket of snow tends to absorb the noise of nearby groups. Check with the Park Information Office for snow and ice conditions at (705) 633-5572.

Fen Lake Trail (Map 44/D6)
The Fen Lake Ski Trail is located near the West Gate of Algonquin Provincial Park. There is a total of 18 km (11 mi) of trails that are groomed on occasion. There is also a warm-up shelter and toilet at Fen Lake. A detailed map of the trail is available at the West Gate, off Highway 60.

Leaf Lake Cross-Country Ski Trails (Map 45/G4)

The Leaf Lake Trails are fully maintained. There are 46 km (28.5 miles) of trails here, the longest of which is the difficult 12.4 km (7.7 mile) David Thompson Loop.

Linda Lake Snowshoe Trail (Map 45/A2)

Although you can snowshoe virtually anywhere in Algonquin Provincial Park, there is one designated snowshoe trail, the 8 km (5 mile) experts-only Linda Lake Trail. Since most of the route traverses frozen waterways, it is important to be wary of ice conditions. In fact, the ice from the beaver dam at Cannisbay Lake to the first winter portage is often unsafe. Travel on the west side of the bog.

Minnesing Mountain Bike and Cross-Country Ski Trail (Map 44/G3, 45/A3)

The Minnesing Mountain Biking and Cross-Country Ski Trail is comprised of four interconnecting loops for a combined total distance of 55.3 km (34.3 mi).

Arrowhead Provincial Park Trails (Map 43/C7)

Arrowhead Provincial Park is located off Highway 11 north of Huntsville. The park offers four easy trails that are groomed for cross-country skiing. One section is lit for night skiing.

Batawa Ski Hill (Map 12/G4)

This small community ski hill was originally built by workers at the Bata Shoe Factory. The hill now has three lifts and seven runs. The longest run stretches 762 metres (2,500 ft) with a vertical drop of 174 metres (571 ft).

Bondi Village Resort Trails (Map 34/G2)

Bondi Village Resort is located off Highway 35 on Muskoka District Road 21 and offers about 15 km of groomed and track set cross-country ski trails. Non-registered guests can use the trails for a fee. Be sure to check in with the office on trail conditions heading out.

Bracebridge Resource Management Centre Trails (Map 34/A6)

North of Bracebridge off Highway 11 at High Falls Road, the Bracebridge Resource Management Centre offers an 8 km (5 mi) series of cross-country ski trails.

Canadore College Education Centre Ski Trails (Map 62/D1)

There are three similar sized trails here, which total approximately 10 km (6 mi) in length. The trails vary in difficulty from easy to moderate and travel through a mainly birch forest past a few wetland areas. There is also a small warming hut available on the trail system.

Copeland Forest Management Area Trails (Map 14/G3–15/B3)

North of Barrie the 1,754 hectare Copeland Forest Management Area can be accessed from one of the two parking areas off Ingram Road. This forested area offers over 35 km (22 mi) of easy to moderate trails that can be used for both snowshoeing and cross-country skiing.

Devil's Elbow Ski Club (Map 10/B3)

Located minutes away from Peterborough, Devil's Elbow has six chairlifts, including four quad lifts. The lifts service 11 runs on the 106 metre (350 ft) vertical hill, including a disproportionately high number of expert runs (almost half). Nordic skiers will also find 8.5 km (5.3 miles) of trails.

Driftwood Provincial Park Trails (Map 66/G4-67/A3)

There are three ungroomed trails for cross-country skiing here. The access points can be found at the parking areas just past the park office.

Earl Bales Ski and Snowboard Centre (Map 1/F6)

Formerly the North York Ski Centre, this urban ski area has four runs, serviced by a double chairlift and a rope tow. It is lit for night skiing and has snowmaking equipment for when Mother Nature is not so generous.

Frost Centre Institute (Map 35/C5)

There are 12 km (7.5 mi) of trails here. Due to the difficult terrain, the trails to the east of the centre are for snowshoeing use only. Across the highway from the centre, cross-country skiers will find 21 km (13 mi) of trails. A detailed trail map is available at the centre.

Georgian Cross-Country Ski Trails (Map 41/A6)

The Georgian Nordic Ski and Canoe Club own and operate 30 km (18 mi) of ski trails. The trails are regularly groomed and include 7 km (4.3 mi) of skating trails. Other facilities include a concession stand and posted trail maps throughout the system.

Glebe Park Trail (Map 36/B7)

There is approximately 20 km (12.4 mi) of ski trails here. Most of the trails are easy although with the longer trails are more difficult. Donations are encouraged to help maintain the trails.

Gravenhurst KOA Nordic Trails (Map 25/A2)

The Gravenhurst KOA offers over 17 km (10.6 mi) of interconnected cross-country trails with varying degrees of difficulty and distances. There is a marginal fee for use of the facilities, which include a main warm up area and a trail warm up hut.

Haliburton County Rail Trail (Map 26/G5–36/B7)

The Haliburton County Rail Trail is a 36 km (20 mi) one-way route along an old rail bed between the towns of Kinmount and Haliburton. The popular snowmobiling route can also be used for cross-country skiing and snowshoeing, but be wary of sledders who often run the route as a means of transportation between the two towns.

Haliburton Nordic Trails (Maps 27, 35, 36)

The Haliburton Nordic Association maintains a series of nearly 100 km of groomed trails around the county. Featuring both skate and classic trails, there is a 1.5 km lit-loop for night skiing, a good variety of easy trails and some of the most challenging terrain for cross-country skiing in the province. Ski passes are needed to explore the many different systems that range from the Leslie Frost Centre (Map 35/F3) to Moose Woods (Map 27/C1), from Glebe Park (Map 36/B7) to Camp Wanakita (Map 27/C1). The many local resort trail systems are also open to the public.

Hardwood Hills Trails (Map 15/C4)

For a marginal fee, you can access over 86 km (53 mi) of trails that range from easy to difficult. There are two main trail systems, the Olympic System, for experienced users and the recreational system, for beginners and intermediate users. The system is open for night skiing on Wednesday evenings.

Heights of Horseshoe Ski Club (Map 15/A4)

Located an hour north of Toronto off Highway 400, this private ski club boasts of short lift lines and the longest ski season in Ontario. Enjoy the 28 runs and half pipe covered covering 41 hectares (102 acres) that are aided by snowmaking. The downhill runs range from green to double black diamond. There are also 35 km (22 miles) of cross-country ski trails north of Horseshoe Valley Road West (County Road 22) as well as a snow tubing area.

Hidden Valley Highlands Ski Area (Map 34/D1)

Hidden Valley Highlands is located 6 km east of Huntsville. There are ten runs here, serviced by four lifts. The hill has a vertical rise of 100 metres (327 ft) and portions of the hill are lit for night skiing.

Kawartha Nordic Trails (Map 19/D2)

Found off Highway 28 north of Burleigh Falls in the Peterborough Crown Game Preserve, this is a well-developed trail system. Offering 34 km (21 mi) of groomed classic trails, 13 km of skating trails and 10 km of wilderness trails there is something for all levels of skiers. They also have a 10 km snowshoe trail that follows a scenic loop from the Woodfine Chalet to the Laderach Cabin and back. The interconnecting trails are patrolled on weekends and there are four warm up cabins with stoves throughout the system.

Kerr Park Trails (Map 25/A1)

Located off Highway 4 on Beaumont Drive are a series of easy 2.3 km (1.3 mi) trails for skiing or snowshoeing. Kerr Park is also a regular area for bird watching and there is a bird-viewing platform along one of the trails.

Lake St. Peter Provincial Park Trails (Map 37/E1)

There are two ungroomed trails available, totaling approximately 5.5 km (3.4 mi). Permits can be picked up at the gate and parking is available at the trailhead.

Laurentian Ski Hill (Map 62/E1)

Laurentian Ski Hill offers one main chair lift to service several runs. At 95 metres (310 ft), Laurentian's longest run spans 427 metres (1,400 ft). The upper lodge of the ski hill can be reached from Airport Road, while the lower lodge can be found on Ski Club Road, off Highway 11/17. For more information, call (705) 494-7463.

Long Sault Conservation Area Trails (Map 9/F6)

Found off Regional Road 57 on Durham Road 20, skiers, snowshoers and hikers will find four great trails to explore. These trails cover about 17 km (10.5 miles) and there is a small chalet available.

Madawaska Mountain Ski Hill (Map 47/E5)
Also known as Radcliffe Hills, this small ski hill boasts the 6th highest ski vertical in Ontario, mile long runs and small lift lines. There are 12 runs, 2 surface lifts and a total skiable area of 78 hectares (193 acres). Visitors will find a full service pro shop, rental facility, ski and snowboard lessons. This quiet hill is well known for its great snow and good mix of easy and challenging runs.

Mansfield Outdoor Centre (Map 6/A4)
For a small fee, this outdoor centre offers 40 km (25 mi) of groomed trails, plus a 10 km (6 mile) dedicated skate skiing loop.

Mansfield Ski Club (Map 6/A4)
This small ski area has eight lifts and four terrain parks for skiers and boarders. There are 15 trails with some advanced terrain near the Summit Quad Chair.

Mattawa Golf and Ski Resort (Map 65/A1)
The resort offers over 20 km (12 mi) of cross-country ski trails that vary in difficulty from easy to difficult. For trail information call (800) 762-2339.

Midland Mountainview Ski Club (Map 23/D6)
Midland Mountainview is a privately owned cross-country ski area and mountain bike centre located off Highway 93 near the town of Midland. There are four well-maintained cross-country ski trails, totaling about 18 km (11 miles) groomed for both classic and skating techniques. They offer low annual fees, easy access to lessons and many social events to encourage more members.

Mount St. Louis Moonstone (Map 15/A2)
Serviced by three six passenger lifts, one express quad, three quads and two triple chair lifts, this is one of the largest downhill ski areas in the region. There are 40 runs, half of which are rated intermediate and the mountain has one of the higher verticals in Cottage Country, at 167 metres (550 ft). The mountain features two super pipes, two terrain parks and snow making equipment.

Nordic Inn Trails (Map 35/B3)
The Nordic Inn Trails are a rustic series of interconnected trails, totaling over 23 km (14 mi) in length. Some of the longer routes are harder.

North Bay Nordic Cross-Country Ski Club Trails (Map 62/G2–63/A2)
The North Bay Nordic Cross-Country Ski Trails are located east of North Bay, off Northshore Road, on the north side of Trout Lake. There are over 42 km (26 mi) of skate and classic trails. Nominal day fees apply for use of the trails.

Oshawa Ski Club (Map 10/C7)
This club-run community ski hill has 22 named runs, half of which are open for night skiing. There are three quad chairs and seven tee-bars servicing the 100 metres (300 ft) vertical ski area. The hill is aided by snowmaking.

Port Sydney Cross-Country Ski Trails (Map 34/A4)
The Village of Port Sydney has 11 km (6.8 mi) of groomed cross-country ski trails. The trailhead can be found off Muskoka Road 10 on Clark Crescent, just past the tennis courts.

Quinte Conservation Area Trails (Map 13/D4)
Located west of Belleville, visitors will find a 6 km (3.7 mile) series of easy cross-country ski trails.

Rotary Greenway Trail (Maps 10, 11, 19)
One way, this easy paved trail traverses over 20 km (12.5 mile) and travels along a portion of the old railway line that travels from Beavermead Park in Peterborough past Trent University towards Lakefield.

Samuel de Champlain Provincial Park (Map 64/B2)
The roads throughout the park are transformed into a groomed cross-country ski trail system. The trail lengths vary from year to year and difficulties range from easy to moderate.

Simcoe County Trails (Map 14/F6)
The Simcoe County Trails are located on the site of the old tree nursery located just west of Midhurst. There are 6 km (3.7 mi) of easy trails to explore.

Sir Sam's Ski Area (Map 36/C5)
Located north of Haliburton, there are six lifts servicing 12 runs at this small ski hill. Snowboarders will enjoy the series of jumps, boxes and rails, while cross-country enthusiasts can explore the popular 3 km (1.8 mile) intermediate trail that climbs alongside the ski runs to a viewpoint over Eagle and Moose Lakes.

Ski Dagmar (Map 2/G1)
Located 21 km north of Ajax, Dagmar Ski Resort has six lifts servicing 14 runs. In addition, there are 25 km (15 miles) of cross-country ski trails. The majority of the downhill terrain is rated easy or intermediate.

Ski Lakeridge (Map 8/F7)
This popular ski area has 23 runs spread over 28 hectares, three terrain park areas and a tubing park for your winter enjoyment. During summer the resort offers adventure camps and mountain biking.

Skyloft Resort (Map 8/F7)
In 2008, Skyloft Resort introduced a new product called Dryslope; a snow substitute that they say will allow the terrain park to remain open year-round. While it remains to be seen if people are interested in year-round snowboarding, it is an interesting development and one that could change the future of snow sports. The mountain has a 100 metre (300 ft) vertical, with 18 runs and trails serviced by three lifts, including one quad chair. The terrain here is divided almost evenly between beginner, intermediate and expert runs.

Snow Valley (Map 14/F6)
Located near Barrie, Snow Valley caters to family skier. In addition to the eight lifts servicing 20 named runs, there is a large tubing area, as well as a fairly extensive snowshoeing area.

South Himsworth Trails (Map 62/G6)
This 10 km (6.2 mi) cross-country ski loop is set amidst a charming forest. The trailhead and parking area is found on the south side of Linquist Line, north of Powassan.

Springwater Provincial Park Trails (Map 14/F6)
There are three cross-country skiing trails here. Facilities at the park include a covered picnic area, washrooms and two warm up shelters that each furnish a wood stove and a good supply of wood in winter.

Tawingo Nordic Trails (Map 34/A1)
There is over 15 km (9.3 mi) of groomed cross-country trails here. There are no fees for use of the trails, although donations for trail maintenance are always welcome.

Trent University Wildlife Sanctuary (Map 11/A1)
There are currently three trails available for cross-country skiing or snowshoeing in this nature area. The sanctuary parking lot is located near the Trent University Campus off Nassau Mills Road on University Road in Peterborough.

Upland Ski Club (Map 1/F5)
This small ski club is located in Thornhill, just south of the 407. There are 18 trails, serviced by 8 lifts.

Vanderwater Conservation Area Trails (Map 21/E6)
The Vanderwater Conservation Area offers 15 km (9.3 mi) of easy to moderately difficult ski trails for visitors to explore. They are well maintained and loop through mixed forest tracts.

Warsaw Caves Trails (Map 19/D5)
The Warsaw Caves Conservation Area is located off County Road 4 on Caves Road. It offers over 13 km (8.1 mi) of trails for hiking, snowshoeing or cross-country skiing. The Cave/Scenic Lookout Trail begins at the parking area off Caves Road and is an easy 4 km (2.5 mi) route. The Limestone Plain Trail is an easy 7 km (4.2 mi) route that travels along the Indian River for a large portion of the trail.

Wasaga Beach Trails (Map 14/A4)
Ski Wasaga is a fantastic facility in the east end of Wasaga Beach. The trail system includes a moderate collection of interconnected loops that total about 19 km (12 mi). Picnic tables are available and a small fee is required for usage. The provincial park also offers over 26 km (16 mi) of cross-country ski trails.

Wasi [East Ferris] Cross-Country Trails (Map 62/G4–63/A4)
The Wasi Ski Club Trails are located just south of the city of North Bay. There are six different loops, which total over 47 km (29 mi) of groomed ski trails. A warm-up hut is also available at the parking area to take the bite off those extra chilly winter days.

Wye Marsh Wildlife Centre Trails (Map 23/D7)
The Wye Marsh Wildlife Centre offers a series of interpretative trails for year round use. During winter, cross-country skis and snowshoe rentals are available. The centre is located southeast of Midland off Highway 12 and charges a nominal fee.

The index location references consist of a **page number** and a **letter, number combination**. In the example found below the city **Cornwall** is found on page **26/F4**.

The grid lines found in the example below are used for illustrative purposes only, the blue grid lines found on the maps refer to UTM coordinates.

Also Note that **bolded** entries in the index represent cities and communities.

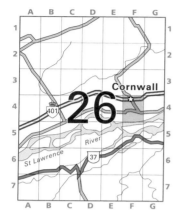

IMPORTANT NUMBERS & WEBSITES

Highways Report 1-800-268-4686
..... www.mto.gov.on.ca/english/traveller/conditions/
Resorts Ontario ....(705) 325-9115
.... www.resortsofontario.com
Travel Ontario..............................1-800-ONTARIO
.... www.ontariotravel.net
Ontario's Wilderness Region 1-800-461-3766
.... www.ontariowildernessregion.com
Updates .... www.backroadmapbooks.com
Weather Conditions ....
.... www.weatheroffice.ec.gc.ca/canada

Ministry of Natural Resources

General Inquiry .... www.mnr.gov.on.ca
........1-800-667-1940 | (800) 667-1840 (French)
Crime Stoppers (Poaching Violations)...................
.... 1-800-222-8477
Invading Species Hotline 1-800-563-7711
Outdoors Card Customer Service ....
.... 1-800-387-7011
Sportfish Contaminant Monitoring Program ....
.... 1-800-820-2716

Parks

Ontario Parks (Reservations) 1-888-668-7275
.... www.OntarioParks.com
Parks Canada...
.... http://www.pc.gc.ca/eng/index.aspx
(Reservations) 1-800-839-8221
Algonquin Provincial Park 705- 633-5572
.... www.algonquinpark.on.ca

Clubs & Associations

ATV Ontario.................................1-877-889-8810
.... www.atvontario.com
Canoe Ontario .... www.atvontario.com
Cross-Country Ontario ....www.xco.org
Cycle Ontario .... www.cycleontario.com
Ontario Federation of Anglers and Hunters ....
.... 705-748-6324
.... www.ofah.org
Ontario Nature 1-800-440-2366
.... www.ontarionature.org
Ontario Snowmobile Federation 705-739-7669
.... www.ofsc.on.ca
Ontario Trails Council .... www.ontariotrails.on.ca
Trails Ontario 1-877-ON-TRAIL
.... www.canadatrails.ca

ONTARIO DISTANCE CHART

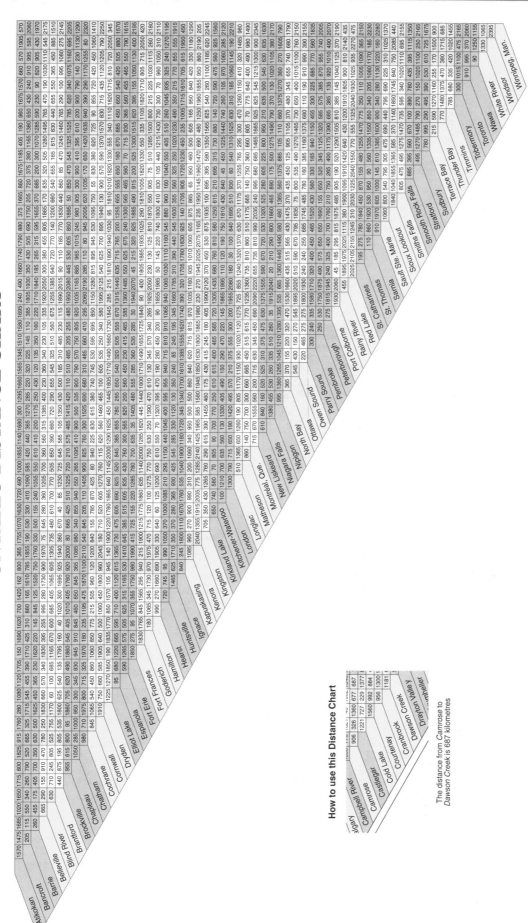

How to use this Distance Chart

The distance from *Camrose* to *Dawson Creek* is 687 kilometres

1 Kilometre = 0.621 Mile   1 Mile = 1.6 Kilometres

SPEED CONVERSION CHART

Backroad Mapbooks
...THE START OF EVERY ADVENTURE!!

Northwestern Ontario

Northeastern Ontario

Eastern Ontario

Manitoba

Nova Scotia

Canadian Rockies

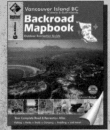

Vancouver Island, Victoria & Gulf Islands BC

Southern Alberta

Northern BC

OTHER PRODUCTS

Eastern Ontario Fishing Mapbook

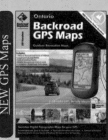

Ontario Backroad GPS Maps

Algonquin Provincial Park Recreation Map

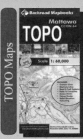

Cross Canada TOPO Map Series

Published By:

Mussio Ventures Ltd
#106- 1500 Hartley Ave,
Coquitlam, BC, V3K 7A1
P: 604.521.6277
F: 604.521.6260
Toll Free: 1-877-520-5670

...and much more!

For a complete list of titles visit our website or call us toll free **1-877-520-5670**
or visit **www.backroadmapbooks.com**